The Adolescent Experience

Elizabeth Douvan & Joseph Adelson

University of Michigan

The Adolescent Experience

John Wiley & Sons, Inc., New York · London · Sydney

Library of Congress Catalog Card Number: 65-25853
Printed in the United States of America

For Kate, Tad, Paul, Ted, and Larry

PREFACE

The reader deserves to be warned that this book is perhaps an uneasy attempt to mix two genres of psychological writing—the discursive essay and the research monograph. The opportunity to write it grew from two national surveys of adolescents conducted by the University of Michigan's Survey Research Center. Our early temptation was to limit ourselves to technical writings offered to the profession through a monograph or a series of research papers. This was one of those temptations, as it developed, that was not hard to resist. It may be of some interest to say why.

When we first surveyed the literature on adolescence, we were struck by the peculiar lack of connection between discursive writings —general theory, casual or naturalistic observation, speculation—and systematic research. As one of us has noted elsewhere:

. . . this literature . . . contains on the one hand a set of broad, extremely interesting and humanistically informed ideas . . . and on the other, a scatter of empirical studies, some ingenious, some dull, some good, some bad, but most of them unified only in that they bear little connection to the literature of large and synthesizing ideas. Thus we have two cultures in a single country; they coexist, but not dialectically; they neither enrich nor regulate each other. The empirical literature, most of the time, is directionless, following a current fancy, or simply following its own nose. The other literature, the literature of large ideas—and many of the great names in the social sciences are represented here—does not find the empirical writing to be relevant to *its* concerns, and so it, in turn, remains stagnant, feeds off itself, becomes insular and even eccentric (Adelson, 1963).

No doubt these words, written for a rhetorical occasion, rather overstate the case. Yet the case remains, we believe, not only for the psychology of adolescence, but also for psychology as a whole, as many recent writers have argued. Therefore we have been particularly eager to offer a discursive context for the research data. We begin most chapters with a general discussion of the topic, and only then proceed to findings. The fit between discussion and data varies from chapter to chapter. In some cases they fit closely, in others not so well or not so clearly. In these latter instances we have usually wanted to offer some reflections on a topic, or to indicate the range of relevant concern, although we have been unable, through limitations of cost or ingenuity, to translate these reflections or concerns into operational form.

The tables have been placed at the end of the book. We hesitated over the decision, recognizing that it might inconvenience some readers, but we hope that this is outweighed by the increased latitude and flexibility permitted in organizing and commenting upon the findings.

The Research

The research is based on two national interview studies conducted by the Survey Research Center in 1955 and 1956—the first on adolescent boys and the second on adolescent girls, sponsored respectively by the Boy Scouts and the Girl Scouts of America. Technical details about the studies—on sampling design and interviewing methods—are to be found in the Appendices. Here we want to describe briefly and nontechnically the scope and limits of the research, to orient the reader to the data, and to our use of them.

The sample. Sampling for these studies presented some intriguing technical problems, but also allowed a somewhat simpler design than can be realized in sampling the adult population. We sampled and arranged our interviews through schools; consequently we could reduce call-back and nonresponse rates to a minimum. We insured representation of different kinds of schools through stratification, that is, by grouping private, parochial, and public schools before selecting schools to be included in the sample. (More specific details appear in Appendix II.)

The sample, then, represents adolescents in school. Youngsters in penal institutions and hospitals are not represented, nor are those who have dropped out of school. At fifteen and beyond, dropouts are a sizable group, and they are, disproportionately, from the deprived socioeconomic strata. Thus our sample underrepresents "problem" children in the population at large, particularly at the upper end of our age range. We have tried to keep this fact before us while making inferences and generalizations from the data; but it is hard to tell whether and where we have been successful, so the reader is asked to bear in mind that many disadvantaged youngsters are not included in the sample.

In all we (the research team and the Center's interviewing staff) interviewed some 3500 adolescents, if we include children seen for pretesting, interviews with children not designated for the final sample, and those with sample members. The final sample consisted of 1045 boys, aged fourteen through sixteen, and 2005 girls in grades six through twelve.

Interviewing. Each adolescent selected was interviewed by a member of the Survey Research Center's field staff. Interviews were conducted individually in school and lasted from one to four hours. The schedules used appear in Appendix I. The questions ranged widely in both form and aim: some were focused, specific inquiries on objective aspects of the respondent's life; some were broad, open-ended, or projective, designed to gain some insight into the youngster's subjective or tacit ways of defining reality.

When we were first planning the research we had more than the usual degree of uncertainty about the interviewing process. Would it be difficult to gain rapport with our respondents? We knew that adolescents are often guarded or diffident in clinical contacts with adults, hard to reach during clinical diagnosis and psychotherapy. Our own experience was, happily, very different: our youngsters were, on the whole, lively, open, and apparently candid.

The most vexing problems have to do with the validity of the interview data. Even if we grant that our subjects were, as they seemed to be, straightforward and accessible, we are left with a number of questions. To what extent were they offering plausible yet unwittingly misleading accounts of themselves and their circumstances and feelings? To what degree were they trying to please the interviewer? And beyond that, how safely can we generalize from what they tell us?

There are, of course, no easy answers to these questions, as the vast literature on the interview and on the nature of inference will attest. We did exercise certain cautionary means in the hope of minimizing gross errors of inference and interpretation. We relied heavily on indirect and projective questions, and in particular tried to make use of concordances and discrepancies between direct and projective information on the same topic. Thus, to cite one example, in the appraisal of family dynamics we examined not only what our respondent told us directly, but also treated his response in relation to projective responses dealing with family interaction. Whenever possible, we attempted to increase reliability by combining responses into indices and using these as the measure of a trait. Another check we employed, although an indirect and often complex one, was to assess the validity of a response through its analytic usefulness. If we predict from theory that two variables show a specific relation to each other, and if we can confirm that prediction, we gain some added confidence—although no certainty—in the validity of both the measures and the theory.

Finally, we have tried to maintain a certain humility in recognizing the extraordinary complexity of the adolescent experience and the limits of the interview in capturing that complexity. We have slighted some topics we know to be important—for example, certain aspects of peer relations—in the conviction that the interview is not the method of choice for some problems, and that our interview time would be better used elsewhere. Still, we do not want to be apologetic about the interview as a method. It has unique strengths and agilities, and we hope we have been able to exploit these in allowing adolescents to tell of their experiences.

ELIZABETH DOUVAN
JOSEPH ADELSON

February 1966

ACKNOWLEDGMENTS

N*ational studies* such as those on which this book is based require extraordinary cooperation from a large number of people. The adolescents who were interviewed, the school personnel who extended hospitality and made arrangements for interviewers to talk with their students during school hours, the sponsors who supported the studies, members of the Survey Research Center staff—interviewers, field supervisors, sampling specialists, coders, and tabulating and computing experts—all contributed to the studies and all have our gratitude.

We should like to acknowledge our special debt to Dr. Angus Campbell, director of the Survey Research Center, to Dr. Stephen B. Withey, program director for the Center's studies of children and youth, and to Dr. Gerald Gurin, all of whom gave personal trust and organizational support for studies that were at the time somewhat offbeat, outside the spectrum of the Center's dominant concerns.

Dr. Carol Kaye, who assisted in directing the study of girls and contributed a great many ideas to the total project, conceived and conducted the analysis of girls' vocational plans.

In the course of the two studies we had the good fortune to hire under the umbrella heading "research assistant" a series of talented students who brought zest and devotion to every task, whether challenging or routine. We feel a presumptive (perhaps presumptuous) parental pride in the list: Dr. Esther Newcomb Goode, Dr. Zelda

Gamson, Jane Faily McCant, and Kristine Rosenthal. We are deeply grateful for all their help.

The typing of study reports and various forms of this manuscript was done with good humor, care, and interest far beyond duty's demands by Joan Weir Alexander, Mary Hartman LaPrade, Norman Wilkinson, Christine Moore, and Bette Erxeleben.

To our colleagues in Psychology at the University of Michigan we are indebted for an intellectual climate rare in its combination of stimulating criticism and respect for differences, a climate we have found ideal for work and growth.

Our families offered the unsolicited gifts of love, patience, and humor without which authors would never survive and books would never be written.

E. D.
J. B. A.

CONTENTS

CONTENTS

The Adolescent Experience

ONE

Introduction

W_e *witness* these days new images, new appearances of the adolescent. Until fairly recently, he had little weight in our collective imaginings, in fiction and the mass media. He would ordinarily be imagined as a figure of fun—callow, flighty, silly, given to infatuations, wild enthusiasms, transient moodiness. Prototypes: Andy Hardy, Henry Aldrich. Or he might be seen as a latter-day and rather harmless Werther: sensitive, emotionally afflicted, sentimental. In either case, the figure was treated sympathetically: lovable, often exasperating, but not to be taken too seriously. He would get over it—whatever "it" might be—in time. Let us call this type the adolescent as Fool. The Fool exists outside the world of adult happenings; he is blessedly innocent of complication, guilt, or responsibility. He is a fool not in being duped, but because he is not yet related to the intrigues and corruptions, or the moral seriousness, of adulthood. He inhabits an Eden of preresponsibility.

More recently two new images, weightier and more ominous, have superseded the Fool figure, and between them they divide the contemporary sense of the adolescent. One of these images is the adolescent as Seer. He is distinguished by a purity of moral vision which enables him to perceive or state the moral simplicity hidden by adult complication. The Seer is generally a Victim as well (prophets usually are); he is betrayed, exploited, or neglected by the adult world. His needs may go unrecognized by adults too busy to give him the concern he requires; or as an innocent bystander, he may get in the way of adult corruption and be hurt or destroyed; or he may be the direct victim of adult malevolence. Prototype: Holden Caulfield.

The Seer-Victim is passive and powerless in relation to the adult world; his only resource is knowledge, and the strength which may

1

eventually accrue from it. His antitype is the newest and most disturbing representation of the adolescent, as Victimizer. Leather-jacketed, sinister, cruel, amoral, he is the nemesis-hero of a new genre of fiction and film. A recent short story depicts him in the following narrative. A man incurs the hatred of some hoodlum youths by challenging their arrogance. They threaten to hurt or kill him. He appeals to the police for protection, but they are impotent to help him. The story ends as the night closes in, and the man, isolated and vulnerable, awaits helplessly what will befall him. The story's mood is paranoid. The adolescents are the persecutors, the killers. These adolescents stand in utter contrast to the Seer-Victim type: one is innocent, the other evil; one is powerless, the other omnipotent.

We are not at all sure why these countertypes have emerged; it is easier to find facile answers than truly persuasive ones. But it is very clear that the adolescent now occupies a peculiarly intense place in the American consciousness. As prophet and victim, he joins and replaces the child who once played these parts. As victimizer, he is the carrier of projections: sadistic and sexual motives are increasingly imputed to him, and he joins or replaces the gangster, Negro, and other external enemies. Nor is it in the imaginative media alone that these adolescent types hold so central a place. A very high proportion of recent social criticism sees in the adolescent's situation a key to our moral and social pathology: for example, *Growing Up Absurd* and *The Vanishing Adolescent* (Goodman, 1960; Friedenberg, 1959). Curiously, it is in the use of the adolescent that the social criticism of the Left is joined by the social criticism of the Right; both see our youth as reflecting what is worst, what is most dangerous in our times.

We have no wish at this time to join any of these arguments, or to comment on the validity or utility of any of these images of adolescence. We do want to stress their simple presence, for the existence of these images—highly charged, contradictory, tendentious—complicates the task of understanding adolescents in their often all too homely variety, and in their often all too mundane particularity. The several *mystiques* of adolescence—as whipping boy, visionary, and sacrificial hero—must be recognized and set aside; otherwise they obscure our vision.

The Memory for Adolescence

The fretful national preoccupation with the promise and portent of youth is but one barrier to coming to grips with the adolescent experience. Another is that most of us find it so painful to recover the emotional quality of our own adolescent years. Recent psychoanalytic writing has recognized a specific amnesia for adolescence (Freud, 1958). Childhood amnesia is well known (Schachtel, 1959). The adolescent amnesia is distinctive in that the events of adolescence are not ordinarily forgotten; rather the emotional intensity of this period comes under repression, where it is blocked out, muted, or misremembered.

When we work therapeutically with adults we generally have no trouble in obtaining a plausible account of the events of adolescence. After some while, however, it becomes clear that the account is affectively false. The patient may remember easily enough that he had been stirred and disrupted by feeling in adolescence; but usually he will go no further. So he may adopt a lordly, amused, indulgent attitude toward the emotional storms of that time, gently mocking his "puppy love," his outraged sense of injustice, the secrecies and intimacies of close friendship—but unwilling to take them seriously, to re-enter adolescence psychically. It was too passionate a period: hot, angry, sentimental, lustful, guilt-ridden, sullen, anxious, bitter, elated, tormented. The adult, living in a relatively mellifluous, homogenized affect world, seems to tell us, in his emotional quietude, that he has had it, thank you, and will have no more of it.

This stubborn burial or isolation of affect is one way in which the memory for adolescence does us false; we want to call attention to another. For many persons, the events of adolescence stand out vividly in memory. The affective texture of the period may be lost, but the details of the adolescent narrative are sharp, clear, immediate. They have an ordered, coherent sense of the trials and vicissitudes of the teens. Why is this so? Partly, we imagine, because of the very isolation of emotion, which allows concrete detail to be present in consciousness. But a more salient reason, we would guess, is that these remembered events are identity-linked. For many of us the self—what we are now—begins at puberty. Childhood (until and unless it is explored in psychotherapy) is felt to be prehistory, pre-identity. The autobiographical fiction, the myth of the self in time, the narrative of what we were and then became are all, in some distinctive sense, dated from adolescence. We view childhood as a preparation. The true life, the true self began when childhood was over, at eleven, twelve, thirteen. Nowadays people (especially when they are patients) have that half or quarter knowledge of psychoanalysis which leads them, dutifully, to tell their stories from early childhood—the earlier the better. But if they are naive enough, or if we can get them to be naive enough, they will date the self (the present self) from puberty.

We force our adolescences into the autobiographical fictions we construct for ourselves, and in doing so, give meaning and coherence to the self's career in time. Hence we can recall even the shameful and distressing moments of adolescence, just as long as they can be placed in the narrative of identity. Those were the temptations I struggled against; that was the weakness I conquered; there was the abyss I rose from. We write a personal *Bildungsroman*, and begin it, as the fictions of that genre usually do, at adolescence.

So the deceits in the memory for adolescence are of two kinds: an amnesia for the affective intensities; and a hypermnesia for the events, truly or falsely understood, which are identity-relevant. We have a great deal at stake in maintaining this sense of our personal history, and the adolescent, in his painful actuality, may make us remember the emotional tempests we want to forget, or may force us to re-imagine the fiction of our adolescent origins. Because we feel ourselves so close to the adolescent, and would like to feel ourselves remote from him, we are likely to respond to him falsely. We are prone to spurious empathy, or misplaced sentimentality, or reactive indignation, or excessive anxiety, or heightened detachment—any of these, and all of these. Even the psychotherapist, devoted to an ethos of self-knowledge, may find himself emotionally invested (as he ruefully recognizes later) in his adolescent patients—stirred, irritated, indulgent, and overprotective; wanting to take sides, to console, to argue; or finding himself strangely distant, unmoved, or bored. It is an age hard to know truly.

An Overview of Concepts

We shall begin by introducing, rather briefly, some of the concepts and perspectives which guided this research into adolescence.[1] The discussion will be succinct and preliminary, since later chapters will treat these matters in fuller detail.

Psychosexuality

The biological changes at puberty undo a balance between ego and id which has, in most cases, been maintained in the latency period, roughly between six and twelve years of age. As the instincts gain in

---

[1] Excellent discussions of psychodynamics in adolescence can be found in Blos (1962), Stone and Church (1957), and Pearson (1958).

vigor, the rather fine articulation between drives and the control processes is endangered.

The two sentences above sum up, however grossly, some of the basic elements in the psychoanalytic approach to adolescence; and at a first glance, they do not seem to depart excessively from nonpsychoanalytic views of the period. All schools recognize the importance of the erotic intrusion for the psychic life of the adolescent, recognize the guilts, tensions, and confusions which arise with the appearance of the sexual motif. The psychoanalytic view is distinctive in making further assumptions about instinctual life in adolescence. We begin by surveying these.

1. The instincts are defined to include more than genital sexuality. Pregenital drives, oral and anal impulses, for example, and aggressive drives are held to be of great importance in the adolescent instinctual upheaval, and indeed are felt to produce far more intrapsychic disturbance than genital eroticism.

2. Sexuality does not arise anew in adolescence. The youngster has experienced an earlier meeting with the impulse life in the first years of childhood. His reaction to the adolescent instinctual revival repeats and reflects that previous encounter. In adolescent sexuality, the past reemerges and must be dealt with again.

These two assumptions give a distinctive cast to the psychoanalytic understanding of adolescent instinctual phenomena. Consider the ubiquitous problem of masturbation. No one will deny or make light of the agonizing difficulties the adolescent faces in coming to terms with masturbation *as it is,* that is, a disapproved practice, carried out in secrecy, and violating the ideal one holds of one's self. The psychoanalytic emphasis recognizes what we might call the existential sources of masturbatory shame and guilt; but it also insists on the part played by unconscious, pregenital, and regressive drives. Thus masturbation is a source of distress because it may be accompanied, for instance, by unconscious incestuous fantasies. It causes trepidation too because of the adolescent's earlier struggle with masturbation, a struggle which now may be unconscious. Here is a fairly commonplace example: an adult woman confessed, after great resistance, that she occasionally masturbated (occasionally meaning once a year or less). The mortification she felt in telling about it seemed, at first, to stem from her belief that "grownups don't do that sort of nasty thing." Later it appeared that other feelings were involved. As a child her masturbation had been accompanied by intense penis envy, with the fantasy of being a boy and doing the sensual, wicked things a boy does. The guilt and shame she felt about adult (and adolescent) masturbation reflected her earlier situation. It reflected the rage, mortification, envy, passion, and guilt of her infantile fantasies.

Pregenital tendencies "attach" themselves to the genital upsurge; one might say that they ride piggyback on the genital instincts. The pregenital drift is accentuated by the fact that in early adolescence there is no ready outlet for the expression of genital sexuality; the instinct life moves backward, regressively, to the fantasies, wishes, and dispositions of early childhood. As a result, adolescent behavior is rife with derivatives of pregenital and aggressive drives. Orality shows itself in many ways: compulsive eating, food jags, compulsive dieting, loss of appetite, food faddism, and so on. Anality also appears variously: ostentatious slovenliness, frenzies of cleanliness, ritualistic orderliness. The adolescent's increased aggressiveness may be manifested directly, in surliness, irritability, temper outbursts, or in more subtle forms of cruelty, or defensively, in a heightened kindness and overconcern with being good.

These drives may not show themselves (or conceal themselves) quite so obviously. In adolescence, as in other stages of life, the instincts appear in displaced, disguised, or distorted forms. The oral motives may be seen not only in characteristic attitudes toward food and eating, but also in other modes of consumption, such as in compulsive reading. Or we may see an intensified passivity, the youngster querulous and demanding of attention, affection, care; or we may get a brisk movement against that very passivity, the child showing himself autonomous, aloof, vigilant against any temptation toward dependency and helplessness. Similarly, anal motives may be expressed in behaviors which are not so directly "anal"—in being obstreperous, touchy about being pushed around, defiant toward constituted authority; or in the reverse, in obsequiousness, excessive compliance, rigid goodness; or by a high degree of interest in painting, pottery, mathematics, or any of a hundred other sublimations.

It should be understood, as it is not understood in primitive or mechanical versions of psychoanalytic theory, that the instincts express themselves in the *psychosocial* context of adolescence. The pregenital impulses of the adolescent are distinct from the pregenitality of the child or of the adult. Instinct life in the adolescent participates in, modifies, and is modified by the psychosocial realities of adolescence. It is incomplete and, indeed, incorrect to say that an adolescent boy's sullenness is due to his aggressiveness, or his swagger due to heightened narcissism. He is defiant, to his father, for example, because of an intensified aggressiveness; because the Oedipus complex is revived; because his status, between child and adult, is blurred; because the defiant adolescent is a common model of behavior; because he feels it secures an uncertain masculinity; because he is warding off passive tendencies; and so on. We are saying that adolescent behavior is overdetermined and that instincts and their vicissitudes do not offer us a sufficient apprehension of its sources.

A stress on the instincts alone is misleading in another way, for their significant manifestations are *interpersonal*. The revival of oral, anal, or other drives is important primarily in its influence on the adolescent's relations to others. Suppose that the instinctual crisis of the period is expressed in an oral regression. There may be, as we have just said, some appearance of the oral motives in food and eating pathologies, which are not primarily interpersonal (though symbolically they are, as Harry Stack Sullivan would insist). By and large, however, the oral dispositions would be manifested in perception of and conduct toward others. Other people would be seen and reacted to, unconsciously, as givers and deprivers of supplies.

Here is another example, taken from the stormy adolescence of a young woman in psychotherapy. Her adolescent years had been very nearly chaotic, marked by intense hostility toward her mother; seductiveness, flightiness, and bitchiness toward boys; and much more. The sources of her behavior generally could be reduced to a feeling of having been victimized orally, cut off from the breast, and to a determination to make others pay for her having been so deprived. Thus she would not go to school, since she would not "give" of herself unless and until she was sure of receiving something in return. Despite a high intelligence she worked as a waitress, thus identifying with a bountiful mother and at the same time reproaching the mother who had failed to give her enough. ("I give to others as you should have given to me.") There were occasional outbreaks of rage against her mother; at one point she went on a rampage in which she broke all of her mother's dishes. Her relations with boys had a recurring pattern: she would be swept off her feet in an infatuation, feeling that the boy could give her something infinitely desirable. Then her feeling would sour into disappointment and then hatred. She would revenge herself by exploiting the boy, forcing him to spend more and more money on her while she in turn gave less and less, until he, confused and disgusted, would stop seeing her. At seventeen, she married a boy a year older, with whom she entered a mother-daughter relationship, she being the daughter.

She stayed in bed most of the day; he fed her, took her to the toilet, did the housework. Then he was drafted, and she took this as a deliberate rejection on his part, and petulantly divorced him.

The behavior here was extreme, but the dynamics are nothing if not commonplace. We see in this young woman a rather vivid demonstration of pre-Oedipal, instinct-dominated object relations. There is, one might say, nothing specifically "adolescent" about this case history: a passionate orality was visible before puberty and symptoms continued into young adulthood, when she entered psychotherapy. The point we want to make is that pre-Oedipal and Oedipal forms of interpersonal relations are rather regularly found in adolescence. Even "well-adjusted" adolescents show in their behavior and feelings the impact of these regressive pulls. The common "eccentricities" of the adolescent always have behind them the influence of revivals of primitive interpersonal patterns.

Of these revivals the most common and most important is the Oedipal. Erotic and aggressive motives, and defenses against them, infuse the conduct and attitudes of the adolescent toward his parents, and toward others as well. Consider the boy's case—it is simpler to describe than the girl's: the youngster's sexuality is dangerous to him in being incestuously "tainted," and adolescent eroticism is thus prey to castration anxiety. Unconscious wishes for the mother, an unconscious fear of and not-so-unconscious rivalry with the father tend to color behavior in the family. Indeed the ramifications of the Oedipal renascence extend far beyond the family, for displacements of and defenses against the Oedipal constellation contaminate relations with nonfamily peers and adults.

How the adolescent handles the Oedipal crisis depends on a multiplicity of factors—his preferred defenses, his talents and ego skills, what the environment allows, encourages, and forbids, how peer and adult models behave, his superego structure; also the ideologies and values he is exposed to, and his earlier history in coping with instinctual crises. The variations are nearly infinite, and we shall discuss some of them in the course of this chapter and later in the book. We may note here that the adolescent Oedipal resolution differs from the earlier one in the critical respect that the youngster now has alloplastic (environment-changing) opportunities open to him. In childhood, in the original Oedipal situation, autoplastic (self-changing) solutions are more common; the child handles the conflict by modifying himself, borrowing parental strength through a decisive identification with the father which tames the impulses. In adolescence the peer group is available for the discharge of erotic drives—especially so in America, with its emphasis on the fetid, flamboyant, and yet fake sexuality of adolescent dating.

A final comment before we leave the topic: it is important to maintain the clinician's skepticism when we appraise the adolescent's sexuality. Much of the time, perhaps most of the time, it is not what it seems to be—a simple discharge of heightened sexual tension. Bear in mind that adolescent sexuality is so infiltrated by pregenital, pre-Oedipal components that a great many unconscious anxieties are activated. The genital sexuality of the adolescent is often a pseudosexuality, a defensive sexuality, whose aim is to ward off these anxieties. The sexual swagger of the adolescent boy may reflect a counterphobic solution of castration or other fears. The girl's promiscuity may be her only defense against homosexual temptations.

Ego Processes

THE DEFENSES

Our understanding of defense mechanisms in adolescence is based on observations made by Anna Freud (1936) more than a quarter of a century ago. Not very much has been added since. The instinctual revival at puberty, she pointed out, upsets the *modus vivendi* between ego and id which had been maintained during the latency period. The defenses are now under strain; the defensive mechanisms stiffen, coarsen, and become more rigid. The adolescent reacts to the threat of the drives in any number of ways. In some cases, the defenses are exacerbated to the point of caricature. The moderate intellectuality of the latency period deepens to a pathological, even bizarre hyperintellectualism; modest reaction formations stiffen to become grotesque rigidities of attitude; mild tendencies to blame others curdle into bitter grievances. At other times we may see oscillations between radical and radically opposed stances toward the impulses. The most apparent of these is the adolescent's tendency to swing between an implacable asceticism, in which pleasure of any kind is fiercely renounced, and libertinism, where the drives are indulged, and then back again. There is also some reason to believe that a greater variety of defenses is employed in adolescence than at more placid periods of the human career. Because a great many primitive drives are activated, drives which derive from a number of earlier periods in the person's development, there is likely to be a wide use of defenses which are not in the "normal" repertoire, but which are tied to these drives, and are called upon to cope with their emergence.

Miss Freud has amplified her earlier work (Freud, 1958) by calling attention to the defenses against infantile object ties. This new emphasis is in line with the theoretical emphasis we noted earlier, which stresses the interpersonal context of the impulse life. The critical problem for the adolescent lies in the fact that the drives are attached to the parents, and that these ties must be severed. Miss Freud specifies several defensive maneuvers (in order of gravity): displacement of libido, wherein the child withdraws emotionally from the parents and transfers libido to peers or parent-substitutes; reversal of affect, in which feelings toward the parent are changed into their opposites—from love to hatred, from dependence to defiance—and where we may find a further development (via projection of hatred, for example, or turning against the self) into grave states of paranoia or depression; withdrawal of libido to the self, where we may get grandiose beliefs, or hypochondriacal preoccupations; and regression, the most extreme of these, in which there is a return to primitive ego states, and a psychotic withdrawal from reality.

One aspect of the defenses relatively neglected in discussions of adolescence is the defenses against affects, or emotions. The instinctual revival activates the emotions, especially the affects of anxiety, shame, and guilt. In some cases the defenses are deployed primarily against these devastating feelings, against traumatic panic, against mortification, against an overwhelming sense of inner badness. The adolescent experience is often dominated by eccentricities of emotion: intense and confused outbreaks of feeling, inappropriate blandness, and so on. If we examine these closely we find they are due to massive defenses against the affects. Certain emotions, felt to be dangerous, are bottled up until such time as they can be displaced, and we then get a sudden outpouring of feelings which are inappropriate in time and place. The adolescent boy may react to anxiety by denying it, by showing a coolness or dullness of mood which seems psychopathic. The overwrought adolescent who seems to be living out affects all too freely may, paradoxically, be warding them off, substituting "safe" affects for dangerous ones. Thus, a guilt-ridden youngster may behave provocatively, insolently, to block the eruption of guilt into awareness. In a later chapter we shall give some attention to the warding off of guilt—the renegotiation of the ego-superego relationship—which seems to us to be of vast importance in adolescent development.

Our understanding of defense dynamics in adolescence is, all in all, fairly adequate, especially so if we compare it with our grasp of other ego processes. Nevertheless, there are a great many gaps in our knowledge. We want to mention only one of these: that we know too little of the defenses as they function in nonexceptional adolescents. Our knowledge is excessively based on neurotic youth, delinquent youth, and, to a lesser extent, gifted, sensitive, or intellectual youth. Many discussions of adolescent behavior make much of the intellectualization mechanisms—the overabstractness, the philosophical musings, the creative (or pseudocreative) tempests. Yet if we consider the core culture American adolescent—*le jeune moyen sensuel*—we are not at all impressed by the frequency or intensity of these qualities. To the contrary, we often note a retreat from introspectiveness of any sort. We find more commonly a marked use of character defenses, such as ego restriction, and a heavy reliance on interpersonal conformity. These adjustments, despite their commonness and their social acceptability, represent defensive reactions to the impulse, object, and affective tensions of the adolescent period, and we should know far more than we do about them.

THE ADAPTIVE EGO FUNCTIONS

The adaptive aspects of the ego encompass a formidable range of functions: thinking, the orientation to reality, memory, social perception, will, creative activity, and many more. Their importance is self-evident, although they were neglected by personality theorists until fairly recently (Shapiro, 1963). Our knowledge of them, in their relation to the total personality, is meagre, and our understanding of their operation in adolescence is even more meagre. We do know that these functions expand in adolescence, sometimes extraordinarily so, and we know too that during this time they are especially vulnerable to conflict. We will be able to speak of the adaptive functions in general terms, although we will be unable to spell out the vicissitudes of their operation with any specificity. Indeed, it is somewhat misleading to treat the adaptive functions as a group. Thinking, memory, and social perception, for example, are separate (though related) activities, each of which would be, were our knowledge greater, analyzed separately. (On the other hand, there is good reason to believe that there is some degree of "common destiny" among them. A failure or underdevelopment in one of these functions, more likely than not, is found with defectiveness in another. A youngster who is functioning well in one area is likely to perform well in others.)

The latency period is marked by a steady and impressive maturation of the adaptive ego functions. The quiescence of the instincts, together with the autonomous growth of ego capacities, and the parental emphasis on work, learning, and self-discipline, join to assure the child's educability, and thus the cultivation of the adaptive ego functions. At adolescence the instinctual intrusion may interfere with the efficiency of the functions in various ways. The function can be invaded by the drive derivatives, lose its adaptive utility, and be bent to serve the drives. For example, the thought processes may become erotized; there have been instances recorded where intensive thought—on abstract matters, such as mathematics—proved erotically stimulating to the point of producing orgasm. More often it is not the function per se but the contents of thought or perception which are invaded. Hence, a preoccupation with sexual matters may disturb the accuracy of social perception, as when girls experience mild and transient erotomanias, convincing themselves that males are interested in them only sexually, and so misinterpreting the most innocuous encounters. Even more frequently, the defenses against the instinctual intrusion inhibit the functions. Blockings, inhibitions, distractedness, and inattention, all attest to the interferences of defense. An adolescent boy cannot concentrate on his studies; unconscious wishes threaten to emerge in the passivity of reading, and he can ward them off only in physical activity or ritualistic busywork.

Severe disruptions of the ego capacities rather obviously indicate the presence of instinctually based conflict. Yet we must expect some distortion, some degree of inhibition in the process of normal development. We have learned to be wary of overplacid, oversmooth adolescent adjustments. Efficiency and smooth functioning are purchased at the expense of a necessary growth in personality, a growth which requires the endurance of some inner turbulence. When we fail to find it, we suspect some premature hardening of the character, or else a delay in the adolescent crisis. In these cases the instinctual side of the self is kept at bay, and the youngster undergoes a remarkably untroubled adolescence. Later in adolescence, or in young adulthood, the adaptations give way, the efficient, smooth functioning of the ego crumbles, and the youngster may sink into an acute crisis, marked perhaps by a total inability to work and by frenzies of self-doubt.

An example: a young woman near graduation from college. She had been a model adolescent, the pride of parents and teachers for her energy, devotion, and competence. She performed at a straight A level through high school and college, and had what appeared to be a normal social life. In her senior year in college she fell into a severe panic, convinced that she was stupid, knew nothing, was a fake, and would be found out by her teachers. The sources of her work collapse were many: sexual fantasies about her teachers, the unconscious meaning of graduating and being "adult," a delayed rebelliousness toward a guilt-inducing mother, and so on. We want to mention only one side of the matter, the role played by the adaptive ego functions. Our young woman's belief that she was inept and would be discovered had, in fact, a germ of truth in it. As she advanced through college (and looked forward to graduate school) the demands upon her changed. Increasingly she was called upon to do work of some individuality. She was asked to think for herself, and not merely to restate or synthesize the work of others. She found that her devotion, her immaculate habits of work, were now far less useful than they had been, and she was bright enough and honest enough to recognize it. These good habits of work, these apparent sublimations had not been wrested from conflict, were not truly won. Rather, the adaptive ego functions were at the behest of the superego, and deployed against the instincts. Thus we had a partial failure in ego growth. We saw in this young woman an asymmetry in development, a heightened capacity for routine and compliant work, but at the cost of imaginative capacity. We found these partial failures elsewhere in the girl's life. She dated frequently, but in fact kept young men at a distance, afraid to become even mildly involved with them; she seemed to be forthright and direct in ordinary social behavior, but behaved mechanically, insensitive to the emotional nuances of social interaction.

We have limited ourselves to one side of a duality. If at adolescence the instincts jam the adaptive ego functions, it must also be stressed that the latter are of inestimable importance in the taming and dissolution of the adolescent instinctual crisis. The youngster who comes into adolescence with a well-established repertoire of ego resources, resources which serve as sublimation media, which secure the tie to others, which serve as a source of self-esteem and as a haven from the pressures of the world and the body—that youngster will be able first to resist, then temper, and finally absorb the instinctual onslaught.

These resources are a major heritage from the past, from the identifications of the Oedipal period and before, and from the learning and leisure opportunities of the latency period. How well they will thrive in adolescence depends in some part on the quality of this heritage. But it will also depend on the opportunities of adolescence. The ego competences are plastic, responsive to what the milieu will tolerate, encourage, and forbid. The social order, through the peer group and culture, through the family, through official and unofficial ideologies, through its intangible moral climate, and through its all too tangible system of economic rewards and priorities, defines which of the adolescent's competences are to be used and unused, encouraged and slighted.

The Self and Identity

At adolescence the self is, perhaps for the first time, felt to be tractable. The youngster can step away from himself, separate into subject and object, a "me" and an "I," and then hope and intend to change himself. The self is no longer the implacable being it has been up to this point, and we sometimes find not merely a belief in the possibility of self-transformation, but a passionate wish for it. Thus we find the adolescent changing clothes, hair style, accent, manners, mannerisms, posture, muscles, figure, attitudes, beliefs. The self is Procrustean.

This yearning to change the self is one reflection of the heightened self-consciousness of adolescence. Everything in adolescence contributes to self-awareness. The body is in constant, bewildering change; new wishes and feelings emerge; psychosocially the youngster is transitional, in a status between statuses. Add to this the fact that other people are instinctually needed, and yet out of reach. Instinctual energy flows back to the self, contributing to the irritating and often insufferable vanity and exhibitionism we find among so many adolescents. Not that we find the entrenched narcissism common to certain character neuroses; adolescent narcissism is a variable and transient phenomenon. The self is not set apart from others. Indeed, there is the constant temptation (and danger) to lose the self in others, to merge with others psychologically, by taking in the ego qualities of others in radical acts of internalization, by the extraordinary empathy the adolescent is sometimes capable of, by putting oneself psychically in thrall to the other. Introjections and projections, infatuations and sudden revulsions, intense closeness and utter detachment—these oscillations reflect the unsteady state of ego and self during adolescence.

Our understanding of the adolescent self has been enhanced through the invention, by Erik Erikson, of the concept of ego identity (Erikson 1950, 1956). The concept "self" is rather closely tied to consciousness; the identity concept encompasses this sense of the self, and includes unconscious determinants and aspects of self, ego, and character. Technically speaking, the identity concept is not altogether satisfactory, since it is allusive, complex, and connotative. Its connotativeness is explicitly recognized by Erikson, who prefers to let "the term identity speak for itself in a number of connotations. At one time, then, it will appear to refer to a conscious *sense of individual identity;* at another to an unconscious striving for a *continuity of personal character;* at a third, as a criterion for the silent doings of *ego synthesis;* and, finally, as a maintenance of an inner solidarity with a group's ideals and identity."

Identity does not begin at adolescence. The child has been formulating and reformulating identities throughout his life. As significant identifications succeed and overlap each other, as psychosexual crises are traversed, as ego qualities arise and are absorbed, as environmental demands are encountered, childhood identities are constantly changing. At adolescence, however, the commitment to an identity becomes critical. During this period, the youngster must synthesize earlier identifications with personal qualities and relate them to social opportunities and social ideals. Who the child is to be will be influenced (and in some cases determined) by what the environment permits and encourages: identity possibilities for the lower-class Negro adolescent (of whatever capacity) are different from those for the white upper-middle-class Protestant youngster. Identity is influenced as well by the child's talents, needs, sublimations, and defenses. The girl who discovers that she is attractive to boys will define herself differently than will the girl who senses (or mistakenly assumes) that she is not. The highly intelligent youngster is confronted with identity opportunities (and pressures) different from those which will be met by the youngster of average intellectual competence. The identity concept, in short, concentrates on the fusion of these elements (identifications, capacities, opportunities, and ideals) into a viable self-definition.

THE TEMPO OF IDENTITY CRYSTALLIZATION

Adolescents vary in the pace of identity formation. It is impossible to discover a "normal" pattern here, but it *is* possible to speak of premature and delayed crystallizations. Some children crystallize identity too early and too narrowly; the motive in some cases is to avoid the anxiety inherent in identity diffusion; in other cases the impetus is to settle an instinctual conflict quickly and decisively. When we find unusual endowments supported environmentally, as for example, the star athlete who gains much attention from his activities, the youngster may be tempted to define himself exclusively along the lines of a special but narrow skill. Or we may have the young "genius," of a clever turn of mind, who cathects intellectuality in order to ward off the dangers of interpersonal intimacy. At other times the child may rush prematurely into a "normative" identity in order to avoid a tempting and feared identity alternative.

At the other extreme we find those cases marked by a delay in identity crystallization, those adolescents who cannot "find themselves," who keep themselves loose and unattached, committed to a bachelorhood of pre-identity. Erikson sees the late adolescent period, in our times, as a "psychosocial moratorium," a time set aside for the youngster to try out identities, to discover what fits him best, to find the articulation between identifications and talents on the one hand, and role opportunities on the other, which can be synthesized into a satisfactory sense of inner coherence. In a number of cases the period is insufficient. The youngster resists crystallization and seeks out enclaves where noncommitment is possible. As Erikson puts it: "They come, instead, to psychiatrists, priests, judges and (we must add) recruitment officers in order to be given an authorized if ever so uncomfortable place in which to wait things out."

There are any number of causes for delayed identity crystallization. Often the reasons are those we have become familiar with in clinical work with adolescents: the feasible identities are those which seem to involve instinctual danger, as in the case of the boy who delays "growing up" because it involves the unconscious danger of replacing his father. In other cases, however, instinctual conflict, while it may be present, is not the central motive for delay. The youngster may feel unable to actualize his capacities; he feels unused and unrealized. The roles which seem available do not engage his true talents or do not gratify his need-linked capacities. In these cases the youngster may give the appearances of identity, dutifully going through the motions, but betraying, if only in his mechanicalness or lack of zest, the absence of genuine identity engagement. In other similar instances the youngster may sense where his dispositions lie but feel pressured to achieve an occupational or social identity which cannot utilize them.

IDENTITIES: NORMATIVE, NEGATIVE, ACHIEVED, ASCRIBED

Identity formation is also influenced by the normativeness of the identity chosen. Certain identities are well defined, common, and socially approved. In certain milieux the youngster is under almost unbearable pressure to choose these, and to develop within a fairly limited range of possibilities. In these cases the socialization processes are so closely articulated with socially defined ideals and opportunities that identity choice is automatic. We are likely to find an easy crystallization toward a well-defined social identity—as we have it, let us say, in the "golden youth" of American society—the upper-middle or upper-class youngsters who pass from the best preparatory schools to the best colleges to the best brokerage houses. In such instances we can speak of the identity as ascribed. Within certain social strata and ethnic groups we are likely to find that identities are both normative and ascribed. An identity which for some individuals is ascribed may for others have to be achieved, generally through upward social mobility. Those individuals whose ascribed identities are normative may find themselves during adolescence striving to achieve socially deviant identities. In the extreme instances (described brilliantly by Erikson) the youngster may feel that he can be something, or be himself, only by the choice of a deviant identity. The child may in fact be driven to the choice of a negative identity, composed of feared, yet fascinating, qualities. Ordinarily, however, the choice of socially deviant identities is made, we feel, to actualize inner potentialities which cannot be realized in the normative and ascribed identity; thus we see the scion of an aristocratic family choosing a Bohemian or other deviant role.

MASCULINE AND FEMININE IDENTITIES

The processes of identity formation in boys and girls are in fact much more dissimilar than the discussion so far has suggested. The problem of sex differences is both complex and largely unexplored, and we shall only concentrate on some aspects of it. Boys tend to construct identity around the vocational choice; in most cases the girl does not. For most boys the question of "what to be" begins with work and the job, and he is likely to define himself and to be identified by occupation. But there is more to the total identity than occupation, and the stress placed on vocation tends to conceal, both from the onlooker and the child himself, some of the vicissitudes of identity formation. Through a precocious vocational choice the child may factitiously crystallize identity. The necessary delays, the necessary diffusion and confusion of the adolescent period may be forestalled, an outcome which may either hinder the full development of personal qualities or simply postpone the identity crisis until a later and more inappropriate moment. The precocious choice may produce a narrowed, overdefined personality, impoverished through a premature foreclosure on experiment and experience; postponement may produce those cases marked by late anguish, where the person sees himself boxed into a life path he does not feel committed to, filled with bewilderment or disgust, or trying abortively to retrace the path or undo it.

The boy tends to concretize identity through anchoring it in an (often premature) vocational choice; the adolescent girl does not ordinarily have this opportunity. Girls tend to keep identity diffuse, and misty. The boy is made to feel (however much he may doubt it, deep down) that his identity is in his own hands, that the choice of vocation and with it, of a life style, will define him. The girl cannot count on this degree of active preferment in identity; her identity is bound up not so much in what she is as in what her husband will be. Someone has spoken of marriage as a "mutual mobility bet." We may add that for the girl it is equally an identity bet. It is for this reason that the girl, unless she is one of the rare ones who remain committed to a work ideal, seems unrealistic and romantic, often foolishly so, when asked to imagine a future life for herself. She tends to retreat into stereotyped notions of the future, imagining a life of suburban idyl. She seems more comfortable in the present; her vision of the future is necessarily dim; and to this extent identity formation (so far as it depends on an anchorage to the future) is likely to remain incomplete.

SOCIAL CLASS

A central component of the sense of identity is the sense of social status. However we define ourselves, whether we imagine ourselves as we are, or were, or will be in the future, the sense of ourselves carries with it some placing of the self in the social system. At adolescence the child loses whatever innocence about social class he had remaining to him; the period is, if anything, more class- and status-sensitive than any other. The youngster plunges into the dead-serious game of grading and appraising himself and others; he does so on a hundred dimensions, but the most important, perhaps, is social status. The status game at adolescence can be cruelly damaging; the youngster is as vulnerable as he will ever be, and it is his very vulnerability which causes him to turn status against others heartlessly.

It is not only social class as such which enters into identity; it is, quite as saliently, social class-to-be—involving expectation, hope, and dread. The child's emergent sense of himself reaches into the future; the identity is, let us say, not so much "electrician's son" as it is "electrician's son who will be an electrical engineer"; or "sales clerk's daughter who may marry a junior executive"; or even "doctor's son who will not be good enough to be much of anything." Identity, then, encompasses both the past-in-present ("What I am through what my parents are") and the leap from present to future ("What I deeply hope to be, what I deeply dread being"). Fantasies and imaginings of social class and social mobility reflect some of the earliest identities of childhood—that is, class and mobility (aside from their objective significance) are the media through which the adolescent expresses yearnings and despairs rooted in the object ties of childhood: to rise, to fall, to maintain oneself—behind these and informing these are those constructions of the self which began in the Oedipal situation, and earlier.

Conscience and Values

These terms are less closely linked than we might think them to be; and together they encompass so vast and obscure a realm of experience that we can hope to touch it only lightly here.

We shall begin with conscience and the superego. It is thoroughly evident that the upsurge of instincts early in adolescence puts the ego under considerable pressure from the superego. Through the course of adolescence the youngster will learn, painfully, to work out means of direct instinctual expression, and to do so without being shattered by guilt. Here we are likely to think of sexual experimentation and its consequences in remorse; but it is only the most visible part of the matter. Not only sexuality, but also such motives as aggression and dependency, can incite the superego. And the superego may show its hand not only by pangs of conscience—painful as they may sometimes be, they are a relatively benign expression of the superego's presence—but also in darker and more insidious ways. The adolescent may fall into apathy and depression; he may be driven to damaging himself—either directly, through accidents and the like—or more covertly, by trying to ruin his life chances; or he may turn against the superego defiantly, by an estrangement from conscience in reckless or "guiltless" behavior.

Guilt and the avoiding of guilt have not been given quite their due by students of the adolescent experience. Many of the more striking qualities of adolescence are sufficiently grasped only when we see that they involve ways of attenuating the ravages of the superego. The most obvious of these are the inhibitions, where the youngster, not altogether wittingly, puts aside temptation, and thus guilt, by denying to himself the instinct life and things connected with it. The occasional asceticisms and rigidities of the adolescent, and the moral self-righteousness which accompanies them, are no more than ways of thwarting guilt by a simple thwarting of the drives which might evoke it. It is a device which, as we know, is often self-defeating, for the superego can act paradoxically, in that the repression of drives intensifies them and thus increases the unconscious sense of guilt.

Other maneuvers against guilt are less direct. We may note that the intense friendships common in adolescence offer, among their other functions, a means of assuaging (or fortifying) conscience. By sharing secrets with a friend, we can make him into a partner in crime, an accomplice before or after the fact; or we can establish him as judge and jury, whose verdict on conduct provides an external guide to moral behavior; or we can use him as a counselor whose assurance and sympathy mollify guilt. Another response to an uneasy conscience is the tendency to projection commonly found in adolescents. In the early years especially, the youngster will discover wickedness everywhere; this attentiveness to the moral failures of others (particularly those in a social outgroup) diverts the superego's pressure outward. Finally, to complete this brief survey, we note that some youngsters handle moral dilemmas through a vigorous identification with admired adults; by borrowing adult moral strength the youngster fortifies himself against temptation.

Although our understanding of superego activity in adolescence is neither complete nor secure, it is better developed than our grasp of values and value change. This despite an enormous amount of public concern on the fate of values in adolescence, indeed, this concern has if anything served to muddy rather than clarify the problem. Changes in style and taste from decade to decade are generally mistaken for changes in values; and the hortatory character of much of the discussion has led to asking wrong and irrelevant questions. At any rate, our knowledge of value vicissitudes in youth is plainly quite spotty.

It seems probable that the adolescent years are, potentially, very receptive to value change, as much or more so than any other period of life. The break-up of ego-superego patterns accounts for some of the fluidity; so does the intellectual growth of these years, which allows the child a more abstract understanding of value issues; and so does the youngster's movement toward personal autonomy, which drives him to a peer group where new values (or old ones newly stated) may be current. But it must be stressed that the potential for acquiring a fresh look at values is not often realized, for reasons we will suggest in a moment. Indeed we are just as likely to see a momentary retreat from whatever ethical and value sophistication the youngster has so far achieved. The anxieties of adolescence can force him back to simple-minded moralisms, rigidly held, and to the tried and true tritenesses of belief. Even when we see an apparent change of values we have reason to suspect it; in early adolescence particularly, value ferment is basically a reaction to intrapsychic conflict. The ego does not absorb the new values, but uses them in a struggle with the drives or to accomplish interpersonal aims (for example, to ratify one's solidarity with a clique).

So we would surmise that the more genuine and reliable value changes, if they occur at all, will take place in later adolescence. At that time they are less influenced by instinctual needs and defenses against them. The choice and use of values will be ego-mediated and ego-syntonic, the child choosing and using not blindly, reflexively, or defensively, but in line with basic interests, dispositions, and perspectives. As we have said, there is little reason to feel that there is more than a sluggish movement in values for most adolescents, or that value choice involves much more than an automatic assumption of the conventional pieties. To break with or to challenge more than modestly the value commitments of the milieu may be the most perilous thing a youngster (or an adult too, for that matter) can venture, and it takes an unusual personality in unusual circumstances to succeed. He will need, in most cases, liberal (or themselves dissident) parents, and above all, the strong (even if silent) support of like-minded peers or adult models.

Yet some do manage it. A small number of adolescents, small but infinitely important, become so strongly committed to new values, or undergo such marked value crises as to give their generation its peculiar ideological identity. The adolescent elite—the intelligent and influential, or more often the intelligently and influentially disaffected—develop whatever ideological tone the generation will be identified with. It is because of this that the college experience is so important. The intellectual leaders of the new generation, separated from home, under the impress of new ideas and idea-exemplars, can produce the guiding ideology of the future.

TWO

Orientation Toward the Future

The metaphor commonly chosen for discussion of adolescent development has the bridge as its central image. The child at this period is pictured between two worlds, closer to childhood, but with his back turned to it, facing the adult status that lies ahead, on the other side of the adolescent pass. The conception is clear, simple, and apt in some ways. But we would suggest that the adolescent's relationship to these two worlds is less simple than the picture implies. There is, first of all, the fact that the passage between the two worlds is not simple and unidirectional. There is a great deal of wavering, backtracking, and even simultaneous movement in both directions (as though the youngster were trying to encompass the whole transitional span by widening his step, avoiding complete commitment to either side). In addition to these complexities of pace, we would add another condition about the child's relation to the future adulthood which makes the metaphor even less descriptive. The fact is that adulthood is not just a prospect that the child sees ahead of him. It is also a crucial component of his activities and life as he makes the adolescent transition. The outlines of his personal future are roughly established, although they are not filled in or realized. The future enters adolescent identity like a crucial piece omitted from a picture puzzle. The color and content of the piece are missing, but the shape is established, and bears an intimate relationship to bordering pieces. If the piece is really crucial—as the future *is* in adolescent identity, the whole puzzle depends for its interpretation and meaning on what the piece will look like. To make any meaningful assessment of adolescent personality, we must look at the shape of the future as it enters and conditions the formulation.

We can think offhand of a number of alternative ways in which adolescents in our culture orient toward the future, making use of it or

22

managing to avoid it. Some youngsters hold a general conception of their future life, or an element of it, which they invest with some importance and use as a guide in current decisions, interests, and activities insofar as these bear on it. In such cases, one has the feeling that the future is managed with some sense of proportion—there is neither a denial of its importance nor an overinvestment in it at the expense of appropriate adolescent interests. The future concept in these cases is more often general than specific, more often partial than complete and detailed. It is a recognition that the future is important within the present, but not a denial or exaggeration of either aspect of time.

Contrast this use of the future with other postures: the child who has no operating concept of future time but is totally absorbed in the adolescent present, and the child whose concept of the future is so concrete and elaborate, so highly invested that it effectively insulates him against *any* involvement in the problems and pressures of his own age group. One adolescent may have a clear notion of the immediate future and a blank beyond that point, another may be vague about the immediate future and have a detailed picture of some later period. The degree of detail he supplies for one period or aspect of the future may be only slightly related to the degree of emotional investment or color the adolescent places in that phase.

The normal adolescent holds, we think, two conceptions of himself —what he is and what he will be—and the way in which he integrates the future image into his current life will indicate a good deal about his current adolescent integration.

To explore adolescent conceptions of future time and of adulthood, we used two general types of questions. One type consisted of direct questions about plans and expectations for the future. We asked boys and girls what kinds of decisions they think they will have to make in the next few years, what kind of life plan they hold, whether they plan to finish high school and what other educational plans they have, what kind of work they think they will go into and why. In all these questions we asked specifically about the youngster's conception of his future life and about the most articulated aspects of this conception—the verbalizable, intelligible plans and expectations. In all of them we asked about the future within a clear reality context.

The second set of questions approached the future concept somewhat less directly. Here our effort was to pose questions that would give us some insight into the less formulated and intellectual aspects of the youngster's image of the future, the visual and emotional qualities of that image. We asked about daydreams and about adults whom our subjects admired and would like to be like. We asked them to tell us what they found exemplary about these particular adults. We asked them to tell us the most wonderful thing they could imagine happening to them, and the worst thing that had ever happened to them. And we asked what they would like to change about themselves or their lives if they had the power of their wishes. These questions deal with hopes and dreams rather than expectations, and they ask for visual and concrete references rather than intellectual and abstract ones. They approach the child's future concept in a context of fantasy rather than asking him to discuss it realistically.[1]

We expected that boys and girls would differ in their handling of future time. The identity problems posed for the two sexes differ sharply, and since the use of the future is guided by identity considerations, this too, we thought, would differ. For the boy, identity revolves around the questions, "Who am I? What do I do?" The nature of his occupation plays a crucial defining role in a man's identity. The girl, on the other hand, depends on marriage for her critical defining element; she will take her self-definition, by and large, from the man she marries and the children she raises.

This difference has critical implications for the adolescent work of identity formation. The occupational issue which forms the core of masculine identity is to a large extent an issue of individual choice and action; it arises during or shortly after the adolescent era, and preparation for the choice starts during adolescence itself. The boy in adolescence can begin to choose and prepare for work, and this activity can focus and stabilize many of the problems and conflicts that arise for the child in transition. The girl faces a more ambiguous task. Marriage is not a matter of simple individual choice, and for most girls it lies not in the immediate future but beyond in some relatively undefined time. It lends itself neither to rational planning nor specific preparation since it involves the decision and initiative of another person. A girl who plans and prepares explicitly for marriage may be thought aggressive and

---

[1] These two levels, the fantastic and the realistic, are not always clearly distinguishable. Some children, we shall see, have vocational aims that the hard-headed outsider must feel are fantasy-based. And in talking with girls about their ideas of marriage, we can hardly expect that they will not present fantasy; since, except for very few girls, they have no real experience from which to discuss the future reality of their married lives. We can, on the other hand, differentiate most of the questions we asked into those that refer to hopes and dreams and those that ask about plans and expectations. It is useful to maintain this distinction where we can, and consider other questions frankly ambiguous, falling, as they seem to, somewhere between the two levels of discourse.

ungraceful, and she may also be courting disappointment and embarrassment since there is always the possibility, however slight, that she will not marry. There is also the fact that the identity task of the girl, tied as it is to marriage, revolves directly about her sexual identity. Far from relieving the anxieties and conflicts of adolescence by providing them focus and outlet in some neutral ground (as occupational choice and preparation may), this issue very likely intensifies the normal problems of the era.

We expected, then, that boys and girls would assume quite different postures toward the future and toward the work of integrating a concept of adult identity. We expected the boy to have a relatively extended time perspective, to have some concept of his adult role, and to connect that concept to the present by a more or less coherent and developed notion of intervening steps, of choices and actions instrumental to achieving his ultimate goal. We thought that some boys might overuse the future, that is, might use a highly concrete and specified concept of adulthood to avoid some of the more unsettling aspects of adolescence (for example, the erotic fantasies that their psychosexual status stimulates). We did not expect avoidance of the future to be a common pattern among boys.

Our notions about girls' use of future time were much less specific than this. They might, on the one hand, have no clear concept of the future—absorbing themselves, rather, in current adolescent activities and concerns. Or they might turn their interest in the future to a relatively immediate future—the period of education and work that commonly precedes marriage for girls in our culture. In this case we might find a displacement of emotional energy from the central issue of marriage to these more immediate but secondary interests. What we find, in fact, is a variation of this pattern.

The clearest form in which the sex difference appears in our interviews is in the degree of coherence between fantasy and reality conceptions of future adulthood. In the boys we find that dreams and plans are either similar in focus or at least appropriate to each other. Girls, on the other hand, show a marked discontinuity between fantasy and reality planning. When girls discuss their plans, they concentrate on events in their lives before marriage. They talk of educational decisions, occupational plans, and so forth. When they describe their daydreams and hopes, or when they describe ways in which they would like to change themselves, they do not emphasize individual achievement or seek changes relevant to a future work. Fantasy for them revolves around other interests. Marriage, which is surprisingly absent from their plans, does appear in dreams. Glamour and physical beauty assert an influence in daydreams which is not expressed in any realistic efforts toward change.

Boys stress education and work in their plans, and in line with this focus, they dream of outstanding achievement, choose adult ideals on the basis of their talents and work skills or the success they have achieved. When they imagine changes in themselves, the changes reflect their dominant reality interests; they wish for more of the qualities and characteristics which they relate to success in the adult role they hope to achieve.

Boys' Plans and Future Expectations

Our culture urges the boy to begin his search for a work identity early. We take it to be a sign of initiative and energy when the little boy says he will be a fireman or policeman; we feel he has learned one of the important lessons about male existence when he underscores the work side of life. We may well be pleased with him, for this does, in some sense, indicate that he has taken an important step in consolidating a masculine identification. By the time he reaches high school, we hope that the boy will have experienced enough of the world to begin more serious exploration of work images. He may change his aims many times still, but we expect him at least to try out in his imaginings some specific aspects of his future work.

This stress and its effects show clearly in our interviews with boys. Throughout their discussion of the future, the boys reveal a consistent preoccupation with choosing and preparing for a future vocational role.[2] The most general question we ask in this area—about decisions to be made in the next few years—launches them into discussion of jobs and career paths. A large majority of boys (86%) refer either to a direct vocational decision or to a decision about the armed services and the draft (which, we shall see, is inseparable from the vocational context for most boys). Most of the boys we interview will not enter active work life for some years to come, but it is a salient area for them, one in which they feel they must begin making choices. For many boys, rough eliminations have already begun; they know, for example, that

[2] Paul Goodman (1960) has drawn a compelling picture of the importance of vocational plans and the confusion that results in boys' development when their chances for meaningful contact with the occupational world are undercut.

they will or will not go to college, and they have narrowed the range of jobs from which they will eventually choose.[3] Decisions around schooling—whether to go to college, which college to go to, and what courses to take—represent a second focus of boys' concerns. Three out of four boys describe some educational question they need to decide in the next few years. Boys' realistic concerns center on the task of choosing and training for a work future.

The particular jobs they are thinking of reveal a good deal about the boys' orientation toward the future. We find, first, that achievement is the dominant theme in these job aspirations. Over half the boys name a professional or semiprofessional job they hope to reach; one boy in ten wants to be a businessman—an owner or manager; 29 per cent think they will be manual workers, and the large majority of these choices fall in the highly skilled trades and crafts. Only one boy in fourteen thinks his future lies in semiskilled or unskilled work.

The striving implicit in these job choices is more apparent when we compare the jobs boys want to those their fathers now hold. When we look at all urban boys, where it is possible to make a direct comparison, we find that nearly half of them (47%) select jobs which are higher in skill and status than the jobs their own fathers hold. Over a third (37%) choose jobs equivalent in skill and status; and one boy in six (16%) chooses a job lower than his father's in these respects. If we look only at those boys who have a chance to move in either an upward or a downward direction from the father's job (that is, if we ignore boys whose fathers hold jobs at either the very top or very bottom of the hierarchy of skills) the proportion of boys who are apparently hoping to achieve status rises to slightly more than half the group (52%).

Our tradition has it that every boy should have the opportunity to develop his talents and to profit by this development. We encourage the young in the dream of success and hope that we build into them drives appropriate to this value. This is not an idle fancy or a simple matter of taste; the functioning of an open-class system and a democratic society depends on talented children from all strata being recruited for leadership roles. This means that they must be provided access to the training and routes for positions of prestige; and it requires that they, in turn, should want the rewards available from these

[3] The growing pressure on children in our culture is for early commitment to an occupation or at least to a class of occupations. This pressure appears in vocational counseling courses in the schools which now begin as early as the fourth grade in some cities.

positions. Past mobility figures indicate the availability of opportunity; and our interviews with boys reveal that our effort to train children to want these opportunities is successful in a high degree.

Aside from the strong achievement theme, boys' occupational aspirations are marked by a second characteristic—this is the concrete and realistic quality of their planning.

We are not using as our criterion of reality some notion of what the boys in our sample will actually do for their living in future years.[4] What we mean, rather, is the active spirit with which they approach the area, the degree of energy and thought committed, and the specificity and coherence of their plans. The boys show a high degree of sensitivity to the occupational sphere, and they are testing and trying their own suitability for various jobs.

We see this active engagement, first, in the fact that most boys are concerned about choosing jobs and making work decisions. Almost all boys can say what it is they currently think they would like to work at when they are grown. Only one boy in thirteen will say that he has no idea what work he would like to do.

Very few boys name glamour jobs or aspirations that are patently those of very young boys not yet sensitive to the work life. Professional sports are chosen by one boy in a hundred, and one in a hundred chooses a job in the entertainment field. Only 2 per cent want to be pilots. In some cases even these job aspirations are more realistic than they look at first glance (for example, one boy who wants to be a dance band musician is the son of a man who is in this field). The important point is that the job categories we can by any reasonable criterion consider glamorous attract the serious consideration of very few adolescent boys.

Their actual job choices are dispersed over a range of occupations. Boys name everything from doctor to carpenter to millhand; they include highly unusual jobs like barber, and highly specified work like ornithologist and physicist (rather than the more general and ambiguous "scientist"). Only three specific jobs attract sizable groups: farmer, engineer, and mechanic. About 15 per cent of the sample

---

[4] Such a procedure would require a careful comparison of boys' job aspirations with some indeterminate combination of the distribution of occupations in the actual job market and corrective terms for changes which will occur in this distribution in the next fifteen years; changes that will be affected by automation and other technological changes. In terms of the current distribution of occupations in our society, one must find boys' aspirations unrealistic—for example, the proportion of boys who want professional jobs is four times as large as the proportion of adult males who hold professional positions at the present time.

choose each of these jobs; no other single job attracts over a 5 per cent choice. We may argue that if an area is vague and ambiguous, individuals will more easily succumb to popular images and stereotypes. If boys knew little about work and had thought little about jobs, we might expect their job choices to cluster heavily around a few highly visible and publicized occupations, as indeed very young children's do. Firemen and policemen are chosen by five-year-old boys partly because they are important symbols of authority, and partly because little boys are ignorant of meaning and variety in the occupational sphere. The fact that boys select a broad variety of jobs, that no one or two jobs dominate the scene for them, and that the jobs they choose are highly specified, all lead us to conclude that they have a degree of sensitivity that implies active involvement.

Nine out of ten boys have a fairly realistic idea of the training required for their particular job choices. Only one boy in ten, in discussing his own plans for schooling, pictures an educational future that is inappropriate to the job aspiration which he gives later in the interview. Their plans for schooling mesh clearly with their expectations of a future work role. Furthermore, most of the boys have a work model —that is, they know someone in the field of work they have chosen. A quarter of them choose work models within their own families (father, brother, uncle, and so forth), and most boys choose jobs held by some personal acquaintance. By and large, they choose jobs about which they can potentially observe something at first hand.

Boys are bound to their aspirations by an interest in job content. Seven out of ten refer to an interest in the work itself as a reason for choosing a particular vocation, and when we offer a choice of job features and ask boys to select the ones they consider most important, "interesting work" is chosen along with job security by about half of the group. A quarter of the boys also choose job aspects that we called "work style" features: working outdoors and being one's own boss, which implies freedom from restraint and independence to decide policy. These answers, like an interest in work content, refer to qualities inherent in particular jobs, and discriminate among various work roles. They contrast with criteria like "steady job" and "high pay" which can be met equally well by a wide variety of jobs. Again we find evidence in their emphasis on discriminating criteria that boys approach the choice of work with a reality-tied, attentive spirit.

Most of our respondents think of their job aspirations as trial runs rather than certain choices. They say they are fairly sure they will go into the particular line of work they name; a sizable group (29%) think they are more likely to change their ideas. Only one boy in twenty says he is very sure he will continue working toward the same goal. Most want further vocational counseling: only 12 per cent of our respondents say they would not be interested in learning "more about different kinds of jobs."

Before moving into the area of boys' fantasies about the future, we should look somewhat more closely at their plans and expectations about schooling. Nearly all of the boys in our study expect to finish high school; and half of them plan to go beyond high school, to college in most cases. Only four boys in a hundred plan to take training in a trade, while almost half (46%) of the entire sample want to go to college.

These college plans, despite their ambition, have a realistic cast. For one thing, they are congruent with occupational aims, and, in most cases, with the boy's own capacities, insofar as we can judge these from our data.[5] The boys who seek higher education by and large choose job aspirations for which college is the necessary and relevant training. Less than one per cent of the boys who hope to enter college have occupational plans that clearly do not require college preparation.

The specific tie that many boys make between education and occupation is apparent in verbatim answers to the question about education. Half of all the boys who name college-level training attach specifications: they plan to go to college and medical school, to engineering school, agriculture school, or to a theological seminary. In other words, they ask for college training geared to particular job aspirations.

This clarity about the nature and purpose of the training they want is again a reflection of the fact that boys focus quite clearly on content in looking at future activities. Just as they choose future jobs primarily because the work content commands their interest, so their view of college is to service certain concrete vocational interests they hold. College can and traditionally has served other more general needs. It may, for one thing, help the young person to crystallize his own interests by exposing him to a variety of experiences against which to test his interests. Undoubtedly many of the boys in our sample will use higher education to this end. But they apparently approach college with some developed interests which at least provide them motivation

[5] The plan to go to college is closely related to measures of verbal skill. Twenty-nine per cent of the boys who say they will go to college are rated higher than average in verbal skill by interviewers, 36 per cent are judged so by coders. Of those who do not plan to go to college, 8 per cent rank high on interviewer ratings of verbal skill, 11 per cent on coder ratings.

relevant to the educational aims of institutions of higher learning. These interests also serve to pinpoint areas in which they can begin the trial and elimination procedures by which young men move toward a final work identity.

An additional indication of boys' strong investment in the occupational area comes from our developmental data. When we analyze vocational attitudes and expectations in relation to age, we find according to the criteria we use that older boys are more realistic than young ones. The choice of glamour occupations decreases with age (from 7% at 14 to 4% at 15 and 1% at 16), yet the range of jobs chosen increases (27 occupations are chosen by 14-year-olds, 34 by 15-year-olds, and 44 by the 16-year-olds). Older boys often say they are fairly sure they will continue in their present aspirations (65% at 16, 57% at 15, and 48% at 14), and they have more detailed and specific conceptions of the preparation required by the jobs of their choice (32% of the 16-year-olds give descriptions of preparatory steps judged by coders to be "accurate and detailed," compared to 19% of the 15-year-olds and 14% of the 14-year-old group).

Older boys also base their job choices more directly on the nature of the work involved; they seldom use criteria which do not discriminate among various occupations. The boy at fourteen has begun to form notions of his occupational future. He is committed and attentive to the problem. By sixteen this commitment has led him to more vivid and differentiated conceptions of what that future will be.

Boys' Fantasy Conceptions

We have seen that boys conceive the future in terms of work, and that they integrate the future identity to their present lives by means of plans and expectations for education and preparation for the future work goal. We noted two themes that dominate their thoughts about future jobs: achievement strivings and a strong and active reality orientation.

In what ways do their fantasies support this system of plans? In general, we find that the two systems match remarkably closely; the fantasies focus on work and personal achievement. In other words, the same organizing themes come through in fantasy, although, of course, at a less articulate and specific level. Their plans are also supported, in other more subtle ways, by fantasy elements.

We asked respondents to tell us about their adult ideals—who they would like to be like, and what qualities they admire in the ideal they choose. Forty per cent of the boys specifically refer to work skill as a characteristic they particularly admire; another 28 per cent mention character traits like perserverance and resourcefulness, which are most meaningful in the context of achievement. The dominant theme in their choice of models is work relevant.

When we ask boys what they would like to change about themselves if they had a free hand, we find realism marking their thoughts in two ways. On the one hand, we find that their concern with work and personal achievement dictates the areas of desired change. On the other hand, we find a reluctance to indulge in the kind of fantasy this question requires, an indication, we think, that boys use their strong reality tie at least partially to avoid fantasy.

The largest group of boys (38%) say they would not change anything about themselves or their lives. This may be a sign of self-acceptance, but we take it also in part as a trenchant refusal to enter the realm of fantasy. For surely if given unlimited and magical power to change, there are few who would not find some element in themselves that needed a little improvement. Many of these boys, we feel, are reluctant to let go of the limits of reality long enough to speculate about changes. Among the boys who do answer the question, there are few who give entirely fanciful answers; the changes they wish for are usually ones they could effect themselves, such as personality changes or increased social skills.

Most of the changes are relevant to an image of the future work role. Boys would like to be more responsible, have better personal controls, and more facility in meeting and handling social relationships. These characteristics would help in day-to-day interaction with people in their current lives—parents, peers, and girlfriends, but also they are similar to the qualities they admire in adult ideals, whom they regard in the context of the work role. One boy in ten explicitly wishes for greater ability or talent for personal achievement.

Two questions about boys' current concerns fall between the specific area of plans and the fantasy-based images: they ask what gives the boy a sense of self-esteeem, and what kinds of things worry boys. The answers are interesting in their consistency with the other levels we have discussed.

Self-esteem depends on work and skill: half the boys gain satisfaction from contributing to a work group—most often the family in its work functions. Thirty-seven per cent say they feel important and useful when they achieve something through their own skill—such as doing well in school. And 30 per cent gain this sense of self from assuming adult-like roles—either on a job or in the home.

The worries they have also center on work and achievement: they worry about doing well in school, about passing and graduating, and about going to college. Sixty per cent of the boys adduce one of these concerns, 29 per cent worry about reality pressures on themselves or their families. Many of these reality problems also have implications for the boy's work life now and for his future plans for education, implications which some boys raise in their answers.

To summarize, boys orient to the future primarily in terms of an occupational identity. They plan concretely for this future, and their plans are marked by an active striving for achievement and by a relatively realistic assessment of the job world and of their own capabilities. They show concern about work and achievement in their realistic expectations, and also in more general and fantasy-like preoccupations. Continuity and coherence characterize the relationship between boys' expectations and fantasies—with essentially the same concerns dominating both levels of thought.

Girls' Plans and Future Expectations

Our culture's expectations for the girl are less simple than for the boy; they are both more ambiguous and less consistent, perhaps because of a recognition of the complexities of feminine development. We want the little girl to play with dolls, and we want her to develop feminine goals. At the same time we recognize that she is an individual with her own talents and potential, and we want to insure that these qualities are not lost to the child or the society through lack of training. We must teach the girl attitudes and skills for her central feminine goals, and at the same time give her the kind of training that will permit her to choose appropriate individual or egoistic [6] goals as well. A problem arises in the fact that the two sets of goals—and the skills and attitudes required for their realization—are often, perhaps always, conflicting. The individual talent or skill may require years of cultivation, training, and preparation. Because the woman's role in marriage is both

[6] The term "egoistic" is Helene Deutch's (1944, 1945). Although it has some unfortunate connotations, we borrow it because it also clearly indicates that the goals we have in mind stem from the unique qualities and talents of the girl, apart from her sex role, and are goals that distinguish her and set her apart from, rather than joining her to, others.

a sex role and a work role—because she assumes the job of maintaining the home and family—her cultivation of an individual talent cannot readily proceed after marriage unless she has the freedom to make special arrangements for home and family care. There is no inherent conflict for the man between work and realization of his sex role in marriage and parenthood, but there is for the woman. The culture's ambivalence emerges at exactly this point.

On the one hand, there is the general prescription that no matter what talents the girl may possess, she should in all cases of serious conflict prefer the feminine goals of marriage and child care to individual goals outside these areas. On the other hand, if she makes a clear choice in either direction, the girl in our culture is likely to feel somewhat uneasy. If she remains single and devotes herself to a profession, she feels that she has failed as a woman, since our culture recognizes only one path to feminine fulfillment. On the other hand, a decision not to work outside the home creates, at least in many educated women, a measure of guilt and a sense of worthlessness. The problem of the full-time homemaker is expressed monthly in the women's magazines. Here we find articles in abundance telling the housewife how important her job is: in providing strength and support for her husband in his day-to-day worldly combat, in helping him win success by entertaining graciously, in raising children who bring credit to the family. The role, in short, is a complicated executive-administrative one. Only two things about these articles lend a false note to the exuberant self-assurance they mean to inspire: they are too insistent, and they always measure the importance of the role by what it contributes to the husband's work or reputation. One gains from them the impression that American housewives need support, that they do not have a simple sense of the worthiness of their work, and that the authors cannot find anything in the role itself that serves as its justification.

Many American housewives share these suspicions and guilts about their position. And so we get the pattern of the housewife-citizen, the woman working hard in community activities to keep busy and assure herself that she is "worth-while." Among college girls, we find the explicit aspiration to be "well rounded"—to combine homemaking and some individually-based activity.

The spinster image is undesirable because it puts a woman's femininity and desirability in question (in addition to depriving her of central life experiences). The housewife-mother choice—if it is an exclusive one—has its own difficulties because it touches on the ambivalence and anxiety our Puritan culture exacts for idleness. Even the idle rich in America keep busy; we can not expect the middle-class housewife to be idle with ease.[7]

At adolescence the girl begins her task of integrating individual goals and femininity, or at least arranging a workable truce between them. She has been taught to want marriage, and has been trained to some extent in the feminine qualities and skills that will help her to reach this goal. She also has been through a period of education devoted to individual development; she has learned to set goals and work for them, to find interests and develop them, to strive for excellence and compete for honors. Now, as marriage age approaches, she must begin to set priorities and arrange alternatives.

The girl's integrative task can also be phrased in terms of activity and passivity, and, in fact, is often phrased this way by adolescent girls. At this period the girl's interest centers on being chosen by boys—as a date, a steady girl, or a future wife. The question arises how active a girl can be in seeking the prize of popularity. Too little activity means dullness, and too much activity can win her disapproval on grounds of unfeminine aggressiveness. She must be fun and interesting, yet she can easily lose the prize if her activity is either competitive with boys or too clearly designed to attract them.

This is the adolescent phrasing, but the problem continues throughout a woman's life—the need to maintain a balance between the active and passive modes. Too little activity makes her incompetent in this day of station wagons and PTA committees; maintaining a high activity level may endanger her femininity—or, at least, society's view of her as feminine (which, in itself, has important determinative power).

We should point out in this connection that the boy has different problems with activity-passivity because the culture allows him virtually no choice. The boy must choose activity, no matter what the personal cost, or be suspected and disapproved by his society. Nonetheless, the approved path for the boy is at least clear and unambiguous, whereas the girl's choice or solution is always something of an individual invention, and seems never to carry complete approval.

The task for the girl, then, is subtle and complex. The work begins in adolescence, and we may appropriately look at our interviews with girls with these questions in mind: "How do girls manage this task?

[7] Wyatt and Hoffman (1960) have developed some interesting ideas about the relationship between anxiety over leisure and the increase in the size of American families.

What means do they use to integrate the two sets of goals? How does the duality of their task influence their concept and use of future time?"

Within the age span covered in our study, girls begin to move from high activity and egoistic goals to greater passivity and the feminine goals. But they by no means give up the side of activity: the reality plans they hold are remarkably similar to boys' plans in their emphasis on the occupational role and relatively slight attention to marriage. The decisions they think they will make in the next few years cluster in the same areas as boys'—occupation and education. Thirty per cent of the girls in the fourteen to sixteen year age group do refer to marriage decisions; this is more than twice the proportion of boys who give such answers. But the overriding concern is with occupational and educational planning: 73 per cent of our sample of girls mention some job-related decision, 84 per cent talk of decisions regarding school.

Even when we phrase the question more openly—when we ask girls what kind of plan or picture they have of their future lives—we find the heavy stress is on the premarriage stage of individual development through school and work. Although adolescence is defined as the time of transition to feminine goals, girls in fact continue to focus largely on the more individual and active work role.

How do girls plan within this context? Do we have here the same desire for achievement, the same active testing and information-gathering that we noted in boys' plans? We do not. Rather, we find that girls focus on the masculine world of work, but in a way that converts this world into a vehicle for expressing predominantly feminine interests.

Girls clearly invest less in an image of their future work than boys do. They have a less differentiated picture of the world of work, a less discriminating view of the content of the particular job to which they aspire. They choose jobs that permit expression of traditionally feminine themes, and jobs that will provide a pleasant social setting in which they can make friends and meet young men to marry.

The greater vagueness of girls' occupational plans emerges in a number of ways. For one thing they are less definite about their aspirations, more often naming a number of occupations they might like. They have not as often settled on a single job preference. The range of jobs girls choose is much more restricted than the range covered by boys' aspirations. Their choices cluster in a few highly visible and traditionally feminine occupations—secretary (34%), nurse (21%), and teacher (17%), while we have seen that boys' job choices are not dominated by popular images. Girls choose glamour jobs more often than boys (10% compared to 3%), and manual occupations less frequently (2% for girls, 29% for boys, excluding farming which claims another 14% of boys' choices), although a large proportion of jobs available to women fall in the category of manual work.

The content of the job chosen is less important to girls than to boys. When asked their reasons for choosing a particular job, they adduce interest in the job content less frequently than boys do.[8] They give the following reasons for choosing jobs more frequently than boys do: social service aspects of the work (23% of girls, 6% of boys); nice co-workers (17% of girls, 6% of boys); a desire to work with children (11% of girls, no boys). Girls choose from listed alternative job qualities nice co-workers as crucial more often than boys do (53% compared to 32% of boys). Girls tend to stress job qualities which are not highly differentiating; nice co-workers can be found in many jobs. They do not as often focus on content skills or on qualities specifically associated with a particular job.

Girls are less realistic than boys in their plans for job preparation. We note ambiguities and inconsistencies in their educational plans. In general, their educational aspirations are almost as high as those of the boys. Ninety-seven per cent of the 14- to 16-year-old girls plan to finish high school; 60 per cent intend to seek additional training. A smaller proportion of girls than boys plan to go to college (34% compared to 46%). But the plan to go to college, even within this group, is vaguer in its purposes than it is for boys. A small proportion of girls (4%) say specifically that they want teacher training in college, but no other specific contents or specialties are mentioned. This contrasts strikingly with boys' college plans, which frequently include plans for particular content training.

A comparison of girls' educational and occupational plans reveals a lack of coherence which also distinguishes them from boys' plans. Over a third of the girls who plan to go to college have vocational aspirations for which college would overprepare them. We wonder how a girl can both want to go to college—where she will presumably broaden her interests and develop a taste for intellectually demanding activity—and at the same time want to be a telephone operator, bookkeeper, or secretary. The answer is that it can be done, with no appar-

[8] Girls choose "interesting work" as an important criterion when it is explicitly offered as an alternative in a question, but they do not think of it immediately or spontaneously when rationalizing their own job choices. We have here a measure of salience, and the boys clearly regard job content a more salient issue than girls do.

ent difficulty, if there is little investment or involvement in work, and if college is not conceived in vocational terms. The girl may indeed develop her tastes to a high point for use and satisfaction in the life area that is important—that is, marriage and family life—and be perfectly content to work at a job that is essentially nondemanding and nonfulfilling. At least in theory—and this, after all, is the level of planning currently available to these girls—it is a feasible scheme.

This is the central fact of importance about the planning girls do for their future: although they focus on work and schooling, very few of them are strongly invested in work or school per se. It is interesting to note in this connection that despite the broader age range of our sample of girls, we do not find an age shift in realism or coherence among girls that compares to the increased realism of the older boys.

We have seen, so far, that girls are not as reality-oriented or as discriminating as boys are in their conceptions of work. What of the other striking theme in the job plans of boys? Are girls as eager for personal achievement as boys are? We suspect that they are not on the basis of what has already been said. If they invest little in the image of their future work, it is not likely that they are primarily seeking individual achievement, fame, or the rewards that follow unique accomplishment.

However, the answer to this question is not quite so simple. Although girls do not have as intense motivation for individual achievement as boys do, they nevertheless want and expect their share of social rewards. They desire social mobility, indeed, their mobility aspirations are more pervasive and intense than boys; on the other hand, they do not tie their hopes for mobility to their individual efforts as clearly as boys do. In this they are unquestionably realistic, since women in our culture characteristically acquire status through marriage rather than through individual professional performance.

Our conclusion that achievement motives are not so crucial to girls comes primarily from analysis of fantasy material. In answers to projective "wish" questions they do not show nearly the same absorption with personal achievement that boys do. But even in direct discussion of work, they stress achievement and its rewards less: high pay and status are less often given as attractions of the jobs they want; and from a list of job criteria, girls less often choose signs of success as important to them (16% of girls choose such job qualities; 28% of boys).

Girls' choices do reveal a desire for social status: although somewhat fewer girls than boys aspire to professional jobs (30% compared to 40% of boys), practically all girls want middle-class jobs of one sort or another. Thirty-seven per cent choose semiprofessional work roles like nurse and airline stewardess, and 39 per cent want white collar clerical jobs. Very few girls want to work in the manual or service fields (2% of girls pick such jobs, compared to 29% of boys, excluding those boys who want to be farmers). Other findings indicate that girls' occupational aspirations express a general desire for a middle-class way of life rather than a specific desire to achieve eminence or outstanding skill in a profession: that is, the status rewards of the job are more crucial than intrinsic work satisfactions.

For one thing, most girls are not particular about the specific content of the job they choose. And if we group occupations on the basis of the commitment they require, we find that only about 10 per cent of adolescent girls want jobs that involve strong commitment or can be considered careers (compared to 47% of boys); most of the middle-class jobs they choose are those that demand modest commitment, which require little skill and continuing contact in order to maintain skills once they are acquired. Forty-five per cent of all girls' choices fall in this category. Another 45 per cent of the girls choose jobs that imply no career commitment whatever.[9] With this little commitment, it seems to us that the jobs girls choose are more often a function of status-striving than of a desire for any outstanding personal achievement or work gratification.

At this point, we turn to the theme that does dominate girls' job choices: fulfillment of the feminine role.

Regrouping girls' job aspirations by the nature of the actual work involved—that is, the functions and the way these are defined by society—we find that the bulk of girls' choices (95%) fall into the following four categories: [10]

I. Personal Aide: doctor, nurse	27%
II. Social Aide: social worker, teacher, librarian	19%
III. White Collar Traditional: sales clerk, secretary, bookkeeper	39%
IV. Glamour: fashion designer, model, stewardess	10%

[9] We are not attempting through this grouping of occupations to predict whether girls will continue to work throughout their lives. It may be expected that some trained for an occupation listed in "strong commitment" will drop out of the labor force, while some working in occupations listed under "noncommitment" will continue. We are attempting an estimation of the appeal of occupations which are commonly perceived as "careers" and those which are perceived as "jobs."

[10] This analysis of girls' occupational choices was designed and conducted by Carol Kaye.

In Personal Aide jobs, the worker establishes an immediate relationship with an individual who needs help and support for physical difficulties. In Social Aide occupations, the worker is also helping others, but in the area of social development. In this field, she helps others to mature and to develop the capacity to face and handle new knowledge and responsibilities, rather than lending support and assistance for physical difficulties.

Both of these occupational groups represent elements of the girl's future mothering functions. They represent responsibilities which women in less complex times and societies have met within their own homes. As these functions have been delegated to agencies outside the home, women have moved into the relevant occupational roles, and have continued to perform them. Together the two job categories account for about half of girls' job choices.

Another large group of girls (39%) want jobs in the White Collar Traditional category. The main choice here is secretarial work. The image of the secretary consists primarily of a helper aiding and assisting an important man in a variety of tasks. In popular literature and the comics we find fantasies of the indispensable secretary who is confidante and aide; or the alluring secretary who carries on a flirtation with the boss. The image obviously permits and encourages expression of a variety of feminine needs and interests. Although most clerical jobs do not offer satisfaction of these needs, the more desirable white collar jobs may approximate the fantasy.

Ten per cent of the girls in our sample express an interest in a group of Glamour occupations: fashion designer, model, dancer, singer, airline stewardess. These jobs, like traditional white collar jobs, require relatively little training or career commitment. They are occupations rarely entered by men, and are the realm of the particularly attractive girl. The image of the Glamour occupations expresses themes of personal attractiveness, romance, and sexuality.

A few remaining categories attract small numbers of girls, which suggests that the needs and interests these occupations promise to meet are less widespread.

Creative occupations—chosen by 6 per cent of our sample—include science and the arts. The central image here is one of self-expression, opportunity for discovery, and fame. Two per cent choose jobs in the Entrepreneurial category (as for example, buyer, store owner). The themes of security, self-determination, and achievement that these occupations evoke are not, as one would expect, crucial to girls.

Another small group of girls (2% of the total sample) are attracted to military service. We called this category Transitional since the chief characteristic of military service is that it permits the girl to suspend normal role obligations, and to assume a new identity on her return to civilian life. The religious life, which implies a more permanent retreat from role demands, appeals to a small group of girls (1%).

Few girls select working class occupations, which carry a negative image and may indicate a negative job choice. That is, as reality pressures increase and girls are forced to yield their original aspirations, they may retreat to working class jobs. This possibility is suggested by the fact that working class choices are more common at the upper age levels.

The overall pattern of our findings indicates that girls are attracted to a few occupations out of the total range of possibilities. The highly selected areas (Personal Aide, Social Aide, White Collar Traditional, and Glamour), have a number of elements in common. They are highly visible jobs, portrayed extensively in mass media. The publicity they receive has led to a popular and broadly held conception (frequently grossly glorified) of the work and relationships they involve.

The images of the highly chosen jobs all involve themes associated historically with the woman's role. Feminine receptiveness and sensitivity to the needs of others are important in the White Collar Traditional and Personal Aide images. Aspects of motherliness stand out in Personal Aide, Social Aide and in some of the images associated with White Collar Traditional. Sexual themes of romance, flirtation, and beauty characterize Personal Aide, White Collar Traditional, and Glamour occupations.

This analysis of the content of occupational images casts a new light on girls' relative concentration on job plans rather than marriage. The occupations girls choose represent extensions of traditional feminine roles. Their emphasis on occupational plans and decisions does not indicate any lack of interest in marriage. It seems, rather, a means for containing and expressing this interest at a time when more direct expression would in reality be premature and in our society might be thought unseemly and inappropriate.

Feminine themes in girls' plans emerge again in answers to the questions "Why do you think you might go into (this occupation)? What would you like about being a (name of job)?" Girls want to perform social service and help others, to work with children, to have the opportunity to meet and work with nice people. The characteristic feminine view defines a desirable job as one which provides a pleasant, congenial social setting and activities that are interesting and varied, and requires some skill and feminine sensitivity. The job activities usually represent aspects of the traditional feminine role of helper-nurturer.

The girls, then, focus their plans on the work role and educational preparation for work, but they use work plans as a means through which to express needs and interests appropriate to marriage, and not to express any binding commitment to a particular field of work or any strong drive toward individual achievement in a career line. In the details of their work plans they reveal the interest in feminine goals which is so strikingly omitted in their general discussion of the future. They express covertly and indirectly the aim they slight in more direct discussion of the future.

It is apparent in answers to a direct question that marriage is a major goal for girls: 96 per cent of all girls eleven to eighteen years of age want to marry. A few girls hedge their desire to marry with some condition or qualification, but only 3 per cent say that they do not want to marry, and one girl in a hundred has not decided whether she wants to marry. We shall see later, in fantasy material, more evidence of the salience marriage holds.

What picture do most American girls have of marriage? We asked about the kind of person they wanted to marry and the kind of jobs they would like their husbands to have. For most girls in our study, marriage is still some years in the future, and we can expect that their conceptions will be in large part made of dreams. We shall use the discussions of marriage as an entree to their fantasy.

The desire for social status and for a middle-class life style is a key to understanding the girl's picture of married life. In America we value the personal tie between two young people and use this as the crucial criterion for marriage. Social considerations like the boy's family background or his prospects of inheritance are supposedly irrelevant to the marriage decision. If a girl or her family openly consider these matters, they are censured as snobbish, as lacking feeling and understanding about the really important things in marriage. However, to consider a boy's occupational future, is not as strongly tabooed. A boy's aspirations and achievements reveal his character, morality, and stability, and evaluating these character traits is considered a legitimate part of the marriage decision. Such evaluation often contains and disguises an assessment of his current social status as well.

We find that girls' ideas about occupations for the future husbands vary a great deal. A sizable group (27%) consider the problem from the boy's point of view: they want him to do "whatever he likes" or "what he does well." This answer which implies a confidence in the future husband is more common among older girls (34% of girls over 16, 25% under 16) who have a clearer and more mature view of the marriage relationship. Such answers do not necessarily imply neutrality about social status however. Many girls who leave the occupational decision to the husband would probably, nevertheless, consider only young men whose aspirations were consistent with their own parents' status. Within this limit, however, the choice of a particular job is his.

When girls do choose specific occupations for their husbands, the choices provide another measure of the social status girls want for themselves. Over a third of the girls want their husbands to work in high-status, middle-class occupations (34%), primarily the professions like medicine, law, engineering. One out of five girls pictures her husband working at some middle-class occupation of medium or low status (17%), the most common of which is white-collar work or office work (12%). Some girls phrase this as a rejection of the idea of their husbands holding blue-collar (factory) jobs, rather than as specific white-collar choices. Only a small group of girls want their husbands to work in factories or at trades or crafts (7%). Girls over fourteen choose blue-collar jobs (5%) less often than do girls under fourteen (12%). A small group of girls mention occupations like farmer, FBI agent, minister, or pilot in which status does not seem to be the important criterion.

Approximately six out of ten girls (58%) mention an occupation or occupational class for their husbands that has middle-class status. Fewer than 10 per cent choose working-class occupations. The status that most girls want for their husbands thus corresponds neatly to their own plans for college and for middle-class jobs.

We asked each girl what kind of person she would like to marry. Answers to this question have also been classified according to social class connotations. In this analysis we distinguish between a middle-class and a working-class conception of marriage and the husband's role. Traits assigned to the middle-class image are those that stress a close reciprocal marriage relationship, cooperation in the home, skill in social situations, and autonomy. Traits classified as part of a working-class image are those that emphasize stable job performance, respect for the institutions of marriage and family (rather than consideration of the mutual quality of the marriage relationship), and control of negative impulses.

A third of the girls in our sample mention some characteristic falling outside this social class system. These consist of references to physical appearance (20%) and concerns about the young man's church membership and religious convictions (16%).

When girls stress status-related characteristics, these most often fit a middle-class image (75% of all such answers). One girl in five mentions some virtue that conforms to a working-class image, but only 10 per cent mention exclusively working-class traits.

The answers girls give vary with age: older girls give more responses, indicating that they have a more formulated and detailed conception of marriage. They also give answers that differ in kind from those of younger girls.

Only the young girls—who have not yet begun to date—think of physical appearance as a crucial consideration. Older girls name more middle-class social and personal traits. The kind of relationship a man offers is much more important to them and they more commonly stress shared interests and personal resources as important characteristics of their future marriage partner. In all, girls over sixteen have a more developed picture of marriage, and their ideas about what they want in a future husband have a more personal, emotional quality than do those of the younger girls.

The ideas girls have of their future husbands correspond to the jobs they want these young men to hold. They are looking for men who have social skill and consideration for others, intelligence and responsibility, all characteristics that are tied to success in middle-class professional jobs.

We cannot fail to be impressed with the consistency that marks girls' views. They want to attain middle-class jobs for themselves, they want their husbands to have high status jobs, and they have a personal image of the future husband which conforms to the requirements of these same occupations.

Apparently young girls today will not be troubled by the problem of yielding romantic, princely fantasies in favor of choosing a real man. Romantic fantasies have little part in their thoughts about marriage. They may, however, face a problem in adjusting their status fantasies to the conditions of life in the real future.

Girls' Fantasies

In the less refined, the vaguer realm of fantasy, we find that girls shift dramatically away from the reality areas of jobs and education, and omit altogether the strong achievement striving which would support their plans for work. In this respect girls show considerably less coherence between reality and fantasy than boys do. They worry about achievement much less than boys: 17 per cent of the girls compared to 57 per cent of the boys list this as a source of serious concern. When given the fantasy opportunity to change themselves, girls are less likely to think of a change that would affect their work lives (for example, they seldom wish they were more responsible or had greater ability). An interesting sex difference appears here in the fact that girls almost universally can think of some way in which they would like to change, whereas a sizable group of boys (38%) say there is no way in which they wish to be different. We judge this finding to reflect the generally greater intraceptiveness and self-critical nature of the female, and also to indicate girls' stronger investment in fantasy, as compared to boys. They have no difficulty in shifting their thoughts away from reality when this question is asked. Many of them wish for changes which they cannot expect to effect themselves. To all questions that require fantasy production, girls give more responses than boys. They seem more familiar with the fantasy world and apparently find the path from reality to fantasy a well-worn, easy route.

In choosing adult ideals, girls pay less attention than boys to character traits like responsibility and resourcefulness (18% compared to 28% of boys), and they less often choose ideals on the basis of work skills (22% of girls; 40% of boys name work skills as the quality they admire in the ideal). Nor is personal achievement as likely to be named by girls as a source of self esteem (25% of girls; 36% of boys).

We do not mean to imply that girls have no interest in individual achievement. A small proportion of girls do show a consistent preoccupation with their own development and accomplishment; and a sizable number are, as we have noted, strongly attracted to a way of life which will represent an increase in social rewards. But what we miss in girls' answers, which is striking in interviews with boys, is the mobilization of interest and individual effort to attain these rewards. They choose jobs that are relatively high in social status aand rich in rewards; but the reward is more important than the particular skill required in the job. Their plans for attaining these goals are not well integrated to the goals; they show a relatively undifferentiated view of channels—in comparison to boys. And fantasy, for them, does not form around themes that will supply energy for realistic efforts to achieve the goals.

This difference between boys and girls in the modes of approach to the future reflects an important difference in the realities the future implies for them. A boy must have a clear picture of how he will get to his goals; he must reach them, by and large, through his own skills and talents, by his own industry. This fact acts in some way as a check on the boy's tendency to dream. The girl, on the other hand, will reach her goal primarily through marriage.[11] It will not be her own efforts alone that realize the goal; she will find her goals by working together with her husband or acquire them through her husband's efforts. The next steps for her have less to do with personal achievement than with being chosen as a mate by an appropriate young man. The question we may ask, then, is whether girls' fantasies contain themes which form a bridge between the present and the future and reflect the fact that women reach status goals by marriage rather than by the use of work channels?

The themes that dominate girls' fantasies are femininity, personal attractiveness, and popularity. Even in fantasy, only a minority of girls are specifically preoccupied by thoughts of marriage: a quarter to a third of the girls fourteen to sixteen say they daydream about marriage or having children or name these as "the most wonderful thing that could happen" to them. But a more general feminine theme—the desire for personal qualities necessary for feminine adjustment and for performing the roles of wife and mother—is prominent in girls' fantasy. And along with this run emphatic desires for personal beauty and glamour, and for popularity.

The stress on femininity is apparent in the qualities girls admire in their ideal adults: 76 per cent of girls in the fourteen to sixteen year age group admire the ideal for personal qualities like kindness, understanding, generosity, and thoughtfulness (compared to 34% of the boys). The capacity to meet, understand, and relate to other people kindly and sensitively is the essence of a traditonal concept of femininity. A wife and mother is good at her life role, and is approved for her performance, to the extent that she is skilled and sensitive in ministering to the needs of others. She must be giving and she must be tactful in handling interpersonal relationships.

The girl's self-esteem is anchored to interpersonal relations more often than to achievement, work, or skill. Compared to boys, they are more likely to give popularity, acceptance by others, and adult recognition as the things that make them feel "important and useful." Popularity and glamour appear as dominant concerns in answers to a num-

[11] In addition to the findings we have presented in the text, other differences between boys and girls confirm this basic distinction in their approach to the job world. For example, in choosing job aspirations, a number of boys spoke of what they would like to do, but added certain doubts about their ability to attain their goals.

ber of questions. Achievement is the major worry of boys, and physical appearance and popularity are the center of girls' concerns. Seventy-three per cent of the 14- to 16-year-old girls worry about acceptance by peers (particularly popularity with boys). This compares to 29 per cent of boys who name this as a major concern. Issues of personal attractiveness concern 62 per cent of the girls, while no boys indicate this source of worry. The ways in which girls wish to change themselves reflect the same preoccupations: 59 per cent would like to change some aspect of physical appearance (compared to 27% of boys), and over a third wish for greater skill in social situations; the kinds of skills which would presumably gain them greater acceptance. (Twenty per cent of the boys wish they had more social skill.) When describing the reasons for choosing adult models, about a fifth of the girls say they admire the ideal for her beauty or attractiveness. Boys do not choose ideals, at least not consciously, because of physical characteristics.

These fantasy themes, while they are disjunctive with the surface content of girls' reality plans, are consistent with implicit themes we have noted in girls' conscious plans. Their job aspirations and their plans express implicit desires for a middle-class life pattern and also strong feminine themes. They approach the occupational sphere with a desire for activities traditionally associated with the feminine role, seeking gratification for feminine needs, and for an active social life that will lead to marriage.

It is her feminine concerns—implicit and not quite directly expressed—which gain reinforcement in the girl's fantasy. Feminine interests are revealed directly in the choice of adult models: girls choose women on the grounds of particularly feminine qualities. But even their fantasy desires for glamour and popularity feed into and derive from girls' strong desires to marry, to have homes and families of their own.

The process by which the girl reaches her future goals (both marriage and the social status she characteristically wants) involves being chosen by an appropriate young man. This will not happen for a number of years for most of our girls, and this fact accounts for some of the vagueness we note in their concepts of the paths to future identity. But, in the meanwhile, there is something they can do toward the goal of being chosen; they can make themselves as attractive as possible to boys. Popularity becomes a guarantee for the future; a proof and talisman against the fate of being unwanted.

The desire for popularity, reinforced by the values of the adolescent peer culture, tends to turn the girl's attention to the external world, toward surface characteristics which attract or fail to attract favorable attention, and toward the reactions of other people to her. This tendency toward "other-direction" is a consistent distinguishing characteristic of interviews with girls. We shall see again and again in various areas that boys are more directly concerned with internal problems during adolescence. Individual choice of goals and gearing of efforts to service them, development of internal controls, and standards and attempts to meet them, are the principle concerns of the adolescent boy. Girls, in contrast, are more sensitized to interpersonal relationships, to the opinions of others, to meeting the demands and judgments of important people in their surroundings. These concerns are functional to the adult feminine role—they are adaptive for the wife and mother— and they also reflect the process by which the girl achieves her identity. Since she must be chosen as a mate, she must develop the art of pleasing.

A look at answers from two sample interviews may clarify some of the differences in the way boys and girls approach and conceive the future. These are not to be construed as typical interviews. They are in many respects quite unusual. The boy whose interview we quote is softer and more passive in his stance toward reality than most boys. The girl we look at is among the small minority of girls who choose traditional professions in their job aspirations (although, in our case, the girl names this relatively masculine goal along with other occupations that represent extensions of the traditional feminine role). But the interviews, for all their uniqueness, do serve to illustrate and concretize some of the contrasts we have discussed as general trends: the unifying thread between boys' plans and fantasies, the discontinuity between these two levels in girls; girls' larger, more direct investment in fantasies, and the fact that boys' fantasies, even when they are rather well developed, borrow structure and language from the reality problem of occupational choice.

Both of these interviews are with middle-class youngsters. Both respondents intend to go to college, and they both clearly expect to live the middle-class pattern that is currently theirs by virtue of the parents' status.

The boy is a 14-year-old who lives in the northeast. His father is a personnel manager in industry; his family consists of mother, father, and three sons. This boy is the youngest.

The young man wants to be an ornithologist some day. His answer to the question "What kind of work would you like to do as an adult?" reveals a taste for the field and some indication of the source of his interest: "I'd just love ornithology work. It seems to be in my family."

This boy is young, and he does not have much information about the field of his choice yet: "I don't know exactly what they do though—whether migration work with birds or what." He thinks that other fields may claim his interest in the future. When asked how sure he is of his choice, and whether he would like to learn more about various occupations, he shows a degree of objectivity and self-awareness. "That's what I can't tell. I'm sure of it now, but you know how teenagers are. But I think I'll stick on it." ("Like to know about other jobs?") "Well, yes. I don't know which is which. There may be something I don't know about which would be very interesting."

Despite his youth and his awareness of the limitations of his knowledge of the field, his ideas about preparing for a career in ornithology are fairly detailed and not inaccurate except, perhaps, in emphasis. He plans to go to college, to forestry school, and he thinks he will need to study "Latin—for bird names—zoology, biology, and, of course, ornithology. Sciences of all kinds." He assesses his chances of becoming an ornithologist: "That depends upon whether I can get a job in the field; and if the job suits me. With what my determination is now, I think my chances are pretty good. I know I'm going to college, and I'll just go along these lines."

These work goals and educational plans are supported by a strong achievement drive that comes up at several points in the interview. When asked what job characteristics would be most and least important to him, he chooses "interesting work" and "good chance for promotion" as most important, and "job in home town" and "leader of other people" as least important. He is attracted to a job with risk and opportunity more than one which provides security but less opportunity for individual achievement. He thinks boys worry about success and achievement, and the self-changes he would like to effect are work-relevant: "I'd like to have better study habits and get more done in less time. I'm working on this, and I'll have to get better at it before I get to college."

We have seen up to this point that this youngster is visualizing a future job, and is judging it in relation to his taste and aptitudes, mechanisms for moving into the field, and his limited knowledge about it. The job idea concretizes his concept of future time. The particular job choice links his future back into the present. He states the linkage when he tells us why he has chosen ornithology as a job aspiration:

"I've always liked the study of birds. I just like to get outdoors and hear them sing; find a new bird and find out what it is. It's fun to find rare birds where they don't belong—[at this point in the interview he told about two mocking birds which nested in his yard the previous summer]—I keep a bird chart—name, date seen, where, who saw it."

He knows an ornithologist: "One of the Scout leaders at summer camp. He's almost blind; identifies them by sound and tells how far away they are." At the outset of the interview when asked to suggest activities for a new club, he had already introduced us to his vocational interest in a set of remarkably egocentric suggestions: "Me, I like the outdoors very much. My hobby is birds. Go on hikes. Most boys like nature. Some like mechanics—but I don't especially."

We find the same theme dominating answers which are less closely tied to reality. The first answer is to the question "Are there any other things [in addition to the thirty-one listed leisure activities] you enjoy doing in your spare time?" He says, in response to this: "Yes, hiking —and just plain sitting out on nice afternoons and listening to sounds. You see more birds just sitting still than looking around for them." The second is his choice of an adult ideal, and his justification of the choice: "Audubon." (Question: "Why?") "How he painted pictures of birds. How he carried on when down and out and became famous that way."

The girl whose interview we have chosen is from a middle-sized midwestern city. Her family has upper-middle-class status (the father is an executive in a large industrial organization) and consists of father, mother, our respondent (15 years old), and a younger sister (13 years old). This girl wants to be a "doctor or a nurse"; she chooses these jobs because she is interested in medicine, and "[I] would like to help people, especially children." The criteria she thinks would be most crucial in judging a job are its social setting ("nice people to work with") and job content ("interesting work"). She would least desire a job in which she would be "a leader of other people" or her own boss. She would rather have a secure job than one offering less security but an opportunity for individual success.

Her plans and decisions regarding the future revolve around school and vocational plans: When asked what decisions she will make in the next few years, she answers "I have to decide whether I'll go into medicine or teaching. I'll definitely go to college, but I don't know whether I'll go to junior college or go away. My parents would like me to go away for at least one year. If I definitely decide to be a doctor, I'll go away, or I may go to the University for nurses training. Her "plan or picture of the way [she would] like life to work out for [her]" includes an allusion to marriage, but does not focus strongly on marriage or motherhood: "I'll finish school and go to college. I'd like to become a doctor or teach, and have a nice job helping people and getting to know different kinds of people. I'd like to get married, but I think I'll work anyway, at least for a while."

When we look at other parts of this girl's interview—at her less reality-tied conceptions of the future, at her current interests and preoccupations, at her ideals and attitudes toward herself, we find little to support these professional aspirations. Within the plan itself we can note some discrepancies, but this might be explained by the fact that she is young and has not yet settled on a single occupational goal. The more significant discontinuity occurs between the discussion of future plans and the rest of her interview: nowhere do we find evidence of the kind of commitment or motivation toward individual goals which her plan would seem to imply and require. She shows none of the personal ambition we might expect; individual achievement is neither a source of concern nor a focus of current interests.

In these regards she looks like girls in our modal category: she is concerned with personal attractiveness and a feminine social facility, she is interested in popularity and particularly popularity with boys. She thinks the most wonderful thing that could happen to her is "to be really popular, be asked out a lot, and have a steady boyfriend I really like." What would she like to change about herself? She would like to be "a better conversationalist, . . . be able to talk to everyone easily . . . [and] not have to wear braces." When asked what girls worry about, she says "Boys mostly. Some kids worry about their families—kids whose parents don't get along or fight. But I don't have to worry about anything like that. Sometimes a friend gets mad at you, and then you worry."

She chooses her mother as an adult ideal because "she's fun and understands young people. She jokes with us and doesn't think everything we do is juvenile or silly. She always looks real nice too." Her major sources of self-esteem revolve around acceptance by others and feminine helpfulness. She feels important "doing something with my club, especially when I know they wouldn't have as much fun without me. And I feel important when I do something for my girlfriend— help her with her work or talk to her when she's worried." (Probe: "Worried?") "About her boyfriend or her school work."

The theme of achievement occurs once in this interview, when the girl is talking about the kind of man she would like to marry. She thinks of high occupational aspirations for her future husband, just as she does for herself, but in connection with *his* work she alludes to the kind of motive base in achievement that we miss in her own plans. "I've always thought I'd like to marry a doctor, but mostly I'd want him to do the kind of work he likes and is best at. I'd like him to have some aim in life like medicine, and the ambition to make good." She also wants to marry someone "with a sense of humor, someone who enjoys the same things, not tired and grouchy." (Probe: "What kind of things?") "Play with the children, help me, go out in the evening after the work is done."

To reiterate the central differences between boys and girls in their posture toward future time: the feminine stance is characterized by a sharp break between fantasy and reality conceptions, and by a concentration of affect and color in the fantasy realm. Girls' reality plans for the future slight and disguise the feminine goals which are crucial to them, and they fail to integrate present and future time. Girls' adolescent preoccupations with personal attractiveness and popularity as well as their fantasies about themselves and their future lives feed into and support feminine fulfillment, but are discontinuous with at least the manifest content of their reality plans.

The boy's future conceptions are more likely to be all of one piece and heavily infused with the rhetoric of reality. He plans for a vocation; his fantasy conception of himself and of future time feed into and support his plans. He may use reality planning to escape the dangers of fantasy (by evasion or by restructuring fantasy in the less dangerous terms of reality). But he does not, as the girl does, invest directly in fantasy and cover the investment by a detached second bet, a conventional gesture. He either avoids fantasy through concentration on reality or reorganizes fantasy in the terms of his real plans. The girl can maintain the two systems independently—the reality plans clear and articulate but uninvested, fantasy carrying her emotional investment and establishing continuity with her current preoccupations.

THREE

Social Mobility

Until a few years ago social scientists commonly made two assumptions about social mobility in America. The first assumption was that the American class system is more fluid than the European, so that upward social movement is more pronounced in this county than in other industrialized nations of the West. The assumption has been challenged and refuted by recent sociological analyses which show that the major Western countries show remarkably similar rates of occupational mobility. (Lipset and Rogoff, 1954; Lipset and Bendix, 1960)

A second assumption, a more covert one, concerns the motives and character of those who rise socially. It has often been suggested that upward-mobile persons pay for their success in psychopathology. Supposedly two processes are at work: those who select themselves for mobility are driven, anxious or cold personalities; and the strain of striving for success exacts its price in tension and insecurity. The pictures drawn of the upward-mobile vary, yet they are alike in being odious: they may be seen as smug, provincial Babbitts; as vulgar, reactionary *nouveaux-riches;* as hard-eyed, cold-hearted men, remote from human values other than success and acquisition; or as miserably driven and anxious souls who burn themselves out in body and spirit in a wretched, self-destructive passion to succeed.

These images of the socially mobile reflect, we think, one of the central arguments in American thought. It is a commonplace that the "dream of success" (Lynn 1955) has been a major force in the American experience; and in turn the success motif has generated its own antithesis, in that mode of thought—more fiercely held in America than anywhere else—which bitterly opposes the common preoccupation with acquisitive motives and material success. The dream of success remains, we believe, viable and indeed potent at most levels of

American society (although, as we shall suggest in a moment, it is no longer as ingenuously held as it once was); but in the intellectual community at large it has for some time—certainly since the latter part of the 19th century—been the object of attitudes ranging from fascinated ambivalence to outright contempt. The tendency to see status-striving as injurious to inner serenity and full personal development reflects, at least partly, a more general opposition to acquisitive values.

There is no question that a great many of the upward-mobile are indeed anxious and driven, or cold and manipulative. There is a substantial body of reliable research which puts the matter beyond reasonable doubt; this view of the mobile personality has more than ideology to support it. But we question whether these studies provide us with a complete enough understanding of the psychodynamics of mobility. These researches have for the most part concentrated on unusually mobile persons, those who have devoted a great deal of energy to the struggle for success—big business leaders, successful career women, and so on. It remains problematic whether we can generalize safely from this type and degree of mobility to mobility in general. If we do so, then we treat upward mobility as genotypic, as though all (or most) instances of status ascent were of the same order in origins and extent. We reason implicitly that extreme and moderate mobility are actuated by similar motives, that the poor boy who ends up owning a diamond as big as the Ritz is akin, let us say, to the electrician's son who rises to become an engineer. We would argue that markedly different processes may operate in the two instances. Most mobility is moderate; that is, it does not involve a sharp rise in status. It is, we think, moderate in another sense as well; the individual's aspirations are reasonable to begin with, and these aspirations do not exceed his capacities. Let us put this in another way: in one conception of upward mobility, the person is driven to rise just as high as he can; how high he rises is a matter of luck, opportunity, and talent, but is not limited by ambitions, which are limitless. In another conception of mobility, the person sets limited goals for himself, goals which are reasonable in that they are within reach and within personal capacity. There is nothing profound or original about this distinction—it is fundamental to Alfred Adler's thinking, and to the empirical work on level of aspiration and on the achievement motive—but it is often ignored or overlooked in sociological research.

We also want to point out that the meaning of status and success has undergone distinct changes in recent years. We have had the habit of equating status-striving with an interest in achieving money, power, and the deference of others. This identity does indeed hold for a great many persons, and for a great many of the upward-mobile; but it is by no means universal, especially as other than acquisitive and power values rise in potency and change the meaning of status and success. A person may want a higher level of work for other reasons, perhaps, because it promises to be more interesting and challenging, or pleasanter, or (somewhat paradoxically) more secure. In many sectors of the middle class, certainly, the naked and unabashed striving for material success is rather out of fashion. Beardslee and O'Dowd (1962), for example, find that among college students the valued and prestigious occupations are those, like medicine, which combine a certain degree of affluence with more "idealistic" desiderata, such as intellectuality or service to others. There is nothing new or startling about this, but again, a consideration of these new meanings of status and success has not altogether been felt in much of the theory and research on upward mobility.

Upward Status Aspiration in Boys

For reasons which will become clear later we want to discuss this topic separately for boys and girls. Since we could not measure actual mobility among adolescents, our interest is restricted to aspiration; we shall defer until later a discussion of the connections between aspiration and true mobility.

In approaching this topic, we were interested in developing a view of status aspiration which would not neglect what we felt to be its true complexity. We believed there were no single set of motives and personality qualities which determine the wish to rise in social status. It is one thing when we have a highly intelligent and energetic lower-middle-class boy whose interest in a professional career is perfectly plausible because of his gifts; it is quite another when a less gifted boy of the same social origin is driven by his parents to opt for a level of professional work he will be unable to attain. In both cases we have upward aspiration, but the motives and consequences are clearly different. From previous work on the sources in personality of upward aspiration we developed a tentative typology of mobility patterns.

1. The first, and simplest, of these can be termed "fear of failure." Here we have the scrambling go-getter, desperately pursuing success, and finding self-esteem in success alone. Ackerman and Jahoda (1950)

have suggested a typical source of this pattern. "Most of the mothers of our cases . . . apparently did not tell their children 'be happy' but rather 'make money.' . . . Success is measured by comparison with others rather than by actual achievement. . . . There are always some who have done better, who have more money and more social prestige; and there is always the danger of being pushed down the social ladder by a competitor."

2. In a second pattern, "ambivalence toward success," we find more complex dynamics at work. In these cases we generally find success and status assuming great importance because of the child's defensive identification with the parents' (usually the father's) dreaded power. The youngster can feel safe only by becoming like the parent, being on top, being "boss." At the same time, success may unconsciously mean a rivalry with and possible defeat of or by the father; in either case, success is both highly valued and extremely dangerous. A common variant of this pattern is one where we find an ambitious mother and a passive or easy-going father. Success may then take its meaning from the Oedipal fantasy, often stimulated by the mother, of taking the father's place and redeeming the mother's disappointment; here again the achievement of status is simultaneously valued and dreaded. One well-known outcome of these situations is the character type Freud termed "those wrecked by success"—those who pursue success relentlessly, yet who go to pieces when it is within reach.

3. The preceding patterns of satatus striving undoubtedly account for the most dramatic, and psychologically the most interesting cases. The achievement of success is so highly invested with unconscious meaning, so closely tied to the deepest roots of conflict, that status and success have all-or-none, life-and-death meanings. But there is no reason to believe that these patterns are in fact representative. We would argue that the dominant pattern of upward status striving, that is, the most common, is one we call (after the need achievement studies) "hope of success" (McClelland et al., 1953).

In this pattern the interest in success is relatively conflict free, governed by the rational side of the ego. Goals do not exceed capacity or opportunity, nor are they unlimited or illusory. The wish for success is neither obsessive nor prepotent. Mobility aims are objectively moderate, that is, they do not involve a dramatic upward movement in status; and if they do, they are not altogether unrealistic, for they are founded on the youngster's knowledge of unusual talents lying within himself.

We would expect the boys to come from families who value

achievement, but value it without being consumed by it. The parents transmit to the child a value which is both common and central in the culture, a value they hold matter-of-factly, neither desperately nor with undue ambivalence. The family allows the child to find and hold a higher status identity without implicating him in conflict; he will not feel himself to be betraying his past. The parents provide, permit, or encourage identity models consistent with the status the child aspires to.

The boys would, we thought, give signs of effective ego functioning. In relation to the outside world, we would expect them to be realistic and well adapted. We also conceive them to show a good capacity for neutralizing impulses, to be energetic, well sublimated, and in control of drives. We expect too to find a good articulation between ego and superego forces, so that the boys would be neither inhibited by excessive guilt nor driven to acting out by an externalized morality.

Downward Status Aspiration in Boys

The ambivalence we mentioned about upward mobility is not easily found in American attitudes toward downward mobility. To be sure, failure holds a certain fascination for us, even a certain appeal; when we can imagine it chosen willfully, defiantly, in protest against whatever rat-race a society has designed; or when it demonstrates to us the workings of *hubris*, when a hero, driven by passion or pride, falls from the heights, as for example, Oedipus, Lear, Anna Karenina, the Baron de Guermantes. There is also an interest in failure which stems from a sentimentalizing of lower-class life, where it is felt that life at the depths is simpler, more spontaneous, more direct, where the lower orders are idealized in a protest against the sterility or artifice or hypocrisy of aristocratic or (more recently) bourgeois society.

But these attitudes toward failure or social descent are, we suspect, artificial, abstract, imagined, and literary. They are rarely reflected in everyday convictions about social status. Certainly there are sectors in our society where the pressure to rise is low, where the child is not particularly encouraged toward upward mobility. But it is uncommon, we think, for downward mobility to be positively valued, or even to be taken in stride. Generally it is seen as a misfortune, an occasion for pity or commiseration, to be blamed perhaps on bad luck; and it is often the subject of moralizing scorn, seen as an outcome caused by indolence, self-indulgence, moral weakness, and the like.

Because downward mobility is widely disapproved, we did not expect to find many boys choosing an occupational status below their fathers'. We knew that a certain proportion of our subjects would eventually move downward in occupation; but we believed that this would overtake the boy, overcoming his conscious aims in the matter. We thought that even were the boy to imagine or portend, secretly, a decline in status, he would keep that possibility to himself alone, and keep it from an interviewer. We were badly mistaken. To be sure, downward aspiration is a deviant pattern, but it is by no means rare. Fifteen per cent of the sample chose occupations which are below those of their fathers; it was rather startling to discover that one in seven adolescent boys anticipates a step downward in vocation.

What causes a boy to expect, or choose, social descent? One possibility is that the expectation is a realistic one. Our subjects were between 14 and 16 years old, in high school or near to it, and had had by that time ample opportunity to appraise their talents and opportunities. The downward-mobile boy may sense himself to be less able academically or socially than his peers; he may have had any number of experiences, of failure or of marginal performance, to make it apparent to him that his chances are not good. So he may decide to spare himself disappointment, and to aim low but realistically.

Another possibility, one we thought to be more likely, is that downward mobility reflects not a realistic and passive acceptance of one's limitations, but rather an active, hostile seeking of a lower status, representing in some cases a determined (if mute) protest against the values taught by the parents or by society at large. In these instances downward mobility reflects and expresses the boy's demoralization. Alienated and anomic, the boys are captured in an infantile, ambivalent tie to their parents. Ego functioning is immature and conflict-ridden. We find failures in impulse control, a poor articulation between ego and superego, and a disturbed ability to cope with the more complex aspects of reality.

The Findings

We measured mobility aspiration in boys by comparing each interviewee's occupational choice with his father's present job. Farm boys were omitted from this analysis because it was difficult in too many cases to determine what their job choices represented in the way of mobility. We typed every urban boy, then, as upward, stable, or downward in aspiration by comparing the status and skill level of his work choice with his father's. We then restricted the analysis by limiting the sample to those boys who could move in any direction; that is, we removed those subjects who could not rise about their fathers', the upper-middle-class occupations, and those who could not fall, the un-skilled working class. In the end we dealt with a group of boys from lower-middle and upper-working class homes. They fell into mobility types as follows: 277 of them are upwardly mobile in aspiration; 168 choose jobs at the same level as their fathers'; and 73 aspire downward.

The Upward-Aspiring. It will simplify our presentation to treat up-ward and downward mobility separately. In almost all of our compari-sons the stable group occupies a position midway between the two mobile types. We feel we can most clearly transmit the psychic mean-ing of mobility by taking into consideration first one and then the other of the mobility types.

We begin with the themes of *work and achievement*. We are not surprised to learn that the upward aspirers show a distinct interest in achievement, and a relative lack of concern with security. When we put these alternatives to them in a forced choice question—asking whether they would prefer a secure job or one less secure but with a better chance for success—they are more likely than the other groups to choose the possibility of success. Their concern with achievement seems to pervade other areas of their thinking. For example, when we ask them what they admire about their adult ideals, they are more likely to mention the work and achievements of these adults (56% of upward-aspirers compared to 23% of the downward-mobile). And when they are asked what they would like to change about themselves, they more often cite changes which would equip them for greater achievement.

The interest in achievement is present, and easily discernible; yet to focus on this aspect alone is to ignore an equally important feature of upward aspiration—an absorption in the work for its own sake. When we ask our subjects an open-ended question about their reasons for choosing their job aspirations, we find that the upward-mobile are more likely to mention interest in the work itself. In choosing from a list of job criteria, the upward-aspiring emphasize two things they would ask for in a job: how will it reward me, and does it fit my tastes and interests? It is interesting to contrast them with the downward-mobile who (to anticipate our discussion) turn out to be concerned both with status and security. In fact, the downward-mobile are almost as interested in the rewards of the job as are the upward-mobile. The difference is that they are relatively less concerned about the work it-self and its relation to their own gifts. The downward-mobile boy seems to be interested in two separate aspects of reward (status and security) and less concerned with the content of the work or its interest to him. He is more concerned with the extrinsic than the intrinsic qualities of the job.

A much-noted aspect of the achievement syndrome is the willingness to forego immediate pleasure for the sake of longer-term rewards. In a sense, the upward-aspiring boys show this quality almost by definition, since their choice of work requires a commitment to a long period of education. Another indication of this pattern is shown by the fact that more often than other boys they report saving the money they earn or get through allowances.

Let us turn now to an even more important dimension—the degree of *personal integration*. We reasoned that the dominant "hope for success" pattern derives from (1) an adequate internalization of parental and cultural values, and (2) the successful resolution of key developmental crises which in turn allows the youngster to use his energies effectively and realistically. We thought that these youngsters issue from benign, conflict-free families which encourage their children to develop personal controls and to move easily toward autonomy. We expected them to be socially mature, poised, self-confident, and energetic.

There are two classes of data we shall want to look at here: those relating to the superego and those reflecting ego processes. We begin with the former: our findings show that the upward-mobile more often display a rational and internalized morality. We asked a series of questions designed to tap the ways in which our subjects formulate and react to rules. One of the questions asked when a boy might break a rule; the upward-aspiring are more likely to cite either an emergency situation, or a boy's decision that he is old enough to use his own judgment. More important, we feel, are the answers they give less often than other boys: that one might break a rule rebelliously, or because of an irresistible impulse, or because one could get away with it. These last responses suggest, variously, a high degree of hostility to authority, difficulty in taming impulses, and an externalized view of authority. As we shall see, they are quite frequently given by the downward-mobile. In another item we asked, "What kind of rule (they) would never break." The upward group more often mention those involving "responsibility to others" and less frequently say that they can think of no rule they would not break.

The upward-mobile group's emphasis on internalized morality again emerges in response to a series of projective cartoons: in one of these pictures an adolescent boy is seen in conflict between a promise he made to his parents (to be home at a certain time) and peer pressure that he break the promise. In their answers this group is more likely to mention the bond of responsibility and trust between the boy and his parents; they less often say the boy would go home because he is afraid of what the parents might do to him. We next asked whether the boy would tell his parents if he did break his promise. The upward-mobile more often say that he would.

To all of the items which allow us to make inferences on the nature of moral integration, the upward-aspiring respond in such a way as to suggest that they govern their behavior through internal standards. We recognize that one might interpret their pattern of answers to reflect that kind of "goody-goody" approach to moral issues which we find when the boy is excessively tied to his parents' apron-strings. In fact the opposite is true; the upward-mobile consistently display a greater degree of independence from the family.

In one set of six questions, we asked boys whether they would seek the advice of parents or friends on a number of specific issues (for example, what clothes to wear, what to do about a serious personal problem). The upward-aspiring stand out in autonomy; nearly a third of them break through the format of the question at some point and tell us they would look neither to parents nor friends, but would use their own judgment. Only 15 per cent of the other groups do this. The upward-mobile boy is also more likely to agree that "a friend can be as close as a member of the family." And when we ask him to name the adult he most admires, he will more often choose someone outside of the family. We consider this last finding to be of some importance, since it tells us that the boys in this group are more likely to have given up the immature overidealization of the parents. Havighurst and Taba's (1949) study of adolescence noted that the replacement of intrafamily by extrafamily models is a key indication of emotional autonomy. The small evidence we have suggests that the independence the boys display is more than verbal, for a higher proportion of them make up their own minds how to spend their money. This datum also suggests to us that the autonomy the upward-mobile show is acceded to (and probably encouraged) by their parents.

An impressive set of differences emerges when we examine those items having to do with ego resources. (Actually, we have been dealing with ego functioning all along; the findings on morality are not findings on "the superego" so much as they are data on the ego's relation to superego forces.) A critical criterion of conflict-free ego functioning is to be found in the degree of disposable energy available to the individual. The conflict-ridden personality has so much of his energy tied up in defensive processes, in maintaining an intrapsychic "steady state," that there is not enough left over for either work or play. Often the conflict shows itself not by active assertion, so to speak, as in the production of neurotic symptoms—but rather negatively, in a general passivity, apathy, inertia, dullness, or easy proneness to fatigue. Energy level, then, is one important indicator of ego functioning; and we discover that the upward-mobile are far more active than other boys. They have more leisure activities (48% of them, compared to 34% of other groups report 20 or more activities); they date more often (66% compared to 57% of the other groups); they read more (17% of the upward-mobile do not report any leisure reading, compared to 27% of other groups); they belong to more organizations (43% of the upward-mobile belong to 2 or more groups, compared to 28% of the other groups). Is this because they less often have part-time jobs? No, for as many of them report outside work as in the other groups (49%, compared to 48% of other boys in this analysis). A spirited zest for activity shows itself in other responses: they are more enthusiastic about the things they have done than other boys are; they more frequently mention activities other than the thirty-one listed, that they would like to try if they had the chance; and they suggest a larger number of activities for a hypothetical boys' club.

We have no trouble in adding to this (by now oppressive) catalogue of virtues. They handled themselves very well in the interview. Interviewers were asked to rate each of their respondents on a number of traits. The upward-aspiring were rated higher on all of the desirable qualities: they were more poised; they were more self-confident; they showed a greater sense of humor; and they displayed a greater lucidity and coherence in speech. And from other (nonrating) data, we know them to be more self-accepting, and to be more objective about themselves. Finally, the upward-aspiring boys show a more extensive time-perspective. When we ask them to name the most important decisions they will have to make in the next few years, they less often mention any in the immediate future (before high school graduation) and more frequently cite decisions to be made in the more distant future. The presence of the remote future seems to us to stem from an eagerness for adult status; in response to another question—what makes you feel important and useful—the upward-mobile more often mention activities in which they take over adult responsibilities.

We have one more general topic to consider—family relationships.

There are important questions here, for the varying theories of up-ward mobility have frequently turned on differing ideas of the mobile child's feelings about his family. The upward-aspiring are, after all, "leaving" the family of origin, in the sense of leaving a given station in life to seek another. Do they do so because they reject the family and its values? Do they internalize the family's own self-hatred about its station and go out to fulfill a vicarious parental wish for success? Does the drive to achieve come from a defensive identification with uncon-sciously hated parents? As we suggested at the beginning of this chapter, we believe that these kinds of genetic conditions would probably turn up, perhaps frequently, were we to undertake a deep and far-reaching study of mobile persons. But we feel that the modal pattern is one marked by a fairly amiable tie to the parents, one which provides enough freedom for the child to go and grow his own way.

We have already seen some of the evidence bearing on this matter—in the greater degree of autonomy the upward-mobile boys show. They display less dependence on the parents, and are less likely to idealize them. They also feel freer to express dissent from parental opinion; more of them report that their parents have some "old-fashioned ideas, or ideas they disagree with." They more often tell us that they have disagreements with their parents about money.

We can take these data—the readiness to disagree, and the relative emotional detachment from the family—to be either the surface ex-pression of a deeper hostility, or the reflection of a congenial, conflict-free relationship to the family. Our other findings suggest the latter. For one thing, in the projective materials—where we might expect covert hostility to show itself—the upward-mobile portray parents as less harsh than do other boys; for another, they more often report sharing leisure activities with the parents. Finally, there are striking differences in the types of punishment they receive; the upward-mobile group contains very few who are punished physically; there is a higher frequency of psychological methods (for example, "a good talk-ing to"). As we shall see in a later chapter, these psychological meth-ods appear to encourage the development of effective internal controls, and certainly they reflect a more tempered hostility on the parents' part.

All in all, we can characterize the modal upward-aspiring adolescent boy as showing a high-energy level, advanced—even precocious—social maturity, effective internal controls, and an unusual degree of autonomy. We would expect, theoretically, that these qualities derive from, or are synonymous with, good ego functioning, which in turn would appear in a family milieu which allowed the youngster to give up the infantile, or ambivalent, attachment to his parents. The parent allows the child to become independent (to be his own man) and to do so without feeling guilty, alone, or neglected. All of our evidence suggests that the course of development culminating in upward status aspiration in most cases follows this pattern.

The Downward-Aspiring. The reader may remember how surprised we were to learn that about 15 per cent of our adolescent boys expressed downward-mobility aspirations. The pressure to succeed, to rise in work and social status, is fairly strong in our society; but it is weak when compared to the pressure against status failure. In some subcultures there is not too much anxiety about the fact that the child ought to improve himself. In fact, Kahl's (1953) and Strodtbeck's (1958) studies on social mobility have shown that there are a great many families who do not value higher education to any great extent, who have limited ambitions for the children, and who feel it is perfectly fine that the boy does more or less the same work the father does. But as far as we know, the pressures against downward mobility are both general and intense, so tacitly assumed, in fact, that there is very little overt concern about it.

Given this state of feeling about downward mobility, we felt that downward aspiration would in most cases reflect an acute personal demoralization, that it would stem from a profound discouragement about one's self, or a deep embitterment choosing social descent as one of its expressions. We expected to find some failures in personal integration—failures in the ego's capacity to handle impulses, to achieve an internalized morality, or to cope adequately with the more subtle and complex demands of the environment. We assumed that these flaws derive, in turn, from failures in the parent-child connection, such that the child was unable to escape an infantile tie to his parents. We thought we might find a high degree of ambivalence, an intertwining of dependency and hatred—failures in identification with the parents producing alienation from them and from common values generally; and an incapacity for autonomous, sublimated ego functioning.

We did not, of course, have the data to test each of these suppositions appropriately; but the findings we do have make a strong case, we believe, for this general approach to the psychic sources of downward aspiration. In almost all particulars, the downward-oriented boys are the obverse of the upward-aspiring; the almost tedious picture of competence, energy, and maturity we saw earlier in the upward-mobile is exactly reversed in the downward-aspiring, where we find a bleak, depressing style of life, marked by listlessness, alienation, psychic meagerness and (perhaps) an inchoate resentment toward others.

Let us begin with *work and achievement*. As we have already stated, they are not greatly interested (relative to others) in what the work is about; that is, in the interest that the work holds and, presumably, its fitness for their talents. Rather, they stress the extrinsic aspects of work: its money rewards, the security it offers, the ease of obtaining work in the field. They look to vocations where they feel jobs are plentiful and easy to come by. They would like a combination of high pay and status along with security, and they do not appear to recognize the possible contradiction between these two desiderata. We had considered the possibility that the downward-aspiring might be boys whose genuine interests led them to choose work which, although it represented a status decline, nevertheless offered internal rewards—for example, the son of a white-collar father who might choose skilled labor because of a mechanical bent and absorption. But our data on the downward-mobile suggest to us that, if this motive does exist, it is rare; most of these boys seem instead to be overly concrete and unrealistic in their conceptions of work. Their emphasis on ease—ease of obtaining work, ease of rewards—shows up too in the absence of the gratification-delay mechanism we find in the upward-mobile. The downward-aspiring rarely save any part of their own money, and, of course, their truncated educational aims imply no self-denial in the service of long-range goals.

When we turn to the topic of *personal integration*, we note, first, that these boys show an externalized form of morality. In responding to the projective cartoons, more of the downward-mobile subjects think that the boy in the pictures would "behave" out of a fear that his parents would uncover and punish any misdeed. Few of them feel he would confess his transgression later if he did stay with his friends. When we ask them when a boy might break a rule, more of them stress rebellion, or an irresistible impulse, or whenever he was sure his parents would not find out. More of them say that they can think of no rule, or that there is no rule they would never break.

Signs of the social immaturity, low-energy level, and meager ego resources of this group appear throughout the interview. The downward-aspiring are less active in all areas of social life; they belong to fewer groups, date less frequently, and report fewer leisure activities. As a group, they hold jobs as often as other boys do, but in every other respect they are less often engaged in activities of any kind. More often than other boys, they report no independent reading, and what they do read is more likely to be immature, for example, comic books. They do not offer a good appearance in the interview. The interviewers more often rated them as having little self-confidence, as lacking a sense of humor, and as relatively disorganized. In talking about the future, these boys show a constriction in time-perspective which, as we shall see, appears elsewhere in their lives. More than other boys do, they prefer all-boy clubs to coed ones. The picture we get of listlessness, immaturity, and gaucheness, has a counterpart in the picture the downward-aspiring have of themselves. When we ask what changes they would make in themselves if they could, these youngsters are more likely to mention changes so great or so central as to suggest a despairing self-alienation. They more often wish for changes that are intrinsically impossible to achieve; only infrequently do they mention changes they might effect through their own efforts.

All in all, it is a sad story—even a grim one. How did these boys get that way? What were the circumstances which produced this depressing picture of failure? Short of a thorough clinical investigation, we cannot say with great confidence; but there is enough information on family relationships to allow us some educated guesses. We find here the pattern we shall see again in the course of this book, the style of family interaction marked by hard punishment, high dependency, and low autonomy. This pattern produces, we think, a marked ambivalance toward the parents which (1) infantilizes the child, (2) aborts the normal growth of his ego resources, and (3) distorts the usual course of identifications, in turn, producing failures in sublimation and in the learning of internal controls.

The downward-mobile more frequently report physical punishment (such as being slapped, beaten, or kicked), and less often say that their parents use "psychological" means (for instance, being reasoned with, or being asked not to do it again). These boys also seem to be less free to decide things for themselves. Our only direct evidence for this is the fact that they less often say they can use their spending money as they see fit. But their limited autonomy shows in another way, in that they less frequently cite their own taste or judgment when we ask them to choose between friends' and parents' advice.

Now we might expect these boys to be resentful and disaffected. So they are, but *only covertly*. We have already seen how, in answer to projective questions on rules, they answer in terms of rebellion, impulsiveness, and "getting away with it." On the projective cartoons they more often picture the parents as harsh, arbitrary, and suspicious. But when we put matters to them directly on questions of family milieu, they present a blander picture. They more often deny having differences with their parents. They do not believe they can be as close to a friend as to their family. Indeed, they often consciously idealize the family, in that they are more likely than others to choose an admired adult within the family. As we have seen, the upward-mobile do exactly the opposite. They are willing to speak critically of their parents, but reveal, in indirect or projective questioning, an easy and equable relationship to them.

Some Final Thoughts and Problems

The differences between the mobility types are so marked, they are among the most substantial we shall report in this book, that there is little to be gained in discussing their validity. The interpretation we have chosen to give the findings is another matter. We have offered a "psychodynamic" reading of the differences, but other readings may be more plausible or parsimonious.

Age Effects

The age range of the boys was between 14 and 16. When we first studied the differences between the upward- and downward-aspiring it seemed possible that the latter group might contain a larger proportion of young boys. Downward-mobile boys respond as younger boys do; for example, their lower dating frequency, their preference for all-boy clubs, and their more frequent reports of physical punishment—all these are tendencies common to younger boys. It seemed conceivable, then, that the differences between the upward and downward groups might be an artifact of age differences between the two. When we compare the age distribution within the mobility groups, however, we find no significant differences.

Nevertheless, it is a datum of some interest that the downward-aspiring respond similarly to younger boys. It suggests that the downward-mobile, although chronologically mature, are socially and emotionally immature, and that the differences we find between the mobility groups reflect differences in "maturity" defined in this manner. We do not consider this interpretation to contradict our own. The psychodynamic complications reflected in downward-mobility can quite plausibly be seen as "immaturity," a failure to meet the psychosocial and intrapsychic timetable of adolescence. Our approach has spelled out, we believe, some of the sources of that immaturity.

Intelligence

Can the differences be accounted for by the operation of intellectual differences? Are the upward-mobile more intelligent and the down-ward-mobile less intelligent, and if so, cannot the differences we found be explained more parsimoniously as an effect of I.Q.? This is a vexing question, first, because we cannot answer it from the data we have; and second, because even if we could, the answer might not turn out to be simple or parsimonious.

The upward- and downward-aspiring do seem to differ in intelligence. The latter are less likely to read, they are less articulate, and they more often fail to respond to questions. While these signs are not definitive, they do support the idea of a difference in intellectual competence between the groups. And in fact, findings in other data (Lipset and Bendix 1960) point to an association between intelligence and the direction of social mobility. We can safely assume that the relationship also exists in our sample. But this fact does not carry us very far. The downward-mobile are alienated and disaffected. Does low intelligence produce alienation, or does alienation produce "low intelligence"? Paul Goodman's *Growing Up Absurd* (1960) offers a penetrating analysis of "stupidity" in young men; it is an outgrowth of resignation, of the feeling that life has too little to offer. Our dispirited, despairing downward-aspiring may show very little alertness, very little curiosity, and very little zest because the game is not worth the candle, and not because their innate capacities are so limited. When we look at it this way it allows us to take a coherent view of the findings as a whole; for example, why should the "less intelligent" have parents who punish them physically, and why should they spend less leisure time with the family? If we interpret the differences between the groups as an outcome of intrapsychic and psychosocial differences—that is, if the downward-aspiring are viewed as suffering deficiencies in ego functioning and in a sense of rapport with the milieu—we have a more inclusive, a more unified and thus a more parsimonious understanding of the findings.

Social Status

The upward-aspiring respond very much as higher status groups do; that is, they are "like" upper-middle-class boys in their answers. The downward-mobile respond "downwardly," as lower-class boys do. We might wonder then whether the differences between them reflect objective differences in social status. We included in our sample boys from the skilled and semiskilled working class and from the white-collar sector of the middle class. Might it be possible that the upward-mobile come from the "upper" stratum of these classes, and the downward-mobile from the "lower" stratum? To check this possibility we made a close examination of parental job level within each of the classes (semiskilled, skilled, lower-middle, and middle-middle) and found no differences between the mobility groups.

Aspiration and Mobility

We have not yet treated the relationship between the two, but we have implied that aspiration, up or down, will culminate in mobility. Is this too simple-minded an assumption? Will the boys who hope to rise make it? Although we have no way of knowing, what we do know argues for a fairly close relationship between aspiration and achievement. As we have seen, boys talk about the future realistically, and choose jobs which make some sense in terms of their gifts and their life chances. Even more important is the fact that the upward-aspiring show those personal qualities which produce success—drive, competence, social presence, and the like. The downward-aspiring appear to lack these very qualities, and here too we would expect aspiration to portend outcome.

This does not exhaust the question, however. The correlation between upward aspiration and achievement will be reduced by the fact that more boys hope to rise than can, given the opportunities the economy will provide. Assuming that those who ascend in status are drawn from those who aspire upward, we may wonder which of the upward-oriented will succeed, and which will fail. Our guess would be that actual mobility will come to those who possess a greater share of the motivational and ego qualities mentioned above; but this may be too smug an assumption. What happens to the others—to those who aspire to a status rise and do not achieve it? How do they adjust to it? Do they become disaffected, resigned, or embittered? We raise these questions not to answer them but to indicate their neglect. In the vast literature on social mobility, there have been no systematic studies, to our knowledge, of the relations between mobility hopes and outcomes. The effects of actual social mobility on social attitudes will be fully understood, we believe, only when prior (for instance, adolescent) expectations and hopes of mobility are taken into account. Those who are disappointed in their status hopes should react very differently from those who never aspired to upward mobility; but both are treated as "stable" in sociological studies of mobility. Some of the ambiguities of current mobility research may be clarified once we get longitudinal studies which trace the interrelations between aspiration and outcome.

Mobility Aspirations in Girls

We should not expect social mobility to have the same meaning for girls as it does for boys. For boys, work, the job market, and work talents are central to the self; boys are realistic, even over-realistic, on these matters; and it is only the demoralized boy who is fanciful or childish in his understanding of work. We have just seen that the mobility expectation of the boy tells us a great deal about him. But for girls the future seems to exist in a misty haze, a limbo made up of dreams and sentiments, in many cases those promoted by the mass media. To say this is not to say that girls are unrealistic. We might argue instead that given the world as it is, they are more realistic, fundamentally, to be "unrealistic." They sense with considerable prescience that in important ways their futures are not entirely in their own hands, that what they will be will depend as much on who chooses them as on their own efforts.

The boy who is of a mind to rise in the world takes stock of his talents, sizes up his opportunities, and tries to fit them together. The girl so minded cannot be so purposeful. Her "talents" are relatively vague—beauty, charm, and "personality." Her opportunities are also obscure—an unknown boy of unknown quality in an unknown future. To ascend socially, she must make a "good" marriage; and the adolescent girl is likely to be uncertain enough whether she will make any marriage at all, let alone a "good" one. Furthermore, while the boy is encouraged to be ambitious, the girl must pretend not to be. Officially she must marry only for love; any concern with status must be kept underground, lest she be considered predatory. Nevertheless the girl feels under pressure to achieve status, and we have a situation wherein a goal—social mobility through a successful marriage—is highly cathected, but where the means to the goal are obscure and even slightly illegitimate. The result, as we shall see, is a retreat to fantasy which marks the attitudes of adolescent girls on social mobility.

The Problem of Measurement

How does one measure mobility in girls? Because of the nature of their mobility aspirations (as we saw it), we thought it appropriate to measure by the discrepancy (if any) between the father's occupation and the preferences girls have for their husbands' occupations (rather than their own). We decided to do this on the basis of our presuppositions about the meaning of social mobility in women; but as a matter of fact we would have been forced to use some such measure in any case, since, as it turned out, it proved very difficult to make a status contrast between the girls' own job preferences and their fathers' occupations. Many of the jobs girls choose are so distinctly feminine that they fit poorly into the status hierarchy of the standard masculine occupations. Does fashion-designing demand greater or lesser skill than managing an insurance branch office? Is airline stewardess a higher status job than automobile salesman? After trying to answer questions like these for hundreds of comparisons between girls' preferences and fathers' jobs, we felt that our judgments were so uncertain that we gave it up as a bad job. We would have been forced to drop so many cases because of ambiguities and uncertainties that we would have ended with too few subjects for the analysis we wanted to do. (We did use the criterion of the girls' own job preferences in a later refinement of the mobility analysis. We shall describe this later in the chapter.)

Once we settled on this method of determining mobility orientation, father versus future husband, we promptly discovered that this too produced problems. Despite the fact that a great many girls use status imagery in talking about their future husbands and the married life they look forward to, they often will not, when asked directly, tell us what kind of job they would like their husbands to have. They say, instead, that they have no preferences, that it is his own business, that he ought to do whatever he likes or does well. The older girls especially were loath to name a specific occupation for their imagined husbands. Consequently we lost a substantial number of cases using this method of determining aspiration (although not so many as we would have in using the girls' own job choices). Our findings, therefore, are based only on the thousand girls (about half the sample) who would answer the question.

There is one more point on methodology. We did a second analysis of girls' mobility strivings in which we used educational rather than vocational criteria. We measured the girl's status aspiration by comparing her educational goals to the actual educational level achieved by her father (and, in another phase of the analysis, by her mother). Here too we had our problems. While adolescents usually know what their fathers do, they are often quite hazy about his education. Fourteen per cent of the girls interviewed could not tell us how far their fathers had gone in school, and 8 per cent could not give us this information about their mothers. Nonetheless, we could measure educational mobility for most girls and we used this measure to check our findings on occupational mobility (husband vs. father). However, we shall not present the data from the educational analysis separately, since it yielded no substantial findings beyond those we get in the occupational analysis. The findings on educational mobility are akin to those based on occupational mobility, although somewhat smaller.

Boys and Girls

We begin by comparing mobility aspirations in boys and girls. The striking fact here is that upward aspiration is far more common in girls than in boys, regardless of the index we choose. For example: 47 per cent of urban boys choose jobs of higher status than their fathers, while 64 per cent of the girls (that is, of those who will express an opinion) want their husbands to be of higher vocational level.[1] *Girls are almost never downward mobile in aspiration.* Only three girls in the entire sample mention husbands' jobs that represent a status decline; 15 per cent of the boys make such choices for themselves. Our educational measures yield much the same contrast: 54 per cent of boys hope to go farther in school than their fathers did; 61 per cent of the girls want more schooling than their fathers had; and 67 per cent more than their mothers had.[2]

---

[1] The distribution of mobility patterns for boys is almost identical to the one Hollingshead (1949) reports in *Elmtown's Youth*. In an earlier study one of the authors obtained comparable results on questions dealing directly with social class aspirations. Twenty per cent of a group of 100 high school boys place themselves in a lower class position than their fathers. Girls, in contrast, never do this, and very often think of themselves as having higher social status than their parents. These last findings appear to answer questions that have been raised about our mobility analysis; that is, about the legitimacy of assuming an aspiration when our only measure consists of a discrepancy between the boy's job choice and his father's position.

[2] The reader may question these comparisons on the grounds that the sample of girls includes an older and more select group of girls. Since girls over 16 who are still in school are probably highly motivated, we ran the analysis again using only the 14 to 16-year-old girls, with almost identical results. Sixty-six per cent are up-

We have suggested that, given the ambiguity of their future lives, given their dependence on being chosen rather than on becoming, girls are, almost inevitably, less "realistic" in their status orientations than boys are. The high rate of upward aspiration, and the absence of downward aspiration, tends to confirm this. The girls are governed by hope; the boys also hope, but their hopes are tempered by their sense of capacity and opportunity, and by the knowledge that, in the occupational area, they cannot afford to be governed by hope alone. They cannot think of status abstractly; once they settle for an occupational goal, that choice produces decision and breeds commitment.

We see this quite clearly in the data on vocational preparation. Recall that boys showed a close correspondence between the job they wanted and the education it needed. When a boy told us what job he hoped to have, he could also tell us, fairly accurately, what steps he would have to take to achieve it. This close articulation between ends and means is not as commonly found among girls. The upward-aspiring girls do not plan to attend college more frequently than nonmobile girls; although they choose professional jobs for themselves somewhat more often than do the nonmobile—the difference is not a very large one (28% upward, 24% nonmobile). In any case, the most commonly chosen job for the upward-aspiring is secretarial-clerical work, which is also the work most often chosen by the nonmobile.

In our analysis of upward mobility in boys we noted that their educational plans were, appropriately, high—quite in keeping with the jobs they hoped to attain. We felt, in fact, apologetic in reporting this finding as it seemed so obvious and redundant. But when we turn to the girls' data we find that the apparent tautology does not hold. The girls who desire high status have no higher educational aims than nonmobile girls; and their goals, on the one hand, and plans, on the other hand, are no more articulated than those of other girls. They are just as likely as the nonmobile to have inappropriate educational aims.

The upward-aspiring show little of the achievement orientation which was so marked in their male counterparts. They do not choose status or success as job desiderata any more than nonmobile girls do, and they choose it far less often than mobile boys. Another difference from boys is found in girls' conceptions of college. For the upward-aspiring boy going to college (whatever other meanings it may have) is viewed primarily as a necessary step to a vocational goal. For the upward-mobile girl what matters about college is "college life"—

ward-mobile by the index of husband's occupation; 60 per cent want more education than their fathers had; and 68 per cent more than their mothers had.

made up of house parties, football weekends, and dazzling popularity. For the upward-mobile boy, college is one part, a most important part, of an achievement sequence; as such, it may represent a postponement of gratification. For the mobile girl, however, going to college is the gratification sought, an end in itself.

There is one more bit of telling evidence on the different meanings of mobility in boys and girls. It is rare for a boy to hope for extreme upward mobility; for example, it is uncommon for the son of an un- skilled worker to aspire toward professional work. Only 11 per cent of the total sample of boys hoped for jobs involving more than a one-step mobility rise. Girls make such choices far more often. Of those who express a preference concerning their husbands' work, 27 per cent choose jobs that are more than one step above the father's job in status. This represents fully 42 per cent of all upward aspiration in girls. To use the example already given: 39 per cent of the girls who come from unskilled laboring backgrounds want their husbands to have profes- sional or managerial jobs; among boys of this background only 18 per cent express such a job choice.

What do these findings mean? We can safely conclude from them that the mobile girl does not generally see the achievement of status as dependent on her own efforts in work. A minority of girls do see themselves involved in careers, expecting to make their way through personal accomplishment. but they are a minority. Most of the girls hoping to have high status as adults apparently believe it will happen through the men they marry. Are mobile girls less realistic than mobile boys? The answer depends on what is meant by realistic. We might question whether the question, "who is more realistic?"—is a very rea- sonable one. The boy is permitted the conviction, or, if you insist, the illusion, that his own efforts can win the rewards that life has to offer. The girl is drawn to the vision of a blissful middle-class domesticity, but is not offered a map of the terrain. She cannot take specific meas- ures leading to that vivid, yet elusive, goal. Indeed, her very activity might endanger her winning it, or she may think so. If she is too active —too intelligent, too competent, too resourceful—she may become the kind of girl boys shy away from. What it means then, is that the girl, captured by the dream of success, is driven back to the Cinderella fan- tasy. The mobile boy confronts a state of affairs in which he is encour- aged to choose activity as a way of life. The girl is also influenced by the ethic of success, as much as the boy is; yet she is asked to rely on passive—that is, regressive and magical—means for making it happen. Wishing will make it so. The upshot is that more girls than it is pleasant to contemplate live in a "Cloud-Cuckoo Land" as far as the future is concerned. They are girls, mind you, who are level-headed and sensitive about themselves and the interpersonal world they inhabit; and yet they will prattle on in the silliest way about their future lives— how they will go to college and then go to work as a bookkeeper, or how they will finish high school, go to work in the bank, and then marry a surgeon. Statements as foolish as these are not typical (although we almost never find them in boys and we do get them from girls), but even the more "realistic" answers of girls tend to collapse once we examine them more closely. They are realistic in that these girls speak of obvious "typical" jobs, nurse, teacher, secretary, which represent the giving of lip service to the idea that one intends to be "useful," somehow, and "do something," yet which do not engage any deep involvement on the girl's part. (The jobs do, of course, but the girls do not really feel involved.)

Because mobility is less real to the girl, because it does not necessarily have any consequences for her present life and activity, because "succeeding" may mean anything from a Cinderella dream to a carefully planned career—we did not expect mobility to be as salient a factor in girls' personal integration as we found it to be in boys'. For the boy, the intention to rise socially (and the intention not to rise at all, or to slip downhill) is an important element in identity building. It tells us something of the way the boy views himself in time; it implicates him in decision. For the girl the intention to rise socially may mean everything, anything, or nothing. It may reflect a realistic aim to make a satisfying future; it may signify an empty, conventional answer to the relevant question; it may, even, be a defense against reality, a flight into fantasy to dull unpleasant happenings in the present.

We assumed, then, that upward aspirations do not have the nuclear significance for girls that we find in boys; so we did not expect mobility, in girls, to be associated intimately, as it is in boys, with indices of effective ego functioning. To test this supposition, we asked the following questions: does the upward-mobile girl show a greater degree of autonomy? Do they show a higher level of activity? Do they give signs of a distinctive pattern of identification with parental values? Do they, in short, show the same psychic constellation we found in upward-mobile boys?

They do not. Our data yield no significant differences in any of these dimensions. Mobile and nonmobile girls are indistinguishable (or differ only slightly and inconsistently) on various measures of autonomy, value internalization, and the quality of family interaction. In one general area, however, we do find nonsignificant but consistent differences. The mobile show a somewhat greater degree of social maturity. They are slightly more active in leisure activities; they more often date and want heterosexual friendships. They show a more extended time perspective, a greater desire to assume adult roles and responsibilities. They are rated higher by the interviewers on self-confidence, and on organization of thought. They show more self-acceptance, and objectivity about the self. We want to stress, however, that these are only trends; the differences between mobile and nonmobile girls are not large enough to attain statistical significance.

An interesting set of differences between upward-mobile boys and girls emerges when we compare their adult ideals. The mobile boys, you may remember, underprefer intrafamily figures and more often (than non- or downward-aspiring boys) choose extrafamily adults, particularly those who represent such qualities as achievement and competence. Upward-aspiring girls, on the other hand, do not differ from nonmobile girls in the degree to which they mention intra and extrafamily models. And it is intriguing to note that the upward-aspiring girls differ from their nonmobile peers in two ways: within the family, they more often choose their own mother as a model; and without the family, they more frequently mention "glamour figures." The first of these findings, the choice of the mother, raises the possibility that, as a number of writers have argued, it is the mother who motivates the child to social mobility. If this is so, it may involve the boy in some degree of conflict, since it suggests to the boy that he surpass his father. But the desire for social status will not necessarily produce such a conflict in the girl; in desiring to rise she is "being like her mother." The fact that mobile girls choose "glamour figures" is especially striking in contrast with mobile boys, who definitely avoid such choices. "Glamour figures" are, for girls, mainly movie stars, and this preference is, according to Havighurst and Taba's (1949) age analysis of such choices, a relatively immature choice. When the mobile boy goes out of the family for a model he chooses a plausible figure, and he rarely chooses a "hero"—a baseball player or the like. On the other hand, a certain proportion of mobile girls make such a choice; and it suggests to us that among the upward-aspiring girls we find a number for whom mobility is something of a daydream. In the boy, the choice of a model is in some sense instrumental, pragmatic; in the girl it may not be so; it may rather concretize and personalize a Cinderella fantasy.

These data remind us once again that the mobility group in girls is probably made up of subgroups showing diverse, even contradictory, qualities. We wanted to see whether we could isolate out of the total mobility population those girls for whom the search for status serves the integrating function we found it to have in boys. What we did was to select girls who want high-status jobs for their husbands, and who also choose such jobs for themselves.[3] We compared these girls with the nonmobile girls (and, by elimination, to the other girls in the original mobility analysis). Our numbers get discouragingly small in the two upward-mobility groups, but we nevertheless obtain some stable findings.

We discover in this analysis that this special mobility group—let us call them the *personally mobile*—shows a *statistically significant* degree of difference from the nonmobile in those areas where the total mobility group showed only a slight degree of difference. To put it another way, we find that when we limit the meaning of upward aspiration to this group, the relationships found earlier are now increased (despite a severe loss in numbers). They are significantly more active than the nonmobile girls in all areas covered by our measures; they are also more eager to reach adulthood, are more self-confident, self-accepting, and poised. We also find differences in achievement motivation which we did not see at all in our previous analysis. They more often dream of individual achievement, and they judge prospective jobs by success criteria more often than do the nonmobile girls.

Not a single one of the personally mobile girls chooses a movie star or other "glamour figure" as an adult model, a fact which provides a minor validation of the category, in indicating that it has eliminated many of the subjects for whom mobility is a matter of fantasy. The personally mobile girls are, however, different in an important way from mobile boys in their modeling attitudes. The upward-aspiring boy, you may recall, does not choose his father as a model; the personally mobile girls choose their mothers as models even more often than nonmobile girls do. We are reminded again of the critical importance of sex difference in mobility. Apparently the boy must in some sense abandon his father psychically in the course of moving upward in status. Not that he will, necessarily, give up his affection for his father; but since the masculine identity is closely tied to vocation, he will

[3] Specifically, we chose all girls who were in the upward-mobile group (that is, had named jobs for their future husbands which were higher in status than their fathers' jobs) and chose professional job aspirations for themselves. We avoided the ambiguous decisions about semiprofessional and white-collar jobs in relation to the skilled blue-collar work which many of the fathers do. Our refined mobile group is, then, a very pure group of striving girls.

want to learn the mechanisms and forms of status from someone who, unlike his father, has achieved the wished-for status. The girl seems able to avoid this pattern. The identification with the mother is likely to be (to use Parsons' distinction) along "expressive" rather than "instrumental" lines (Parsons and Bales 1955). Her mother's status need not interfere with her modeling needs, since her mother is not linked to a vocational role. The girl can easily imagine her mother's fitting into a higher status had she married someone else.

The personally mobile girl's ability to avoid a psychic separation from her parents appears again in the data on family relationships. Mobile boys differ from the nonmobile boys in a greater degree of autonomy from the family. The personally mobile girls are no different from the rest of the girls sample in this area. They do show a slight precocity in the internalization of values, and they are somewhat more self-reliant in behavior controls (although not significantly so). But on all questions relating to autonomy per se, they show just as strong and unyielding a dependence on parental regulation as nonstriving girls do. Indeed, on some measures they are somewhat more compliant than other girls.

In concluding our comparative analysis of mobility in boys and girls, we should note that even when we get significant differences between personally mobile and nonmobile girls (in achievement motivation, ego functioning, and ego skills), these differences are not as great as comparable differences in the boys sample. The personally mobile girls do not show the same degree of clear and active realism in regard to mobility. The girl's future must in some sense remain ambiguous—it depends so much on sexual realization and on being chosen in marriage— and this ambiguity clouds the issue of status achievement. This is true, as we have seen, even for girls with fairly well-developed goals.

The girl's future is, psychologically, foreshortened. She can envision that part of the future which lies before marriage. She cannot plan, or even imagine, realistically for marriage and beyond; and since her adult identity depends so heavily on the self as wife and mother, we find in girls some delay, some marking time, in the crystallization of identity. How the boy sees himself in time—whether he is planning or not planning for it, whether he is sensible or foolish about it—tells us a great deal about his contemporary, adolescent adjustment. The girl's image of the future is less relevant, and how she sees it, and what she is doing and thinking about it—tells us little about how well she exists in the present.

FOUR

Values and Controls

A*dolescence is a decisive period* for the fate of personal morality. The youngster must accomplish two major tasks: consolidate his pattern of internal controls and move toward new values. While the tasks are related to each other, they are by no means equivalent. In the first case, the adolescent must learn to meet and live with heightened impulses; he must find a balance between desire and constraint which will allow enough to each side. In the second case, the youngster must construct an individual moral philosophy, a system of values and moral conduct which, however tacit, is his own, his own in the sense that it is not a simple copy of what he has been told to believe, but rather a guide to conduct and valuation appropriate to his own circumstances. He may achieve one task well and yet not the other. Many adolescents (and adults) find a viable pattern of internal control, but do not develop an antonomous personal philosophy; and some are able to establish coherent and differentiated values, but are unable to sustain these in the realm of personal conduct. Nevertheless, controls and values are closely enough linked in general so that we shall find ourselves discussing them together, although both our theory and data on controls are so much more complete that this topic will dominate the chapter.

Let us begin by putting the problem of personal morality in the psychosocial context of adolescence. We may start from a point of view shared by psychoanalysis and sociology—that an advanced society would not be viable were man incapable of the superego. The social system requires an efficient means of regulating the conduct of its members. Without an internal agency for assuring moral control, a far less efficient system of external coercion, a police state, would be required. Given the capacity for the superego, the person is self-regulating, common social tasks are more easily accomplished, and the need for direct social control is minimized.

To put the matter so baldly is to simplify things to the point of vulgarity; but it serves as a useful way of stressing why it is that controls become so urgent and problematic at adolescence. The youngster's encroaching maturity means that he is physically competent, mobile, capable of impregnating or becoming pregnant—all in all, afflicted with the burdens and hazards of maturity. The adolescent's impending maturity works several ways at once. He feels himself compelled to move toward a greater degree of independence as he senses that his identity, his self-realization depends on decisive, although perhaps symbolic, gestures of freedom. And even when these inner, existential pressures are not strongly felt, both the family and the community at large will make it plain to the adolescent that he must give up some of his ties to the family. The parents may feel some uneasiness about letting go of their child, but sooner or later they recognize that the child must be encouraged to become his own man—and if they do not, the child's own clamor for autonomy, or the community's censure of "possessive" parents will force them to swallow their misgivings and allow—or even encourage—the child to move away from his dependence on them.

In America more than elsewhere, adolescent autonomy shows itself in sheer mobility, in the access the child has to the automobile, and an immersion in a peer group psychically and physically remote from adult overview. The adolescent is no longer within the precinct and purview of the parents, nor, indeed, in the immediate vision of adults. Until this period he could expect, most of the time, some warning or intervention, from parents, teachers, or neighbors, should matters get out of hand, should spirits or tempers run dangerously high. Now he finds himself ever more in situations where he cannot automatically count on adult intercession to keep things under control. The adolescent may tell us and himself that he prefers this new freedom and responsibility, but there is a part of him not so breezily self-assured, which remains anxious that in the absence of adult control matters may indeed get out of hand.

The adolescent's circumstances are riddled with ambivalences. His parents, and the community at large, want the child to take and master autonomy, and yet remain uneasy that the youngster, not really ready for it, may lose control altogether, and in one rash act damage his total life chances. For his part, the adolescent pushes on for independence, and yet often frightened, unsure, ready to run back to the sweet, simple life of the child. These ambivalences are important in giving us a sense of the emotional turmoil of the adolescent experience, but they are not ultimately important, for in the not-so-long run the adolescent does decide for autonomy. And once he does, he commits himself to internal rather than external controls. If he is to cope with internal drives and external demands, if he is to take the decisive leap into adulthood, he must accomplish that final act of socialization in which he regulates himself through his own internal resources.

However, we must not imagine that there is an abrupt shift from external to internal controls. External controls by no means vanish, although the locus of authority does tend to shift from parents to the peer group. Nor do internal controls suddenly appear, for the system of internal regulation has in fact been developing since early childhood. What we see in adolescence is a change in emphasis more than a decisive change in structure, but it is no less momentous for being that. The source of sanctions and norms increasingly moves from the family to friends; and the intrapsychic control structure undergoes a radical proliferation and strengthening.

The Psychosocial Parameter—From Parental to Peer Norms

No one will question that in adolescence there is a shift in valence from the family to friends and the peer culture locally and at large; yet its character is so variable and its processes so subtle as to make it difficult to grasp and formulate. We think most writers have overplayed both the potency of peer norms and the amount of discrepancy between parental and peer standards. For most adolescents there is, appearances aside, no great dissonance between what parents and friends believe. We say "appearances aside" because we sometimes observe a great hue and cry of conflict between the child and his parents over "values" and "norms" which are in fact trivial. The so-called adolescent rebellion in these cases exhausts itself on issues of manners and tastes; for example, we know a family in which the father and son locked horns in a bitter dispute about popular music. No doubt the struggle "stood for" more, yet, its outcome was, on the son's part, a rebellion which might have been psychically necessary, but which produced no real examination of, challenge to, or departure from parental values. Thus a pseudorebellion helps to forestall any serious appraisal of serious value issues. Perhaps it is asking too much to expect adolescents to do more than make mock revolts, but one sometimes wonders whether the parent and child enter into a tacit understanding to disagree only over "teenage" matters, just as we often suspect that college authorities and college students mutually agree that they will get exercised over collegiate horseplay and the like, in that way making sure that nothing serious, for example, education, comes up for discussion.

The ambiguous quality of adult-adolescent opposition appears elsewhere, where we find that an apparent discrepancy between parental and peer standards involves far less conflict than meets the eye. Presumably parents encourage sexual control in their adolescent children, and so they do; but it would be a mistake to imagine, as we sometimes do, that there is an implacable opposition between the family and the peer group on matters of sexual morality. Here too we find unspoken understandings between parents and their children. The parents know, and the children know that the parents know, that the child "makes out," more or less, with an occasional prayer or hope on the parents' part. Here we have another form of the mutual conspiracy of silence which informs so many of the negotiations between the generations. The parents are unable to discuss the child's sexual behavior openly, and cannot officially encourage his or her erotic experiments. Instead these are given the tacit consent of silence; parents look the other way and hope for the best. In the words of Sydney Smith they "take short views and trust in God." Because there is so much covertness in this arrangement, and thus so much ambiguity, all parties are likely to feel more tension than they need to. The parents uneasy lest the children go too far, the youngsters imagining themselves to be more wicked and defiant than they are, and the observer believing there to be more conflict in sexual codes than is actually the case.

By stressing these ambiguities we mean to caution against an oversimple or overschematic view of parent-peer conflicts during adolescence. Such terms as "the conflict between the generations" have dramatic force, and help us to highlight a problem, and even contain some measure of truth; yet to take them literally is to be misled by appearances, and to miss the elaborate systems of *play*, of obfuscation, deception, and role-playing, which are involved in the parent-child transactions of adolescence.

Another common error in defining the relations between parents and peers is to imagine, as we generally do, that the former represent self-control, morality and other superego qualities, while the latter represent indulgence and the instincts. In this metaphor the adolescent is the besieged and lonely ego caught between two warring forces. In fact, the peer group is itself a moralizing, socializing agency. It sets standards, exercises a pattern of external control, and states expectations for self-control. Furthermore it may, in certain areas, be far more insistent on self-control than the family is. For example, some parents are fairly lenient about displays of temper or sullenness by the child. Let us say they are too ambivalent to suppress the child's aggression, or that they enjoy it unconsciously, or they feel that this is the way the child "is" and that there is nothing much they can do about it. When such a youngster finds his way into the adolescent peer group he may discover that the pique and petulance permitted by the family is prohibited by his friends. They will insist that he not give in to his moods, or that he may do so only at certain times and places. The peer group will demand that its members acquire an elaborate code of tactfulnesses, sensitivity to others, and prohibitions of impulses and emotions. In doing so, it socializes the youngster toward the achievement of self-control. To be sure, other nonfamily agencies have done so previously —the school, and the preadolescent peer groups. But given the adolescent's intense attachment to his peers, their expectations assume an extraordinary importance.

So the peer group will demand forms of self-control that the family does not; of course the opposite is also true. The adolescent's friends will permit an emotional leeway that the family may forbid. This side of the matter needs little elaboration, since we commonly recognize this function of the peer group, as an arena for the display and discharge of drives the family suppresses. We mention it in order to make the point that both parties, the family and the peer group, are dialectically entangled in the adolescent's career in controls. Each party allows certain modalities of instinct expression; each sets standards and values; each provides sanctions and controls; each demands of the youngster that he show self-control. These separate "moralities" are, as we have emphasized, not only opposed, but also overlap and reinforce each other, and what is perhaps most important, they differ in valence, in stressing different—not necessarily opposed—ideals and values.

It then becomes clear that the adolescent faces the problem of synthesizing these separate (although intertwined) moral communities; indeed, we believe that *ego synthesis* is probably the most useful concept we have for formulating the growth or stasis of controls and values in adolescence. Adolescence, we might say, is critical precisely because the ego must undertake such prodigies of synthesis, and no more so than in the areas of impulse control and moral valuation. With so much in flux, the strain on the synthetic function is enormous. The youngster must integrate prevailing social norms, his own early moral codes (the superego), early and late ego ideals, his ego dispositions and defenses, these and more, into a coherent pattern of moral belief and conduct. So far we have limited the discussion to a single, although central, aspect of this extraordinarily many-sided problem of synthesis —the integration into some functioning unity of the separate moral "worlds" of family and peers. We should also note that there is no single act of synthesis. During the adolescent period, we find continuing resyntheses, as the peer group increases and the family wanes in emotional significance, as the values dominant in the peer world change over time (for example, in boys from the "latency" interests of early adolescence, in athletics and a world without women, to the more heterosexual concerns later in the period), as the peer groups themselves are changed by the child as his own needs and interests change.

What is remarkable is not that the synthetic processes in adolescence often fail, but that they are ordinarily successful. We become aware of the synthetic function only when it does fail, when the child is unable to absorb and tie together the needs, demands, and ideals which envelop him. More often the syntheses are successful enough to be "silent"—there are no agonies or outbursts. There is a gradual, almost indiscernible accretion of new controls and values.

The synthetic process is eased when we have an objective absence of conflict between parental and peer norms. We have already suggested that this is true most of the time. Parent-peer conflicts are less severe and general than they are reputed to be. Some discrepancy of values is sure to be found, since the two generations differ in perspectives, but for the most part, we believe, core values are shared by parents and peers, and conflicts center on peripheral or token issues. This muting of conflict helps produce a fairly untroubled adolescence, in this area at least, and from the point of view of personal adjustment the concordance of values between parents and the peer culture is a desirable thing. But there are other points of view than "good adjustment." An absence of tension between values also tends to produce the bland, docile youngsters who make up the majority in our high schools and colleges, and who forever remain morally and ideologically parochial. On the other hand, those adolescents who are caught in a struggle between family and nonfamily (usually peer) norms may suffer intense personal disturbances; but they are also more likely to be capable of those fresh or deviant or relativistic perceptions of social reality which make innovation possible. Until fairly recently America had, in the sons and daughters of its immigrant families, recurrent instances of adolescents enmeshed in just such struggles between competing norms. These generations did in fact show a high rate of emotional turmoil; and they also produced an unusual number of those who, given propitious circumstances, were capable of high achievement and originality.

When the adolescent finds himself torn between conflicting norms or values, the strain on the synthetic function may be severe enough so that he abandons any attempt to integrate them. Instead he may opt for one and give up the other, clinging desperately to one system and totally rejecting the other. Thus the adolescent may commit himself deeply to the family and abandon nonfamily standards and ideals. On the contrary, he may flee from the family psychically, to cleave to peer or other nonparental values. Another solution may be to work out a synthesis based on splitting, dissociation, in which the two moral communities are kept apart, the youngster living in one and then in the other. These splits sometimes work out without apparent stress. We know of a Latin-American girl from an aristocratic and rigid family who was sent by mistake to a progressive American college. (The mistake was made because her parents chose the most expensive college they could find, assuming it would therefore be the most carefully regulated.) This young woman found she could switch from one milieu to the other without much sense of strain, one day being a casual, rather bold college girl, and the next (given a fast plane) a demure, eyes-lowered scioness, complete with entourage of duennas. She could not say why this was easy for her, nor in fact can we. Certainly this great plasticity to the milieu is not common. At this college girls from less remote provinces, such as Texas, often found they could not abide the freedoms given by the school, and fled.

In these examples we have an "objective" difference between competing norms and values; and as we have suggested, the presence of such dissonances strains the synthetic function. But it would be wrong to suppose that most adolescents caught in normative conflicts have these imposed on them by circumstance. On the contrary, value conflicts are often "chosen" by adolescents for internal, and usually unconscious, reasons. Intrapsychic factors may play the leading role, in that the struggle between family and extrafamily standards and values expresses an internal crisis, although a crisis which may have "external" referents, as when a boy chooses lower class friends to torment his ambitious parents. It is often difficult to disentangle the interaction between genuine conflicts in values and the personal dispositions which lead the youngster to use the "conflict of generations" motif in resolving some part of the adolescent crisis; and it is easy to be "bamboozled" by the rhetoric which these conflicts occasion. A specific case is an adolescent boy, highly gifted intellectually, who suddenly lost interest in school work, opted for the "beat" life, and was preparing to go on the road. When he was taken to a psychological clinic by his parents, he offered a compelling indictment of the fakeries of the "Organization" society, sounding very much like Paul Goodman, and the intake interviewer (also *au courant* in these matters) was persuaded that this was a social-philosophical rather than a personal crisis. The clinic staff thought something was fishy, nevertheless, and urged a more searching interview, which revealed that the boy's loss of interest had been preceded by a homosexual seduction by one of his teachers. Going on the road was simultaneously a flight from homosexual arousal, an unconscious seeking to repeat and master the trauma, a way of punishing the "elders," a self-punishment for having yielded, and no doubt much else. This tale is told not to debunk Paul Goodman, or anyone else who believes that the prevailing ideology of adolescent discontent tells us a great deal about the culture and about those adolescents attracted to it; nor is it meant to refute the "reality" of the protest or of adolescent values in general. Rather we mean to caution against simplistic appraisals of parent-peer conflicts, which are always a mixture of the "social" and the "psychological," the real and the unreal, the objective and the personal.

Internal Controls

In our discussion so far, of the relations between parental and peer norms, we have stressed the elusiveness, ambiguity, deceptiveness, and complexity of matters, and in doing so have doubtless sacrificed the lucidity of plain statement. We shall continue in this vein as we move to our next theme—the nature of internal controls—for here too things are less straightforward than they seem to be. We are in the habit of speaking of "good" or "poor" controls, implying a continuum of control effectiveness. Hence we deem certain persons to be impulsive, instinct-ridden, or out of control, others to be overcontrolled, still others to show good or effective control. These terms are useful descriptively, as a verbal shorthand, especially for the rough-and-ready purposes of clinical communication, when we want to sum things up quickly.

For analytic purposes, however, this model of controls is not at all adequate. For one thing, it reduces the variousness of control styles to a single and rather crude dimension. A person may be "well controlled" in relation to some drives and not others, and in some situations and not others. He may be overcontrolled most of the time and then explode into impulsive action; does he then show better or poorer controls than the person who is mildly impulsive most of the time? This conception tends to make us lose sight of the many-sided sources of control. If we ask ourselves what produces good control, we find ourselves tempted to say "strong defenses," or "a reasonable ego," or "a strong superego." These concepts themselves may obscure more than they illuminate; for example, to speak of defenses as strong or weak elides the problems we should be dealing with—how defenses relate to each other; the connections between defenses and adaptive ego functioning; the sources of defense preference; and the linkages between specific impulses and specific defenses. The defenses *are* involved in control, as are the ego and superego processes in general; and if we are to achieve an adequate grasp of how controls work, in adolescence and elsewhere, we shall have to recognize that control is a complex process, related to a multiplicity of processes—defenses, ego states, superego functioning, the ego-ideals—each of which, in turn, requires a differentiated treatment.

An Incident

To get our discussion going, let us imagine a single instance of loss of control. Ordinarily when we think of failures of self-control, our minds run to flamboyant examples, as for instance, girls who cannot say no at the critical moment, or boys whose violence makes them a menace to others. Our present purposes are better served by a more representative example. Imagine a group of adolescent boys sitting around bantering with each other about this and that. Imagine too that the mood of the group has been fairly low-key, so that there is no question of group excitement or contagion. Unexpectedly, one of the boys turns to another and says something too personal and too cruel. The victim flushes, the group falls into a discomfited silence. What has taken place? Let us take this as a representative anecdote, from which we can survey what may be involved in control and its failures.

The first hypothesis that comes to mind is instinct-excess. Perhaps the boy had had a series of rebuffs during the day; perhaps the conversation had touched on something that excited anxiety—what may have been critical was an unusual strengthening of the impulse, to the point where it surmounted control. We would also wonder about the state of the defenses. The boy may be able ordinarily to keep himself from recognizing the presence of hostile wishes or feelings; this capacity may have been weakened momentarily, perhaps because of a sudden surge of drive, or perhaps because of other factors which may have eroded the usual efficiency of the defense processes. Even when impulses are known, the person need not yield to them. We shall also take into account the executive aspects of the ego, to consider whether (and for what reasons) the ability to delay drive expression may have failed.

Perhaps the boy's sense of social reality was at fault, either momentarily or as a general state of affairs. He may have been (or may usually be) obtuse to the demands of social interplay, insensitive to group feeling. Perhaps he had intended to be witty, and misappraised the effect of his words, or the probable response of others. In any case, we must consider as a source of control-failure a defect in judgment, anticipation, and the like, any one of a number of adaptive ego functions.

Another possibility to bear in mind is that the boy's "loss of control" exists only in the eye of the beholder, that the boy may view himself not as rude or tactless, but rather as frank, candid, outspoken, and unhypocritical. His hostility may be ego-syntonic, in that it may reflect some ideal of the self. What is pertinent here is that impulse-control is related to a social role, ego ideals, and ego-identity. Many so-called failures of control are not ego-alien disruptions of behavior, but are rather expressions of the social personality; and it is important to keep in mind that impulse expression and control are influenced by the roles and identities the adolescent assumes.

This survey is by no means definitive, but it offers us some feeling for the great range of phenomena which are involved in controls. Let us turn now to a more detailed and extended view of the mechanisms of internal control.

Control and the Defense Mechanisms

It is a fairly common tendency to view controls and defenses as, more or less, synonymous. When the defensive system gives way, we often see a failure of control, and in these cases the two concepts may appear to be equivalent. Nevertheless, the defenses are more correctly understood as an important system within a larger, more ramified system of controls. As we shall see in a moment, in some instances the defenses more or less dominate the control process. But control can, and usually does, involve more than defenses. Indeed, one criterion of good controls is a minimal reliance on defenses exclusively. To illustrate why this is so, we can do no better than revive Freud's early metaphor of the censorship in a society. A well-functioning nation can do without censors, for seditious views can be broadcast without endangering political stability. A society under stress may have recourse to a censorship if its rulers feel there are no mechanisms available for containing or adjusting to dissidence.

Analogously, the person who is functioning well instinctually, who senses himself competent to achieve drive discharge without anxiety, who can delay or postpone the instincts until ready, can also allow himself to "hear" them. He fears no internal disruption. When these resources are unstable or sorely tried, he may feel compelled to treat the instincts by refusing to recognize them. Control and defense then do indeed become equivalent, in that the burden of control is assumed entirely by the defense mechanisms.

If the defenses operate successfully, other mechanisms of control need not come into play. This is precisely the state of affairs we find in a great many individuals whose psychic functioning in the area of controls is dominated by defenses, and who have few other techniques of impulse inhibition. Unfortunately, the advantages of defense are purchased at some cost to the total personality. An excessive reliance on defenses reduces the flexibility and differentiation of the total personality. The person may be inhibited, either generally, or in certain areas of his life; he may show rigidities of attitude, feeling, or response; he may develop certain eccentricities of thought and behavior; frequently he is in some respects "washed out," drained of the richness and complexity he might otherwise enjoy; often he is emotionally and intellectually shallow. Furthermore, a heavy commitment to the defenses tends to burden them excessively. The defenses become brittle, and the person endangered by a potential eruption of the drives. Hence, the "well-defended" personality may seem to show "good control" in the short run, yet be unable to endure tension over the long run.

It is characteristic of adolescence that precisely these costs, sacrifices, and failures dominate the picture. A great many of the peculiarities, excrescences, and eccentricities of adolescence are the result of putting too many of the control eggs into the defensive basket. When the youngster turns hyperascetic or hyperpious, when he suddenly is unable to work or when his work becomes ritualized, when he swings between extreme shyness and frantic exhibitionism—in these and dozens of other cases, we can recognize clearly enough stiffenings and falterings of the defenses. Because instinctual pressure is so great at this period, adolescence is a good laboratory for observing the defenses under strain, and it is probably no accident that Anna Freud's classic book on defense mechanisms gives so much attention to adolescence. The instinctual upheaval at this time produces a number of changes in the work of the defenses. They take over a larger share of the control function; and they become more rigid, and influence the total personality more completely (see below). In a great many cases, the existing repertoire of defenses is inadequate to handle the instinctual pressure, and "new" (that is, more primitive) defenses take up the slack, often at a great cost in adaptation. For example, it is not at all uncommon to see adolescents develop a high degree of suspiciousness and hypersensitivity, or transient social phobias, due to the fact that projection replaces other defenses.

In these examples we emphasize the symptomatic costs of the defenses. But it should be clear that this is only one side of the matter. The defenses are ubiquitous. They are always problematic for the adolescent—for all adolescents (adults too, of course) and not merely in producing symptoms and not only for "disturbed" adolescents. We want to stress that the defenses are at all times relevant to psychic functioning, and to the person's relation to the milieu. In appraising the influence of the defense mechanisms we would therefore want to consider the following questions.

1. *Do the defenses interfere with the adaptive ego functions?* When the defenses play too central a role in internal control, and thus assume dominance psychically, one common consequence is that we get an enfeeblement of the sublimations, and a subversion of the adaptive ego capacities—judgment, memory, thinking, and the like. It is a clinical platitude that those who depend too strongly on repression tend to become far too naive and ingenuous, and frequently cannot learn or remember as easily or as well as they might. The intellectual work of adolescence, then, may be inhibited by a heightening of repression. If the youngster tries to solve an impulse problem by projection, and grows suspicious of the motives and good will of others, or sees sexual license all about him, then his ability to see the world truly, accurately, is in some degree diminished. If the isolation defenses become rigidified, the adolescent's emotional life may become stiff and artificial, and his cognitive life arid and ritualized. Any of the major ego functions can be invaded, distorted, and crippled if defensive urgencies dominate the control processes.

2. *Do the defenses "force" an identity?* If over a long period of time the defenses maintain priority in control, the character structure as a whole may arrange itself about them, so that personality is essen-

tially an outgrowth of the defenses. The choice of ideals and values, and of models which personify these, may "follow" the defenses; the defenses are then the nucleus about which an identity forms. For an example we need only turn to our own discipline, where we sometimes find students who opt for the "hard" side of psychology because it suits an obsessional demand in the self. Ideals, values, identifications, even personal and collective utopias, are then encrusted over the obsessional defenses to make up an obsessional style of being. Another example is found in those girls who respond to the instinctual crises of adolescence by beating a retreat to hysterical repressiveness. Repression then is the rock upon which a certain style of character is built, as for instance, in the Dumb Dora. One of us has seen clinically a *naif* of this type, a confused, bewildered, dizzy innocent who, as it turned out, had been in childhood a sharp, saucy brat. In adolescence a series of instinct-object dilemmas had led her to rely heavily on repression, and with it, "dumb Doraism" as a way of life. During the course of her psychotherapy another personality, pert and witty, first peeped through and then stepped through the curtain of wide-eyed innocence.

3. *Do the defenses fit the milieu?* This is not a question we ordinarily ask, since it is our habit to think of the defenses as locked in a solitary relationship to the impulses. A good deal of recent work has, however, stressed the external sources of the defenses; the defensive style is to a great degree acquired through identifications; and defense preferences reflect social class level. The middle-class way of life is based not only on certain values, but also on defense mechanisms which both support and reject these values, for example, reaction-formation, isolation. Extending this line of thought, it is plain that the individual's defensive style may, or may not, fit the demands or preferences of the social environment. Such discrepancies are especially important during adolescence, where the peer group can be severe in demanding a uniform personal (and thus defensive) style, and where the youngster is vulnerable to peer pressure. Imagine an adolescent boy whose defensive style centers on reaction-formations; imagine him to be polite and fussy, somewhat timid. Now imagine him in a peer milieu where direct aggression, or a degree of studied slovenliness, is normative. Some strain may result; his friends may chide or mock him for his fussiness and timidity; or he may himself find his friends' attitudes disquieting, even intolerable. Perhaps we ought not to overemphasize the importance of these discrepancies, since most urban and suburban high schools offer the youngster a sufficient range of opportunities for friendship so that he can ordinarily find a viable peer group. Neverthe-

less, sometimes we come across adolescents who are, defensively speaking, isolates. Recently we saw clinically the adolescent daughter of a professor, living in a lower-middle-class fringe suburb. The girl's sense of difference from her peers involved not only values and ego traits, but also her (intellectualizing) defenses, which set her apart from most of the girls she knew, in whom the predominant use of repression had produced the usual mixture of prudishness and shrill coquetry. The girl, we felt, was a perfect fit, defensively, for Shaker Heights, Ann Arbor, or Newton; but her characteristic defensive style deepened her isolation from the peer milieu.

Control and the Ego Processes

The topic is vast, extraordinarily complex, and in some aspects obscure; we shall survey only some central problems. In discussing the defenses we have already touched on one important part of the ego's role in control. Now we want to treat the nondefensive side of the ego —the adaptive ego functions, the sublimations, the processes of rational control, giving particular attention to how these function and change in adolescence.

Let us begin with those ego functions not directly involved in control—judgment, thinking, memory, the appraisal of reality, and so on. We may state as a general principle that the more intact these functions remain the more effective will control be; conversely, loss or failure of these functions will in most cases interfere with control. We see this clearly in cases of gross disturbance of ego function, as in the psychoses and severe character defects. The loss of the reality-testing capacity ordinarily makes good control impossible to achieve; if the person cannot appraise the environment accurately, his capacity to act rationally is most problematic.

It is when we turn to less extreme examples, in normal or neurotic behavior, that the principle is eroded by exceptions and reservations. Consider again the problem of reality-testing. Once we begin to examine closely the vicissitudes of "normal" reality appraisal, the concept seems to dissolve before our eyes. There are extraordinary variations in the way people cognize the external world—in the conceptual schemata they employ—and these variations do not necessarily interfere either with adaptation or self-control. Indeed, a highly accurate appraisal of reality may at times interfere with adaptation. Imagine the not-too-hypothetical case of an adolescent whose understanding of some sides of reality is more differentiated and subtle than that of his peers; his very grasp may hinder his relations with friends, who do not assess the "real world" as carefully as he does. An excess of virtue, here as elsewhere, may get in the way of "good adjustment."

On the whole, however, the principle holds. In adolescence the instinctual upheaval often leads to an invasion of the adaptive functions; these functions—thinking, judgment, and the like—lose some of their autonomy, their freedom from conflict, and they begin to serve the instincts or to help ward them off. Their clarity may be lost, and with it, some of the capacity for control. When the youngster can judge truly and think coolly he can keep out of difficult situations; he can judge what is and is not possible in the way of gratification; he can avoid unbearable frustration, and so on. When these talents are diminished, as they often are in the course of adolescence, control itself becomes more uncertain.

A related issue, and a most important one, concerns the fate of the sublimations in adolescence. Sublimations transform pregenital instincts, and in doing so, ease their pressure on the apparatuses of control, both defensive and rational. When sublimations fail, the defenses are burdened, leading to the costs and consequences previously discussed; the processes of rational ego control (to be considered below) also are placed under strain. We have already mentioned that the latency period shows an extraordinary development of sublimations, so that the child ordinarily enters adolescence with a remarkable repertoire of sublimation channels, which permit a conflict-free discharge of instincts. The instinctual revival of puberty threatens the integrity of the sublimations.

We have recently begun to recognize that sublimations are not an either/or matter, but are arranged along a continuum in their degree of freedom from direct instinctual discharge. Some sublimations are close to the drives, for example, the person who "sublimates" his voyeurism by photographing nudes. It frequently happens in adolescence that precisely this sort of "slippage" takes place, that an activity remote from the drives may be invaded by them, hence be subject to conflict, and hence lose its utility. The activity will become dangerous, so that the child "loses interest" in it or abandons it altogether. Or the activity may become so infused with instinct-derivatives that its "quality" deteriorates. We know of a witty adolescent boy, gifted at satire, who gave up writing precisely in this way. His wit became heavy-handed and cruel, and he could not resume his interest in writing until well past adolescence.

Paradoxically sublimations, which are a substitution for defenses, may serve defensive purposes, especially during the adolescent years. The youngster may invest too heavily in a single mode of sublimation, so much so that it "forces" an identity, as the defenses sometimes do. We have in mind here the not uncommon adolescent development wherein the child loses himself in a single line of activity—mathematics, for instance, or one of the sciences or arts—to the exclusion of all else. This may happen for a number of reasons; sometimes external persuasion is involved. The child's talents coincide with parental (or school) support, as often happens in the middle class; or child, family, and school concur in viewing a gift as a path to social mobility, as often happens in the working class. The youngster's identity then crystallizes about a given sublimation medium, and at once a number of dilemmas are resolved. He can contain some share of the impulses, support his self-esteem, achieve role, place, purpose, and identity, and win the environment's support. But so heavy an investment also protects the adolescent from too much of life; sublimation serves as a defense against experience, and the ego's ability to endure instincts, affects, fantasies, and external challenges, is never tried and proved. Other potentialities, other realms of experience, are uncultivated, and the child grows into only a part of what he might otherwise be. Furthermore, the "control" that the child wins over impulses may be false, in that it is a postponement rather than a solution of the instinct crisis. We have seen enough instances where the precocious and one-sided development of a talent did no more than borrow time. In late adolescence or early adulthood, or even later, the instincts finally assert themselves. The person has not acquired a range of techniques for dealing with them. The outcome may be an acute impulse disorder, where the person runs wild, partly in order to make up for lost time; or there may ensue a regression to more primitive methods of instinct-control, culminating in a neurotic "breakdown" of some sort.

It might be said that the examples we have chosen do not represent true sublimations, but counterfeits of them. We agree, and would add that the counterfeits are commonly mistaken for the real thing, largely because "sublimation" in any form tends to be valued automatically. Let us close this section by reasserting that the true sublimations are indeed valuable; their integrity is an enormous asset for control. By allowing the diversion of pregenital drives they make possible rational control. Indeed, the state of the sublimations is probably our best index of the quality of control and of adaptation in general. Both acting-out and overinhibited adolescents usually show a poverty of sublimation-channels. And a loss of interest in these channels is a fairly regular precursor of acute emotional disturbance, in adolescents and in others.

Now we shall discuss the processes of rational control, a difficult and elusive problem.[1] We have approached it by stressing a distinction between defensive modes of control and the rational modes. The former are automatic, inflexible, unconscious, involve the expenditure of psychic energy, and produce the costs and sacrifices we detailed in an earlier section. The latter are harder to characterize, but seem to involve the following: an ability to delay pleasure, and to tolerate that delay; the ability to achieve minimax solutions of common human dilemmas, that is, to find a satisfying compromise among instinctual, environmental, and moral demands; and a heightened consciousness of one's own motives. (Of these, the last, self-awareness, is perhaps the least important, despite the prestige which is attached to it. Many people achieve rational control despite a rather shallow understanding of their motives. In any case, it is doubtful whether many persons, outside of those who have had intensive psychotherapy and a few highly perceptive souls, have a deep understanding of the forces which move them.)

We ought to bear in mind that the distinction between defensive and rational modes of control is somewhat factitious. Here too we do not have an either/or proposition. The defenses, as we said earlier, are ubiquitous, and even among those who show an exemplary judiciousness we expect to find a considerable reliance on defenses. Presumably the defensive processes would be relatively less important in the overall functioning of the control apparatuses than they would be among those whose style of control is less rational. Yet even this way of putting it, as a contrast between defensive and rational emphases in control, involves a gross oversimplification. In any close clinical examination we see an astonishing mixture of modes of control—the defenses (in all their variety), sublimations, other displacements, inhibitions, avoidances, character attitudes, and suppressions—arranged in idiosyncratic patterns. In adolescence the pattern is ordinarily unstable. The prevailing style of control may emphasize at one moment certain defenses, then shift to inhibitions, or sublimations, or other defenses. In adolescence the processes of rational control are weaker than they will eventually become, once instinctual, identity, and self-esteem questions have been, somewhat, settled.

Perhaps this is a good place to say that we do not view control as an

[1] The extraordinary complexity of the problem is surveyed in Heinz Hartmann's paper, "On Rational and Irrational Action" (1947).

ultimate good, especially in adolescence. When one is writing about the difficulties, failures, and costs of control, as we are, one gives the impression that the achievement of good control is the purpose and meaning of the adolescent experience. Now there is no question that the development of controls is a central item in the agenda of adolescent development, nor can there be much doubt that failures or excesses of control—as we find them in impulse disorders, on the one hand, and neuroses or character constrictions, on the other hand—are less desirable than a modulated self-regulation. But we must keep in mind that there are goals other than good control, and that the achievement of these goals may require some slight turmoil, some loosening of the control system.

We have in mind here the impressive findings which have emerged from the Vassar studies (Sanford, 1956). These show that impulsivity increases in the course of the college experience, and that the capacity for impulse expression relates well to such traits as social maturity and independence. College girls who are moving toward autonomy are more likely to be "troubled" and "upset," and we are sure the same is true for other adolescents. The bland life, the life of serenity within and without, is admirable only when we contrast it with agonizing inhibitions or explosive lack of control; it is not nearly so impressive when we compare it with the tenser, less harmonious, yet perhaps richer, more various, more complex life of those who exist in some degree of conflict with impulses and the milieu—where control is constantly under test, where it must every day be won anew.

Control and the Superego

The superego may well be the most frequently misunderstood concept in psychoanalytic theory. Two related errors are commonly made. Superegos are deemed "strong" or "weak," (we earlier noted a similar tendency in conceptualizing controls) and they are taken to be the executive of control. Thus we sometimes hear it said that so-and-so acts out because of a weak superego, or is morally exemplary because of a strong one.

The difficulties involved in putting it this way are apparent when we recall Freud's (1928) paper on Dostoevski. He points out that Dostoevski fails as a moralist because his moral pattern was to sin and then undergo periods of deep remorse. Freud comments wryly that a truer morality consists of not sinning in the first place; there is something suspect in a moral righteousness which has so little influence on wickedness. But what shall we say of Dostoevski's superego or, for that matter, of the superegos of so many of the personalities he created? The superego in these cases is "strong," in producing prodigies of self-reproach; yet weak, in failing to induce constraint. (Indeed, as Freud pointed out, the sin-to-expiation pattern may become fixed, so that the person commits sin in order to enjoy the purifying effects of remorse.)

The point is that the ego is the executive of action, and thus of control, and the superego's part is to be a critic of action, either before or after the fact. Hence it is more accurate to avoid speaking of superego strength, and instead to characterize the articulation between ego and superego processes. What relationship do these processes show to each other? What contract is established between them? The ego, in choosing a path of action, must take into account the price to be paid in guilt. In aiming for certain pleasures, the ego's choice, ordinarily, is to spare itself reproach by foregoing gratification, or to take the pleasure and later take its medicine in guilt.

The topic is replete with paradoxes. For example, a vindictive superego is frequently found among delinquent personalities. Unable to bear the pressure of unconscious guilt, they isolate the superego (that is, dissociate the ego-superego linkage) and act on an apparently guilt-free basis. They then offer penance not by suffering remorse, which would be unbearable, but by self-damage, such as, being caught, being ruined, and so on. Closely allied are the "criminals out of a sense of guilt feeling"—those who seek "real" punishment in order to ease the torment of unconscious guilt. The superego can act silently and indirectly, exacting its tribute not only by remorse and feelings of moral worthlessness, but also by producing "objective" suffering, as in the neuroses of destiny, wherein the entire life pattern is arranged to produce failure or misery. Another paradox is that the superego will act against the ego not necessarily for deeds done, but (some say more frequently) for deeds not done but wished. Thus those who sin least may suffer most, for the fear of guilt prohibits the quest for pleasure, and yet the prohibition of pleasure increases temptation, in turn increasing guilt and the further prohibition of pleasure.

These paradoxes are by no means empty. They go to the heart of the matter, in allowing us to define the supergo's often peculiar role in the adolescent's control problem. The emergence of instincts activates the superego's force vis-à-vis the ego, producing, as we shall see, some extraordinary complications of the ego's job in assuring control. As ego-superego tension is increased, the ego may find it more, rather than less difficult to achieve good behavior. Indeed, what may appear at first to be an instinct problem may turn out, on closer study, to be a problem in adjusting to an untamed superego.

An habitual delinquent of seventeen who was seen in a juvenile detention home, affords an example. His delinquent career had begun at the age of twelve; in the five years between he had been out of detention for a total period of three months. Typically he would be released from a reform school, commit some meaningless, "impulsive" crime, a minor one, and be back in custody within the week. The circumstances of his arrests plainly showed an interest in being caught. For example, he had one time broken into a service station, then gone to sleep (with the loot beside him) in an automobile parked right in front of the station. His most recent crime was the following. He had been free for two days. He borrowed his brother's car and began riding aimlessly through the city. Noting that the fuel gauge was running low, he decided to siphon some gas from another automobile. He chose a car parked on a residential street, and managed to make so much noise while siphoning that the car's owner looked out the window, saw what was going on, shouted to him to stop, and threatened to call the police. The boy paid no attention, but calmly finished the job and then drove off. Several blocks later he remembered that he had left the siphon hose at the scene of the crime. He drove back to retrieve it, straight into the embrace of the police who had arrived by then.

It would be hazardous to generalize from this example, either to the sources of delinquency or to the nature of the superego in adolescence. Yet it does illustrate, however extremely, the effects of ego-superego tension on control. A superficial look at his history might lead us to say that he is instinct-ridden. But in fact the containment of impulses was not a severe problem for this boy, not in the ordinary sense; for example, he was a model (that is, docile) prisoner (which accounted for his frequently being released from detention). A deeper examination made it clear that he was driven to achieve external punishment in order to escape the presence of a ferocious, vindictive superego. This pattern had been mildly evident before adolescence, and was intensified then. The force of the instincts produced the danger of overwhelming guilt; and the ego had opted for punishment and prison to relieve superego pressure. In Franz Kafka's phrase, he was "a bird seeking its cage."

In the genuinely impulse-ridden personalities we can again discern the hidden and disruptive effects of unconscious guilt. Impulse neurotics seem to show superego absence; in truth, the opposite is the case. They are generally so tormented by massive superego pressure that their impulsivity is a desperate attempt to "cure" a depression. The impulse neuroses are, paradoxically, closely allied to the depressions, and we find in intensive therapeutic work with the impulse-ridden a depressive nucleus. In treating those who act out impulsively we have to keep an eye out for depressive and even suicidal reactions once the acting-out symptoms have been breached. These personalities do in fact show superego presence, in severe self-reproaches after the fact, in intense feelings of inferiority (due to internal self-criticism), or in a life pattern marked by failure and self-destructiveness.

What bearing does all of this have on adolescence? Just as certain adolescent careers are best understood by using as a model the symptom neuroses, so are others understandable as transient, age-specific impulse disorders.[2] The activation of drives leads to failures in control, not because the impulses overwhelm the defenses but because they activate archaic superego forces. The ego then defends itself not against the id but against the superego, using impulse-expression in a flight from guilt.

In a therapy of a young adult woman, the following adolescent pattern was reconstructed—with the onset of puberty she became a "bad girl." She chose shady friends, dressed provocatively, talked "shamelessly," and gave so delinquent an impression that she was the cause of much hand-wringing by concerned adults. It was all a sham. She did nothing "bad" and in truth was extremely prudish. She managed to give the appearance of being "foul-mouthed" when in fact she was phobic about saying dirty words, so much so that she was into her second year of therapy before she could bring herself to say them. Her provocative behavior involved a direct denial of intense shame and guilt. By appearing to be "bad," she was able to say, "See how unashamed I am. I do not feel guilty"; at the same time by being "good" she enjoyed the sense of being unjustly accused. These are only part of some very complex psychodynamics, but the operative motive throughout was the need to escape the sense of guilt. In other cases we have seen the pressure to escape the superego produces real acting out and not the sham variety this girl showed. The superego may induce severe inferiority feelings, for example, and "loss of control" may actually be a means for restoring self-esteem; a girl may be accessible sexually in

[2] It has been suggested that recent social changes, affecting both the family and the conditions of adolescent life, have made acting out a more common adolescent pattern, and that we are seeing the disappearance of the "neurotic"-like adolescence.

order to feel loved and thus repair the mortification produced by hostile introjects.

In summary, the superego probably causes more problems in adolescent control by its "strength" than by its "weakness." As we have seen, when the superego's criticism injures self-esteem, or when it threatens to produce a catastrophic sense of badness, the ego may react by a defense against guilt—isolation, denial, and so on—behaving in a way that may at first appear to be without conscience. And just as the impulse neurotic handles the depressive danger by yielding to the drives, so may the adolescent, facing the onslaught of internal badness, attempt to keep things in balance by throwing himself defiantly into the impulse life.

We have chosen examples from the pathological extremes of ego-superego interaction. Normally ego and superego are more harmoniously articulated, enough so to work in concert for control. But it would be a mistake to imagine that ego-superego dissonance will be found only among disturbed adolescents. To the contrary, it is normative for some tension to develop between the two structures; adolescence almost always brings with it a need to renegotiate the ego-superego compact. Since the resurgence of instincts activates infantile prohibitions, the adolescent ego must learn to temper their force, must strengthen itself against the superego, establishing a new and viable relationship with it. For example, suppose the Oedipus complex was resolved in childhood by a vigorous disavowal of sexuality. When erotic impulses reappear at puberty they must be allowed some release. The superego's prohibition of sexuality, if it is not tempered, will hinder the full growth of the personality. So the ego must learn to unlearn the superego—more precisely, some parts of it—as one of the intrapsychic tasks of adolescence.

Control and the Ego Ideals

How does it come about, how does the ego overcome the archaic prohibitions of the superego? It does so largely by taking unto itself new ideals, ideals which oppose, replace, or are synthesized with superego injunctions. These new ideals come from the peer group, for the most part, although they are present in the peer culture at large, and are likely to be supported, if only tacitly, by the parents as well. Consider the example we just gave—prohibitions on sexuality stemming from the Oedipal superego. The adolescent absorbs new ideals—"popularity," let us say, for the girl, and "masculinity" for the boy, which act as counterideals to the older negatives. The importance of the peer group is in no small part due to its being the carrier or spokesman of the ideals; and the ideals themselves are valued, or overvalued, as the peer group may be, in the need to overcome some part of the superego constraints.

Before we continue let us pause to examine, cursorily, the ego-ideals. Their role, and their definition, have never been formulated clearly, primarily because Freud developed the concept on his way to discovering the superego, and later absorbed the ego-ideal into the superego, rather loosely. The ego-ideals remain obscure, we think, because they are defined so variously, sometimes being understood as close to the superego (the "do" of the superego's "do not") and thus unconscious, "deep" and infantile, and sometimes as close to conscious values. We shall propose the following conventions for this discussion. First, that the superego and the ego-ideals are to be treated as distinct (while recognizing that some ideals are quite close functionally and genetically to the superego). Second, that there is no ego-ideal, but rather a more or less loosely synthesized collation of ideals. And third, that these ideals differ greatly in depth, intensity, extensiveness, centrality, and so on. Thus, some ideals are archaic and outside of awareness, and others are fully conscious. Some are more highly cathected than others. Some are more extensive than others (that is, some govern a large context while others are narrowly applied, even situational). We shall not be punctilious on the distinction between ideals and values, since in the present context they can be treated as synonomous.

In adolescence we see a desynthesis of the system of ideals and attempts toward resynthesis. We cannot stress strongly enough the importance of these processes for almost all aspects of the adolescent experience. The integration of new values supports the ego in its interplay with the drives, and as we have just seen, it aids the ego under duress from atavistic prohibitions from the superego. The ego-ideals strengthen the child's will toward autonomy from the family, and they also guide vocational and role commitments. The ideals influence the forms of sublimation the adolescent chooses, and vice versa. Altogether, it is hard to imagine a phase of adolescent life unrelated, directly or indirectly, to the resynthesizing of the system of ego-ideals.

The task of resynthesis is by no means easy to accomplish. To understand what is involved, let us spin out a metaphor from architecture. In designing new buildings for a college campus, the architect generally confronts older styles, either a hodgepodge of styles—a

Gothic library here, a Georgian dormitory there—or a unified style—Gothic or Tudor, for instance,—but in either case unsuited to contemporary doctrines of style. He has several choices. He can design buildings in the established pattern—pseudo-Gothic or what have you; he can break with the past altogether, demanding that the old buildings be abandoned or razed to begin a new campus from scratch; he can design new buildings to sit side-by-side with the old, without any attempt at stylistic unity; or he can design contemporary buildings which have some of the mood of the older style, as in Eero Saarinen's American Embassy in London, designed to blend into the Georgian style of Grosvenor Square.

The adolescent, as the architect of ideals, faces similar problems and chooses roughly similar solutions. He may absorb only those ideals which are close copies of the existing pattern of morality and valuation. He may abandon the past altogether, living exclusively by the new ideals of adolescence. He may accept new values to co-exist with the old but without coherence between them. And he may try to choose and modify the new ideals to blend easily with the old.[3] The form of synthesis chosen has considerable bearing on control. If the old ideals and prohibitions are dominant enough to bend the newer values to their pattern, we may have an overinhibited adolescent, or one mired in the past and incapable of growth. If there is a lack of coherence between older and newer ideals we may see the dissociations we mentioned early in the chapter, in which a Jekyll-Hyde morality emerges, or a fragmented identity appears.

The synthesis once established bears on control in another way, in that it provides a model of behavior which directs the adolescent's ventures in gratification and constraint. For certain ideal identities the control vector is easily apparent—the young gentleman, or the chaste young maiden. But most ideals contain tacitly some image of control, even when it is not obviously present. Consider an ideal of masculinity common in American culture—the strong silent type, as we see it in Gary Cooper. At first we may be struck by the toughness and the strength of this ideal, but when we look again we note that the image also implies a particular style of control. The model synthesizes strength and constraint, in stressing a reticent toughness—the man who walks quietly but is sure of his resources, who does not initiate violence but can take care of himself when provoked beyond endurance

[3] If this metaphor were not already overextended, we would point out that the designs of buildings must take into account the site (that is, environmental demands), existing services and utilities (ego capacities), and so on.

(in the Western—Cooper, John Wayne, Matt Dillon; in detective fiction—Humphrey Bogart, Sam Spade). In these fictions a contrast is established between a hero who can control himself and a villain who cannot. In the "showdown" it is the villain who is unable to tolerate, delay, abide tension—he shoots first. Even in those adolescent subcultures characterized by violence, this ideal of control asserts itself. In the ideology of urban street gangs there is a great deal of stress laid on the testing of one's own and the enemy's capacities for control. In the lower-class game "the dozens" the idea is to trade insults, the loser is the first to lose control. However, we must also note some erosion of this ideal. The once-firm line between a restrained hero and a trigger-happy villain is being blurred. The hero shows a lowered threshold for violence, as we note in The Untouchables, let alone Mickey Spillane.

The foregoing discussion of controls has avoided, except here and there, any general consideration of differences between boys and girls. We had of course expected the sexes to show differing patterns of control, if only because they have different problems of control. What we were not at all prepared for was the extraordinary degree of difference. It is here, we suspect, that our data make their most striking contribution. Not only do the findings spell out markedly separate orientations toward control by boys and girls; but also suggest that the psychology of control is male-centered which may be irrelevant for feminine behavior and experience.

We first came to this realization in the course of exploring our developmental data, which are, as the reader knows, limited to the girls sample. We had developed a set of expectations concerning the interaction of impulses and controls over the adolescent period. Since these expectations did not work out empirically, we shall only summarize them here. We thought that the use of defenses would change during adolescence, with repression, projection and similarly more "primitive" mechanisms appearing more commonly during the 14 to 16 year period, to be replaced by a greater tolerance of the drives in later adolescence. We also expected to find a more self-conscious awareness of controls growing as adolescence progressed, so that the girls would increasingly rely on internalized authority. We also expected to find a bristling, self-assertive insistence on one's right to self-government, with a concomitant edginess and rebellion toward adult authority. We saw the early adolescent girl as a young Puritan, somewhat rigid in personal standards. The humanization of both values and controls would not, we thought, make its appearance until later in adolescence. In general, we anticipated an acute sense of awareness of the difference between one's own standards and those of the parents, and we thought the sense of difference would become clearer as the girl moved through our three adolescent substages.

Generally, the developmental analysis yields findings which do not support these assumptions. The "crisis" in the 14 to 16-year-olds does not on the whole materialize; defensiveness, rigidity, and defiant self-assertion are not markedly different here than elsewhere. We do find age changes, but these consist in minor and straight-line relationships. For example, we expected the 14 to 16-year-old girls to be more tightly defended against sexual drives than the younger and older girls; now there is some evidence of this, but in the main we find a gradual and continuous development in impulse tolerance over the total range of the adolescent years, from eleven to eighteen. More important is the evidence that the degree of change (measured by the proportion of subjects who reveal a conscious acceptance of impulsivity) is modest indeed. Only a small proportion of the total sample at any age meet our criteria (to be detailed in a moment) for impulse tolerance. We do not find much evidence of changes in defenses or in the operation of internal controls. (There is one exception; when control questions are phrased in a peer context, we do find some of our expectations met: a major growth in controls, and some brittleness in the mechanisms used during the 14 to 16 year period. We shall discuss this later.)

Now let us look at the evidence. Many of our questions allow and even encourage the girl to make allusions to sexuality: questions on dating, on sources of popularity, on the reasons girls are liked and disliked, on parental expectations, on rules, and so on. We find that only a small percentage of our subjects give answers which recognize the existence of sexuality; furthermore, the proportion of sexual references does not change, except slightly, with age. For example, the subject of "steady dating" is discussed, even in the mass media, in sexual terms; it is widely felt to be undesirable in encouraging erotic intimacy. But when we ask our girls about it, they reject steady dating on much more innocuous grounds, saying, for example, that steady dating keeps the girl from knowing many boys or excludes her from the fun of ordinary dating. Only 3 per cent of the girls talk about steady dating in a way which alludes to sexuality, and even here they use a flat nonsexual, sometimes ambiguous language ("it might get too serious").

The same avoidance of sexual references is found in responses to other questions which might elicit them: "All parents have ideas about how they want their children to behave. What are the most important things your parents expect of you?", or again, "What kind of [parental] rule would you *never* break?" We had expected these questions and others like them to invite some degree of concern about sexuality. But only 7 per cent of the sample in the first case and 4 per cent in the second make even oblique sexual references. When we ask a more general, more projective question—"What would happen if parents didn't make rules?"—only 1 per cent refer to sexual consequences, such as that girls would marry too soon, or become pregnant out of wedlock. We get little sense, from the answers to this question, that impulses in general are much of a problem—most responses stress the confusion and disorientation which would follow the release from parental restraint.

One projective question was specifically designed to draw sexual references—"Gladys feels terrible because she did something she thought she would never do. What do you think it would be?" This question did indeed elicit more responses concerning sexuality than any other, just as we had hoped, and yet the proportion of girls is, we think, surprisingly low even here—18 per cent. Developmentally, we find some support for our assumption that the middle period of adolescence shows the greatest concern with impulses. Sexual references are 12 per cent in the 12 to 14 year group, 24 per cent in the 14 to 16 group, and 20 per cent among late adolescent girls. Our own reaction to these findings was one of some surprise at the fact that sexuality, here as elsewhere, breaks through so infrequently. Using a simple cumulative index of ten questions in answer to which any sexual responses occur, we found that only one-fifth of the girls ever allude to sex during the interview. And if we exclude the projective question just mentioned, nearly all direct sexual references are made by 5 per cent of the sample— this small proportion of girls is distributed evenly over the age range.

When we turn to the question of the aggressive impulses we find, as we might expect, that the girls talk about them more easily than they do about sex; but one is also struck by the fairly mild quality of the discourse. We do not get the sense that the girls feel that controlling hostile feelings is a major problem (as we do in the case of the boys). The girls mention hurting a friend or one's parents as a shameful act, about twice as often (42%) as they mention sexual misbehavior. They are also aware of disagreements in their relations to family members— parents and siblings. But the tone of these is moderate; only about 5 per cent of the sample talk about their disagreements so as to suggest that these are more than differences of opinion. And between a fifth and a quarter of our sample deny any disagreements at all.

We shall continue to see in this chapter and later, that girls tend to picture the family milieu as pleasant and harmonious. Their discussion of peer relationships does, however, generate a more active awareness of hostility, not in themselves, but in others—specifically in the quite frequent concern about gossip. When we ask what a friend should be like, or the sources of a girl's popularity with other girls, or the reasons why a girl might be excluded from friendship—we get the gossip motif in about one-quarter of the answers. Our respondents are often apprehensive about being victimized by gossip. We suspect that this concern is partly real, partly projective, that the fetid world of peer relationships—with its cliques, rivalries, petulances, and making and breaking of friendships—becomes the arena in which both sexual and aggressive impulses are most frequently engaged. The girl's sensitivity to being gossiped about is undoubtedly based on her knowledge that her friends do gossip, and also on her guilty awareness of her own tendency to gossip about others, which is then projected outward. Interestingly, the concern about gossip is more marked in middle adolescence (14–16) than later on, and here at least it would seem that our early expectations about the developmental fate of the impulses are borne out, that the 14 to 16 age period sees a higher vulnerability to impulses and thus a use of projection to ward them off. Some further evidence along these lines is to be found in the tendency of girls in this age group to be projectively sensitive to sexuality in other girls. When we ask if there are some girls they would not go around with, we find that 11 per cent reject girls who are boy crazy, 39 per cent reject those who have acquired "bad reputations," and 4 per cent reject those who have "gone too far with boys." Girls in middle adolescence are more often preoccupied with the issue of reputation than either the younger or older girls (39% of the middle group, compared to 15% of younger girls and 18% of older girls, said they would exclude a girl if she had a bad reputation).

Let us pause here to recognize that much of the preceding evidence lends itself to variant interpretations. In our own reactions to the findings on impulses we were impressed by the general placidity of tone, by the absence of a preoccupation with drives and their control that we had expected to find. At the same time, we are quite aware that the evidence does not decisively support this view of the feminine adolescent experience. The dearth of sexual responses, and the muting of aggressive responses (except for two items dealing with peer relations) may occasion little surprise in those readers who feel that the interview situation simply did not encourage or even allow the emergence of the impulse tensions which are in fact present. One might say that an interview set in a school, administered by an unfamiliar and (generally) matronly interviewer, would tend to check the appearance even of oblique sexual allusions, and would produce a dampening of any signs of rancor, especially in regard to one's family. Perhaps so; we can offer no decisive counterargument. But we were aware beforehand that this might be the case, and so placed a good deal of emphasis on indirect and projective questions, wrote codes so as to maximize the scoring of "impulse" laden answers. Our own interpretation remains that the sexual and aggressive drives in girls are more firmly contained than is commonly believed, at least more than *we* believed, and we unrepentantly maintain that the interview, ceding its limitations, would otherwise have yielded more than the mere whisper of impulse-striving that it did. And finally, we think we shall be able to improve our case when we examine the boys' data.

Let us turn now to a topic where the findings are, we think, less ambiguous: on the internalization of standards and controls. We find that girls do not show much self-conscious concern about self-control, that they are not much preoccupied about achieving autonomy and self-direction. A negligible few (less than one-half of one per cent) think of control issues (for example, control of temper, irresponsibility) when asked to mention what they worry about. Only about 13 per cent, when asked how they would like to change themselves, say they would want to be more self-reliant, responsible, or self-controlled. In describing their adult models, only one girl in ten mentions as admirable these or related qualities. There are no age trends in any of these questions, no indication that older adolescents are increasingly concerned with self-direction.

We had originally believed that adolescent girls would be actively interested in distinguishing between their own standards and their parents' dicta; and we imagined we would find evidences, however covert, of a struggle between child and parents as this process developed. But we find few signs of rebellion or conflict. The girls largely feel their parents' rules to be fair, right, or lenient. Only a quarter of them state *any* reservations, however mild, about their parents' rules, and only 5 per cent consider them to be unjust or severe. About half the girls in the sample tell us that they have some part in setting the rules at home; and we find, to our great surprise, that whether or not she participates in rule-setting has no effect on the girl's feelings about parental rules. Those who have rules made for them are as happy about this state of affairs as those who are consulted about rules. Indeed, even those girls who have highly restrictive parents show no strong tendency to resent or rebel against their situation—at least consciously. We isolated those girls who report that their parents expect them to be obedient and to respect authority, and who, to a projective picture, portray parents as controlling and authoritarian. This group of girls view their parents' rules as benignly as the rest of the sample.

We could go on at some length adducing evidence which gives further support to the girls' tendency to adopt a compliant attitude to parental authority; but some of the data will appear later in this chapter, when we make a direct comparison between boys' and girls' orientations toward impulses and controls; and some will appear in the chapter on the family. We sum up the findings as follows: girls look to their parents for guidance, yield to whatever demands are made by the family, and tend to identify with parental authority. Girls do not generally feel that their parents want them to be independent or show initiative, or take over the task of self-control; nor do the girls find within themselves any strong urge to do so. From the girls' reports, we feel that their parents supervise them rather closely, and that the girls do not object to this control, and in fact even want and justify it, identifying themselves with parent motives and attitudes.

What it adds up to is that one common model of the adolescent experience—instinctual turmoil; the opposition between will and constraint; and the consequent emergence of a self-governed set of controls—is of little use in understanding the feminine experience. Our girls seem to have the instincts well under control; only rarely do they show the oppositional attitudes we associate with adolescence. Decorous, compliant, seeking love, support and guidance, they bend easily to parental regulation. What is perhaps most striking is the absence of age trends either in impulse acceptance or in the work of internalization. From early to late adolescence we do not find the girls showing visible increases in concern with personal controls, nor do they show any growing need to define personal standards individually or independently. We see few signs of that rebelliousness, those cries for freedom which we ordinarily think of as preceding the development of autonomous controls and values.

Throughout adolescence, girls remain compliant to parental authority. The major changes we find are not in the fact of compliance but in its style. The younger girls accept parental direction unselfconsciously. They tell us that parents expect them to be obedient and to respect authority; they say the rule they would never break is to be obedient; they believe parents make rules because children need them. Older girls seem equally dependent on the standards and controls their parents set, but their compliance expresses itself in an articulate identification with the parents' point of view. They more often than younger girls tell us they would not break a rule if it meant hurting or bringing grief to their parents; they feel parents make rules to help children mature, to teach them what is expected of them, to give them standards to live by. Now these latter answers are more sensitive, more sophisticated; they show an empathic understanding of the parent role and viewpoint; but they are, after all, answers which imply the child's dependence on the parents. One example may serve to demonstrate the girl's growing identification with her parents. We asked the following projective question: "Jane wishes her parents were different in some ways—more like the parents of her friends. What does she have in mind?" Younger girls more commonly mention a dissatisfaction with parental restrictions; older girls say that Jane wants a closer relationship with her parents. But the difference we want to highlight concerns not the content of the answers, but rather the respondents' attitudes toward "Jane's" criticism. A number of girls commented spontaneously that Jane's dissatisfaction was probably unjustified, merely the normal grumbling of children, proof only that "the grass looks greener in the next family." Through the recording of these side remarks that justify the parents, we find that they increase markedly with age. The proportion never rises above a minority, this is always the case with answers we get as a bonus in spontaneous remarks, but the differences among age groups are larger than most others we found in this topic area: 6 per cent under 14; 14 per cent of 14 to 16 year-old girls; and 26 per cent of those over 16.

To sum up, we may say that the line of moral development in girls moves from a rather passive, childlike acceptance of parental authority to an identification with the point of view of that authority. As far as we can tell from our evidence, the transition is effected without an intervening phase, in which the girl defiantly asserts her own values and controls before moving closer to those of the parents. As we have already implied, the transitional period of defiance, generally thought of as "typical" of adolescence, is probably found in adolescent boys; it appears that different processes obtain in girls.

To understand why the feminine pattern is different is no simple matter, since we find here (as elsewhere) not a single factor, but a confluence of forces, some of them obscure or hard to articulate. To begin with, there is the fact that girls are in general more compliant, and long before adolescence. The sources of their readiness to submit are still not thoroughly understood. Certainly one element is that girl children are expected to be submissive, and so are socialized with that model in mind. There is no really satisfactory evidence as to how the socialization process works, why in most cases it takes; perhaps there is a subtle yet decisive process of coercion and reward which the mother uses to train out "impulsive" or "defiant" behavior and train in "lady-like" and "submissive" patterns. Probably this is not the whole story. We must add the possibility of very early modeling—the girl, even at a very early period, learning that it is the mother's softer pattern she must incorporate. And we must also bear in mind the possibility of constitutional tendencies, the nature of which is still unknown. However it happens, by the time the girl reaches adolescence she is in most instances more docile than the boy is. The ideals of decorousness and compliance have been reinforced countless times by the examples of both peers and adult models, parents and teachers.

The "masculine" theory of adolescent conflict is based on certain assumptions concerning the impact of the biological changes at puberty. These bring a new and formidable intensity to the child's impulse life, endangering childhood controls; in turn, this new intrapsychic state demands firmer, more articulated controls; the childhood dependency—relying on external constraint—can no longer work effectively. The girl's internal situation differs in several ways. For one thing, the sexual drives differ between the sexes. In boys they are imperious and biologically specific; in girls they are more likely to be diffused, ambiguous, even mysterious. The boy cannot deny the existence of the sexual drives. He must confront them directly, consciously, find within himself the means of obtaining sexual discharge without excessive guilt, and means of control without crippling inhibitions. The struggle over masturbation, ubiquitous at least in the middle class, is, from one point of view, the crucible within which the boy's pattern of control, pleasure, and guilt is worked out. For the girl a limited, temporary denial of sexual impulsivity is not only feasible, but may indeed seem to her to be a most comfortable adaptation. We have here something of a "chicken-egg" dilemma. Are the girl's sexual impulses veiled and ambiguous because of the operation of massive defenses? Or is the nature of the impulses such that they lend themselves to repression? Probably both alternatives, in interaction; the girl's sexuality—receptive, reactive—lends itself more easily to the repressive controls which, for reasons we shall examine soon, the parents of the adolescent will more often impose on the girl. But in any case at puberty the girl's sexuality, as Freud noted, undergoes a wave of repression. Sexuality is then not experienced as such; it very easily becomes spiritualized, idealized, etherealized. It may be transformed and displaced into schoolgirl "crushes," or into vanity, or into a great many other disguises. From our clinical work with adolescent girls, and in the reconstruction of the adolescent period with adult women, it often appears that sexuality is more often than not secondary to other motives. The promiscuous girl at adolescence is generally frigid; promiscuity is a defense against pregenital drives, or a disguised repetition of pre-Oedipal relationships, or a seeking for various reassurances, and so forth. In the more normal girl, the sex play of this period may afford little in the way of truly erotic gratification; rather it serves other motives—self-esteem, reassurance, and so on.

Another source of sex differences in controls and character involves the ego-superego balance. As we know, the boy resolves the Oedipus complex through a decisive act of renunciation; he internalizes the father's prohibitions and constructs a well-articulated superego; the motive is castration anxiety. The girl's Oedipal situation is more complex —since she is strongly influenced by pre-Oedipal longings for and fear of the mother. The girl child has a less compelling motive for disavowing her Oedipal feelings. In many cases her incestuous feelings are not so much renounced as transformed; she identifies not so much with her mother's moral standards as with her mother as a loved object, and makes herself over into a to-be-beloved. Superego formation is not so well articulated; the girl is less likely to act at the behest of principle or abstract justice. Of course this is not to say that she is not "moral"; but the question of moral behavior is less a matter of being "good" for abstract, internalized principles, and more a matter of "goodness" for the sake of retaining the love of others, or of maintaining a "good reputation."

At adolescence, with the revival of the Oedipal constellation, the boy is more likely to react by a heightening of ego-superego tension. Superego pressure will not necessarily keep him from discharging some share of the forbidden drives. But the presence of strong superego forces may cause him to feel severely guilty. The processes we discussed earlier may become apparent. The ego may yield to the superego, so that the boy is inhibited by the knowledge of guilt (before he accomplishes his wickedness), or he may become preoccupied with abstract ethical concerns; or he may feel acutely guilty afterward; or he may "isolate" or externalize superego pressure, the ego reacting to the possibility of severe guilt by erecting defenses against it. In either case the necessity to come to terms with the superego, to renegotiate the ego-superego compact, is likely to emerge as one of the important items of the adolescent boy's agenda.

In contrast, the girl will more often respond to the instinctual upsurge of the period by an intensification of the earlier pattern of compliance and decorousness. Not altogether, of course; certainly she will have her moments—pique, sullenness, aggressively provocative behavior toward her parents, and so on. But the basic polarity will be between being willful, on the one hand, and seeking to restore the love tie on the other. The boy is more willing to lean on his own controls, and in fact may be eager to test and strengthen his controls. The girl will continue to rely, and now even more urgently, on the support and control of her parents.

We cannot leave the question of sex differences in the adolescent character crisis without giving some attention to the social forces which influence the development of controls and character. These factors are, in a sense, more "superficial" than the deep and often muddy intrapsychic forces we have been discussing; but they are equally important. The consequences for the girl in acting out sexually are so severe that the family will maintain a greater degree of protectiveness throughout the adolescent period. Furthermore, the peer group itself generally acts to maintain the girl's good behavior, through gossip (and the fear of it) and the high value given to reputation. Here again we see an emphasis on external controls; the girl's fear that her friends will withdraw their respect from her is in some senses related to the earlier fear that parents may cease loving her. Mild social phobias of this type, expressing themselves in a hypersensitivity to moral censure, seem to us to be far more common in girls than in boys.

In summary, a number of related factors coincide to distinguish the girls' experience in controls from the boys—a greater degree of compliance; the more diffuse quality of sexual impulses; the previous construction of the ego-superego relationship; the more thorough controls imposed externally. All of these forces coincide to make the development of internal controls a somewhat less salient, less pressing matter for the girl than for the boy. To confirm this assumption we made the following predictions about sex differences:

1. That adolescent girls will reveal a more compliant relationship to the parents; will show more identification with their standards; will be less openly troubled by the problem of containing impulses, and will

give less evidence that they differentiate between personal and parental standards and controls.

2. That the quality of moral integration will be of greater importance in the overall adjustment of boys than girls.

A comparison between boys and girls of the same age (14 to 16) offers unequivocal evidence that boys are more preoccupied by problems of self-control; in fact we shall see that some of the largest differences between the sexes are to be found in this area. We get the distinct impression from the data that boys feel themselves to be engaged in a fairly constant struggle to keep impulses penned in; girls generally show far less concern about an explosive loss of control.

Boys more often worry consciously about controls (12% of the boys, 1% of the girls), especially controls over aggression (7% of boys' answers to less than 1% for the girls). When we ask what they would like to change about themselves if they could, personal controls are chosen by more boys (28% of them mention it, compared with 16% of the girls).

It is in the sequence of questions about rules that some of the most interesting differences appear. Boys are more likely to think of rules as a means parents use to control errant behavior; girls see rules in a more positive, more nurturant way. When we ask why parents make rules, boys underscore the parental motive "to keep children out of trouble" —36 per cent of the boys offer this reason, while less than half as many girls do (17%). On the other hand, girls are more likely to stress the educative and guidance motif, more frequently saying that parents want to teach their children how to behave, give them standards to live by, or let them know what is expected of them (46% of girls, and 27% of boys).

"What would happen if parents didn't make rules?" Here again marked differences appear. For one thing, boys give about twice as many answers as girls do, a rather striking phenomenon, since girls are generally far more talkative than boys in the interview, and it is only in the rules area that boys find themselves stimulated enough to out-respond the girls. In their answers boys emphasize the antisocial consequences—the things that children would do. They imagine that children might run wild (45% boys, 36% girls); that they might get in with bad companions (40% boys, 8% girls); that they might stay out late (15% boys, 7% girls); and in what is probably the largest difference of the entire research, that children would not go to school (33% boys,

2% girls)! We sense in the boys' answers a high degree of impulsivity, ready to make its appearance once there is a failure in external constraint; at the least, they seem to imagine the situation in these terms. But girls more often mention the effects of absence of rules on the children themselves. They more frequently say—"Their lives would be ruined; their health would suffer" (31% of girls, 18% of boys). This response, we feel, reflects the girl's identification with the parent's nurturant point of view, as though the girl were in one part of herself seeing herself in the parental role.

"When might a boy [or girl] break a rule?" The boys' answers are either more impulsive and defiant, or more autonomous morally than girls'. They more frequently mention an emergency situation, or some circumstance which makes the rule inappropriate—that is, they deem it proper to break the rule on the basis of a personal judgment; at the same time, more boys than girls mention such motives as uncontrollable impulses, rebelliousness, or pressure from peers. Girls' answers to this question are striking in one respect: a surprisingly large proportion of them (25%) misunderstood its intention, did not specify the causes for breaking a rule but rather detailed a strategy for doing so. What they did, essentially, was to tell the interviewer how one might break a rule without getting caught. We interpret this parapraxis to reflect something distinctive in the quality of feminine rebellion. When girls resist parental authority, they may be more likely to do so quietly—if you will, covertly, perhaps deviously—while maintaining a ladylike conformity. In the masculine mode, rebellion is explicit and direct. The feminine orientation to morality may involve a distinction between public and private behavior; if the girl wants her own way, she may also want to remain on good terms with her parents and other audiences, and so she may be led to deal with moral issues as though they were a form of gamesmanship—being (or doing) one thing while appearing to be or do another. (We may be reminded here of the Wolfenstein-Leites (1950) discussion of the good-bad girl in American films; in the movies the girl appears to be bad but turns out really to be good. In her real life the American girl may want to be bad but must at all costs give the appearance of being good.) Perhaps we are making too much of the matter. Still, this misunderstanding of the question recurs in one-quarter of the girls' answers, and is never found in boys'.

The willingness to confront authority directly, and in some cases to confute it, is everywhere in evidence in the boys' interviews, far more so than for girls. For example, girls more often than boys say they have never broken a rule, or that they *think* they broke one once. It is much harder to find a boy who has not broken a rule; the prototypic answer was given by one young man who stared at the interviewer in disbelief and said: "You kiddin', lady?" A more representative indication of sex differences in the stance toward authority is provided in the answers to a series of projective pictures. A boy (or girl) is shown with his parents, who are setting a limit for the child. One-quarter of the boys had the story hero question the parents' restriction—not resentfully, but with a freedom that tacitly assumed the right to question. Only 4 per cent of the girls of the same age react in this way. On the other hand, something of the feminine style of meeting restraint is suggested by the fact that one-third of the girls have the heroine reassuring the parents, using such phrases as: "Don't worry," "I'll act like a lady," "You know I'll behave." Boys almost never reassure the parents in this way. Another answer to this item comes only from girls: 10 per cent of them say that the girl would be hurt, taken aback, or surprised by her parents assuming she might misbehave. Boys never tell us this; they seem to take parental suspicion, or foreboding, very much in stride.

Girls are in general more compliant to authority than boys are. They show a greater degree of reliance on authority not only in relation to the parents but to other adults as well. And in a later chapter we shall see sex differences in peer relations when the issue is the stance toward authority. Boys view the peer group as a source of support in the struggle for independence from adult control; girls rarely concern themselves with this issue, and instead look for a close friend with whom to share secrets.

In summary, the findings clearly support our expectations. Adolescent boys are actively engaged in establishing their independence from parental control; they are acutely aware of personal control as a problem, as a goal, as an issue. Adolescent girls are less frequently, less intensely, preoccupied with these issues; maintaining a compliant-dependent relationship to their parents, the problem of personal control is of less moment in their lives.

Our second prediction concerns the part played by moral integration in the overall adjustment of boys and girls. Do the differences we have just discussed—in the development of personal controls, and in the relationship to authority—have different consequences in the total personalities of boys as against girls?

We guessed that the style of moral integration would be more salient for boys than girls; that is, we believed that differences in moral style would show a more significant relationship to other aspects of behavior within the boys' sample than these same differences would reveal within the girls' group. To test this expectation, we did the following analysis. We first developed a measure of internalization-externalization, designed to reveal whether the subject treated moral issues as an internal problem, or whether he saw them as a matter of external control. An exact description of this measure will be found in Appendix C; here we need only report that the measure was based on responses to three questions, replies to which could be coded as "internal" (that is, making moral decisions on the basis of an inner morality), or "external" (making moral decisions on external criteria, such as the fear of being found out), or "neutral" (showing neither of these tendencies). We then isolated extreme groups on this measure (those who responded "internally" to all items, and those who had responded "externally" to all), and investigated its relationship to other measures of personal behavior and experience.

The results are, we believe, of great interest. They show that the internalized boys are distinguished from the externalizers on a substantial number of items which suggest effective ego functioning. They show a high achievement level; a high level of activity; self-confidence combined with realistic self-criticism; and independence of judgment. They show an effective organization of thought and a capacity to bind present and future time. The externalized boys are deficient in these aspects of ego organization.

Now when we make the same comparisons for highly internalized and externalized girls, we do not find the same relations between moral style and personal integration. The two girls' groups do not differ significantly in achievement level, independence of judgment, energy level, or self-confidence. Neither do they differ in thought organization or in time perspective. In short, the type of moral stance, internal versus external, does not serve as an efficient predictor of ego organization for girls.

Let us press these findings further. Might these sex differences stem from the fact that the internalization-externalization measure does not tap the same processes in boys and girls? We tested this possibility by comparing the internalization groups (I vs. E) on other items dealing with rules. Relationships among rules items are generally lower for girls than for boys, suggesting that this area is less coherent for them; nevertheless, internalized and externalized girls do differ in the kinds of rules they would never break, in their views on parental regulation, and in adherence to parental morality. These differences run in the same direction, and support the conclusion that the I-E measure does indeed distinguish between internalized and externalized girls. In this sense the index appears to measure moral style in girls as it does in boys.

The question remains: how do we account for the apparent dissociation between moral style and ego integration in girls? Several possibilities emerge from the line of thinking we have followed. It may be that the group of internalized girls is made up of different types. Some of the internalized girls may be similar to boys in that their controls are both internal and autonomous; in other cases what may seem to be internalization may reflect an identification with parental standards rather than internal differentiation of standards. If our measure of internalization does not distinguish between these, if it counts either pattern as internalized, then relationships between the index and aspects of ego strength would be obscured. Another possible explanation of the disjuncture between moral style and ego functioning might be found in the suggestion we stressed earlier—that compliance to external standards is a common mode of orientation in adolescent girls. Since parents tend to maintain close supervision of the adolescent girl, the tendency to see moral issues "externally" may be less likely to reflect personal disorder or an unduly deviant family structure.

We have some evidence to suggest that the internalized group indeed contains two types of girls, one which has autonomous standards, and one which is overidentified with parental standards. When we break down responses to the question, "What kind of rule would you never break?" we find that the group of internalized girls contains a high proportion who—as highly internalized boys do—mention general or impersonal rules (referring to the larger society's moral code), and rules involving a responsibility to self and others. But the internalized group also contains a very large number of girls who say they would not break a rule that reinforces adult authority. This category included such responses as "I would never disobey my parents" and "I wouldn't do anything my mother told me not to do," responses which reflect a strong reliance on parental control. The internalized girls group also contains a high proportion of girls who have the heroine of the projective cartoons tell her parents not to worry, that she will behave like a lady.

The pattern of authority-compliance is modal in the group of internalized girls. This fact supports a supposition we incline to on other grounds—that for girls (and not for boys) the pattern of internalized morality derives from a strong identification with the parental point of view. "Autonomous" morality—in which personal standards are based on a differentiation from parental standards—is more commonly a masculine pattern.

Although an "anaclitic" morality may be normative for internalized girls, there is still some reason to believe that some of the internalized girls do show the "autonomous" morality we assume to exist in internalized boys. Here again we have some evidence which, while slight, is intriguing in its implications. We thought some of the internalized girls might show a "masculine" pattern, and indeed we do discover that this group includes a disproportionate (although still small) number of girls who choose a masculine ideal. When asked to name a person whom they would want to be like, 14 per cent of the internalized girls name a man. This compares with 6 per cent of the total population of girls, and *none* of the girls who rely on external controls. (Since boys almost never choose feminine ideal figures, a sex comparison was not possible.) Furthermore, the internalized girls are more likely to show masculine trends in job preferences. A choice of the traditional professions occurs in 25 per cent of the internalized girls, 11 per cent of the total feminine population, and only 6 per cent of the externalized group. Finally, the same tendency appears in response to the question "Do you ever wish you were a boy?"

FIVE

The Family

The guiding *term* for this chapter will be *departure*. Here, indeed, is one of the universals of the adolescent experience. It is the time when the child prepares to leave home. In folklore and in heroic fiction, we find the recurring pattern—the adolescent hero, having received some sign, an inner stirring or an outer call, gets ready to leave the family. The paths to departure vary. Some must struggle to leave, others must flee for their lives; some leave vindictively, full of hate, thrashing the father or mother, while others are themselves beaten or betrayed before they leave; some leave in high expectation, carrying the family's hope for fortune or redemption, and others leave at dead of night, in disgrace, bearing the family's curse. The hero's journey begins with an ending—the breaking of the connection to home.

At adolescence the interaction of parent and child is conditioned by their mutual knowledge, however dimly and remotely held, of the child's eventual departure. The family's task is to rehearse the child for it and help him rehearse himself. In our time it is not easily done. We have not developed those ritual circumstances that in simpler times helped ease the strains inherent in a profound psychosocial transition. The family must take on tasks of socialization more subtle than they have met before; at the same time it must know how to yield gracefully to such competing socializers as the peer group. It must accommodate itself to the implications and dangers of the child's sexual maturity; it must adjust to his extraordinary, nerve-wracking ambivalence; it must face and respond to his clamor for autonomy, distinguishing those demands which are real and must be granted from those which are token and are used to test the parents or to bargain with them. Above all, the family must allow the child to abandon it, without allowing him to feel that he is himself abandoned or an abandoner.

Already we have written about the psychosexual situation at adolescence. We want to look at it again, this time examining its impact on the family and on the child's life in the family. As we mentioned earlier, before Freud adolescent sexuality was thought to be an entirely discontinuous event in the human career. Psychoanalysis taught us the error of this view, by demonstrating that the sexual emergence at puberty is in some respects a re-emergence, a second coming. In the first flush of revelation, the repetitive elements in adolescent sexuality were not only stressed but also overstressed, so that in the first period of psychoanalytic thought, the adolescent experience was considered to be little more than a reworking of the earlier Oedipal crisis.

Time has changed these views in a great many ways. For one thing, as Spiegel (1951) points out, we now recognize that the ego undergoes a considerable maturation during the latency period; the child at twelve is not merely the child at five grown taller and heavier; he confronts the instinctual eruption of adolescence with a new and sturdier array of ego resources.

Another change is in our understanding of the instinctual situation at puberty. The earlier tendency was to focus on the sexual drive itself, and on its connection to Oedipal fantasies. We are now very much aware that the adolescent must learn to meet not only phallic sexuality, but also an upsurge of earlier, pregenital impulses—orality, sadism, and so on. And it is not only the Oedipal conflicts which are rearoused; more primitive ties to objects make their appearance—homosexual feelings, for example, or tempting and dangerous dependencies. For the pubescent boy, then, the mother may figure in his unconscious fantasies not only as the dangerous seductress, but also (at other times) as a merciless castrator, a poisoning witch, a devouring ogress. His father may figure not only as the dark stranger of the Oedipal period, but also variously, as devourer, poisoner, or beloved. The child is besieged by drives and feelings from all levels of the infantile experience, and personifies his parents in a bewildering variety of ways. The emotional quality of family life is influenced, not only by the reappearance of Oedipal motifs, but also by the child's expressions of and defenses against a constantly changing assortment of pregenital drives. The adolescent is now dirty and then clean, one day eating everything in sight and the next picking at his plate morosely, today childishly dependent and tomorrow crying for freedom, now abusive and then sweet.

Still, it is the Oedipus complex which figures as the dominant source of conflict in adolescent psychosexuality. What complicates the matter is the child's growth, his actual and impending maturity. The 5-year-old's incestuous and aggressive feelings are taken seriously only by himself; ordinarily they go unrecognized; even when they are detected (as in the more *au courant* of upper-middle-class families) they are more likely than not to be treated only as occasions for wry amusement. There are, to be sure, those instances where the parents are neurotically sensitive to the Oedipal in the child. The mother who gets uneasy and angry at her daughter's coquettishness with the father, the father who feels compelled to quash his 5-year-old son's assertiveness, but these are exceptional. The reawakening of erotic feeling at puberty takes place in a new social context; the incestuous and aggressive fantasies of early childhood are dominant in a genitally maturing individual. The adolescent faces not only tabooed drives, and fantasies, but also the discomfiting realization that he is reaching a point where he can, theoretically, do something about them.

For the parents there is the simple fact that the household now contains one more sexually mature personality, and one toward whom there has been a long history of intimacy and affection. Incestuous temptations can, in short, run both ways. This side of the matter, the parental side, has not been given the recognition it deserves in the literature on adolescence.[1] Yet we know, both from clinical practice and everyday observation, how common it is that the parents of teen-agers are clearly moved and disturbed by the emergence of sexuality in their young. A father's (often comic) anger or suspiciousness about the boys who date his daughter, a mother's agitation about the loss of her youthful looks, her sudden penchant for dressing just as her daughter does; and of course those extreme and all too obvious instances, as when a father finds and runs away with a girl "young enough to be his daughter." For the most part, however, the development of incestuous feelings on the parents' side is handled by defenses, such as repression and denial, which prevent a fatal recognition of motive and yet do so without disrupting adaptation. In some cases these devices are not adequate to the task, and we find the use of projections and displacements, defenses which are more likely to implicate the parent's actual behavior and feelings about the child's activities. The parent may impute his own aroused eroticism to the child or to the child's peers. He may, for example, come to see the peer group as a source of sexual contamination, or become preoccupied by various dangers to the child's sexual purity. In the end the parent may be led to commit him-

[1] An excellent discussion of the *interactional* side of family life can be found in Stone and Church (1957).

self to arbitrary or absurd restrictions on the youngster's activities, decisions which will lead inevitably to increasing bitterness on both sides.

This is the erotic aspect. The Oedipal renascence also brings with it a heightening of aggressive feeling, at least between father and son. Again we have a mutuality. The son is likely to feel himself hemmed in or picked on, the father is apt to bristle at the boy's surliness, contempt, or outright defiance. In the urban and rural jungles of our society we may sometimes find that the hostile interaction between father and son reverts to the ur-situation. The father keeps the son in line through sheer physical force, or the threat of it, until the day the son turns against the father, defeats him, and then either leaves home or stays on to establish a new order. To be sure, nothing like this is likely to happen in middle-class American families. But the point is that the prototypic possibilities persist. Father and son share the knowledge of the son's impending maturity, each senses the imminence of a struggle for a new order. These dim recognitions run under the public discourse, giving it a sharpness, an edge that the topic at hand does not warrant. There is the sense on both sides that statuses are being tested and redefined. Father killing son, son killing father—these are the mythic survivals which give a peculiar energy to the conversation.

Mothers and daughters also have their problems with each other at this time. The girl may become hypercritical or scornful of her mother's ways, vowing silently that when her turn comes she will do things better. Or she may come to feel, as the boy so often does, that she is unjustly hemmed in by her mother's restrictions. We have seen instances where the daughter developed a bitterness toward the mother, a sense of being victimized, which reached a nearly paranoid violence. It is our impression, nevertheless, that the hostility between mother and daughter is, at least on the surface, less intense than that which exists between father and son. Perhaps it is only more complex. A difference between the sexes as regards Oedipal rivalry lies in the strength of oral longings for the mother that exist so frequently and so intensely among girls. In some cases these dependent wishes are so tempting and so dangerous that the girl is driven to turn against them by hating the mother; thus the passionate, almost paranoid resentment of the mother we mentioned a few sentences ago. Blos (1957) has shown that certain instances of sexual delinquency in adolescent girls have their source in the girl's need to act out as a defensive maneuver against homosexual yearnings for the mother. But for the most part, we feel, the girl's need to retain the mother's love is likely to balance and soften the expression of rivalry.

At this point the reader may be murmuring to himself that our account of family life is totally unlike what he has seen and known, that it is more like life in a Gothic novel than a judicious report of the realities of family interaction. No doubt we have given the darkest view of the matter; we have done so not to neglect the prodigies of adaptation we know the adolescent and his family regularly, almost casually, achieve. But we want to stress, as forcefully as possible, the strains and complications produced by the intrusion of instinct on the family scene. It is a hard time for the youngster, moved as he is by drives and feelings he finds difficult either to recognize or contain. The home has become a hothouse. The adolescent must discover a way out, a means of escaping his infantile status in the family and, more urgently, his infantile motives toward members of the family. He seeks a pattern or strategy of disengagement.

Disengagement is one side of the duality of departure. In disengaging, the child escapes the fetid psychosexual climate of the family; at the same time he responds to a hidden psychosocial necessity, by moving forward to autonomy. We see autonomy as a tropic movement toward the adult condition; we shall discuss it later in this chapter. We see disengagement as a flight from a psychosexual irritation. Moravia has illustrated the disengagement motif in his two novellas of adolescence, *Luca* and *Agostino*.

There is of course a great deal that one might say about these remarkable stories. They illustrate the Oedipal entanglements of adolescence with extraordinary vividness. But our interest in discussing them here is that they show two separate patterns of disengagement. Agostino, in withdrawing from the Oedipal temptation, ends in withdrawing from objects altogether, moves into himself, until he is rescued by the loving attention of his nurse. Luca, more clearly aroused by his mother than Agostino, also withdraws, but his tendency is to flee toward others, to find substitute objects. These are two directions of disengagement—moving away from, moving toward. The reader may be reminded of Karen Horney's typology of character trends. We have only to add her third category—moving against others—to designate one more direction of disengagement, which would include the common instances of adolescent rebellion and delinquency.

But we have no desire to impose a system on the reader, especially one which seems somewhat too facile. These three variations of the disengagement process provide only a loose ordering of adolescent behavior. In specific cases we find blendings of these directions or oscillations from one to another depending on mood and circumstance. A

mode of disengagement is likely based on dominant character dispositions, modified by the prevailing social influences on the youngster. In
any case, the direction of disengagement tells us only part of the story.
Just as important are variations in tempo and intensity. Clinical practice with adolescents is filled with these instances where the pressure to
disengage has become too acute, or where the youngsters' resources
for modulating the disengagement process have proved too feeble.
There we have the adolescent crises—the runaways, the delinquents,
the lonely or confused or desperately passionate youngsters—the gamut
of adolescent malaise.

These are the dramatic casualties of disengagement. We also need to
recognize that many of the more familiar or innocuous bits of adolescent behavior may reflect techniques of disengagement. Here is an example. Lionel Trilling, in a brilliant essay on *Lolita* (1958), characterizes the manner of an upper-middle-class American girl toward her
father. "She maintains towards him the common alternation of remote
indifference and easy acceptance." So she does; and we imagine that
she does so in order to keep a ritual distance between herself and her
father. It is a way, we suspect, of becoming (or remaining) disen-
gaged, of keeping things in their proper place, not unlike a stereotyped
joking relationship we might discover between brother and sister in a
primitive society. If we pursue the matter further we may discover
that our young lady's manner toward her father is not altogther unlike her manner toward men in general. Take her "remote indifference
and easy acceptance," mix it with decorous coquetry or wide-eyed en-
thusiasm or some other form of insincerity, and we may find it is the
manner she uses on dates and indeed, will use, with some further variations, in dealing with her husband.

Perhaps we are going too far. The point we want to make is that the
specific disengagement techniques that the adolescent discovers, tests,
and employs contain sources from the past and provide bridges to the
future. The disengagement strategies, and the particular disengagement
tactics, are a crystallization out of past experience, character structure,
and prevailing social influences. Once crystallized, they tend to be generalized and to survive. Not in all cases, certainly. Indeed, the most interesting psychologically are those instances where adolescence is
marked by a disengagement crisis which reverses or arrests or over-
turns the established course of the child's development. Luca and Agostino are examples.

But for the most part disengagement patterns are both ego-syntonic
and in harmony with the demands of the social environment. They en-

able the child to avoid the instinctual complications he finds at home and they do so in ways that engage his ego resources and contribute to his growing sense of identity and competence.

We are fairly certain that the adaptations of adolescence are decisive in the crystallization of adult character. We do not yet have a persuasively precise account of the genetic bridges between adolescent ego growth and change, and adult character. While we can spell out, for the young child, the consequences of this or that or the other resolution of the Oedipus complex, we are still some distance from an equivalent sureness of grasp for the psychic vicissitudes of adolescence.

If disengagement is one major side of the adolescent departure, then autonomy is the other. We can see the two terms as complementary. In the first we stress a reflexive, reactive movement, a retreat from the dangers of the home. In the second, autonomy, we emphasize the pull of the future, a forward movement toward adult status, its privileges, and obligations. We do not want to make too much of the distinction, which we see only as a conceptual convenience. In the particular instance, disengagement and autonomy are generally closely joined. The greatest utility of the distinction, we feel, is that it allows us to separate motives. What often seems to be a clamor for freedom turns out to be, when we search it closely, a cry of terror.

Anyone who puts his mind to the topic of adolescence will sooner or later find himself leaning on the autonomy concept. It soon begins to appear not only useful, but also compelling, inescapable. The direction of adolescent growth is clearly toward emancipation from the family. The period begins with the child almost entirely dependent on the family, needing its say-so for what he can and cannot do, still tied to the parents emotionally, still clinging to their ideas and ideals. It ends with the child reaching into adulthood, freer to make up his mind about what he will and will not do, holding (if he so wishes) his own beliefs and values, and if need be looking elsewhere than the family for love and support.

To be sure, the movement toward autonomy is not exclusively adolescent. The metaphor is viable at all stages of the child's career. As he grows, as his capacities mature, he is constantly demanding, or being granted, or silently assuming a greater measure of freedom. Nevertheless, autonomy is a peculiarly pregnant issue at adolescence, more so than at any other time since early childhood. During the latency period, autonomy demands on the child's part are gradually made, and even more important, are likely to come out of rational needs. At adolescence there is a sharp rise in the number of demands made, and a

distinct change in their quality. Above all, at adolescence autonomy be·
comes important for itself; it acquires a meaning beyond the particular,
concrete issues at hand. The specific issues—what time to be in at
night, let us say, or whether to wear lipstick—are important not only
in themselves but also because they carry such high symbolic value.
The particular freedoms the child wants, or gets, is given, or takes, are
the visible part of a larger conversation between parent and child, having to do with the child's dawning need for liberation. The struggles
over autonomy at adolescence are, in this respect, reminiscent of the
child's stubborn drive for independence during the anal period. When
the two-and-a-half-year-old flies into a rage because his mother has
opened the door for him, when he insists that she shut it again so that
he can then open it, we recognize readily enough that the issue is something other than door-opening. He is concerned, as the adolescent so
often is, with the ceremonial rightness of things, with the gestures and
rituals of recognition.

Here is an excerpt from Toqueville on the adolescent years in America over a century ago:

> But as soon as the young American approaches manhood, the ties of filial
> obedience are relaxed day by day; master of his thoughts, he is soon master
> of his conduct. In America there is, strictly speaking, no adolescence: at the
> close of boyhood the man appears and begins to trace out his own path.
>
> It would be an error to suppose that this is preceded by a domestic strug-
> gle in which the son has obtained by a sort of moral violence the liberty
> that his father refused him. The same habits, the principles, which impel the
> one to assert his independence, predispose the other to consider the use of
> that independence as an incontestable right. The former does not exhibit any
> of those rancorous or irregular passions which disturb men long after they
> have shaken off an established authority; the latter feels none of that bitter
> and angry regret which is apt to survive a bygone power. (Tocqueville, 1948)

We can use Toqueville in two ways: for a knowledge of what has
proved enduring in American life, and also for a sense of what has
changed. This passage suggests that a good deal has survived. To this
day, the European observer is bemused and even astonished by what
Americans take for granted, the degree of leeway the adolescent is
given in making his own choices, the freedom he feels in negotiating
with his parents. But we also remark that distinct changes have taken
place since Toqueville's commentary. One obvious difference is the absence of adolescence he notes. Today we are concerned that the adolescent period is increasingly extended. In Toqueville's time a young,
vigorous, expanding nation could give its young social tasks and social

roles. A great many forces at work in American life today, above all the technological complexity that requires long years of education, have tended to make the adolescent years appear to many a limbo or purgatory, perilously empty of meaning for the young.

There is another difference. Toqueville gives us a sanguine account of the transactions between the generations. Father and son are joined in an implicit recognition of the obligations and uses of independence. Social tasks, life roles were visible and immediate. The child's movement toward independence no doubt had its symbolic undertones, but these were, we imagine, of little moment since the youngster's energy was so soon absorbed by the challenges and responsibilities of adulthood.

When we write on this topic today, we are far more aware of the uneasiness infusing the conversation on autonomy between parent and child. Our attention is held by evidence of ambivalence and even suspicion of each generation toward the other. The ideal of autonomy has remained central in the American ethos; but over time it has lost, we think, some of its clarity in losing some of its relation to the specific tasks and goals of an earlier era. The American, to give one example, has tended to equate freedom with the capacity to move freely in space. To be free meant, in some part, to be mobile, to have the will and energy to leave home and find the frontier. The ideal persists, the passion for movement persists, but it is now all too often dissociated from a viable social or personal purpose. Mobility comes to stand for autonomy, and in the end replaces it. We see this in the work of Jack Kerouac, especially so in On the Road. Here autonomy is at one with movement; the ideal of freedom achieves an ultimate and perverse apotheosis in the central incident of the novel, where the hero drives a Cadillac cross country at high speed, to nowhere, and with no purpose other than the act itself

We find in America today a deepening ambivalence about the adolescent's autonomy; and we think it grows out of a dim, largely unconscious recognition that a cherished value, independence, is in danger of being corrupted. What is problematic to the parent is not whether the child ought to be offered autonomy, that issue is long settled, but an uneasy concern about what the child will do with the autonomy he is so freely given. In the course of the last two decades we have seen a profound transfiguration of our myth of youth: from Andy Hardy to James Dean. These prototypic adolescents express the opposing possibilities of autonomy. Andy Hardy is free in the sense of being carefree; he is, to be sure, as vulgar a figure as only the American movie industry can achieve, but he represents, nevertheless, one ideal of the American adolescence, the freedom from responsibility, from care, from concern—an autonomy which remains innocent. His father, Judge Hardy, is at times cross, or perplexed, but is on the whole, protective, amused, indulgent. Father and son are joined in a mutual, implicit acceptance of the core values. The James Dean prototype is also free from care, not in the sense of being carefree, but in being careless and uncaring. The nonresponsibility of the innocent adolescent now changes to a violent irresponsibility. Autonomy has come to mean nihilism and total loss of control. The father is represented as bewildered, weak, self-indulgent—the generations have lost touch with each other.[2]

To these complications, spun out of collective history, we must add those coming from the parents' psychodynamic circumstances. The child's adolescence announces the encroachments of middle age; the child's vigor is a harbinger of decline. This is difficult enough, and especially hard in a nation which has set itself against old age and death. In one way or another, the parent may involve the child in his struggle with these imminences. In the upper-middle class, for example, we sometimes find the parents refusing to acknowledge the child's youth, and the needs that arise from it, the father turning away to professional

[2] We find this ambivalence about autonomy elsewhere in American fantasy. It expresses itself in the Western and in the detective story. Both hero and villain are likely to be uprooted, restless, free to wander in space. Cowboy and outlaw, private eye and hired killer, are travelers, wandering strangers, unconnected, except by nostalgia, to a home place. The cowboy hero is generally in transit, a stranger newly arrived in town, or about to depart, or both. The outlaw, the killer whom the hero must confront, is sent for or arrives from a distance. (Both of these situations are found in the prototypic modern Westerns, *Shane* and *High Noon*). Those who are rooted to the place, the townspeople, are often represented as passive and helpless (*Shane*), or weakly corrupt (*High Noon*), although in some cases they are stirred to heroism by the hero's example. The danger of the town is that it weakens the spirit; the American hero finds his strength in his ability to keep moving. Similar themes are found in the crime film. Wolfenstein and Leites point out that "the hero is likely to be a stranger in town, or just returned from a journey." But we must also note that traveling freely in space has something counterphobic about it. Space has its terrors; if one is endangered by being too deeply rooted to the place, one is also alone and vulnerable among the empty wastes or on the lonely highway. We see the other side, the phobic side, in the frequency of the ambush theme. In the film, *North by Northwest*, this is vividly presented in a scene where the hero has been lured to a crossroads in the Midwestern flatlands. He is attacked by a cropdusting plane; the danger of empty space here becomes manifest. The integrity of the hero depends on the counterphobic mastery of the hidden terror of being alone and isolated in space.

duties, the mother to country-club pleasures. Generally, however, the American parent does not separate himself enough from the child; instead he will want to live in the child, excessively, trying to re-realize, in the child's freshness, in the opportunity to make a new life, his own lost autonomies. Usually this works out well enough, but the position has its dangers. The youngster at this age may need more distance, more sense of the barrier between generations, than the benign parental presence will allow. Or the parent, living in the child, may impute too much to him; blurring his view of the child by projections, or, in the truly pathological instances, being tormented by his envy of the child's youth and possibilities.

In negotiating with the parents on autonomy, the child enlists the authority of the peer culture. The parents will have had prior experience with the peer voice. The young child, eager to keep up with the Joneses, will announce, strident, querulous, or wistful, that Johnny down the block has an English bike and why can't he, or that the Smith family does things this way, and why can't we. Unless the parents are overindulgent or insecure or simply foolish, they will not be too troubled. The child's claims are likely to be trivial or transient, soon forgotten and replaced. It is a very different matter with the adolescent. He will use the same tactics, adverting to the peer world, pressing its authority on the family. But the matter is different first, because he makes his claims more forcefully, more urgently, and second because he now has a different position both toward the family and toward the peer group. He does not, as the young child does, merely carry a message from the world. He appoints himself its delegate.

He does so by playing on the American family's sensitivity to social change. Knowing how vulnerable his parents are here, sensing their uneasiness about being out of date, out of touch, he represents himself as the champion of new forms and values. He compounds his advantage because he has a reference group while the parents do not. They must find a style of relating to the child's demands without the guidance of an established ideology, and without any firm knowledge of what is normative. They feel they cannot disadvantage the child by restricting his opportunities in the peer world, and yet are chary lest the child abuse his freedom.

The other side of the coin is that both parties in the dispute recognize, however vaguely, that the parent, in the last analysis, must not give in to the youngster's demands. It is in the intergenerational dialectic that while the child must stand for freedom, so must the parents stand for control. The youngster will play Sam Adams, but only in the understanding that the parents agree to play King George. The adolescent, however he may press overtly for more and more freedom, recognizes well enough its terrors. We know clinically that some of the most dangerous situations for the child arise when the parents can no longer tolerate the inherent threat and yield to the adolescent's demands.

Until now we have used the word "autonomy" almost lightheartedly, assuming that both reader and writer give it the same meaning. But once we settle down to more exacting discussion, we recognize the difficulties in the definition of autonomy. The term has been used variously and idiosyncratically, by writers of differing persuasions and perspectives, and its use demands that we make clear from the start just how we intend it.

Our own interest in the concept—and this the reader will already know—centers on *emotional* autonomy, the degree to which the adolescent has managed to cast off infantile ties to the family. Much of the vital psychic work of the adolescent years involves the adaptation to and resolution of instinctual conflicts, particularly where these reinstate infantile motives toward the family. We judge the youngster autonomous in the degree to which he has been able to advance beyond ambivalent attachments to his parents, in the extent to which he is no longer at the behest of unconscious feelings toward them.

In addition to emotional autonomy, we can distinguish at least two other forms: *behavioral* autonomy and *value* autonomy. Each of these will enter later discussions, and each merits at least brief explication.

Behavioral autonomy focuses on behavior and decision. We ask: What can the youngster do on his own? What decisions can he make for and by himself? This approach avoids much of the ephemerality of other approaches. And it is, we should add, no less attractive to the adolescent and his family. As we have suggested, their discussions on autonomy also tend to avoid the underlying issues and instead fix on the immediate and the concrete: when to wear lipstick, buy one's own clothes or a car, what time to be in at night.

There are of course advantages to this approach, but it is also easily misleading. Obviously the 16-year-old who is not free to make decisions for himself is less independent than a child of the same age who is allowed to. But what about the youngster who is given complete freedom—who can, for example, stay out all night if he wants to? Is he more autonomous, or is he being neglected?

In any case, matters are rarely simple enough to fit a calculus. If we look closely enough, we are likely to find that autonomy "items" are patterned, and that differences in the "amount" of autonomy are less apparent (or if apparent, less important) than differences in pattern. Imagine that child A is allowed to choose his own program of studies, his own books, and to come to his own decisions about religion and politics, but is closely regulated in his social activities. Child B may be allowed great leeway in choosing friends and leisure, but little or no leeway in choosing ideas or values. The example is hypothetical and probably overdrawn—very likely there is some generality in the "amount" of autonomy the adolescent has. But it warns us how misleading a simple-minded approach may be. In the example given the patterns of autonomy are clues to something else; to the parental value system. In the first example, we may have an only child of intellectual and overprotective parents, in the second a family eager to promote the child's sociability but parochial in its outlook.

Behavioral autonomy is, in short, a dependent variable. To give it meaning we have to know its antecedents, its sources. In the case of the adolescent we imagine that these are to be found in parental values. What the youngster is free or unfree to do and decide probably tells us less about him than it does about his parents; it tells us about him indirectly, through what it may suggest about the family milieu and the parent's implicit ideology of socialization.

Another approach to autonomy, the last we shall treat, is what we shall call value autonomy. We use the word "value" in the broadest sense, meaning beliefs, attitudes, opinions, ideologies, and so on. What do we mean by value autonomy? It is hard to offer more than a connotative definition: we mean the capacity to manage a clarity of vision which permits one to transcend customary structurings of reality. The autonomous person, by this definition, is able to escape illusion and convention; he does not allow custom to bend his perception of himself or the world about him. Erikson (1950), in another context, has had the best phrase for what we have in mind: "a responsible relativism."

This state of autonomy—perhaps we should say, this state of grace—is a rare enough achievement. We cannot imagine that the youngster begins to approach it until he has at least partially settled some of the early and stringent problems of adolescence—sexuality, vocation, identity—and until he has managed a certain degree of independence from the impulses and from the emotional claims of the environment. Once these are assured—and it will not be in most cases until late in adolescence—the person may then be able to accomplish those qualities of perception and conduct we call value autonomy.

Why is it so uncommon an achievement? Because it needs more than the ordinary intellectual gifts; because it requires a moving encounter with values and ideas contrary to those one has grown up with, either in one's own experience, or through reading, or as they are represented in a loved or idealized figure; above all, because it involves a willingness to endure the loosening of identifications with significant others, and indeed, with one's sense of the community as a whole. Our ties to others, our emotional solidarity with them, is endangered when we dare to give up customary beliefs, so much so that those who do so are able to, ordinarily, only by forming intense attachments to those of like-minded unorthodoxy.

We sometimes see, in clinical practice, individuals who have managed a marked value change: here is a girl from the Deep South, daughter of a staunchly segregationist father and a shallow, hysteroid, Southern-belle mother, who liberates herself from racist orthodoxy to adopt the standard liberal values; here is a son of superstitious, bigoted parents, raised in a brutish rural milieu, who manages to make a scholarly career; here is a young woman reared in Mennonite orthodoxy, who makes her way first to a softer religion and finally to no religion at all. Who are these people? How did they find the way out of their histories? Even the close knowledge of character and circumstance that the therapeutic interaction allows does not give one a totally satisfactory answer. But we note some recurrences: in almost all cases, a penetrating intelligence, and with it the ability to see farther and think more quickly, breeding a secret confidence in one's own judgment and a certain (often secret) skepticism about the opinions of others; in some cases, a parent, or some other esteemed adult figure, who while giving lip service to the official pieties, nevertheless lets known a half-felt, largely unspoken dissatisfaction with them.[3]

Almost always, in the instances we have seen, the college experience was decisive. For a few who had lived sealed off in one or another ver-

[3] In one closely studied case, a woman patient's father was a self-made man with reactionary political opinions. He was appropriately dismayed when his daughter developed, in college, the moderately liberal ideas he termed "socialistic." But his daughter was convinced that this was a pretense, that secretly he was delighted with her, and that he egged her on in her defections from his politics. Her own impression, which seemed to be correct, was that as a young man her father had held advanced ideas, that he had given them up in keeping with his financial success, that unconsciously he half-despised both his success and the opinions that went with them, and that he now used her to live out his lost liberalism. We may have here an ideological counterpart of the hypothesis advanced by Johnson and Szurek (1952), who have argued persuasively that many violently antisocial children act out the unconscious wishes of their parents.

sion of the American provinces, college had meant nothing less than a re-birth in a new world. Others had known, even in high school, a sense of difference and isolation, a groping for something new; for these college had meant not so much discovery, as the crystallization of vague stirrings and portents into the beginnings of identity. The college experience had been able to accomplish its work not only because it offered new values; but also because college had meant leaving home and thus the severing of affective ties to the family and to the peers of the home milieu which could now be replaced by ties to like-minded others. It was not only that one met ideas in college; it was as much that one found in examples living testimony that one could live comfortably with ideas. The college experience for the people we speak of, had all the meaning, all the impact that Henry James describes in Kate Croy's attachment to Merton Densher: "He represented what her life had never given her and certainly, without some such aid as his, never would give her; all the high, dim things she lumped together as of the mind. It was on the side of the mind that Densher was rich for her, and mysterious and strong, and he had rendered her in especial the sovereign service of making that element real. She had had, all her days, to take it terribly on trust; no creature she had ever encountered having been able in any degree to testify for it directly. Vague rumors of its existence had made their precarious way to her; but nothing had, on the whole, struck her as more likely than she would live and die without the chance to verify them."

Relations among these three autonomies are by no means simple and, at least to this point, they have been only partially and generally mapped or studied. In clinical work with adolescents, we learn to be cautious in appraising the surface of behavior, especially where "autonomy" is concerned. The youngster may give every evidence of a spirited independence, and yet we shall learn that it tells us very little about the state of inner freedom. He may have won or been granted a high degree of behavioral autonomy, to move in the environment as he sees fit; yet a searching analysis may inform us that he moves not freely but because of an inner necessity.

It has been in the psychoanalytic genius to uncover the constraint and compulsion which may underlie seemingly adaptive, seemingly normative behaviors; it has been in that genius too to connect, at the level of motivation, patterns which happen on the surface to be unconnected or even opposed to each other. Thus we may find that the counterphobically reckless and the phobically restrained adolescent are in some respects not nearly as apart as they seem. We learn to see them as brothers in castration anxiety. The discovery and annotation of these kinds of paradoxes belong to an earlier (and more exuberant) era of psychoanalysis. Nowadays we are not so bemused by genotypic similarities as to overlook or underplay the importance of the surface.

Our knowledge of the depths allows us, however, to gain a surer understanding of the surface. We can (to continue in the previous example) differentiate a controlled, ego-syntonic sense of independence from a counterphobically compelled "freedom" which may look like it, just as we can distinguish judicious caution from a seemingly similar phobic timidity.

The same kind of connections and contradictions can also appear when we look at values in relation to emotional autonomy. We are familiar enough with the ideologist of anarchic freedom who in the end becomes an apologist for the most orthodox and traditional systems of authority, and we see here that continuity between apparently irreconcilable positions was provided by an underlying need for clarity, for some magical system capable of reducing imponderable complexity to a neat and categorical system.

Nor is this the only form in which we may find discontinuity between emotional and value autonomy. There is the equally plausible opposite situation—the individual who has achieved a high degree of internal emotional freedom, yet because of lack of cultural opportunity has never met a system of values different from the one he has been born to. While isolation of this degree may strike us as rare in contemporary society, we must recognize that the communication of ideas through mass media is of recent origin and that many older people in this country in fact grew to adulthood in very great isolation, in rural America, thirty or forty years ago. Even today there are cultural pockets in this country which are insulated against alien views—remote regions in the South and also, perhaps, certain established upper class milieux.

So the issue of autonomy is complex and it did not surprise us to find problems and ambiguities in our research on the topic. We shall describe findings and our interpretations of them presently; we want first to consider some of the factors which affect the child's progress toward emotional autonomy, the variables in family interaction which determine whether an adolescent can begin to resolve infantile ties, and, if so, the pace and path of his turn toward independence. Here again, in looking at the aspects of family life which can facilitate or inhibit the child's quest for an emotional life of his own—we find ourselves in theoretical wilderness. A few concepts have been staked and studied empirically and our understanding of these only highlights the obscurity of larger regions of American family life which we know only slightly from clinical work and the observations (often keen, but rarely tested) of American and European cultural commentators.

Our own thinking about the problem is far from comprehensive or systematic; it is limited to those areas of family life most relevant to the problem of autonomy, and is in many cases allusive rather than closely ordered or refined. We speak of variables of family interaction, but often we can only point to differences between families which seem large and important, without being able to claim that we have reduced all of the tone and color of the difference to a simple unidimensional scheme.

The concepts which seem to us crucial for understanding family dynamics—as they affect adolescent autonomy—are these: (1) the parents' interest and involvement in his parent role and in his child's development (both the degree and nature of this involvement; (2) the affective intensity of family interaction; (3) the degree and nature of family conflict; and (4) the nature of parental authority.

1. *Parental interest and involvement.* Lack of interest or emotional investment in parenthood is usually thought of in connection with the most deprived and depressed parts of lower class culture. The mother who deserts her children, the parents who leave small children alone in a locked house while they go out with friends—cases such as these, reported with frightening frequency in metropolitan dailies, occur most often in that lumpen segment of the lower class where pathology and poverty run together like hungry dogs. But we must not be blinded by middle-class bias or by the obvious fact that the norm in the middle class is very deep involvement in parenthood. The fact is that there are also middle-class mothers whose involvement in child-raising is slight —whose major interests center on their social lives or careers or on narcissistic concern for their own persons. Often such women are compelled to find legitimate rationalizations for behavior that their social circles tend to view as shockingly nonmaternal—like the upper-middle-class golf enthusiast who has been told by her physician that an incipient ulcer demands that she spend as little time as possible at home with her four children. This only testifies to the imposing value middle-class adults generally place on the parent role and on being devoted, conscientious parents.

For middle-class parents, by and large, consider parenthood among their most important functions, and their children an ultimate test of their own worth. If they have been good parents and their children turn out to be good people (by whatever criteria they may use), then most middle-class adults feel their lives to be successful, to have meaning. And indeed the child often provides the single hope of value or meaning in what is otherwise an unsatisfactory, shadowy, valueless existence. This theme, prominent in American literature is nowhere more sharply, or painfully described than in *Death of a Salesman*. Willie Loman's one contact with his own self, with passion, with anything substantial was his desire for his son's love. This love was inevitably corrupted by the sham that was the man and his life, but for a time, at least, it sustained Willie Loman's humanity. In most cases, we assume and hope, the child of normal middle-class background does not carry so exaggerated a burden of parent investment, but it will be a large share nonetheless.

We have spoken of the parent's investment in parenthood. There is the more specific, the more particularized, version of this same issue— the parent's investment and interest in a specific child. Families are more or less explicit about favored children, about the parent's having a larger stake in one or another of their children. Beyond the question of favorites, parents obviously have different kinds of involvements with their several children, depending on factors like the child's sex and birth order, special talents and handicaps, personal histories, beauty or charm. Folk wisdom (particularly handed down by psychologically sophisticated upper-middle-class folk) has it that involvement will be greatest with the first-born and less with subsequent children, larger for a son (at least for men of traditional orientation) than a daughter, very high in the case of a son born after several girls, and so forth. But individual histories and family circumstances upset these rules and create enormous variation in the patterning of parent investment.

The amount of parent interest is obviously a crucial factor in the child's progress toward independence. If parents are too deeply tied to a child, if they bear a love for him so intense it amounts to dependency, the child's way to autonomy will be blocked or cut off. On the other hand, a child who is loved too little is not by this fact freed from internal struggle or provided an easy start toward independence. Here as in so many areas of parent behavior it is moderation that seems to hold the key to normal, uncomplicated growth. The parent who loves his child and can release him appropriately; this is the pattern that seems from all the empirical evidence to promote healthy development in the emerging adult.

This curvilinear relationship between parent involvement and child development—in which the child's autonomy is promoted by an investment neither too large nor too small—raises the closely related issue of the *nature* of the parents' involvement with the child. That is, the child's meaning for the parent, the nature of the needs which the child serves for the parent.

The needs which can be served by having children are nearly as varied as human motivation. Children may be desired as an economic asset, as proof of potency, as a warranty on eternal life, as a narcissistic extension of the self, as well as gratification for the simpler and more universal needs Erikson groups in the concept of "generativity"—the desire to create something significant that has an existence outside one's own, and the desire to tutor (and in other ways encourage the growth and welfare of) the next generation. What we suspect is that when parent involvement is moderate (and optimal), its central component is this appropriate generative need. When parent involvement is low— where a child is neglected or actively rejected—we suspect a flaw in the parent's capacity for object ties, of which the generative needs are one expression. Such a flaw implies pathology, and we expect growth to be impeded by any family structure infused with pathology. The excessive involvement at the other extreme probably means that the parent expects to get from his child gratification for needs above and beyond the generative system, neurotic cravings, or needs which should be supplied largely outside the parent role. The mother who pushes her child into one of the glamour professions despite the child's opposition, the father who exploits his children's accomplishments in the interest of his own faltering self-regard or for some external reward, the parents who infantilize a child in neurotic and useless efforts to deny the aging process—these are all fairly familiar clinical types, and they all bear seriously neurotic marks.

There are, however, situations in which parents would realize certain needs through their children which, although essentially nonneurotic, may endanger the child's autonomy or health. Some of these problems grow out of culture contact and culture conflict. The European immigrant whose values and expectations about family interaction are completely different from those which his children have learned in their American experience, may make demands on his children which they cannot meet without risking their own autonomy, their adjustment and happiness in their American setting, or all of these. According to our values, the parents should find sources of gratification for their needs (for dependency, companionship, and intimacy) outside their children. They should, in other words, adapt their demands to the American idiom. This is easier to say when a person has only experienced the American idiom, of course.

We see, then, some relationship between the degree of parent involvement and the nature of that involvement. It may be that studies of parent behavior find moderate investment providing the best milieu for child growth because the middle range on measures of involvement taps appropriate involvement, while the upper extreme implies that the parents love their children not only too much, but also in the wrong ways.

2. *The affective intensity of family interaction.* Here we deal with a variable that overlaps parent involvement to a large extent. There is, however, a difference between the two concepts at least in this sense —that parent involvement describes the psychological relationship between the parents and a particular child, while we have in mind here the emotionality in the family as a whole, a kind of atmospheric background within which a particular parent-child relationship exists. It is clearly conceivable that a family may be intensely emotional, and the home atmosphere emotionally dense, without a particular child being implicated or carrying much of the parents' emotional investment. This is the situation of the daughter in *Five Finger Exercise*, who moves as innocent, skirting but never (except accidently) involved in, the tragic intensity of the father-mother-son entanglement which dominates the family atmosphere. In large families the same separation may occur in less neurotic settings.

Or the level of general affective intensity may be quite high in a family but be centered primarily in sibling relations rather than parent-child relationships. This again is easily conceived in large families, and it could also hold in cases where parents, deeply involved in themselves or each other or some intense commitment outside the family, had only modest investment in their children and left them in the care of others or each other for their emotional education. In such cases, the intensity of the parent-child relationship would tell us nothing of the general emotional climate in the home, since the parents would be peripheral to its core emotional life.

Even where the parents are central, we think that their emotional involvement with the children and the level of affective expression will not be perfectly correlated. There are the American Gothic families in which affect is expressed with great restraint, if at all, but where family dramas of great intensity and bitterness are enacted in the approved covert, tight-lipped manner. On the other hand, some parents create a family life in which emotional expression is raucous or deafening, but at the same time permit their children an easy freedom at the appropriate moment—a freedom granted so simply that we must assume that the parents' investment is nonneurotic and appropriate, however flamboyant its expressive style. And this is what we intend by the concept of affective intensity—the style of family interaction. It is a variable more directly observable in family behavior than parent investment, it affects the style in which the child will make his bid for autonomy, and, we suspect that it conditions the outcome of that move rather than determining it directly. To use an example introduced previously, the daughter in *Five Finger Exercise* would in all likelihood develop a relatively large degree of personal autonomy, assuming that her relationship with her parents could recover from the accident of her stumbling briefly into the arena of her mother's projections. Budding independence was clear in this child before the accident—in her precocious wit, her capacity for sympathy and tenderness, her honesty. Even her relationship with her neurotically driven mother borrows meaning and warmth from the girl's original and humorous view of the world, her faith in her own perception and judgment, and her resistance to her mother's efforts to force her into conventional, status-based ways.

Yet the emotional atmosphere in her family is charged with intense pathological (or, at least, primitive) elements, and it is unthinkable that this should have no effect on the form of her development. We can point to some of these effects. She maintains a friendship with a lower-class girl in open (although gentle) defiance of her mother; she has an unusual sensitivity and sympathy for the young tutor whose history of oppression has left him with serious emotional scars.

We do not mean to say that these are bad effects or that they are symptoms of an injured capacity for emotional autonomy. Quite the opposite, we think that witnessing a crucial struggle over the issue of autonomy (her brother's) when she herself is in a real sense privileged against the neurotic side of the parent's investment—that this peculiar combination of intense emotionality and a degree of personal separateness may allow her unusual opportunities for developing autonomy. It provokes consciousness of the issue, without blocking access to the channels for reaching freedom.

This much seems clear—that the same kind of parent investment without the highly charged affective atmosphere would produce a different pattern and degree of emotional autonomy; and, we think, not merely because the particular parent investment could not be duplicated outside the emotional atmosphere which existed in this family. What we are trying to say is that the two variables are separable and can have important and distinguishable effects.

Before we leave this discussion of the intensity of emotionality, it is worth noting that American child-raising literature very often offers an ideal of moderation in emotion as in all things. But the ideal is offered, and adopted, by parents who have the most passionate investment in parenthood and in their children. For most middle-class parents, success in parenthood has become a key measure of personal worth. The problem, then, becomes how to maintain a dispassionate stance in an area where one has a truly passionate involvement. The difficulty of managing this task is reflected in interviews with mothers: the most common criticism women make against themselves as mothers involves loss of control, the expression of anger (Gurin, Veroff, and Feld, 1960). The paradox was expressed very neatly by a sophisticated middle-class clinic patient when she noted that, "It's too bad children have to be raised by their own parents, when we'd probably all do better by someone else's." It is certainly easier to achieve the ideal of balance when we are not so deeply involved in the effect of our behavior.

3. *Conflict in the Family*. This dimension of family relations can be analyzed in a number of ways. We can think of the amount of conflict that occurs, the level at which conflict exists (overt or covert), the particular issues on which it centers, the style of expression (verbal, physical), and so forth. Certain of these variables overlap with other dimensions of family interaction (for example, the level of conflict, its overtness can be subsumed under the intensity of emotional expression, the existence of permissible areas and degrees of conflict will in part define and be defined by the nature of parental authority, and so forth).

The parents' allowance of some form of expressed conflict seems a crucial variable for the comfort and development of the adolescent child. The central internal conflict of the period requires that the child loosen his emotional bonds to the parents and also begin to form his own internal system of authority. These tasks, and the fierce intensity of adolescent instincts, insist that the parent become a target for the child's resistance and resentments, at least for a time. The parent who is either too frightened or too rigidly dominant to allow the child any open hostility courts disaster. The child may turn the anger in on himself, he may lose touch with, and also the capacity to control, his own anger. Or he may manage to keep resentment under control, but only at the heavy cost of personal impoverishment or emotional barrenness.

Aside from the question of expression possibilities, we must recognize that families vary on the basic dimension of degree of conflict. Some families argue or fight a great deal and others very little, even if we eliminate those in which the parents permit the child little or no expression. To some extent this difference can be attributed to the emotional intensity of family members, to temperamental factors. In part the degree of conflict will depend on the parents' capacity to assume the role of authority with sanity and security, to avoid becoming embroiled in conflicts which are essentially the child's expression of his uncertainty and internal conflict. But beyond these factors, we would suggest that the amount of family conflict will also be related to the degree of difference between child and parents on any of a number of crucial characteristics.

The child who is different from his family in intellectual gifts, the child of immigrants who talks to his parents across a cultural barrier, the child of special talent (for example, in an art form) all represent cases in which the stage is provided for emotional conflict by the sheer distinctiveness of the child vis-à-vis the rest of the family.

The case of special intellectual gifts is interesting because the difference is uncontaminated by the emotional factors we want to predict. The fact that IQ looks more and more like a genetic trait means that we may find large parent-child differences only rarely in biological families. The cases we offer as illustration—in which the child's very high IQ led to a sense of separation and to grave parent-child conflict —are first a case of an adopted child, and second, a case in which the child was apparently the product of an affair which his dull-normal mother had had with a man of much higher intelligence.

In both cases the gifted children showed a strong sense of separation, an isolation from the family. The parents, on their side, were totally unable to cope with these youngsters, whom they could neither understand nor mold into the only kind of life they knew by the only techniques available to them. Very early the children seemed to detect their own superiority, and this recognition, in turn, undermined their capacity to respect or rely on their parents in any of the ways taken for granted in normal parent-child relationships. The parents, unequipped to understand or appreciate the child's position, became (in one case) terrified, and (in the other) determined to quell signs of what they interpreted as unchildlike impertinence. Conflict developed and burgeoned. It was as though the intellectual distance between parents and child allowed only one form of emotional interaction—conflict and hostility—since their vocabularies for respect and regard, for ease and affection, were so different.

Such marked intellectual variation is extremely rare in biologically related families. While children may be more or less gifted than their parents, parents are usually in a position, at least, to appreciate and tolerate a degree of difference less extreme than the kind our examples illustrate. But characteristics other than intelligence—as for instances, artistic talent, or a temperamental bent, a developed interest or a physical trait—can and do vary widely within families, and can become the focus for abiding conflict. To be sure, the outbreak of hostility over difference will also depend on the parents' emotional make-up and on the nature of their investment in the child. But the difference must first be apparent—it is a necessary although insufficient condition for conflict.

4. *Parental Authority.* This is the one dimension of family relations which has been the object of extensive empirical research. Following the original authoritarian personality studies, and even antedating them, the social sciences have built a substantial research literature about the origins and effects of certain patterns of parent authority. The California group (Adorno et al., 1950) use analytic categories which describe authority as a complex and multidimensional system. They contrast strong, rigid, and essentially irrational authority with more moderate and flexible power. The anchoring concepts for the authoritarian pattern came from an analysis of a certain personality-value structure and a line of inference (via psychoanalytic theory) extending back into the family patterns which seemed likely to engender it. The nature of the categories, their complexity and descriptive richness, followed the form of the research process.

Since publication of the *Authoritarian Personality*, research on family power has moved in several directions. One line of research has concentrated on sorting out the effects of the various dimensions included in the original categories. From this work we begin to get more refined notions about the effect of power in combination with warmth or coldness. We begin to see that the effects of parental power on the child's developing personality depends on the whole complicated distribution of power within the family (that is, the relative power of father, mother, children) and the larger social system (for example, the effects of a dominant father on child development differ depending on the father's position in the power structure of the society). We are still some distance from a comprehensive understanding of the problem, but it is interesting to note that as research gives greater delineation and refinement to our picture of the dimensions of family authority, the complex descriptive category used to account for development of the authoritarian personality holds up. We are impressed with the consistency with which the same pattern of family variables appear and seem essential for explaining at least this one form of development.

What dimensions within the authority system do we need for anything like a complete analytic description? We can list some which seem theoretically crucial, only a few of which have been studied systematically. There is the question of locus—do parents hold the power for all decisions affecting the child or do they permit the child himself a degree of self-determination? If so, in what areas do they grant such rights? We would like to know, as well, something of the grounds on which parents exercise their power. Do they rule from a position of unquestioned and traditional right which they feel no need to rationalize, or do they rely on greater experience and wisdom as the source of their legitimate authority? The basis of authority should appear in behavior as the accompaniment of power assertion. The traditional parent will neither explain his act nor permit the child to question it. The parent who assumes a rational base for power treats the child as an understanding being, explaining his own acts and responding to the child's questions and arguments, assuming that they signify, at least in some measure, efforts to comprehend parent action.

Another aspect of family authority consists of the sanctions parents use to enforce their rule. In general we draw distinction among physical punishment (in which the message to the child is clear—avoid disobedience or suffer painful consequences if you are found out); deprivation; and methods which aim to eliminate disapproved acts, but also seek to encourage growth of the child's own internal controls. Enlistment of guilt exemplifies the last category.

An underlying dimension of sanctions not completely covered by this kind of behavioral distinction concerns their punitiveness. Ideally we would distinguish harshness from the content of punishment, and analyze the meaning of various patterns. But harshness per se—the message implicit in a particular punishment—is very difficult to assess except by the most intensive and time-consuming observations. Since we can assume a high correlation between type of punishment and harshness, ordinarily we settle for the more easily obtained information about techniques and use this as a rough index of subtler psychological dimensions.

One other dimension of authority has to do with consistency, or what we may call rigidity when we are negatively disposed to a particular authority pattern. It should be distinguished from the centralization of power. A parent may reserve all or only a few areas of power for himself, but this does not tell us how consistent he is in imposing rewards and sanctions in the areas where he does rule. Most analyses of family authority assume some kind of relationship between centralization of power and the consistency with which power is exercised, but —depending on one's theoretical and value position—the nature of this assumed relationship can vary extremely. From a knowledge of the family pattern that produces the authoritarian personality—a pattern combining punitiveness, concentration of power, and inconsistency— we can assume that a more democratic distribution of control will also mean greater consistency. On the other hand, comparing the Victorian ideal—the strong, consistent parent who controls children but also provides them with clear limits and models—with much of what passes today for modern permissive child-raising, we can emerge with a very different notion of the relation between parental dominance and consistency of application. Whatever we hold against Victorian methods, one virtue most would concede the Victorian parent is that he was alert to children's behavior and quick to respond to deviation from the norms he imposed, whereas we sometimes have the feeling that permissiveness can deteriorate into an ideological rationalization for not noticing what is going on, not committing oneself to the hard work and responsibility of parenthood.

These then are some of the major dimensions of family interaction which we would ideally measure in order to characterize family relationships. We did not try to measure all of them in our studies. Some of them (for example, the punitiveness of sanctions apart from the use of particular techniques of punishment) require methods other than the interview for adequate assessment. Others would require interviews with parents in addition to or instead of children. Still others which we felt we could measure we did not because of time and space limits. Any variable that called for too much interview time was likely to get a low priority in our research since our project aim was broad and exploratory rather than intensive coverage of a small area of adolescent experience.

Even where we included certain dimensions in our objectives, we were not always successful in devising useable measures. Of the range of variables we have discussed, we had reasonably good success in measuring the degree of the child's autonomy, some features of family conflict, the extent of parental control, and the style with which that control is exercised, particularly the harshness of sanctions.

Autonomy

Most of our information in the autonomy area suggests that there is a steady drift toward greater independence as girls grow older. Certainly this is true at the behavioral level. The proportion of girls who hold jobs, or date, or have major and independent responsibility for work at home, all increase dramatically during this period. The proportion of girls who spend most of their free time with friends rather than the family increases, although here differences are surprisingly small when we consider the age range covered in the girls sample.

Small increases in independence are all that we can report for most items designed to tap emotional independence. For the most part there are no sudden leaps forward for the group as a whole. We asked whether a girl could be as close to a friend as to her family, and we find a slow rise in the proportion of "yes" responses over time, from 58 per cent of the early adolescents to 68 per cent of those in late adolescence. The proportion of girls who think so is much higher than for boys of the same age (14-16); this may be put down to the apparently greater social maturity of adolescent girls, or it may be due to the greater meaning that friendship has for girls.

In one of the projective items we posed the problem of a girl with a good job away from home who is asked by her lonely mother to leave the job and return home. Somewhat more than half of the youngest subjects have the girl return home. The proportion offering this response declines steadily to one-third of the late adolescents. Only about one in ten of the youngest group flatly refuses to return, but this increases to one-quarter of the oldest group. With increasing age, there is a tendency to suggest conditional and compromise solutions. We almost imagine that some of the girls have thought long and hard on this question, so canny and ingenious are some of the proposals.

We have two other indications of a general trend away from total emotional involvement with the family. In the projective question about a girl who has done something shameful, older girls are less likely to think of mother as a confidante to whom the girl would turn, they more often think of a girlfriend in this role. As age increases we find a steady decrease in the proportion of girls who choose their own mothers or other women in their own families as the person they would like most to be like when they grow up.

As the girl grows older, her attitude toward her parents undergoes gradual but distinct changes. These, again, are more or less in the direction we would expect. The early adolescents show a childlike dependence and submissiveness. They are eager to win the parents' approval; they are ready to defy parental authority only in minor issues, and even then show themselves to feel frightened or guilty. The youngest girls, in responding to the projective picture, tend to picture the heroine as accepting without cavil the parents' demands. As they grow older, we find a rather interesting change. They do not often have the heroine argue with or directly defy the parents; but many of them represent her as being surprised and hurt that she is not trusted.

With increasing age, the parent-peer conflict in the projective pictures is more likely to be settled by need-oriented and group-oriented responses, as against the parent-oriented answers we find among the younger girls. As our subjects grow older, they are less likely to be frightened of their parents. When we ask if a girl who disobeyed her parents would tell them about it later, it is only the youngest group who give a high proportion of "No" answers. The older girls can afford to be candid about minor delinquencies. Interestingly, there are only insignificant changes in the representation of the parents in the projective pictures—they are seen as no more or less lenient or strict by the different age groups. The differences we do find are in the heroine's reaction to the situation.

When we look at items which link autonomy to conflict, we get the impression of an outward arc of autonomy. We asked a series of specific questions on areas of disagreement with their parents. ("Do you disagree with your parents about . . . ?") We find that disagreements peak at different ages, and that the different curves, in suggesting the rise and decline of tension, give us some insight into the girl's serial career in autonomy.

In early adolescence, the greatest amount of disagreement reported has to do with personal grooming—disagreements about clothing and lipstick. For both of these items, conflict is high below fourteen, then diminishes sharply. For items centering on the child's social activities we find a very different curve, one which peaks at middle adolescence, in the 14 to 16 age range. It is during these years that we find the greatest amount of disagreement reported about dating, the choice of friends, and driving in cars. These issues are met and, for the most part, resolved during middle adolescence. After that time the degree of conflict diminishes. Our sixth item had to do with ideology—we asked whether the girls disagreed on ideas, such as politics. Here we find a third curve of conflict, low in early adolescence, rising sharply in the middle period, and peaking in late adolescence.

Our inference from these data is that the reach of autonomy expands as the adolescent grows older. The early conflicts are, in a sense, "narcissistic," centering as they do on issues of personal grooming. The girl is preparing herself for the leap into social activity and is busily remaking herself; the psychic changes are largely silent, the physical changes, through the use of make-up and clothing, engage parental attention and join parent and child in some degree of conflict. These issues won, the girl is ready for the next sweep of the arc of autonomy, which will involve her in the intense, absorbing social life so characteristic of adolescence. The issues of conflict center on the girl's participation in the world of social activity and, implicitly, on her sexual conduct. By late adolescence these conflicts are somewhat settled, not necessarily so in individual cases, but for the group as a whole. In late adolescence the arc reaches out to encompass the world of ideas and values. The adolescent's interest now extends to a suprapersonal autonomy—having achieved a fairly high degree of physical and social independence, she now has both the capacity and desire to challenge, or simply to examine, her parents' opinions and values.

There is some evidence that as the girl grows older her father begins to play a somewhat different role in regard to her. We asked a general question about disagreements with parents, and we coded any spontaneous indications as to which parent was the antagonist. The number of girls who report no disagreement at all declines steadily over time. In early adolescence one-quarter of the girls report the mother as the antagonist. This proportion declines with increasing age, and it is balanced by an increase in references to the father. We infer that the issues of adolescence, for some families at least, are no longer seen as specifically "child-rearing" issues and thus in the mother's province primarily. Larger questions of morality and manner are now at stake, and the family as a whole is more frequently involved in settling them, or at least in arguing about them.

The stress we have placed on parent-child conflict ought not to give the impression that family life is marked primarily by dissension. Most of our subjects thought their parents to be fair. When we asked them to judge the rules in their own families, a majority offered some approving statement (50% or more, depending on age; there is a slight increase with age). Even the negative minority are rarely downright hostile. Most of the evaluations we coded as "negative" were simply cool and unenthusiastic—"O.K., I suppose," rather than bitter and discontented. We are perfectly aware that this high rate of approval may be due in part to the interview situation, but we have a good deal of indirect and projective evidence which also points to the probability that American adolescents generally do not judge their parents to be arbitrary or unjust.

One of the projective questions was specifically designed to produce material on this theme—"Jane sometimes wishes her parents were different. What does she have in mind?" The most popular complaint refers to parental restriction. Somewhat more than half the girls have Jane wishing for fewer restrictions—there are, somewhat to our surprise, only small changes in the choice of this category with increasing age. We do find one striking increase—in the proportion of those who have Jane wish for a closer relationship to the parents; the choice of this category almost doubles from early to late adolescence (from 17% in the youngest group, to 25% in the 14 to 16-year-old, to 32% of girls over 16). It appears that the child's gains in autonomy bring with them, in some cases, a countercurrent of disappointment, a yearning to return to the closeness and intimacy of the past.

As to the parents' authority and the way in which they exercise it— at least as this comes through to the children—we again find slow but steady changes as girls move through the adolescent era. For example, parents make more explicit demands for self-direction as the girl gets older. The proportion of girls who mention this among the "most important things [their] parents expect of [them]" changes from 8 per cent in the youngest group to 16 per cent in the 14 to 16 years group, and 25 per cent in the group over sixteen. We asked whether the girl has any part in making rules at home. Here we find an ascending curve of assent. Not quite half of the girls report this in early adolescence, 58 per cent in the middle period, 62 per cent after that.

Techniques of rule enforcement—the methods parents use to discipline their children—show greater responsiveness to the girl's increasing age than any other aspect of parental authority. There is a sharp decline in reports of physical punishment at the upper age levels (23% of the youngest group reports physical punishments, compared to 8% of the 14 to 16 year group and 2% of the girls over 16), and psychological techniques (that is, verbal, guilt inducing) rise (30%, 31% and 50% for the three groups). Deprivation of privileges is the most common technique at all age levels for both boys and girls, and age changes are less striking for this category than for either of the others.

These are the developmental findings on autonomy and family relations in girls. We have some comparable information for boys, although much less than we would like to have. We can compare boys and girls on the question of the relationship between autonomy and other variables, and we shall do this later in the chapter. Our greatest handicap occurs in trying to make direct comparisons of the extent of autonomy achieved by the two groups because we have only a few questions about autonomy and family relationships that are common to the two studies.[4]

Where we do have comparable items, our findings are ambiguous. We note, for example, that girls are advanced in certain behavioral autonomies. They date earlier than boys do and they start earning money away from home at an earlier age. (In middle adolescence, 56% of girls and 47% of boys hold jobs.) At the same time they stay closer to the family than boys do. A larger proportion of girls in middle adolescence share some leisure activity with their parents (93% of 14 to 16-year-old girls compared to 78% of the boys); in fact the middle adolescent boy reports family activity even less than do girls in late adolescence.

In the sphere of emotional independence from the family, boys by and large outdistance girls. By middle adolescence they seem to have achieved greater emotional autonomy than girls, and the pace at which they are developing seems faster than the comparable movement among girls. So, for example, in choosing an adult model, boys choose their fathers somewhat less often (25%) than girls of the same age choose their mothers (32%). Overall the choice of infamily models is somewhat less common for boys (45% of the boys, 55% of girls the same age). A more impressive finding relates choice of model and age for the two sex groups. The age changes in the boys' choice of the father are steady and quite large even within our restricted age range (31% at 14, 26% at 15, 18% at 16). The decrease in choice of the father is almost as large for boys in a 3-year span as the change in girls' choice of the mother over an 8-year period (from 40% at 11 to 24% at 18), and much larger than the girls change during the same three years (35% at 14, 33% at 15, 30% at 16). In the projective series boys more often than

---

[4] In the study of girls we probed the area of family relationships more extensively than in the study of boys. This was primarily because of our greater experience at the beginning of the girls' study, and the fact that we were willing to use a longer questionnaire than we had originally thought possible or manageable.

girls conceive of resisting parental restrictions, and they are also more likely to say that the boy in the series would tell his parents that he had disobeyed them. In both of these instances, changes in boys' answers over the three year age range are larger than comparable age changes in girls, and about equal to the changes we find in girls from early to late adolescence.

In Chapter 3 we have dealt at some length with sex differences in the internalization of personal standards and controls. In that discussion we presented a number of differences that occur in the series of questions about parental regulation. Our general interpretation of these findings was that girls continue in a compliant relationship with the parents throughout adolescence, while boys seek more actively for independence and self-regulation. The difference we find between boys' and girls' conceptions of adult authority is perhaps illustrated most clearly in answer to the question, "Have you ever broken a rule?" Ten per cent of the sample of boys say either that they have not ever done so or that they cannot remember ever breaking a rule. Twenty-six per cent of the girls the same age give comparable answers. We find that girls continue to give such answers even in late adolescence (27% of the girls 17 and 18 years old) at about the same rate. Whether or not the answer reflects literal truth is less important than the authority attitudes which seem to lie behind it. Even to conceive of the possibility of living with an external authority system without any deviation implies a respect (or even awe) for authority that is somehow inappropriate and slightly unrealistic. This, then, is what we would emphasize about girls' attitudes toward authority and particularly parental authority—that they often bear an unreal and unrealistic stamp, which seems to indicate that the issue is not terribly salient. Since the strain for independence is not as great for girls, they less often come into direct conflict with the authority and have less opportunity to judge it for what it is—a particular set of behavior regulations for which there are conceivable alternatives or substitutes. We shall see later that boys who hold to the more absolute and awesome conception are very immature. But in girls the assertion that they have never broken a rule does not necessarily imply slow development in other respects. The fact is that independence—in the sense of making one's own decisions about moral and emotional problems—is not a crucial issue for most adolescent girls.

There is one other difference between boys and girls in the authority area. Girls are often judged by coders to rely heavily on adult authority on the basis of their answers to questions about adult club leaders—about how leaders should perform and what they especially like about a favorite adult leader.

We shall have more to say about sex differences in the area of autonomy after we present the major analysis of autonomy and family relationships. But even at this point—on the basis of the limited evidence we have—we can begin to see that the issue of emotional autonomy has a salience for the adolescent boy which is not matched among girls.

In general, we find that for both boys and girls the autonomy indices from individual questions hold together quite well. Girls who think that a friend can be just as close as one's own family, for example, are also more likely to spend their free time with friends, they are more willing to criticize parents, they less often think a girl should give up her autonomy and a good job in order to live with her lonely mother, they more often choose ideals from outside the family, and so forth. Boys who say a friend can be as close as a family member tend to accept friends' counsel on issues of taste and personal behavior, and to choose unrelated adult ideals.

And we find relationships between the child's autonomy and certain aspects of family interaction—particularly the nature of parental authority and the style of punishment the parents use to enforce their rule. The one dimension of family interaction which shows inconsistent effects is family conflict. The problem here seems to be that certain of our measures reflect the child's capacity to separate himself from the family, and so tap an aspect of autonomy itself, while others get at more intense and corrosive conflict, of a kind more likely to inhibit the child's developing independence. We were not able to gain a detailed or coherent picture of the effects of conflict on development because of this peculiarity in our measurement techniques.

The clearest demonstration of autonomy differences in girls comes from an analysis of the question: "With whom do you spend your spare time?" For this analysis we contrasted two groups: those who say a friend or friends (28%), and those who say the family (41%). A small group of girls say they spend most of their time alone, and although this response is interesting and useful in other connections, it does not bear directly on the issue of autonomy from the family. We shall contrast the "friend" and "family" subjects, since this dichotomy exposes two fairly separate styles of relationship to the family.

The girls who spend spare time with the family are far less autonomous than those who say they spend time with peers. They less frequently have a part in rule-making. They show a greater tendency to rely heavily on external authority. They are more often punished physically (although they are also overrepresented in the "psychological" category, largely because the "friend" subjects overwhelmingly report deprivational punishments). They are more docile in regard to the parents' statement (on the projective pictures). More of this group denies having any disagreements with the family. They do not believe that a person can be as close to a friend as to one's family; at the same time, they more frequently wish (to a projective question) that a girl's parents would be less restrictive. (The "friend" group more commonly wishes they could be closer to the parents.) The adult they admire most is the mother. They are given somewhat heavier responsibilities at home. They more often say that their parents expect them to get along with others, be pleasant and well liked; the girls who spend their spare time with friends give a higher proportion of "independence" answers to the question about parental expectations. To spend one's spare time with the family is the modal response, as we have seen, so it may be more to the point to put it that the "friend" group is more self-directed.

Large and stable autonomy differences for boys emerged in relation to a simple index we derived from a series of six questions which asked whether the boy would take his parents' or his friends' advice on a number of issues (for example, personal grooming, choice of clubs, spending money). For this analysis we compared boys at either extreme—those who heavily choose parental advice, as against those who prefer the counsel of friends on most issues. This item, we should mention, is susceptible to another type of analysis. A number of boys say on one or more of the issues that they would seek the advice of neither friends nor parents, but would make up their own minds. These boys appear to form a psychologically separate group, but for the moment we shall ignore them to focus on the friends-parents dichotomy.

We found substantial and largely consistent differences between these groups. They respond differently to the set of projective pictures, the friend-oriented boys assuming a less submissive, more willful posture toward the parents. Those who prefer the friends' advice are less likely to accept the parents' suggestion, and more often question the hour. Later in the series of pictures they tend to say the boy would stay with his friends, while parent-oriented boys more commonly say that he would go home. When we asked whether the boy, if he decided to stay with his friends, would tell his parents later, the boys who would take the parents' advice more often say yes.

The parent-oriented boys show their dependence on the family in other ways. They more often deny that a person can be as close to a friend as to his family. When we ask which adult they admire most, they are likely to mention their fathers. And yet their dependency does not necessarily mean the boys enjoy a close relationship to the family; for example, they do not generally share activities with the parents. Their dependence, instead, seems to be part of a more general pattern of authoritarian submission. When they consider the role of a club leader, they show a strong tendency to rely on adult authority. They are docile about the draft, more often stating that they would like it (while the friend-oriented boys more often tell us that they would enlist before being drafted in order to get a good deal). Finally, this group contains an unusually large number of boys who are punished physically; as we shall see later in this chapter, those boys who report corporal punishment make up a distinctly authoritarian group.

The boys who lean heavily on their parents for advice show certain signs of immaturity. They report dating less frequently. Their descriptions of what they would look for in a job are also more immature; they less often cite "interesting work," and more often mention a steady job and having "nice people to work with." They have relatively shorter conceptions of future time and are thought by interviewers to be less confident than other boys.

The boys who depend on their parents' advice are somewhat younger than the sample as a whole, although age is not nearly as strong a force as we might expect. A similarly moderate relationship exists between social class and answers to this series. Middle-class adolescents are less reliant on parents for advice, and more often say they would seek the advice of friends. The relationships we have reported between this series and other aspects of autonomy, social development and family patterns are not attributable to either age or social status. Differences between boys who are parent-reliant and those who look to peers as advisors are stable for both social classes and at each age.

Another "autonomy" group—one which shows somewhat different features than the others we have isolated—emerges in response to the final picture of the projective series. The boys who have the hero stay with his friends (and disobey his parents) differ only moderately from other respondents. However, the differences are interesting and seem to suggest a pattern. These boys less often say they would seek parental advice, and they would more often choose friends' advice. In answering the question, "When might a boy break a rule"? they less often choose "emergency" and more often choose "rebellion." They are low on authority reliance. They tend not to choose the father or family figures as the admired adult. They read less, they date more, they are less likely to belong to clubs. The evidence is ambiguous, but we would guess that the autonomy pattern here is defined by a detachment from the family, accompanied by some mild rebelliousness. They are not the docile, brutalized, ambivalent youngsters who are punished heavily, cleave to the parents, and fester underneath (their punishment pattern is no different from other respondents). Nor do they show the autonomy pattern of the more mature youngster, who enjoys a good relationship to the family while keeping himself autonomous in the things that count. We have the feeling that these boys are heavily invested in the peer group, to the degree that it counts more for them than the family does. There is no sign that they bear any strong resentment toward the parents, although there are some indications that they do not like the parents to interfere too much or too often with their fun. In response to an early picture in the projective series, they have the boy (who will, remember, later disobey the parents) accept the parents' suggestion. They are unlike that group, more overtly rebellious, who challenge the parents' right to set limits. These boys do not report more (or less) disagreements with the family than do other boys.

Still another dependent and immature group of boys emerges in our analysis of the question: "Have you ever broken a rule?" The overwhelming preponderance of our boys say that they have; only about fifty in the entire sample deny it. This latter group then is of no great importance numerically, but they are of some interest psychologically, for they illuminate for us the sources and accompaniments of excessive virtue. They are not, we should mention, distinguished by any particular demographic background features. We thought it probable that they would be mainly 14-year-olds, but this is not the case. They are not younger than the sample as a whole, and they are not predominantly of one social class or from rural backgrounds.

They are distinguished from other boys by certain psychological characteristics and certain features of family interaction. As we would imagine, they are highly dependent on the parents; every item we have which bears on this topic illustrates it. They accept parental advice, and reject friends' advice; they do not feel a person can be as close to a friend as to the family. In response to the series of projective pictures, in every item they picture the hero as submissive—accepting the parents' regulation more frequently, going home more frequently, confessing to the parents more often. They admire their fathers, and also admire other masculine family figures (uncles, grandfathers, and so forth); they underchoose unrelated adults. They more often deny having disagreements with their parents.

None of this, as we implied, should occasion too much surprise. What makes this group of boys stand out is the dreary, constricted picture they present when we look outside their attitudes to the family. They are extremely high on authority reliance. They belong to far fewer clubs than other boys do. Fewer of them date (22%, as contrasted with 60% of those who say they have broken rules). They read less. They more often say they would change nothing about themselves if given the chance. They more often report physical punishment, which we would expect, but they are also overrepresented in psychological punishment, an unanticipated and intriguing finding.

Despite the occasionally "patchy" nature of these findings, we get a plausible picture of the autonomous adolescent, a picture which confirms what personality theory would lead us to expect. Among the nonautonomous, we find a kind of relationship to the family which we have learned to call either authoritarian or infantile—a pattern where the heavy hand of the parents produces that muffling of vitality we call ambivalence. The child is docile and dependent, more so than he should be, past the time he should be. His docility may mask a fretful resentment which may never express itself directly, but which itches or burns underneath, producing, at the least, a distinct inhibition of the limits of personal growth, or edging the personality toward an excess of blandness, on the one hand, or an implicit, cankerous anger, on the other.

Family Conflict

What does overt disagreement between an adolescent and his family mean? Do boys and girls who report a high rate of disagreement with their parents differ in any marked way from those who do not? The answer, for girls at least, seems to be no. With six specific questions, we were able to compare those girls with low, moderate, and high proportions of disagreement. We found very few items in the family area which distinguished these groups. It should be noted here that, on the whole, girls who report disagreement on one issue are more likely to report disagreement elsewhere. By and large, there are positive relationships among the separate disagreement items. One might say that we have groups of "yeasayers and naysayers," (Couch and Keniston, 1960) those who are disposed either to report or to deny disagreement. But high or low disagreement does not appear to be closely related to other aspects of family life. For example, it does not relate significantly to punishment type, nor to most of our measures of autonomy. It shows no clear relation to more subtle measures of family discord.

The same state of affairs obtains in regard to most of the individual items. For example, the girls who tell us that they disagree with their parents on dating—certainly a salient area of concern for most girls in this age group—appear to be no different in most ways from the girls who do not.

There is one disagreement area which is a decided exception to the foregoing. The girls who report that they disagree with their parents on ideas stand out as different in their relations to the family from those who do not disagree and, in most respects, from those who disagree on other issues. They come from more equalitarian homes—reporting a higher level of participation in rule-making; they are more likely to say, to the "lonely mother" question, that they would not return home; they are somewhat less reliant on authority (although, curiously, they more often report that their parents expect them to respect authority). They have lighter home responsibilities than other girls; they are less willing to have the parents deceived (on the projective pictures); and they report less severe punishment at all age levels.

These findings suggest that the girls probably come from those middle-class homes where ideas have enough salience to have come to the child's attention, and enough importance to serve as a vehicle for expressing their independence. We might speculate whether the girls are more "intellectual," in the sense that their conflicts are more spiritualized, or sublimated. In any case, disagreement over ideas—"politics or things like that," as our question put it—is by no means a sign of a rancorous disaffection; to the contrary, it seems to be found among those girls who are more trusting with their parents, who are more self-reliant, and who have an easier time of it in the family.

Two items in the boys study can be interpreted as measures of family conflict: one is a direct question asking whether the parents have any old-fashioned ideas or ideas with which the boy disagrees, the second question in the picture-story series, in which the subject is asked what the boy would say to his parents after they impose a rule restricting his behavior. In answer to this latter question, we get a good break between those boys who accept the parental restriction with no objections, and those who question the restriction.[5] Small groups of boys gave two other answers—some questioned the parents' right to impose

[5] This analysis was not possible in the case of girls, since few girls (4%) question the restriction.

any restriction on the boy, and expressed real annoyance with the parents; another group had the boy accept the parents' restriction but indicated at the same time that he would not, in fact, mind the parents. Unfortunately for our analysis of family conflict, these two groups— which very likely represent family patterns of intense conflict—were so small that they defied systematic analysis.[6]

The two measures we have—the direct question and the picture story question—seem to tap different kinds or levels of family conflict. The direct question, as far as we can determine from our analysis, taps a slightly rebellious attitude toward the parents. What we had intended as a softening phrase in the question, the allusion to the parents' having "old-fashioned" ideas—apparently strengthened the critical tone of the question. Many boys who said they had disagreements with their parents hastened to assure the interviewer that their parents were not, however, old-fashioned. Only 50 per cent of the boys interviewed answered the question affirmatively. They said, that is, that their parents had some old-fashioned ideas or ideas they disagreed with. In light of other evidence from the interview, we interpret the high proportion of "no disagreement" responses to be products of this critical tone we unintentionally imposed by the reference to old-fashioned ideas.

What the question seems to get at, then, is the boy's capacity to assume an objective-critical view of his parents, a capacity indicating independence and also a degree of rebellion. The rebellious quality is overt and relatively moderate, however, and does not imply the deeper and more masked hostility that characterizes certain nonautonomous patterns that emerge in other parts of our analysis.

Boys who say they disagree with their parents' ideas more often say they would seek friends' advice rather than parents' on issues of taste and personal behavior. They tend to see the boy in the projective series resisting his parents' restriction, and they mention rebellion as a basis for breaking a rule somewhat more frequently than the boys who say they never disagree with their parents' ideas. They are not, on the other hand, marked by any general flaw in the internalization of standards and values. In fact they show more conscious concern with personal controls than other boys do. They are more likely to mention an area of personal control in answer to the question about how they would like to change themselves and also the question about things that worry boys most. They show some of the aspects of ego development characteristically associated with autonomy. They tend to be upward-

[6] The numbers in these two categories were as follows: questions parents right 3 per cent; and surface compliance with no commitment 4 per cent.

mobile and achievement-oriented, and to be active in work and dating. While none of the differences in this analysis are large, they consistently indicate a pattern of independence fortified by mild rebelliousness.

The other conflict item in the boys study—reactions to the projective situation in which a boy's parents impose a restriction on him— distinguishes a less rebellious style of independence. The fact that a boy questions the parents seems primarily to illuminate the nature and style of family authority, the parents' accessibility and their acceptance of the child as an individual with the right to independent opinions in areas that directly concern himself and his action.

The boys who question the restriction stand out, compared to those who answer more compliantly, in three respects. They are active, they are independent, and they come from families which apparently encourage autonomy. With regard to activity, these boys read more than other boys, belong to more clubs, and report a larger number of general leisure activities. Their independent spirit comes through on most of the autonomy items. They tend to take the advice of friends more than their parents' counsel; they think a friend can be as close as a family member; and they are generally less authority-reliant than other boys. They more often report some area of disagreement with parents. They say that a boy might break a rule in an emergency, and they infrequently suggest rebellion as a basis for breaking rules. They are generally somewhat precocious in their internalization of personal standards.

Behind this developmental picture we find parents who tend to use psychological techniques of discipline and eschew physical punishment. Boys in this group portray parents (in the projective situation) as permissive more often than other boys do, and they suggest this same picture when they say that if the boy in the projective situation were to disobey his parents, he also would tell them about it later.

What does this all mean? Are we to conclude from the pattern of our findings that conflict between a child and his parents urges the child to an early autonomy? We have seen that boys who report family disagreement and girls who disagree with their parents about ideas do indeed seem to be moving toward independence at an accelerated pace. Yet our interpretation of these results relies less on the notion of conflict than on a picture of relatively easy relationships in a family pattern where the parents encourage independence, permit the child to feel and express his differences and disagreements, and exercise moderate authority which they both explain and allow to be questioned. For what our questions seem to tap is the child's capacity to take an objective view of family relations, an indication in itself that the child has achieved, and has been encouraged to find, a certain degree of independence. The conflict items distinguish a group very much like those in the analysis of family authority (which we shall consider in a moment) who come from homes in which power is both reasonable and rational. They are different from the demoralized youngsters whose family life bears the imprint of hostile, impulsive, or inconsistent power relations. Clues about this latter group come from the analysis of discipline, which apparently taps conflict of a deeper and more disruptive sort than we got at in any of our direct questions.

Parental Authority

Except for the issue of discipline, our information about the nature and style of parental authority is limited to the girls study. While we can infer some things about the parents' use of authority from boys' responses to the projective situation and from the boys' own stance toward authorities in general and the parents' rule in particular, we did not ask boys any direct questions about the ways and means by which their parents control them.

In the girls study we had two questions designed to clarify family authority. The first of these asked the girl about her parents' expectations regarding her behavior: "What are the most important things your parents expect of you?" We coded answers to this question for the traditionalism of the parents and the extent of control exercised.[7] The one category of answers which proved distinctive, and useful analytically, included all those which indicated that the parents stressed independence or autonomy in their child-training: "They expect me to know the difference between right and wrong," "They expect me to stand on my own feet," "Stand up for what I think is right, what I

[7] In the ideal study of family relations, one has access to both parents and children, obtains measures of family discipline and authority from parents, and relates these to measures of the child's attitudes, behavior, and development. We are constantly faced, in our data, with the problem of separating the reality of parental authority from the screen of the child's perceptions. While we cannot solve the problem, and must always interpret our information within the limits of data gathered entirely from the child, we have tried to increase our understanding of family patterns by approaching the area from several directions, asking for factual information about the family as well as for the child's attitudes toward his parents, using both direct and indirect, projective techniques.

believe in." Such answers were given infrequently by girls in the youngest age group, and our analysis is only reliable at the two higher age levels, but in general the direction of difference is the same throughout the entire range. The differences add up to this—parents who communicate this value on autonomy to their children carry their own authority easily and effectively and apparently help their children to exercise and appreciate their own internal authority as well. These parents are portrayed by their daughters as lenient, understanding, and sympathetic. Girls who say their parents expect them to be independent make the parents in the projective situation concerned and lenient —more than other girls do. They characteristically think that parents make rules in order "to teach their children right and wrong," "to help the children grow up, mature." When they think of the person a girl would confide in, they think of the mother more often than other girls do.

To judge from somewhat more factual questions, the parents who expect independence from their daughters support their expectations with child-raising techniques designed to help the children develop controls of their own. The girls report that they have some share in making rules at home, and psychological discipline is the norm in their families. They report physical punishment much less frequently than other girls do.

As far as we can determine, the girls who have this sense of a strong parental value on autonomy are more advanced in emotional independence and the development of personal controls than other girls of the same age. We must always add the conditioning remark that advancement in individual controls for the girl seems to consist of a growing identification with the parents rather than individuation of strongly internal controls. The "independence" group show a strong identification with parental authority and also a respect for their own standards when they say that the girl (in the picture-story) would be disappointed and surprised that her parents feel they need to remind her how to behave. They say—more often than other girls—that parents make rules to help and teach their children, and that a girl who compares her parents unfavorably to the parents of her friends should realize that other parents have faults too. They think a girl might break a rule in case of an uncontrollable emergency. When the girl in the projective story disobeys her parents, they are more likely than other girls to say that she would tell her parents afterward.

Their emotional autonomy comes out in response to the problem of a girl with a good job whose mother asks her to return home. They say the girl would return less often than other girls do, and they more often try to find a solution other than returning or rejecting the mother directly. They also characteristically think that a friend can be as close as a family member, and they spend most of their spare time with friends. In both these respects they seem less dependent on the family than other girls do.

The most specific question we asked girls about family authority was: "Do you have any part in making the rules at home?" We have seen that there is a steady rise in "yes" responses with increasing age. We find that girls at each age level who report participation in setting rules show evidence of greater independence than other girls. They are more likely to feel that they can be as close to a friend as to their family. Furthermore, these girls come from families which seem to encourage autonomy as a value or character trait. They more often tell us (at the middle and late age levels) that one of their parents' expectations is that they behave in an independent manner. At the late age level (17 and 18) those who join in rule-making are less reliant on adult authorities outside the family. In response to the projective pictures, they less frequently picture the heroine as passively accepting the parents' restriction.

These findings point to a pattern of autonomy among girls who come from families which allow at least a sense of participation in setting rules. We have here, it would seem, that sort of autonomy which reflects not an underlying alienation from the family, but rather the opposite, the easy closeness which allows the child to maintain some separateness. On one of the projective questions, for example, the girls who join in rule-making are more likely than other girls to think that the heroine who has done something shameful will talk her problem over with her parents. We also find (at the middle and late age periods) that they more often see the heroine in the projective pictures as informing the parents after she had disobeyed their orders. When we ask when a girl might break a rule, these girls more frequently say "emergency" and less often say "rebellion." The presence of an equalitarian, nonpunitive atmosphere in the home is suggested by the fact that these girls report physical discipline far less frequently than girls who have no share in setting rules.

There are some interesting developmental changes in the relation of rule-setting participation to other variables. Girls under fourteen who share in rule-making are more likely to picture the parents as strict in the projective pictures; in middle and late adolescence these girls more often portray the parents as lenient. We have a similar reversal in response to the question of disagreement with the parents. The girls who join in setting rules report more disagreement below fourteen; there is no difference in middle adolescence; above sixteen, these girls less often report disagreements. The meaning of these changes is by no means self-evident. It may be that girls who share in rule-setting settle their grievances early, that the necessary conflict with the parents takes place early in adolescence and is then laid to rest. Or it may be that these girls come from families which maintain fairly close supervision over the child until a somewhat later period in adolescence, and then relax their controls. Or it may be—this is our preferred conjecture—that "strictness" and "disagreement" have somewhat different meanings in early and late adolescence; that the young girls who do not join in setting rules are docile enough to accept parental decisions without a murmur; the far fewer girls who have no share in setting rules late in adolescence are by then openly resentful and disaffected.

The two groups do differ in the types of conflict they report with the family. Those who do not join in making rules more often have disagreements about dating and about riding in cars. Those who do join more commonly disagree about ideas. This intriguing difference suggests a number of possibilities—that the autonomous girls may be more reflective or "intellectual" (or that their families are), or that their conflicts with parents are more neutralized.

Discipline

If we hesitate at this topic, it is because too much has already been said and written about it. For a good portion of the mass media and the general public, the psychology of child-rearing is equivalent to the theory of discipline in the narrowest sense—what type of punishment to use, or more specifically to spank or not to spank. Specialists, even when they have known better, have found it hard to resist all those eager faces raised in inquiry, and have too often yielded to simplistic definitions of the problem. Anyone who has had the mixed pleasure of addressing parent groups will know what we mean.

These public discussions also make us mindful of what a vast uneasiness there is on the topic. There is too much doubt present, sometimes showing itself directly, sometimes concealed behind a violent self-assurance. This is due partly, we think, to the much-noted fear of American parents that they may be too hard on the children and so lose their affection. For the American family, the trick is to manage that evenness of disciplinary touch which will keep the child from becoming recklessly wild on the one hand, and too constrained, or submissive, on the other.

Adolescence brings with it some decisive changes in discipline, but these tend to appear neither suddenly nor even tangibly. They grow out of the youngster's advances in autonomy, out of gradual accruals in responsibility and self-regulation. The problem the parent faces is in adjusting his loosening of control to the child's capacity to regulate himself, letting the reins slacken at the right time and in the right way, neither holding them so tightly that the child resist nor releasing them so suddenly as to endanger him. In this respect the problems of discipline at adolescence are not much different than those in earlier childhood. What complicates the matter, as we have said before, is the child's own confusions about freedom, control, and responsibility, his newly acquired taste for the sweet symbolic uses of independence, his perplexing oscillations between compliance and defiance, his need to confute and confuse authority for its own sake—all of this will make it difficult for the parent to appraise the child's needs dispassionately.

Another complication stems from the parents' getting (or feeling) out of touch with the adolescent's world; his child now lives his important life out of the home and thus out of the parents' ken; the parent often cannot catch sight of the matters that may need discipline, and even when he does he may not be sure that he interprets them correctly, so uneasy is he about the quickness of social change.[8]

We now want to look at some of our findings on discipline. We asked our subjects this question: "If you do something wrong, how do you get punished?" Their answers were grouped into three categories —physical, deprivation, and psychological. The first two of these presented few problems in coding—punishment was coded "physical" when the youngster reported spanking, beating, slapping, whipping, and so on. Deprivation punishments (which are modal in adolescence)

[8] Here is an example. Not long ago in a Midwestern suburban community the police discovered that over forty adolescents from the best families of the city had been engaged in extensive shoplifting from the best shops in the city. Over a period of months the take—mostly in clothing—ran to many thousands of dollars. One of the questions asked in connection with this incident was how it was that the parents of these children did not recognize what was going on. How could a boy or girl appear at the dinner table with a new thirty-five dollar cashmere sweater without the parents asking about it? The answer is that the teenagers of this setting had the custom of exchanging clothing with each other; their parents, it turned out, were not quite sure at any given moment which items of clothing belonged to their children and which were borrowed. The clothing which had been stolen was worn openly, the parents assuming it had been borrowed.

were also more or less self-classifying. We included any form of deprivation, major or minor. The most commonly reported have to do with mobility—being forbidden to use the family car, to go out at night, and so forth. Psychological punishments offer some difficulties in coding. We included here those punishments based on verbal admonition —being lectured, scolded, reasoned with, told not to do it again— without concurrent deprivation or physical punishment. Our hope was to gather those cases where the parents' aim is to induce guilt in the child, or where this is the outcome whatever the conscious aim. But no doubt the category includes a certain (and unknown) number of cases where guilt-induction is neither the intention nor the outcome.

We are quite aware, as the reader must be, of the inadequacies of this classification. It is restricted to punishment type, and thus is somewhat mechanical. We know nothing directly about the harshness or frequency of discipline. The scheme gives us little sense of the function and context of punishment—what it aims to achieve, the affective atmosphere accompanying it. The categories themselves are crude and somewhat misleading. For example, the deprivation class includes instances of fairly severe restriction, where the parent's intention plainly is to bear down hard and hurt, and also cases where the aim is the induction of guilt.

Despite defects, the classification has its uses. We believe that it reflects differences in both the intensity and function of discipline. Probably we are not far wrong in assuming that parents who continue to use corporal punishment into adolescence do so on the whole impulsively or vindictively, to drive some evil from the child, or to discharge some personal torment. At the other extreme, we take it that the psychological methods are generally calculated to enlist the child's ego, and to encourage the internalization of controls. It is doubtful that they do so in all cases; all of us have known those appalling families where the parents are simperingly, cloyingly, "rational" or where the lightness of discipline conceals a guilt-ridden ambivalence toward the child. But we trust that there are not enough of these in our sample to invalidate our assumption that this method of discipline makes its appeal to the ego, and helps to develop internal controls.

How do the three groups get on with their families and how are they approaching the problems of autonomy? Among the girls those who are physically punished are most distinctive, and submissiveness is the key to their difference. This group is extremely high on authority reliance ("What do you think an adult leader should do?"). They are docile in relation to their parents—in response to the projective pictures, they are the most likely to accept the parents' statement without rejoinder. They more commonly choose an admired adult within the family. They are more likely than other girls to say that a girl should give up a good job and return home if her lonely mother asked her to do so.

Physical punishment is part of a family atmosphere in which the child is allowed little independence. In response to the question, "What do your parents expect of you?", the physically disciplined are the least likely to mention "independence." An even more substantial difference is found in response to the question of whether the girl has any say in making the rules at home; this group is far less likely to join in setting rules than are girls in the other punishment groups (28 per cent, compared to 61 per cent of other groups).

How do the physically punished girls view their parents? They are more docile and more dependent, but these qualities may coexist with overt or covert resentment. Our findings here are by no means unambiguous, but they are suggestive. As far as overt disagreement is concerned, these girls are distinctive in only one respect. They tend to have fewer "intellectual" disagreements with their parents than do girls in the other two groups. Aside from this, they do not stand out on any other specific disagreement item. Their total number of disagreements is no different from that of other girls. Nor do they show a unique pattern in response to the open-ended question on disagreements. However, they do appear to be more willing to deceive their parents. When they are asked whether the projective heroine would tell her parents about disobeying them, they are the most likely to say "no." An interesting difference emerges in their representation of the parents on the projective pictures. They more often picture the parents as extremely lenient or extremely strict, and are under-represented in the middle categories. It is not too surprising that they represent the parents as extremely strict; the use of extreme leniency would seem to suggest that this represents a wish-fulfillment, or perhaps that some of these girls are actually neglected by parents who oscillate between punitiveness and its opposite.

Analysis of the data from the boys study indicates that the effects of particular punishments are similar for boys and girls, with two important exceptions. Boys who are physically punished show a resentment of their parents at the same time that they are dependent and submissive. And they show certain flaws in development which we do not find among the physically punished girls. Physically punished boys, compared to those in the other two categories, are undeveloped in regard to the internalization of controls and social behavior.

As to autonomy, our evidence is quite consistent. Boys who are physically punished are most dependent and submissive in relation to authority; the psychologically punished boys are most autonomous. We asked our subjects whether they felt that a person could be as close to a friend as to his family; the physically punished agree least and the psychologically most often. In the series of six questions, dealing with personal decisions, we find the same trend: 31 per cent of the "psychological," 47 per cent of the "deprivation", and 55 per cent of the "physical" subjects would follow parental advice in 5 or 6 of the situations presented. The physically punished boys choose within family models more often than other boys do, although they choose their own father infrequently. They are also somewhat more likely than other boys to say that they have no adult ideal.

The boys in the physically punished group show similar signs of submission to nonfamilial authorities. We asked subjects to tell us their preferences in an adult club leader, and to describe a leader they had particularly liked; responses were rated for the degree of authority reliance. The differences again are sharp. The physically punished show heavy authority reliance in a ratio of 2 to 1; the deprivation group is evenly split; and the psychologically disciplined show a marked preference for the nonauthoritarian leader (54%–38%).

We examined the data bearing on the boys' feelings about being drafted. Here again, responses are scattered, but they permit grouping into positive, neutral, and negative statements. The physically disciplined are alone in giving a slight preponderance (53%) of positive responses; the other subjects are much more likely to be negative.

Another finding confirms the impression of greater submission to authority among the physically punished. We asked: "What kind of rule would you never break"? One category distinguishes the punishment groups clearly—rules maintaining adult authority (typical responses: "I wouldn't disobey my parents," "I would never disobey a teacher"). Forty per cent of the "physical," 35 per cent of the "deprivation," and 28 per cent of the "psychological" subjects gave answers in this category.

In the physically punished boys we find signs of resentment accompanying submissiveness. We have said that these boys tend to reject the notion of an adult ideal. They show their resentment in the projective series. They picture the parents as strict more often than other boys do, they are more likely to say that the hero in the picture would disobey his parents, and that he would not tell his parents of his disobedience "unless they asked," or that he would tell because "they would find out about it anyway." This is how they react to projective questions. In a direct question about disagreements with their own parents, they are not distinguished by a greater number of disagreements. This set of answers is consistent with the theory of the development of the authoritarian type. The child who is treated badly is more likely to remain tied to parental authority and to cover underlying resentment of that authority by conventional or even idealized conscious attitudes toward the parents.

Up to this point we have discussed the boy's attitudes toward external authority. We next turned to the problem of internal controls —superego structure and dynamics. This is, we feel, the heart of the matter. If we have reasoned correctly, the psychologically punished should show an internalized morality. The aim of psychological discipline is to insure the potency of guilt as a check on action; it persuades the child, through guilt, to regulate himself. The same reasoning led us to expect the physically punished to be defective in internal controls. We imagine a household where discipline is erratic, and controls on violence unsteady. The parents' aim is to show who is boss; punishment is intended to punish rather than to teach. In these circumstances morality becomes a matter of escape and pursuit; we are likely to find that form of conscience and control that we call, somewhat erroneously, an externalized superego.

From a number of different items, we constructed an index indicating the degree of internalized morality. The physically punished score highest on externalization, and lowest on internalization of morality; the opposite is true of the psychologically disciplined; the deprivation group is, as usual, midway between the two. There is a specific illustration of the differences in superego dynamics which are reflected in this finding. One of the items composing the index is, "When might a boy break a rule?" Here are the specific responses differentiating the "physical" and "psychological" subjects:

	Physical (%)	Psychological (%)
Rebellion	15	10
Impulse	11	8
Authority not present	18	7
Emergency	9	25

In addition to this problem in the area of internalization, the physically punished boys show a general flaw in social development. They date less than other boys, have fewer leisure interests, read less, and less frequently belong to organized groups. They are rated low on self-confidence by interviewers, and they have relatively narrow time perspectives. The differences hold up when age is controlled. When we compare punishment types within social class, our analysis is limited of necessity to lower status groups, since physical punishment is virtually never reported by boys from professional and managerial backgrounds. The differences among punishment types do hold, however, within the white collar and manual working groups.

Physical discipline (and the pattern which underlies it) apparently has broader implications for the boy's development than it has for the girl's. This brings us to the last area of our analysis of adolescent autonomy and family relations, relating to the question of sex differences in the significance of autonomy and family interaction for general personality development.

Earlier discussions, in Chapter 3 as well as sections of this chapter, have laid a basis for this analysis, and have previewed its major conclusions: that autonomy is a more crucial issue for the boy, and that family interaction that conditions the autonomy crisis has greater impact on the boy's personal growth and integration than it has in the case of the girl.

We know that independence is a more salient issue for boys—they more often speak of it in discussing their conscious concerns, ideals, hopes and aspirations. They are more actively "on the move" toward independence during the adolescent period, to judge from our developmental data. Age changes in the boys study are greater than comparable differences among girls on almost all autonomy items. And we find consistently that boys who have achieved greater autonomy vis-à-vis the family also have more highly developed and articulated personal integrations. They are generally more advanced in the internalization of personal controls, they have more energy and greater ego resources than do those boys who are still dependent on the family. Among girls, we find some relationship between autonomy and internalization, although differences are neither as large or as consistent as comparable differences for boys. (The index of internalization, our most reliable measure in this area, bears only minor relationship to measures of autonomy for girls.) As far as we can tell from our data, the fact that a girl is dependent or autonomous tells us little about other aspects of her ego development or social development. Measures of autonomy do not bear any marked or consistent relationships to the girl's activity level, self-confidence, poise, or time perspective. The least autonomous girls show some minor differences from other girls in the area of friendship development, but they are minor and also quite inconsistent.

What about the connection between family interaction and autonomy? In general we find similar relationships holding for both sex groups. Children who are encouraged to develop self-reliance and are treated with respect by parents who wield moderate and humane authority do, in fact, achieve greater emotional autonomy. Children treated badly by parents who assert more total power more strictly remain dependent and submissive. Again we must note, however, that the relationships are consistently larger in the data on boys than they are in girls. And one relationship comes through only for boys. When parents are too controlling and harsh, boys respond with some degree of rebellion or, at least, covert resentment, while girls under similar circumstances show no such aggressive reaction—they are no more resentful toward parents than are girls who are treated kindly and with respect. They do not question parental authority, in the projective story or in evaluating their own parents' rule, any more than the girls who are treated well. We might anticipate boys' greater resentment of heavy-handed control, knowing that they are consciously more interested in freedom than girls are. But we must at the same time wonder what girls do with the aggression which would seem so natural a response to their parents. Do they turn it against themselves? Or is the parents' restrictiveness really less frustrating to them than it is to the boy? We prefer the second of these two explanations for several reasons.

For one thing, we find no evidence to support the view that girls from even the strictest families are unusually intropunitive—they do not seem on any of the projective questions involving interpersonal conflict to be more willing than other girls to absorb conflict rather than to express it in hostility. If they were turning hostility inward, we might expect this to be reflected in some internal impoverishment, in, for example, a reduction in usable energy. We find no such signs in their development. There is also the fact, which we consider in detail in later chapters, that much of feminine development during this period occurs in the context of close like-sexed friendship. The kind of activities and sharing that make up this interaction neither requires that the girl achieve autonomy nor provokes any conflict over the issue. And so, we suspect, the fact that parents may not allow a girl much freedom has little of the powerful irritating effect which it has for boys.

The findings on family relationships have been, we recognize, somewhat redundant, but the redundancy is forced on us by the findings themselves. We have seen, time and again, no matter the topic to which we gave our attention, that a certain clustering of variables defines the differences between children and families. Whether we look at punishment, authority, autonomy, or conflict, a distinctive and recurrent patterning of responses makes itself evident. One key to the pattern is found in punishment type—a key not necessarily because it is causal, but because it seems to represent so much else in the connection between parents and child, as though we could see and hear, behind the punishment message, an infinite array of acts and attitudes which together have made up and make up the child's life in the family, and which are distilled and expressed in the act of discipline. Another, equally central, equally suitable, key can be found in the autonomy area—among girls to the question, "Do you spend most of your spare time with friends or with your family?" and among boys to the question of whether they take friends' or parents' advice. Here again, the youngsters' responses seem to represent or sum up the values and experiences belonging to separate family styles.

The pattern most apparent in our data is an authoritarian one. The parents, in this case, are slow to give up physical punishment and slow also to give the child a sense of sharing, if only symbolically, if only in the spirit, in the regulation of his behavior. As we have seen, the consequences generally are a heightened dependence on the parents and beyond that, a tendency to lean heavily on external authority beyond the home, a need or willingness to have teachers and other adults take the lead, set limits, and make decisions. In the case of the boys, there seems to be a concurrent rebelliousness; their docility is balanced by evidence of resentment and conflict, in some covert, and in others on the surface. This is not so with the girls; we do not, in our data, discover clear signs of rebellion or discontent among the coercively disciplined, low-autonomy girls.

The authoritarian pattern is more evident in the working class, and it is especially prominent in the most disadvantaged sector of that class. This finding should not surprise us, since it has been clear for some time now that authoritarianism in general follows class lines. However, the correlation between status and family style causes vexing problems in the interpretation of some of our findings. We would argue that the relationship between, let us say, punishment type and authority reliance is a fairly direct one, in the sense that there are casual linkages between the two, not immediately or mechanically, but in the sense that authority reliance is one effect of a family milieu which expresses itself in, among other things, the act of discipline. But what are we to say about the finding that the physically punished boys are socially isolated and immature, that they belong to fewer clubs, that they have a lower rate of social activity, that they date less frequently, and that they read less and less maturely. Are these relationships "causal" in our special meaning? Or are they an artifact of status? From the analyses we have been able to carry out we infer that there are interactional effects. However, we can say on the basis of these data that outside the depths of the working class (where authority is most severe) the same processes seem to obtain, that the physically punished and the nonautonomous boys show all of the morbid social and psychological qualities that we find in the unskilled working class; indeed, as we saw in an earlier chapter, the authoritarian pattern accompanies downward-mobility aspirations.

Let us confess, however, that we simplify matters excessively when we confine ourselves to the severe, sometimes brutish conditions of that most deprived, depressed stratum of the working class. There we see the authoritarian pattern incised deeply and corrosively, so much so as to permit little doubt of its crippling effects on the youngster's personality. The authoritarian pattern also exists, in a milder, more diffuse form, as one of the common patterns we find throughout the population. We have in our discussions characterized autonomy as one of the necessary developments in the adolescent's relation to his family. Here we may well recognize how limited (relative to what is possible, and, we believe, desirable) that autonomy often is, and how infrequently it appears. As a matter of fact, one intriguing sidelight of the study is in the fact that the proportion of "authoritarian" responses is surprisingly constant. We chose, at random, a series of seven questions to which one of the responses could be considered authoritarian (or at least highly conventional and conforming) and found that in all cases these made up about one-third of the answers in the girl sample.

1. Close to friend as family. No: 35%
2. Parents seen as authoritarian. Picture 1: 31%
3. Coder rating, parents strict or extremely so: 39%
4. Parental expectations; respect for authority: 29%
5. Club leader functions, heavy authority reliance: 32%
6. Admired adult, mother: 34%
7. Participation in rule-making. No: 36%

There is no need to read any great significance into the consistency of these figures; we could easily find other items which show "authoritarian" responses to be higher or lower than one-third. The point we want to make is that so sizable a proportion of adolescents show a distinctively authoritarian orientation that the pattern is normative, that is, one of the prevailing modes of parent-child interaction in the culture. These data remind us that a great many adolescents are unable to accomplish, or accomplish only feebly, that psychic departure from the family that we think of as one of the routine achievements of the adolescent period. The fact is, as a good deal of recent research has shown (Axelrod, 1956), that kinship ties remain central for a sizable share of the adult population; and we would guess that it is the boys and girls who, as adolescents, show this limited growth in autonomy who later make up most of that part of the adult world which has never left home, psychologically, and much of the time, physically as well, marrying in the home town, visiting the parents weekly— shielded, for the most part, from the perils and pleasures of change.

On the whole, however, the American family provides for its adolescents an easy-going, libertarian milieu. The vaunted equalitarianism of the American family is, if we read our data correctly, no mere fiction. One might object that the circumstances of the interview would not allow us to dig out the conflict. But we think not; we get a remarkably consistent picture, both from direct and projective questions. Parents (and adults in general) are seen and characterized as reasonable, lenient, well intentioned; and this more often than not (from one-half to two-thirds of the time, depending on the question). It is not, we want to stress, a goody-goody picture (the Pollyannas are far more often found among the authoritarian subjects); for these boys and girls, parents are neither infallible nor too good to be true; they can be impatient or overconcerned or incorrect.

The autonomous children are over-represented in the higher social strata. The social (and some of the psychic) advantages enjoyed by this group no doubt derives from the more abundant opportunities open to the middle class. But the status factor is not adequate to account for the difference we find. We must also recognize that the leniency and good will these children find at home frees them from much of the paralyzing ambivalence that diminishes the vitality and style of those raised in authoritarian families.

The findings from our analysis of family patterns give us no occasion for surprise. It is simply good sense that adolescents who are treated well by their parents will have a better relationship to them. Nor should our findings necessarily give rise to elation. Autonomy, in the sense in which we have been able to capture it in the questionnaire, often produces no more than affability and a certain bland "adjustment". It does not necessarily produce the deeper autonomy of individualism. The most we can say is that the autonomous have the opportunity for individualism (while the nonautonomous, by and large, do not). There is not much evidence that many, even of the autonomous, do in fact achieve a personal articulation of values, nor do they manage a genuinely individual identity.

SIX

Friendship

In our time the adolescent's departures are partial ones. The child continues to live at home but situates his emotions in the world of peers. In the preceding chapter we examined some of the motives that drive the child to disengage himself from the family; here we concern ourselves with the other side of that process, the child's ventures into friendship. We shall want to consider three aspects: the like-sexed friendship, dating, and the ties to the peer culture. The peer relations of adolescence are part of the preparation for adult love and friendship: by loving and being loved, by making friends and being befriended, the child learns something of the vicissitudes of affection. We think he learns more than that. The particular advantage of the adolescent friendship is that it offers a climate for growth and self-knowledge that the family is not equipped to offer, and that very few persons can provide for themselves. Friendship engages, discharges, cultivates, and transforms the most acute passions of the adolescent period, and so allows the youngster to confront and master them. Because it carries so much of the burden of adolescent growth, friendship acquires at this time a pertinence and intensity it has never had before nor (in many cases) will ever have again.

So we must start our inquiry with the recognition that the study of friendship is at its very beginnings. The words friend and friendship are used to denote a great range of roles and relationships, of styles and forms and functions and meanings; but we have no taxonomy of friendship, nor do we know much about its psychic sources or its psychic functions. We also know little of the varying ways in which societies or social groups influence its definition and practice. Adolescence may be a good place to begin—for one thing, many forms of friendship seem to originate during this period; for another, it is a particularly vital social form at this time. In the fumbling, tortured efforts of the youngster in achieving closeness with others of his own kind we may be able to see, enlarged, some of the processes underlying friendship in general.

Almost everyone who has written on the topic has made the distinction between shallow and deep friendships. Much of what passes as friendship is cordiality in various forms: people come together through the accidents of propinquity, or to enjoy together the more public forms of pleasure. This is sociability, and we do well to distinguish it from intimacy. It seems especially important to insist on the difference when we reflect on American modes of friendship. No doubt we have had in all places and all times a tendency to mistake sociability for intimacy. The gift of intimacy has probably always been rare—both Aristotle and Montaigne make much of this—yet it seems likely that Americans are peculiarly uneasy about intimate relationships.

Americans, we are told, are a friendly people. The European observer, almost without exception, is struck by this. Nowadays it may sometimes appear that our talent for friendliness is exhausted, or under strain. Like an old ballplayer who has used up his resources and is operating on semblance and nerve, the American, if he has lost the knack of easy friendliness, tries to do as best he can with its appearances; and so we get the mechanical smiles, the automatic cordialities —all the false personalizations that David Riesman has described so well. We may sometimes find that the concern with friendliness becomes obsessive. If we listen to the personality shows of television, we hear an insistent, compulsive stress on friendship and friendliness, an ubiquitous, promiscuous use of these words to characterize the most fleeting or the most commercial of acquaintanceships.

Yet we ought not to be too bemused by these occasional failures and excrescences. It takes only a trip abroad to refresh the conviction that there is an American manner: openness and informality, an easiness with strangers, an equalitarian temper. Perhaps the most impressive analysis we have of it is in Kurt Lewin's (1948) classic essay contrasting German and American character structure. Lewin points to the relatively small degree of social distance between persons in the United States. The American is not terribly concerned with maintaining his privacy: doors are left open, people waiting for a bus exchange pleasantries. The American is conspicuously accessible, but this accessibility is confined to the peripheral layers of the person:

The more intimate "central" regions of personality seem to be at least as separated between different persons, and at least as difficult to get access to as among Germans. . . . Compared with Germans, Americans seem to make quicker progress towards friendly relations in the beginning, and with many more persons. Yet this development often stops at a certain point; and the quickly acquired friends will, after years of relatively close relations, say good-by as easily as after a few weeks of acquaintance.

The American, then, passes easily from friendliness to sociability, but hesitates at intimacy. Because of the unique circumstances of the American historical experience, through the commitment to the frontier (or only the myth of the frontier) certain peculiar habits of friendship were established. One had to be prepared to make friends on the run, to settle into friendship quickly, and still be ready to leave it without too much regret. It was not only geographical mobility that helped produce this disposition; but also it was the hope and expectation of status mobility. The American kept himself in readiness to rise in the world, and so perhaps learned not to commit himself too deeply to a particular friend. The question is: did these habits of mind, these reservations about the futurity of friendship, did they in the long run cripple the very capacity for intimacy? It is hard to believe that this did not happen. Friendships of a deep degree of intimacy do appear to be rare in this country.

What do we mean by an intimate friendship? It is hard to define it without seeming abstract, or rhetorical, or sentimental. The friendship we have in mind is characterized by mutual trust; it permits a fairly free expression of emotion; it allows the shedding of privacies (although not inappropriately); it can absorb, within limits, conflict between the pair; it involves the discussion of personally crucial themes; it provides occasions to enrich and enlarge the self through the encounter of differences.

One reason why this depth of friendship seems to be so rare among adults (aside from peculiarly American reasons) is that many of its purposes can be served by kinship ties. The evidence (Axelrod, 1956) we have indicates that for a considerable portion of the population, close personal relations are confined to the extended family. Very often, of course, these ties do not achieve any great degree of intimacy. Conversation will center on the comings and goings of family members, or the growth and gambits of the children, or about such common interests as sports or television or housekeeping. Even in these instances, where conversation does not run much deeper than it might in a casual acquaintanceship, the level of affect, the feeling of ease and closeness, the sense of intimacy may be very deep indeed. The comforts of kinship, its continuity, its familiarity, the often unconditional nature of the bond, will reduce or eliminate the need for intimacy with peers. But it is well to keep before us the understanding that the kinship tie, while it may take the place of the intimate friendship, is in the end an unsatisfactory substitute for it. Ideally, the peer friendship will provide an opportunity for the exploration and extension of the self; the kinship intimacy does not. It is too likely to continue earlier patterns of relationship; it provides comfort and closeness, but offers few occasions for the enlargement or freeing of the self; it keeps the self at the *status quo*.

In many cases kinship ties do not exist in any important degree. The person has moved from the family geographically, to another town, state, or region; or he has remained near the family, but has moved away from it in sympathy by adopting new values and interests. In such instances there is a considerable opportunity to develop that uncommon type of friendship we have in mind. But often it will not work out that way. The very absence of kinship connections, the loss of ties to family and to long-time friends, may drive the person to put such a burden on friendship as to distort it. One may lose the sense of appropriateness and flood the friendship with a degree of affect it is unable to handle. There may be a precocious dispelling of privacies, or an implicit demand that the friend play too many roles at once: spouse, kin, minister. Whyte (1956) has given us an account of situations like these as they develop in the new suburbs. The residents, missing long standing ties to family and friends, may rush into intimacies that they can neither control nor temper, and therefore cannot maintain.

For many persons the barrier to friendship lies in the strength and exclusiveness of the marital tie. This is particularly true now that the wife is often educated to the husband's level, and so we have come to believe it not only proper but also necessary that the marital pair share their leisure and privacies as much as possible: the well-known and roundly cursed "togetherness." It was the absence of this sort of marital intimacy, the limits put on the marital bond, that led so many nineteenth century personalities to cultivate friendship (as well as other things, such as concubinage). It is a delicate thing nowadays even to appear to talk against marital intimacy, but the danger is in the inbred, over exclusive marriage, the marriage as a refuge from the world, which may lead husband and wife, in devoting so much to each other, to cut themselves off from the enlarging experience of intimate friendship.

Apart from all these barriers to the cultivation of intimate friendship, and perhaps more important than any, there is the fact that, for more of the population than we may care to recognize, adulthood, with the settling of impulse and identity problems, brings with it an encapsulation and even retrenchment of the personality. The adult loses both the misery and the advantages that arise from the adolescent's peculiar openness to inner experience; thus, there is little need to examine and share the internal world with others. Adulthood all too often brings with it a retreat into extroversion and, paradoxically, a loss of sensitivity to the other. Aside from those whose work or style of life allows or encourages introspection and insight, the tendency is to abandon the inner resources. To be intimate with another endangers the repression of drives and affects.

Perhaps there is no need to belabor the point; we have been told about this often enough in the jeremiads of psychoanalytic social philosophy, from Carl Jung to Erich Fromm. But unless we keep it in mind, we shall fail to understand the appalling superficiality of so many adult friendships at all educational levels. To a disquieting degree, the adult friendship is no more than a mutual flight from boredom—a pact against isolation, with an amendment against intimacy. The interaction focuses on gossip or on leisure interests; in many cases the friendship centers itself on a game—bridge or golf, let us say, the understanding being that anything that does not bear on the game is gauche, embarrassing, or out of bounds. Those things which are crucial to personal integration, such as a person's history, values, or work, are studiously excluded from the interaction. This is not to argue that the trivial and the merely diverting are not necessary to a balanced life; perhaps we do well to remember that John Milton's first wife left him because he would say only deep or lofty things to her. What is distressing is not the presence of the mundane and diverting, but the absence of anything else.

We are at last ready to turn to adolescent friendship itself; this long preliminary on the generality of friendship, has, we hope, given us a perspective from which to view its particularity in adolescence. In our society, the adolescent period sees the most intense development of friendship. There are a good many reasons for this. Erotic and aggressive drives toward family members become so intense that the youngster must have a neutral arena in which to work them out; he is in process of breaking (or recasting) his ties to the family and desperately needs the support, approval and security, as well as the norms, of a peer group. He is discovering, and trying to interpret and control, a changed body, and with it new and frightening impulses, and so requires both the example and communion of peers. He is about to crystallize an identity, and for this needs others of his generation to act as models, mirrors, helpers, testers, foils.

All in all, it would seem that the adolescent does not choose friendship, but is driven into it. The paradox is that the very needs that drive the child will, if they are not kept in control, imperil the friendship itself. Erotic and aggressive drives, in some degree of sublimation, are the cement of adolescent peer relations. If the sublimations fail (as they often do during this time), the drives spill over into the friendship and spoil it. Adolescent friendships, as we shall see, are based to a considerable extent on narcissism, identifications, and projections. These are tricky processes. If the youngster is too narcissistic, he may be so sensitive to rejection that he cannot abide friendship, or so obtuse to the needs of the other as to be unfit for it. If projection dominates the interaction, it may end in the other being seen as overdangerous. Identifications may become problematic in threatening to blur the all too tentative lineaments of ego identity. These dangers are by no means confined to the adolescent; the adult may avoid close friendships for the same reasons. But the adolescent, generally, will feel these dangers more acutely because of a turbulent intrapsychic situation, and because he has nowhere else to go. If friendship is difficult or dangerous, it is ordinarily less so than isolation, or working these things out in the family. All these circumstances join to make the adolescent friendship a tempestuous, changable affair. Best friends may change in a moment; strange partnerships may come into being. If we look back to adolescence, we may be stupefied to recall friendships with the unlikeliest, the most alien of partners, to whom we were bonded by a momentary, yet critical mutuality of needs. Even our solid and enduring adolescent friendships may turn out, if we remember them closely enough, not to have been quite so unbroken and harmonious as they first appear in retrospect. They may in fact have blown hot and cold, responsive to all the rise and fall of feeling in self and others.

If some circumstances drive the child to friendship, others give him the opportunity to use and be changed by it. There is the simple fact that he is given, nowadays, the leisure and freedom to explore friendship, free from the responsibilities of work and family which will shortly absorb so much time and energy. Society finds his labor expendable, a circumstance that produces a great many complications; it helps to produce some of the adolescent demoralizations we hear so much about. But ordinarily the adolescent's leisure and freedom from responsibility do not work out so badly. It offers him the occasion for making discoveries about himself and others. The youngster needs time, needs the sense of unlimited time, and usually he will find or make the time. Even in the overorganized segment of the middle class, where the child is likely to be hemmed in by the demands of school and official leisure, he will discover his own slow-down techniques, making sure that there is time left over for the bull session, telephone chatter and all the other (well-publicized) forms of adolescent idleness.

So we have a necessity for friendship and, ordinarily, considerable opportunity for it. Another quality of the adolescent must be noted; he enters friendship with a remarkable eagerness and capacity for change. The contrast with the latency child is an instructive one. Before adolescence the child accepts himself as he is; if he is popular or unpopular, if he has many friends or only one or none—this is the way things are; the child may sorrow over it, but he will not generally feel there is much he can do about it. He has not yet made the discovery of the tractable self. Sometime near the start of adolescence, the child develops a consciousness of the self as a social stimulus, modifiable by will and intention. He enters the world of self-help, of books and columns on manners, dating, dress, make-up, chit-chat, the world of rituals and resolutions designed to make or remake the self. He enters friendship with an eagerness to make good, and the conviction that the self can be transformed to that end.

Along with this almost conscious, almost deliberate openness to change, we have another level of openness, to which we alluded earlier, the openness to the inner states of experience; with it comes a psychic fluidity, a vulnerability to conflict, an affective lability which together give adolescent intimacies so much of their characteristic flavor. The very fragility of the defenses may at times implicate the youngster in conflict, but on the other hand (and on the whole) they permit a relation to the other which captures the deepest levels of feeling, and so bind the adolescent and friend into an immoderate and unreserved intimacy.

In the explosion of impulses that dominates the early adolescent period, we find that while a goodly share of drive energy is diverted from the family to peers, a considerable amount of it is directed to the self. The adolescent's narcissism is ubiquitous: it expresses itself in a great many obvious ways—in an excruciating self-consciousness, in the concern with clothing and appearance, in shyness, in raucous exhibitionism, in posturing, primping, preening—and in anomalies of emotion and behavior where the origin is less obvious and direct. The narcissistic orientation, as we said earlier, influences the form and function of friendship at this time. There is the well-known adolescent touchiness, a hypersensitivity to rejection which in some cases can assume almost a paranoid intensity, in the conviction that friends are talking about them, or are out to exclude, wound, and humiliate them. The youngster will put himself at the center of the peer universe; the behavior of the other is overinterpreted; casual happenings—the friend's gesture of boredom, or the passing mention of a third person—will be magnified into events of major interpersonal significance.

Even when things do not come to such a pass, the adolescent's narcissism may make his friendships far less interactive than they first appear to be. His tie to the friend may be no more than the need for a forum where, by mutual consent, each participant is allowed equal time to discourse on the self's vicissitudes. In these cases the friend is expected to offer only the mechanical responses of the listener. We also may see the role of narcissism in the choice of friend—the other is someone who is like the self, or more commonly, someone who can represent certain illusory aspects of the self. In the other, the adolescent can make objective the disavowed or prospective or half-understood qualities of the self.

The mechanisms here are identification and (to a limited extent) projection. These defenses play a conspicuous role in the reconstruction of adolescent personality, not unlike their part in the constitution of the ego during childhood. Both mechanisms allow the person to discharge and tame the impulses; identification also helps in the absorption of ego qualities; the projective identification permits the individual to be rid of distorting drives and yet to experience them vicariously. However, the use of projection is ordinarily limited in the friendship tie; if what is imputed to the friend is too extreme, the friend begins to personify danger, so that the relationship becomes too threatening to be maintained.

We can illustrate the workings of these processes through a simple, if flamboyant, clinical anecdote. A young woman patient reported that when she was sixteen, she had had a prep-school friend whom she did not especially like, but whom she used, and by whom she was used, for the sharing of sexual secrets, and for that purpose exclusively. The patient was impulsively promiscuous; the friend was afraid of defloration, but engaged in fellatio. Each thought the other peculiarly indecent, and it first seemed that they had chosen each other for that very reason, on the principle, apparently, that it is comforting to confess to a greater sinner than yourself. It soon became clear that, for the patient at least, the primary motive for the friendship went much deeper. Her promiscuity (as well as the severe symptoms she later developed) were in the nature of defenses against her own interest in fellatio. By choosing this friend, she was able to disavow, through projection, her perverse wishes, and yet, through identification, gratify them vicariously.

We need not rely on clinical instances for examples of these processes at work. Let us consider a fairly common form of adolescent likesexed intimacy. In this case imagine two girls, A and B, who come together through their common concern with the erotic mysteries. A is more advanced socially (or sexually) than B; A is the active, "talking" partner of the twosome; B the listener. A acts out for B; in the stories she tells of her experiences in dating or petting, B can, at a safe distance, identify with her friend, and in so doing can allow herself to observe, to test and to grow comfortable with areas and qualities of experience she cannot at this moment allow herself.

In this example, the identification elements are conspicuous and projection is minimal. There may be some tendency for B to use A as a screen for the projection of unacceptable drives; but as we have said, the degree and the content of projection cannot become excessive.

If we look at this prototype again, at A and B, we begin to see that there is more motive to the friendship than the vicariousness enjoyed by the listening B. This simple prototype can give us some feeling for the unusual complexity of needs served by the adolescent intimacy. What is A's role in all this? To begin with, of course, there are the narcissistic gratifications afforded by the envy and admiration presumably coming from the avid listener; in particular cases, exhibitionistic aims can be satisfied. A more important gain to the active partner derives from the telling itself: As any dramatist does, she omits, condenses and rearranges, all to the end of ordering experience so as to produce an epiphany of the self. It would be, we think, too superficial to see the dramatist's purpose as merely self-glorification; that motive is there, of course, but a more subtle and relevant one is to achieve some degree of distance from the self in action, and in doing so, to obtain a new conspectus of the self's identity.

Another important function of this sort of intimacy is that it serves as a device for relieving guilt, obtaining reassurance, and establishing controls. The active partner of the twosome will be sensitive to the response of the other. A's tales are to some extent confessions; in her response to the partner, B may provide reassurance, overtly, or even by the sympathetic silence that gives consent. But if A's behavior carries her too far from B's willingness to accept or approve, the identification may become too dangerous for B, who will become uneasy in the friendship. B's uneasiness communicates itself to A, who sees herself in danger of being transformed from Glamour Girl to Bad Girl. Through B's response, then, A is able to find limits for her behavior at a time when external norms are uncertain and internal controls weak and confused.

The same may be true if the partners are drawn together through another theme. Let us say that the key to the friendship is rebellion, a joint unhappiness with parental values and control. Again we have a twosome composed of a bold and a timid partner, one friend more advanced or more articulate in disaffection than the other. The motive of the one is vicariousness, of the other, statement and self-definition. This miniature social system of two also serves to control and limit the impulse to rebellion, in part by expressing and so discharging, in part by the checks and balances we spoke of earlier.

Sometimes it does not work out that way, for reasons we do not really understand. The two-group fails to limit and control the impulse. Instead, a contagion effect develops. Conjoining needs, instead of limiting each other, spark each other to fulfillment. The controlling function fails, and two together will do what each alone would be unable to do. Then we get the instances of joint delinquency, running away from home, as an example. This is precisely the sort of thing the parent is likely to be fearful of; he worries about a contagion effect in the peer friendship, that the child will, with someone else, become inspired to delinquencies that he could not achieve by himself. Generally, this does not happen; one function of the intimate friendship is to allow some discharge of impulse while keeping it in check through the externalized limits set by another.

Until now, we have been considering friendships where there is a dissimilarity of role, although with a similarity of preoccupation. We have, however, stressed the friendship based on dissimilarity not because we hold it to be more common, but because it has given us an opportunity to define more clearly the mechanisms obtaining in the adolescent intimacy. For the most part, we are more impressed by the likenesses governing adolescent social relations. Like seeks like, and while this is generally true at all ages, it is, we feel, more apt to be so during the adolescent period. The young intellectual seeks others of his own kind, as does the young athlete or playboy. We often find during this period an intolerance and contempt for those of a different bent of character and talent more intense than at any other stage of the life cycle. The need is to define personal identity; to accomplish this, the youngster needs the reassurance and mirroring offered by others of the same disposition.

So a pair, a trio, or larger grouping will establish itself through joint sympathies and mutual identifications. The group tendency is to define itself with considerable exclusiveness (the preoccupation with "cliques" and "snobbishness" is very strong during adolescence), the attempt being to confirm identity by insisting on homogeneity. The outside world, and especially other peers, is excluded, and more, becomes the subject of projection. We find, at this time, a tendency to strengthen in-group ties and to reduce their inherent tendencies toward ambivalence, through ascribing to others, to the out-group, those qualities too dangerous to recognize in the self. Of course these projections often cannot be kept outside the group. If the group is large enough, a tendency will develop to exclude temporarily, or to scapegoat, particular members. There is no end to the complexities (and the tedium) of arrangements and rearrangements within the friendship group, particularly among girls: A breaks up a close tie between B and C by retailing to B something she had heard C say about B; so the displaced C will detach D from her intimacy with E and get her to join a vendetta against A and B; it is something like a da Ponte libretto.

Generally, while adolescents choose each other for friends on the basis of likeness, dissimilarity plays a greater role in the functioning of the relation than first meets the eye. Certain general qualities must be alike, social class, interests, taste, morality, but after these likenesses are established, we find that the play of interaction is conducted through differences. Adolescent friendship is based (to some extent) on complementarity (although within a framework of similarity), just as in the case of marital selection as discussed by Winch (1958). Qualities of personality must vary between friends enough to give the relation the zest, tension, and enrichment that comes out of differences.

Finally we come to the art of friendship, the winning of friends—we hesitate at this topic, since it seems to have been pre-empted by the self-help industry. Yet it is clear enough that one of the essential tasks of the adolescent period is learning friendship, learning its demands and responsibilities, its nuances and complexities. Surely, much of what goes into being a friend and being befriended is so much a part of character as to be somewhat removed from learning—warmth, grace, and integrity—these qualities and others like them are too deeply woven into the fabric of personality to be susceptible to change. Although they are not readily lost or acquired, they need to be practiced, tempered, and polished within the framework of personal relations. The child must learn, or sharpen, his discretion, tact, and sensitivity— all that goes into knowing the limits of the other's privacy, acquiring a sense of the implicit. He must learn how to get what he needs from the other, while taking into account (and serving) the other's own needs. He must come to know the tolerable limits of his own aggression, and how much hostility he is prepared to accept without endangering his self-regard; and how to stand up for his rights without guilt and without abusing the rights of the other.

These are just some parts of the interpersonal agenda of adolescence. Of course it could be said, and with some justice, that the child has been learning these things all his life. So he has, but in ways too limited to prepare him for the peculiar exigencies of adolescent friendship. The personal relations between parent and child are intrinsically hierarchical; the relations to siblings are generally ambivalent and competitive; the peer friendships of the preadolescent years are, as we shall soon see, emotionally pallid and not genuinely interactive. The child before adolescence cannot learn, from family and friends, the ego qualities he will need to master the modalities of friendship in adolescence. These relations are the result of personal choice, are interactive, equalitarian, and suffused with the child's deepest emotions. He is only partially prepared by earlier experience; he must now learn the rest himself.

Up to this point we have treated adolescent friendships in a most general fashion, highlighting those processes unique to the period as a whole. Our intention here is to examine the developmental data on girls; through it we hope to understand the forms and functions of the like-sexed friendship as it grows and changes during the adolescent years.

Our data yield clear developmental trends; changes that occur in a simple direct fashion as girls grow older. Beyond this, we find differences among the age groups which are not continuous, but point to distinctive qualities of relationship in the three stages of adolescence.

Generally, we can say the child develops, as she moves through the adolescent era, an increasing emotional investment in friendship, greater sophistication and subtlety in her conceptions about it, a growing capacity for disinterested appreciation of the friend, and greater tolerance of differences within the relationship.

Preadolescence and Early Adolescence:
Girls of Eleven, Twelve, and Thirteen

It is very possible that our conception of the latency period is something of a fiction. We have fallen into the habit of seeing it as a time of life without passion. The emotions and drives, and all the conflicts they bestir, are held to disappear near age six, to be rearoused at puberty. As our knowledge of the latency period increases, we become aware that it is instinctually placid only in contrast with the Oedipal period before it and adolescence after it. It is psychodynamically more complex than we realized. Nevertheless, the contrast is impressive; we can go only so far in refining our idea of latency. Relative to what precedes and follows it, the preadolescent period is indeed low in drive and conflict; the child is absorbed in the quiet growth of ego capacities. Erikson (1950) calls it a stage of life dominated by "industry." The child begins to develop skills—reading and writing, of course, but also the myriad opportunities of a complex culture—sports and games in an infinite variety, the arts and crafts, collections and hobbies, and riddles and jokes.

It is a busy age, then; and the nature of friendship at this time reflects its busyness, its diligence, and its enriching dilletantism. The friends focus more on activity—on what they are doing together, than they do on themselves. The companion, to be sure, may be used as a point of reference—the child judging herself by the other—but there is little interest in the friend's personality as such. We see this in the fact that girls at this period can tell us so little about friendship. When we ask what a friend ought to be like, and what things make a girl popular with others, the early adolescent mentions fewer qualities than older girls do. More important, the qualities she does mention are fairly superficial ones. For example, she wants a friend to do favors for her. She wants the friend to be amiable, easy to get along with, cooperative, and fair. The friend ought not to be a crab, grouchy, mean, selfish or a showoff.

What we miss in this surfeit of adjectives is the sense that friendship can be emotionally relevant. The girl alludes to those surface qualities of the other that promote or hinder the swift and easy flow of activity. The friendship, we feel, centers on the activity rather than on the interaction itself. In this respect, the friendship is not yet relational. One wants a partner who is neither demanding nor disagreeable, whose personality will not get in the way of activity. The personality of the other is seen as a possible encumbrance to activity; later on it becomes the center of the interaction, as the girl becomes concerned with the friend's qualities in their capacity to disrupt, not the joint activity, but the friendship itself. At this point the friendship is still an adjunct to something else, the partnership in work and play.

The preadolescent girl is engaged in the exercise of the ego—the drives and conscience are not yet a source of concern. The child is oriented to the "real" world, to externality, rather than to the inner world. There is little preoccupation with internal qualities, either in the self or the other. The need for friendship arises out of the need to practice and extend the newly won and still growing ego resources. What the child wants is a certain degree and quality of growing room, and if there is any conflict with the family, it will probably be over this issue. The child grown in skills will demand the independence to put them to use; in some cases, the family may be too confined an arena, and a relation to friends may be needed. Most families in our society raise no objection; they may set some limit to the child's demands and the child ordinarily will accept these without fuss. Basically the youngster's emotional commitment is to the family, rather than to friends. Most of our subjects at preadolescence do not believe that they can be as close to a friend as to members of the family. They rarely report conflict with the family about friendship and the choosing of friends. Leisure time is more often spent with the family than with friends.

Boys do not have much importance yet. At least this is what we gather from what our subjects tell us; we may suspect that there is a good deal of anticipation, and no little trepidation, regarding heterosexuality—more than the girl allows herself to think there is, and far more than she will tell an interviewer. Still, as far as overt activity is concerned, friendship means the like-sexed friendship, period. The girl at this age has ordinarily not begun to date. When we put to her a hypothetical question pitting a friendship tie against the possibility of a date, she plumps for the friendship. But if the preadolescent girl does not date boys, she does play sports with them. At this age, the sexes meet on the playground, and judge each other by skill rather than sex. When sex begins to be important, there will be more distinction made between male and female activities than we find at this point. Given this lack of involvement with boys and dating, we are not surprised to find that ethical issues centering on heterosexuality do not play much part in the friendship; soon, however, the girl will be concerned with the ethics of competition for boys, and sexual morality, and the balance to be found between the ties of friendship and the demands of dating.

Puberty and Middle Adolescence: Girls of Fourteen, Fifteen, and Sixteen

The processes we discussed earlier now make their appearance. The child is swept into the erotic mysteries; the body changes and the instincts disturb the psychic equilibrium. The doubts, confusions, anxiety, and guilt evoked by the eruption of sexual urges, the incestuous and aggressive dangers in the family—these, and more, as we have said, drive the child from the family and into intimate, intense and sometimes desperate friendships. But the erotic is still too new and frightening: the child does not know enough yet, either about herself or about the opposite sex. The transition to heterosexuality is made through the like-sexed friendship.

These friendships are very different in style and purpose than those of preadolescence. At this age, our findings show, the girls are less tied to the family, spend more time with friends, and are more articulate about the nature and conditions of friendship. The mere sharing of activity diminishes, to be replaced by a relation that is mutual, interactive, emotionally interdependent; the personality of the other, and the other's response to the self become the central themes of the friendship. The girl no longer stresses the concrete and superficial qualities of the friend. It is no longer important for the friend to do favors for one, nor does popularity depend much on good manners as the younger girl is likely to tell us. When girls past puberty report on their friendships they use a vocabulary that is (relatively) abstract, differentiated, and relational. They want a friend they can confide in, someone who can offer emotional support and understanding. When they describe the popular girl, they define her as one who is able to proffer this kind of friendship—someone who is sensitive to the needs of others.

The girls of this age group are unique in some respects, that is, different from both younger and older girls. What stands out in their interviews is the stress placed on security in friendships. They want the friend to be loyal, trustworthy, and a reliable source of support in any emotional crisis. She should not be the sort of person who will abandon you, or who gossips about you behind your back.

Why so much emphasis on loyalty? We imagine that part of the reason is that the friendship is less a mutuality than it appears to be at first.
The girl is less interested in the other than she thinks; what she seeks in
the other is some response to, and mirroring of, the self. She needs the
presence of someone who is undergoing the same trials, discoveries,
and despairs. The sexual crisis, in short, is handled through identification. In this way, the girl gains some of the strength she needs to handle impulses; and through the other, she has the opportunity to learn
something about her own sexuality. Through the sharing of knowledge
and affects, she is relieved, to some extent, of the anxiety and guilt
which accompanies the emergence of sexuality.

With so much invested in the friendship, it is no wonder that the
girl is so dependent on it. To lose the friend, for the girl at this age, is
to lose a part of the self; those qualities of the other that one has in-
corporated within the self, and those aspects of the self that one has
given to the other, and with which one has identified. Intimacies, at
this time, are often too symbiotic to be given up without pain. The
friend who is disloyal leaves one abandoned to the impulses. Then,
too, there is the fact that in leaving she takes away with her the knowledge of the girl's sexual history and fantasies. The girl is likely to feel
like the woman analysand in that famous *New Yorker* cartoon, who,
getting up from the couch, takes a pistol from her purse, and says:
"You've done me a world of good, Doctor, but you know too much."
It is this sort of feeling, no doubt, which accounts for the anxiety
that the friend may gossip behind one's back.

The erotic preoccupations of this period are also reflected in the fact
that our data show sexual references to be more common between fourteen and sixteen than either before or after. This group of girls is the
most likely to mention sexual immorality as a cause of unpopularity
and as a reason why one would not want to be friendly with some girls.
In these data we see how the sexual impulses are to some extent handled by projection. Apprehensive about the strength of her own controls, the young girl may become engrossed, fascinated, and repelled
by the "bad girl." The advantages of projection are too well known to
need extensive treatment here. It is enough to say that by splitting female peerdom into "nice girls" and "bad girls," one is able to deposit
unacceptable wishes onto the outgroup, and so reinforce one's defenses
against impulse. This device also helps the girl to relieve her guilt for
whatever erotic pleasures she permits herself. She will reason that her
own behavior is shared by the collectivity of "nice girls," and that, in
any case, her own sins pale in contrast with what she imagines are the

indulgences of the "bad girl." Perhaps we ought to say here that the "bad girl" is in most cases no simple figment of fancy; in any high school of size, the girl will have the opportunity to know, at a safe distance, a number of girls who wear tight sweaters and too much make-up and who go with the wrong sort of boys. Later, when the girl has come to terms with her own sexuality, she will be able to take the girls of dubious reputation more in stride. At this age, they represent a degree of impulsivity too dangerous to be casual about.

While the erotic seems to touch everything at this age, there are of course other themes present during this most difficult period of adolescence. The girl is not only unsure of her capacity to settle sexuality; she is also confused and uncertain about personal identity and indeed about her worth as a human being. To a considerable extent, she will look to the peer group's appraisal both to define and evaluate her. It is a time when, in order to consolidate identity, confirm status, heighten self-esteem, adolescents form themselves into cliques which are, as we know, more or less exclusionist. Paradoxically, the girl in this age group gives some evidence of democratic sentiment—she tells us that she admires equalitarian manners and dislikes those who are snobbish and status-seeking. Those who live by the ingroup, as the young girl must, will also live in mortal fear of perishing by it. The girl does not view her own ingroup commitments as snobbish, but she fears a possible exclusion from the group, and so makes much of snobbism. Here we find another reason for the emphasis on security and loyalty at this age—the good friend is one who will not abandon her to social isolation.

Another source of insecurity arises from the fact that the girl ordinarily begins to date at this age. We shall discuss dating later in this chapter. Here we want to say something about its relation to the like-sexed friendship. The friend is needed as a source of guidance, comfort, and support. In the preceding section we discussed the intimate friendship in this function—how the friends share their learning, how, in recounting their experiences to each other, they become able to live vicariously, reinterpret their behavior, relieve guilt, and exercise mutual controls. At this age, too, the girl must begin to come to terms with the ethics of friendship and dating. The girl, needing friendship so desperately, wants to feel that her friend will not abandon her in favor of boys. The dating friendship, at this age, may be seen as competitive with like-sexed friendship. Another form of competition is in the possible rivalry of girls for popularity with boys. The friendship has to recognize and adjust to differential popularity. The girl who is too popular or who flaunts her popularity risks the hostility of her peers. The girl who has won popularity must learn how to accept her good fortune graciously and modestly, so that her friends can learn to temper their envy. We cannot avoid the impression that the adolescent girl is far more concerned about the opinion of girls than of boys. She wants to be popular with boys, for its effects on her appraisal by the peer group of girls.

Late Adolescence: Girls of Seventeen and Eighteen

Our story has a happy ending. The desperate, feverish quality of friendship in the preceding age period now gives way to calmer, more modulated friendships. The girl has become somewhat easier about herself. She has managed to define herself and to find the basis for a personal identity. She has been able to develop fairly secure defenses against impulses and can now allow herself to discharge them in more direct experimentations in sexuality. She has learned how to handle herself with boys, and has acquired the rudiments of social skill. All of these changes relieve the pressure on the like-sexed friendship. Much of the emotional energy that has been invested in girls is now diverted to boys. As her suspiciousness of boys has dwindled, she is able to turn to them for intimacy. As she has gained skill in the dating relation, she no longer needs the friendship as a retreat, or a source of learning, or a cushion for disappointment. As identity is secured, she has fewer needs for identification-based relations with girls.

The passionate quality of friendship recedes, and it is replaced by a more equable tie to the other. By the time the girl reaches late adolescence she has developed a fairly complex understanding of friendship. This group has more to say than any other about its various functions, and what they tell us is at once more subtle and more abstract. Like early adolescent girls, they stress the confiding and sharing aspects— they want a friend with whom they can share important confidences. Yet we sense a new note in their answers—there is some indication that identifications are less prominent than before. There is now a greater emphasis on the personality and talents of the friend, a stress on what she can bring to the relation in the way of interest and stimulation. The girl becomes aware of and interested in her friend's individuality. There is a greater capacity, we imagine, to tolerate differences, and to value the friend for the ways in which she is unique. This stands in some contrast to the preceding period, where the girl, out of the need to confirm identity, might insist on a homogeneity of character, or where she could tolerate differences only when they allowed her to work out some instinctual dilemma. Now it is possible for the friendship to take on a more disinterested, neutral, playful, and diversified quality. It is no longer an apparatus for the resolution of conflict, and for that alone.

The partial solving of the sexual and identity crises brings with it a reduction of the emphases characteristic of the earlier age period. The girls make fewer references to loyalty, security, and trust when they talk about the qualities a friend should have. Needing friendship less, they are less haunted by fears of being abandoned and betrayed. There is also less of a preoccupation with sexual immorality. There seems to be a diminished use of projection, less tendency to divide girls into the good and the bad, and less concern with sexual reputation as a basis for judging, choosing, and excluding friends. Now that she can manage her sexuality, she is less fascinated by it, no longer so sensitive to it in others.

One other finding may be of some interest. When we ask younger girls what age group they prefer to be with in a social situation, they express a marked preference for older girls. We get the impression of a rush to maturity, a desire to know and grow, and a desire to share the sophistication (and the sexual secrets) of older girls. At seventeen and eighteen, this pattern ends, and we now find that girls prefer age groups which put them at the upper end of the age range. Our older girls have the advantage of greater experience and status without the burden of adult responsibility. So they seem to pause momentarily, and slow down, before they begin the transition to adulthood.

The reader may be weary of hearing that, for our knowledge of developmental processes we have had to rely on the study of girls; to those who have just joined us, let us repeat that the data on boys is limited to the 14 to 16 age group, while our interviews with girls extend from eleven to eighteen. So we cannot provide a complete comparison of male and female friendship patterns during the course of adolescence. We do, however, have enough information to know that the differences are considerable.

Before we look at our data, let us note some general differences which influence the contrasting forms of friendship for the sexes. There is the obvious fact that the girl is socialized so as to place great importance on personal relations; her life task, as wife and mother, requires her to cultivate such traits as sensitivity, warmth, tact, and empathy. The boy, to put matters oversimply, is trained toward activity and achievement; he needs to cultivate assertiveness and independence. (Of course we can easily make too much of these differences, and construct a caricature of the sexes, stressing these contrasting traits to the exclusion of all else.) Furthermore, the fear of homosexuality runs so strong among men in this country as to inhibit any display of "womanly" qualities; it also serves to frighten the man away from close ties to other men. Men fear more often than women a breakthrough of the homoerotic if they allow themselves too great a degree of intimacy with their own sex.

There are some less obvious reasons for the different forms adolescent friendship may take in the sexes. Helene Deutsch (1944, 1945) and other psychoanalytic writers have distinguished the differing psychosexual tasks of adolescent boys and girls. The boy's problem is to sever old object ties and form new ones. The development of adult sexual impulses makes it imperative to withdraw drive cathexes from the family and divert them to new and more appropriate objects. This is, of course, the girl's problem too. The difference between them is that the boy has little trouble in understanding his own sexuality. He experiences the erotic as direct, discrete, immediate, and uncomplicated. His sexual impulses are unambiguous; the organ of sexuality is familiar. There remains much to learn, about controlling and gratifying the erotic, about heterosexuality in general, but he is not long confused about the nature of his sexuality.

The girl's sexuality is not known to her quite so simply. For the girl the erotic is diffuse, remote, ambiguous, and complex. She also has the task of controlling and gratifying impulses, but at the same time she must learn their nature. As we have indicated, she does so through intimate friendship, and through complex identifications with her own kind. Not only is the girl attuned to the interpersonal, but also she is driven to make use of it for self-understanding. The intimate friendship, then, is a resource more necessary to the girl than to the boy.

Let us try putting this another way. For the girl we can imagine a reticulate triad: identity, the erotic and the interpersonal. The erotic and the interpersonal are much more closely linked in women than in men. Women in our society are object-dependent; they are compliant, passive, and responsive to the fear of losing love, that is, losing the esteem of the other. The woman cannot easily separate, as many men can, her erotic feelings from her ties to another. The achievement of personal identity requires a synthesis of the erotic and the interpersonal. Each of these terms is linked to the others: to define one's identity means to know the erotic, which in turn means to know the relation between the erotic and the interpersonal.

For the boy, the definition of identity is more likely to depend on such qualities as assertiveness, autonomy, and achievement. If we imagine a triad for the boy it would be something like: identity, the erotic, and autonomy (including in the last term a number of other characteristics, such as those given above). For the boy one problem is to come to terms with authority, neither submitting to it, nor identifying with it, nor fighting it obsessively; another (and related) problem is to come to terms with assertiveness, which means that it must not be degraded into cruelty or crushed into timidity, but must be controlled, refined, and adapted into purposeful activity. The boy's sense of the erotic will reflect and be reflected by, influence and be influenced by the development of activity and autonomy. Whether sexuality is, for example, brutal, or passive, or impotent is reciprocally connected with the boy's resolution of the relation to authority. In turn, both the erotic and autonomy (again, in a broad sense) will interact with identity.

So we may say that the adolescent girl, bred to the interpersonal, must solve problems of the interpersonal, and uses interpersonal methods to do so. (In a moment, we shall present some data which indicates how important interpersonal competence is to the girl's integration and effectiveness.) For the boy, the problem at adolescence is, as we have said, the relation to authority, and all that follows from that. The boy, to some extent socialized against intimacy, is also less dependent upon intimate relations during this period. He needs to assert and maintain his independence against control by parents and by parent-surrogates. To this end he needs the gang, the band of brothers, in alliance with whom he can confirm himself as autonomous and maintain a wall of resistance to authority. Even when the boys' close friendship group is small in number, they are apt to give it a ganglike definition, for example, calling themselves "The Three Musketeers" or "The Four Horsemen." Girls, on the other hand, even when they are part of a large group of friends, tend to form into centers of intimate two- and three-somes.

While girls ordinarily show few signs of the true gang spirit, boys do have intimate friendships, based on identification, much as girls do. We have defined ideal types, rather than differences which exist invariably. Our assumption is not that the intimate friendship cannot be found among boys, but rather that it is less common, and that it does not usually achieve the depth of intimacy usual among girls.

But limitations in our data prevent us from testing this hypothesis. As we shall see in a moment the interviews show that 14- to 16-year-old boys are less involved in close friendship than girls are at the same age. Since our sample of boys does not extend into the later stages of adolescence, we have no way of knowing whether we are dealing only with a slower rate of social development (this is generally true of adolescent boys) or whether, as we believe, there is, among American males, an absolute inhibition of friendship which continues not only into late adolescence but also into adulthood as well. The slow pace of development in itself does not tell us much about the ultimate limits of friendship development.

What we do know, what the interview data make quite clear, is that boys in early adolescence are less sophisticated about friendship and less eager for intimacy than girls of the same age. The findings also suggest that the peer group collectively, the gang, is more important to the boy than to the girl, that it serves to orient and support him.

To begin with, boys are less articulate than girls about the nature and meaning of friendship. To all questions in this area, concerning the qualities a friend ought to have, and the bases for popularity and unpopularity, they give fewer answers than do girls. Neither do they count close friendship as important as the girls do. They will more often assert that a friendship can never be as close as a family relationship: 42 per cent of the boys feel this way, compared to 61 per cent of the girls the same age.

When we ask boys the criteria they use for choosing a friend, and about the sources of a boy's popularity, they name rather concrete qualities. Their answers bear a striking resemblance to those given by the preadolescent girl. They believe a friend ought to be amiable and cooperative, and in general demand little in the way of genuine interaction. They want the friend to be able to control impulses, and here they particularly have aggression in mind. They also mention excessive hostility ("he's mean, a bully, picks fights") as a major source of unpopularity. Apart from exercising a degree of control, the friend is seen as having few obligations in the relationship. Boys at this age do not emphasize, as the girls do, the affective elements in friendship. They make no demands for closeness, mutual understanding, or emotional support. There is less mention made of security, which is heavily stressed by the girls. Since the boys' friendships do not involve the deeper emotions, they are not quite so threatened by the possibility of losing the friend. The support they do ask from the friend is, again, similar to what we find among the youngest girls. They want specific, concrete supplies, rather than warmth and understanding. Their conception of the roots of popularity again reminds us of the criteria mentioned by preadolescent girls, in being specific, concrete, and fairly superficial—good looks and good manners, athletic ability, an amiable, nonaggressive disposition. There is no value placed on sensitivity or empathy; snobbishness and gossip do not figure in their evaluations of other boys. All in all, the boys show little concern with the relational aspects of friendship. Friendship for them, as for the youngest group of girls, involves a tie to a congenial companion, with whom one shares a common interest in reality oriented activities.

Our findings also give us some sense of the relative importance to boys of "gang" life, and of the role of the peer group in helping him to confront authority. Boys are more likely than girls to adduce as a cause of unpopularity the unwillingness to "go along with the crowd." In their view, the failure to conform to peer standards is a more probable basis for peer rejection than it is for girls.

Another difference is in the kind of help one expects from a friend. We have already seen that boys are nearer to the youngest girls in wanting specific, concrete supports. But we also find in the boys' answers a theme which does not get much play from girls—the expected help from a friend when in trouble or in times of crisis. Remember that our preadolescent girls wanted from their friends positive supplies in the form of favors. But boys are less receptive in orientation, and more concerned about possible conflicts with authority. They seem to anticipate being on the spot, or being in trouble. The friend is one who will support you when trouble comes. We feel sure that the trouble the boys have in mind is trouble with the adult world. Another indication of this is in the difference between the sexes as regards verbal hostility. The girls object, as we have said, to gossip, to being talked about by other girls. Here the objection is to behavior which will damage or destroy one's relation to peers. Boys however object to "tattling," that is, to the boy who breaks peer ranks to collaborate with the adult enemy. So the adolescent boy's assertive-resistant stance to adults, which we examined earlier, is also evident in his definition of friendship and peer relations. We shall look at this again when we discuss the peer group later in the chapter.

Finally, we want to consider a finding we deem to be of special importance. We have argued throughout this chapter that the interpersonal is of peculiar importance in feminine psychology, that it plays a central role in the woman's development and experience, more so than for the man. Throughout her life, she meets developmental crises through permutations of the interpersonal—the major motive is the desire for love, the major source of anxiety is the fear of losing love, the major technique in crisis is the appeal for support and supplies from persons important to her. While the boy develops internal controls and strives to meet internal moral standards, the girl regulates her behavior to a greater degree through a sensitivity to signals from key figures in the environment. The boy, to put matters too simply, responds to guilt, the girl to shame. Just as we hypothesized that the consolidation of internal controls is related to personal integration in boys, so we anticipate that, for girls, the degree of personal integration is related to the maturation of interpersonal skills. The girl's talent in relating to objects, her techniques in attracting and holding affection, would, we felt, hold the key to her success in adaptation. Interpersonal skills, we thought, would not be nearly as critical to the boy's integration.

To test these hypotheses, we devised a measure of interpersonal maturation. Using extreme groups, those who show relatively mature attitudes and skills in the area of friendship, and those who are strikingly immature, we compared their responses in other areas of ego development. For girls there is a clear relation between interpersonal maturation and the following variables: energy level, self-confidence, time-perspective, organization of ideas, and positive feminine identification. For boys, however, the degree of interpersonal maturation is not significantly related to energy level, self-confidence, time-perspective, or self-acceptance. In short, we gather that the interpersonal mode is interwoven with the girl's personal integration, while it does not have the same degree of influence in the boy's development.

Peer Group and Peer Culture

We shall not have much to say here about the influence of the peer group and culture on the adolescent's social experience. We discussed peer phenomena earlier in this chapter, as well as in our treatment of the family. As we shall argue later, we do not feel the interview is the method of choice for studying the operation of the peer group. Therefore we did not give this topic high priority in the development of the questionnaire.

We have agreed with most writers in stressing the importance of peer relations during adolescence. The youngster uses the support and example of his contemporaries in making the transition from parental control to personal autonomy. Peer opinion weighs heavily with the adolescent, so much so that the youngster often seems little more than a prisoner of peer norms, slavishly dependent on them for counsel on how to dress, what to say and do, and what to feel and believe. As we suggested earlier, peer opinion invades the parent-child relationship at this time. It is, at the very best, a third party to be heard, if only as a possible veto group.

To say all of this is to ascribe a high degree of influence to the peer group. We feel, nevertheless, that many recent writings on adolescence have gone too far to overestimate the actual power of peer influence. Several possible reasons come to mind. To begin with, the observer's attention is likely to be captured by the more conspicuous enclaves of adolescent culture: to the lower class youngster, who is quickly alienated from the family and who often enters into visible and much-publicized gang activity; and to the upper-middle-class group, also very visible, where we find a high degree of emphasis by the parents on popularity and social success, and thus a particular stress on peer activity. In the "core culture," parental authority is in greater evidence.

Another reason may lie in the fact that the adolescent culture has undergone genuine changes in recent years, most of these in the direction of increased influence and visibility. Many writers, lay and professional alike, have exaggerated the extent of these changes in the very process of highlighting and documenting them. By judging these late developments on the basis of other expectations of the adolescent's place vis-à-vis the family, they have sometimes given us a picture of contemporary adolescence that is, at the best, one-sided and at the worst far fetched. The eccentric views are in some part the work of the professional hand-wringers of the mass media (Whither Youth?); but they also are found in the writings of some of the liveliest and most insightful of social scientists. What we have here, we believe, is something in the nature of a cultural antilag, that is, an alertness to the recent or emergent, an otherwise laudable quickness of vision which may lead the social scientist not only to accentuate the new, but also to exaggerate its scope, power, and significance.

Here we ought to add that the adolescent peer culture, having developed new forms, may not yet have found its final place, its natural level, in American society. The social changes of the postwar era are probably not yet complete; but they seem sufficiently established that we can now begin to appraise them, and to gain some sense of their limits. The social re-emergence of the last two decades produced a number of distinct changes in the conditions of adolescence, the most obvious, perhaps, being the autonomies allowed by a general affluence. The adolescent peer culture and (locally) the adolescent peer group came to enjoy new indulgences and new hegemonies over individual behavior. We have suggested that the extent of these changes has been overestimated, but that does not make them less real. Now we may suggest that some of these changes may turn out to be temporary —for a brief moment in time, the adolescent culture operated in something of a power vacuum; its influence expanded because the countervailing force of other social institutions (themselves involved in change) had not yet come into play; the peer culture's influence extended beyond its inherent strength.

Finally, we may be finding it hard to appraise the actual nature and degree of peer group influence because our perception of it is affected and distorted by the kinds of attention given to adolescence in the mass media. Does this generation of adolescents propose any serious revolutions in morals and ideology? If it is doing so, it is doing it silently. The issues we hear about, the publicized issues, are the trivial ones, having to do with taste and manners. When the delegate from "Teendom" steps before the cameras, he will likely commit his native eloquence to the defense of rock-and-roll. We do not deny that we are are in the midst of one more conflict between the generations; but as often happens in war, the eyewitness cannot easily learn what the fighting is about, where the important skirmishes are being fought, or who is at any moment winning. The mass media, by highlighting the simple or spectacular issues and instances, make the central issues of the dispute that much harder to recognize or understand.

Nevertheless, the peer group is important. During adolescence the child is in process of abandoning his dependence on parental standards and is trying to find his own. He looks to his peers for support and guidance. In rejecting one source of authority, the parent, he substitutes (at first) another, the peers. In both cases he leans on an external agency. The dynamics of control remain the same. Indeed, when the child begins his commitment to peer opinion, he is liable to be more in thrall to it than he is to his parents. He may conform to peer authority (in matters of taste and manners) so wholeheartedly as to give up. momentarily, any will to select or differentiate on the basis of personal judgment. As he moves through a series of peer relations, each representing one more step away from the dependent bond to the parents, he gradually finds and absorbs standards suited to his own taste and circumstance, and so weans himself from a strict allegiance to external norms.

In our chapter on the family we pointed out how the American adolescent's quest for autonomy is affected by the parents' uncertainty about appropriate norms for the youngster. They are likely to be impressed (probably overimpressed) by social change, likely to feel that parent and child live in different worlds, and that they themselves lack the experience to teach the child how to meet and manage his world. We have here something similar to a self-fulfilling prophecy. Half believing he cannot really guide his child, the parent helps the child in his turn to the peer group. This is done, as we said earlier, in an atmosphere of doubt and ambivalence. The parents, on the one hand, are much given to bewailing their child's enslavement to the peer group and culture. On the other hand, they find themselves compelled to reinforce their authority in a great many ways, some subtle and some not so subtle. Success and happiness are defined as popularity and acceptance by the peer group. If the children are successful with peers, the parents feel that they are winning the crucial rewards. The child is encouraged to do what he can to achieve popularity. The peer group is often the explicit norm-setter. In making a decision the parent will ask the child directly (or extract from him indirectly) what other children are wearing, or doing, or spending.

Observers of American adolescence have felt that this source of authority for the peer group is most likely to be found in the middle class. What data we have tends to confirm this supposition. We find that the emphasis on peer acceptance and approval is more prominent in the upper-middle class; the lower-middle class is more often the stronghold of traditional and family-centered standards. Upper-middle-class children are the most likely to be responsive to the judgment of the peer group. Among girls, furthermore, those from professional and managerial backgrounds will most often tell us that their parents expect them to be popular and well liked by peers.

Peer opinion, we reiterate, is most authoritative in those areas that the parents do not deeply feel to be at stake. The adolescent is free to be a "teen," that is, to live in the consumption fairyland, and to follow whatever strange customs the collective adolescent genius can dream up and the media popularize. On issues of morals, where the adults do have a stake, the adolescent remains fairly responsive to parental standards (although we might add here that there is really little conflict here between peer and adult opinion). Almost universally, our data show, the adolescent expects to rely on his parents for help and advice on deeply involving personal problems. There is, of course, a movement away from the earlier dependency on parental standards. Some of our youngsters reported themselves to be aligned with peer standards on moral issues; others have made the transition from parental to internal controls, in some cases without first adopting peer standards. Still, our data suggest that peer influence is more likely to touch specific and often superficial areas of the child's experience.

We do not have so much data as we would like on the quality of the adolescent's attachment to the peer group. In developing the interview schedules we were constantly faced with problems of priority. We had to use the available time and money where we felt it would be most fruitful. The peer group and culture had already been the object of study by many other investigators. We felt, besides, that the interview technique is not particularly suited to the study of some of the more critical aspects of peer relations; for these such methods as participant observation and sociometry seemed more appropriate. Consequently we put our efforts elsewhere.

Nevertheless, we do have some findings that bear on the nature of peer attachments, particularly in regard to sex differences. From the earlier discussion of friendship we can anticipate the different meaning of peer relations for boys and girls. The boy needs the peer group to support him in his quest for autonomy; he wants a band of rebels with whom he can identify and so gain the strength he needs for a stance against adult authority. In the delinquent gang we have the para-digmatic instance—a group which insists on loyalty and secrecy, which has some degree of organization, which ranges itself against competing groups and official authority. In a far more diluted form, these qualities are commonly found in groups of nondelinquent boys.

It is unusual for girls to form into this sort of collectivity. They rely more heavily on a close tie to a best friend, or to two or three good friends. They use the group as a source of narcissistic supplies (being "popular" is a more common goal for girls than for boys) or as a mechanism for finding girls with whom to build a more intimate rela-tion. But they do not generally value the authority or solidarity of the group *qua* group the way boys often do. Nor do they ordinarily defy parental authority openly. The girl will more likely seek to keep peace with the family, deviating from their rules quietly and sedately. The intimate friend will be used as a source of support and a repository of confidences, but not as an ally in open rebellion.

Our data confirm the expectation that the peer group, as such, looms larger in the boy's experience. This is true despite the girls' greater degree of social development. Throughout the interview girls respond far more frequently in terms of interpersonal relations—they are more eager for popularity, they stress good social relations as a motive in vocational choice, they more often desire social experience in clubs and other activities—and we might expect this stress on the interpersonal to obscure the sex differences in peer attachment. Yet it does not. Boys do express a stronger tie to the peer group; they give peer standards particular authority, are more often swayed by peer demands, and use peer opinion more directly in their power negotiations with adults.

Here is some of the evidence. In discussing their feelings about clubs and organized groups, the boys will more often allude to the example and influence of friends in motivating their behavior. More frequently than girls, they tell us that they do not belong to groups because their friends do not. What they like best about their favorite club is that their friends are also members; they have more often dropped out of clubs because their friends had.

We also find sex differences in the degree of authority imputed to the peer groups. The boys are more likely to tell us that peer pressure might lead one to break a rule. In the projective pictures, where the subject is asked to choose between parental regulation and peer influence, boys are more likely to yield to the latter. In an earlier picture of this series, boys more often question the parents about their rules (25% of the boys, 4% of the girls). In doing so, they are more likely to argue that they ought to be allowed to do as their friends do. They look to peer norms for support in the stand against the parents. Girls oppose parental regulation less frequently; but even when they do, they are not as likely to refer to peer example. Earlier in this chapter we described other instances of the boys' tendency to see the peer group as an aid in the opposition to adult authority: their looking to other boys for support in times of trouble; and their rejection of the tattler, the boy who betrays peer trust to sell out to authority.

Finally, when we ask our subjects what might happen if parents did not write rules, we discover that no less than 40 per cent of the boys say that children would "get in with the wrong crowd"—an indication we would argue of the degree to which adolescent boys are preoccupied and tempted by the possibility of joining with others in a stand against order and decorum. Only 8 per cent of the girls give this answer to the same question.

Dating

Dating is surprisingly complex, and far more difficult to encompass and understand than many discussions of it would make it appear. We have discovered, in talking with people about their dating experiences, that they generally take their own histories to be typical, when in fact their histories were distinctly diverse. We shall speak of the dating pattern but it would be more accurate to make it plural. What we find are many different patterns. Even within the adolescent period, the modes and conditions of dating vary sharply with age. There are local variations and differences stemming from social class. In most cases, the dating institution is loose enough to permit marked individual variations.

Another source of complexity is that the dating mechanism serves a number of functions simultaneously. From the broadest, most telic perspective it is clearly a device for mate selection. From this point of view, dating is to be related to the prevailing ideology of marriage. Our social system stresses love as the motive for marriage, and insists on the free choice of partner. The dating institution, then, is an integral part of the courtship-to-marriage sequence. It offers occasions for falling in love and thus finding a spouse. All of this is obvious enough; but to place too much emphasis on this particular goal of the dating system is to misconstrue its actual workings.

Observers of the American dating system, Waller (1937) and Mead (1955), in particular, have shown graphically that dating absorbs and reflects motives and values somewhat removed from marriage per se. Among other functions, the dating mechanism serves in the finding and testing of identity; it is a laboratory for training in the social graces; it provides occasions for sexual experiment and discovery; it is used to chart popularity and success. To be sure these functions are by no means unrelated to the ultimate goal of marital choice, but neither are they isomorphic with it. It is one of the paradoxes of the dating system that its presumably subsidiary goals and values, such as "popularity," become autonomous, lose their connection to the ultimate goal, and may even end in subverting or distorting it. As we shall see, the dating system tends to reward certain personal qualities; these may become entrenched and survive, inappropriately, into marriage. The dating institution encourages certain modes of sexual behavior which, again, tend to survive inappropriately into marriage. It would be both foolish and overfacile to argue that American marital patterns are largely fixed by the rites of dating and by those alone; but there is enough in the relationship between the two to make us want to look closely at dating and its consequences.

Let us begin with an outsider's view. A thoughtful Finnish girl, after a year in this country, tells us she has been unable to feel comfortable about dating. The reason, she has at last decided, is that as a "date" she is not quite herself, not quite allowed to be herself. As a "date" she is, these are her words, a Social Role. "The boy is supposed to bring a date, and it doesn't matter who she is as long as she says and does what's expected of her. The boy brings a date the way he might bring a pair of skis if he were going skiing."

She is being unfair, and we tell her so. She is simply too new to the role, too self-conscious about it, and therefore unable to do much more than discover and try to realize its expectations. The American girl, we say, is socialized to the dating pattern, knows its rules automatically, unconsciously, and so can find within them the elbow room she needs to practice individuality. Our Finn will take some of this reproach, but not much. Yes, there is something in what we say, but on the whole she will let her statement stand. The more sensistive American girls agree with her, and for the rest, they have long since grown into the role, so much so that role and personality have become hard to separate.

Whatever we may think of this conversation, it does remind us that the dating situation is a social form, governed by a complex and sometimes fiercely constrained etiquette. It is no less formal and ritualized for pretending strenuously that it is not, for appearing to be "free" and "spontaneous." All that merry laughter, all that gay, youthful banter notwithstanding, dating behavior is generally as limited and narrowly focused, as predetermined as the courtship reparteé in a Jane Austen novel.[1] That dating is so regulated and constrained does not especially distinguish it; all social behavior follows certain forms and understandings. The point our Finnish girl wants to make is that the American dating code, as she has seen it, works to inhibit and destroy the very type of personal relationship it ought to encourage. She means that dating should allow the encounter of selves rather than roles, that it ought to expose rather than conceal individuality.

What are the reasons it does not, when it does not? Here we meet an apparent paradox. We might believe that dating is designed to bring about liaisons marked by increasing intimacy. So they do: sometimes.

[1] Indeed more so, when we come to think of it, and remember the easy play of wit and nuance in the courtship conversations.

But dating has another side to it, which is the avoidance of intimacy, or perhaps we should say the control of intimacy. The dating situation is potentially explosive, or at least is felt to possess that potential. The external controls provided by chaperonage are absent; the burden of constraint passes to the actors. One function of the dating role, or the dating persona, is to keep the instincts at bay in a potentially unstable setting. The date will generally have its erotic aspect, but ordinarily it is a token sexuality, implacably fixed in its negotiations, designed less to express the erotic than to bring obligations to account. This is especially true when the boy and girl are new to the game. It is during the early years of adolescence that the dating pattern is a means of shielding the youngster from the demands and anxieties of sexuality.

Another problem is self-esteem, so uncertain during this time even among the better adjusted. Dating is a way of measuring the self through the other's appraisal. All too often the youngster will take his success or failure in dating as a portent of his entire heterosexual destiny. The response of the other is used to predict one's future in affection. With so much felt to be at stake, and knowing easily he can be hurt, the youngster retreats to the safety of the role as a way of hiding the "true self" from the humiliations of social failure.

These vulnerabilities—sexual anxiety, the tenuousness of self-esteem—help give the dating system its peculiar emotional tone. The problem is to expose the child to these sources of hurt and danger, and yet protect him from being overwhelmed by them. It is something like hyposensitization for an allergy. The trick is in the controlled exposure to a potentially dangerous substance. The dating pattern, particularly in its early stages, immunizes the child, by allowing him to play at and so learn the techniques of social and sexual interaction. The dating code, the implicit prescriptions for behavior and affect, are designed to keep the relationships casual, superficial, emotionally noninvolving.

There develops a kind of characterological fiction—the "good date." Its dimensions vary somewhat with age, social status, and other local circumstances, but generally, the good date is someone skilled in keeping impulses and affects under control in a situation that tends to stimulate them. The good date, male or female, can keep the ball rolling, is amiable and verbally facile. The overt expression of impulse is strictly forbidden. One must not be directly sensual or aggressive. Indeed, any extreme of behavior, even a "desirable" extreme, is generally felt to be out of place. One ought to be gay and yet not altogether frivolous; one ought to be bright, and yet not serious or intellectual; one is expected to offer comments on the evening's entertainment, the movie, let us say, and yet without vehemence. The boy can exercise some inventiveness in arranging the evening's activities, but not to the point of deviation. The girl's behavior is probably more strictly regulated than the boy's; she is to be the audience to the boy's offerings of entertainment, yet she must be at the least polite and if possible enthusiastic about it, whatever her secret inclinations may be. Similarly both sexes must learn to control the moods they may be in as they enter the evening. One cannot settle into a glum silence because one feels out of sorts.

These controls on the free expression of feelings are of course general to social life and are by no means unique to dating. All social intercourse is regulated by expectations and prescriptions of varying degrees of stringency. One does not tell the hostess what one may really think of her meal, nor yawn loudly during a committee meeting, nor do a thousand other things one may want to on public occasions. It is one perspective on social life to see it founded on a complex structure of deceits, hypocricies, black and white lies, false fronts. In this respect (and allowing for differences in rhetoric) adolescent cynicism-idealism as we see it expressed, for example in the tortured reflections of Holden Caulfield, shows a striking similarity to the solemn observations of an Erving Goffman (1959) on the necessary falsehoods of everyday life. The entry into adolescence brings with it what may appear to be a loss of innocence, in that the child learns to dissemble, and to adjust himself to proprieties which are at the same time, hypocricies. What the child loses in innocence, he gains in tact. Childhood can also be the age without pity, the age of unconscious and casual cruelty.

It is in this sense that we can see the entrance into dating and the learning of the dating code as functional to adolescent socialization. The youngster acquires a wide array of ego skills appropriate to social interaction. He may learn to temper whatever projective confusions he has established concerning the opposite sex. Because dating is to some degree transitory, errors of tact and control are of less permanent consequence than they might otherwise be. The system also provides techniques for terminating unwanted relationships (and for forming new ones) which minimize the loss of face. Later we shall present data which suggest that the girl, as she matures in the dating system, shows a growth in both sensitivity and good sense as regards her relations with boys.

Probably that is the best to be said for the dating pattern as it now exists in this country. There is not much more to be cheerful about. The emphasis on the "dating personality," in a context of intense sexual and personal competitiveness, can drive the American youngster to displays of emptiness, silliness, artificiality, vanity, vulgarity and among girls, outright "tigerish bitchiness," which is truly one of the wonders of the world. Here is a comment from a film review by James Agee:

The March of Time's issue about teen-age girls is worth seeing in the sense that one might examine with interest a slide of cancer tissue. These girls may be no worse than the teen-age girls of any other country, class, or generation, but I would be sorry really to believe that, and am sorrier still to imagine their children (Agee, 1958).

That is all he has to say. He leaves it to our own experience to fill in the rest, and we find it all too easy to do so. This is, to be sure, the American adolescent at his or her worst, but it is an all too frequent worst, and a worst that is likely to be produced by (and show itself in) the dating context.

One reason that the present dating system is (as we think it is) damaging to character formation is that dating begins so early in this country. Our data show that girls typically begin to have dates at fourteen and fifteen, boys a year or so later. We have been unable to find data for the European countries, but everyone we have talked to reports that dating (or its equivalent) begins several years later in most cases. Indeed, the European observer will generally comment on the tender age at which the American youngster is launched on an independent social career.

One consequence of this early entrance into heterosexual social life is that the youngster will become socially precocious. The American adolescent, put out on his own so soon, will often develop a degree of poise and nonchalance which stands in vivid contrast to the shyness, embarrassment, and even gaucherie of the European youngster of equivalent years. The contrast is perhaps especially marked among girls. One of us taught at an expensive women's college which occasionally enrolled Canadian girls, upper-middle class and raised in the British tradition. These young ladies tended to deviate from the American model in one of two ways: either by a high degree of commitment to the "serious" things of life, and a manner half-bluestocking and half-conventual; or by a brittle primness which, under the stress of heterosexual freedom, quickly gave way to the gigglings, gushings, and grand passions we expect in an American 14-year-old, and even then not commonly. No doubt these differences between the borders are the outcome of differences extending through the full range of socialization; but to some degree at least they stem from the fact that the

Canadian girls had had so little immersion in the heterosexual waters, and the American girls so much.

What are the consequences of the American adolescent's social precocity? It seems that the boy and girl readily learn to take command of themselves and each other. They also initiate themselves into the forms of erotic interplay. It is all too easy to imagine that their ease and coolness, their social elan, their erotic dexterity bespeaks a solution of the psychosexual dilemmas of adolescence. On the contrary, we feel that what is learned is only manner-deep, the acquisition of the exterior graces; the deeper bewilderments go untouched. We see a skewed maturation—social maturity preceding psychosexual maturity, and in preceding, influencing it. The American youngster may very well fall back on manner, retreat to the social persona. Initially this is done to temper the anxieties and doubts of sexuality and self-esteem. But the temporary redoubt may become an entrenched position. The adolescent is led to commit much of himself to the achievement of social style, and social style may become a means to delay, inhibit, or distort the psychosexual achievement. The American tendency, we have said, is alloplastic, and it is no more so than in the dating matrix. The American child is led to the use of "external" devices, presentations of the self, as a solution to intrapsychic dilemmas. We have, to be sure, no established way of describing this process metapsychologically, how it is and why it is that the emphases on social face (revealing itself in the stress on popularity, "personality," success), works to abort the subtler, more delicate maturations of character; but something of this sort does seem to take place.

The dating personality is, as we said earlier, a characterological fiction, a beguiling one, a highly cultivated myth of the self, in which only the more agreeable and conflict-free facets of character are shown to the other. Gaiety, charm, masculine poise, or feminine insouciance— these and other ego-ideal qualities are offered for display. The problem, of course, is that these pleasant qualities, so serviceable in casual social interaction, are irrelevant to the needs of marriage. For marriage, more than any other adult relationship, is a projective system within which one's deepest wishes, fears, conflicts, and relational strategies are lived out. Marriage absorbs, reflects, and attempts to settle the object-constellations each partner is burdened with. It attempts to join affection, sexuality, dependency, power, (and much else) in a viable mixture, a feat for which there has been no prior preparation, even in the original family setting. Obviously no myth of the self will long survive a relationship so intimate and so geared to unconscious dialectics.

Another dubious consequence of the dating pattern, as Margaret Mead has so perceptively and forcefully observed, is in its influence on marital sexuality. The dating system, as we find it in the middle class, forces its participants to be their own executioners of impulse. The petting pattern involves stimulation without discharge. For this pattern to work there must be a prior socialization against sensuality, directed particularly toward (or against) the girls. Reinforcing it we have peer and adult pressure, expressing itself in the emphasis on good reputation. The girl, if she is to maintain status (and avoid pregnancy) must count on her own ability to check impulse, and to avoid surrender. The boy is expected to get what he can, although it should also be said that the petting code requires the boy not to pressure the girl beyond a certain point. When the girl says "no," the boy must yield, however grudgingly, and despite whatever ritual protests and persuasions he is expected to offer.

That the system breeds its own pathologies, we know well. In the middle class, the boy and girl find their sexuality fixed to the quasi-erotic patterns established by their dating experiences. The young woman, now a bride, will find it difficult to relinquish the habit of constraint. The young man's sexual pattern, as Mead points out, is influenced by the ideal of pure, unchecked potency. The need to meet the ideal is frustrated by his young wife's failure or diffidence in sexual response. The ideal is in any case fantastic enough that any human being would be bound to court disappointment in trying to achieve it. The young man's disappointment and anger may turn inward or outward, and may or may not reach consciousness. The young woman reacts to her husband's resentment and disappointment in any number of ways. In many cases she avoids the bitter sense of her own failure by putting the blame on her husband, relapsing into an aggrieved disappointment of her own which retraces the path of the earlier Oedipal disappointment. Here we have one of the sources of the marital problem so common as to be endemic in the clinical practices that cater to the middle class. The husband fleeing to his work or some other style of acting out, the wife settling into a martyred resignation, or into the sullen conviction that if she were a man she could do it better, or that someone else, a man rather than the child she wed, could really bring out the best in her.

Dating is the closest thing our culture has to a *rite de passage*. The norms for beginning dating are clear and highly specified. Most girls begin dating at fourteen, boys begin between fourteen and fifteen. We have some indications that the form and function of adolescent social life undergo changes in accompaniment to this crucial shift. A change occurs in the activities boys and girls share. Girls under fourteen are more likely to mention sports and physical activities among the things they play with boys (60% of the girls under 14, 40% of those over 14). When they suggest activities for clubs, the older girls make a clearer division in activities depending on whether the club is to be for girls or for both boys and girls. The girls under fourteen suggest essentially the same range of activities for the two settings.

Preference for coed clubs is at its height in the 14 to 16 year age group. Younger girls are more comfortable with girls, while those over sixteen have plenty of boy-girl interaction outside organizational settings, and are not so anxious to use organized groups for this purpose. The 14- to 16-year-old group are not yet firmly established in the dating system and are eager for coed experience. They look for opportunities to meet boys; the organized group offers them this chance, and at the same time does not imply the responsibility of a direct dating relationship. It provides a structure of activities and other companions, both of which act to cushion the anxiety of early heterosexual social encounters.

We find clear developmental patterns in girls' conceptions of dating and attitudes toward boys, corresponding to the three stages of adolescence. The preadolescent group treat dating as a more or less intellectual issue and give no real indication of emotional involvement with boys except for occasional signs of anxiety about their imminent introduction to dating. Early adolescents are very much involved in beginning dating, have considerable anxiety about it, and take a defensive rather than an interactive stance toward boys. Only in late adolescence, as initial anxieties subside, do girls begin to have true interactive relationships with boys, and bring understanding, sensitivity, and feeling to these relationships. In her early dating, the girl is likely to be absorbed with the problem of integrating new role demands and an image of femininity to the self-concept. As she gains some assurance that she is measuring up to a style of feminine behavior, the girl can begin to seek and find emotional gratification in friendships with boys.

Superficiality marks the preadolescent view of boy-girl relationships. Girls at this stage have not begun to date for the most part, and they are relatively unaware of either the bases for boy-girl relationships or the conditions of dating. Their general attitude is unemotional. When asked what they think of the idea of dating, they do not give strong reactions as older girls do, but refer to conditions for dating, particularly the age at which a girl should begin to date. Some of them (23%)

indicate anxiety about dating when they stress that girls should not start dating too early, or want to postpone the issue until sixteen or a later age. In general their attitudes are less developed. They give fewer responses than older girls do. They have less formulated views about going steady. Thirty-nine per cent of this group, compared to 74 per cent of the 14 to 16-year-olds and 89 per cent of those over sixteen hold definite opinions about going steady.

The superficiality of the preadolescent view is most clearly seen in answer to the question, "What do you think makes a girl popular with boys?" The modal reaction at this age (56%) is that physical appearance is crucial. They do not stress social skills and the dating personality, nor do they emphasize the girl's sensitivity or interest in the relationship.

They show little conflict about problems that arise in dating, again, doubtless, because these problems have not yet much reality. When confronted with a conflict between loyalty to a girl friend and a chance for a date, they resolve the issue with minimal conflict. They are much less likely than older girls to try to work out a compromise solution—some arrangement whereby they can meet their obligation to the friend and still have the fun of the date. Although loyalty to the girlfriend is the modal choice for girls all through adolescence, the youngest girls are more likely to make this commitment. Dating is not yet part of their real experience, so their strong loyalty to the girlfriend is not challenged.

Their ideas about the ethics of boy-girl relationships are also undeveloped and simple. The preadolescent girl typically feels that if a boyfriend of hers began paying attention to another girl, she would break her relationship with him. She is not confused by any tendency to look at the issue from his point of view, nor is her investment in the relationship sufficiently great to create a sense of loss at the idea of a summary break.

In an easy reversal, she takes a different stand in the next conflict posed. In this case the issue is criticism. What should a girl do if her fiancé asked her to change certain of her habits and manners? Now the younger girls do not (as we might predict) refuse to enter into the boy's system and break the relationship. Quite the opposite. More often than older girls they unequivocally say that the girl should change to suit her fiancé. They do not surround the change with conditions. They say simply that if the girl loves him, she should do what he wants.

The girl at this age can take a simple, straightforward, uncomplicated view of each issue raised without any complicating context of experience, without any great need for consistency.

At fourteen, when she is launched in the dating market, a girl's thoughts about heterosexual friendship and love are likely to become more subtle and less decisive. Solutions to conflicts are no longer so easy, since the conflicts now have a more striking reality. This greater complexity shows in many ways in the answers of the girls in the next age category (14-16). They respond to both dating and the idea of going steady with greater affect than the younger girls. They are more enthusiastic about dating than the younger girls are, and more often have strong feelings about steady dating one way or the other.

The older girls are not so concerned with the age at which a girl should start to date or go steady. Their concerns are more subtle. In the question on steady dating, the girls under fourteen concentrate on the simple age condition, but the girls of fourteen to sixteen talk more about the relationship itself. They think steady dating is acceptable if a boy and girl like each other a great deal, or if they do not get too serious or too sexual. They look at the question from inside the relationship, while the younger girls set up a simple criterion and apply it to individual cases mechanically.

The older girls also take a less superficial approach to the question of attractiveness. They do not emphasize physical appearance as the basis of popularity as much as the girls under fourteen do. They have begun to recognize the importance of the dating personality. They stress the way a girl handles relationships, her social skills, and personal charm. "Good personality" is one of the most common responses to this question for the early adolescent group. They still have little sense of emotional give and take in relationships, but they see that attractiveness has something to do with their behavior toward boys.

So girls in early adolescence have some conception of the relationship between a boy and girl. Still, we must recall that many of these girls are in the first uncomfortable stages of dating. The dating institution with its clear definitions and forms serves to relieve them of some of the responsibility and anxiety of their early boy-girl relationships, but it does not wholly dispel anxiety. They are testing themselves in a competitive arena, and we can expect to find some signs of anxiety and defensiveness in their attitudes.

We find, indeed, that this age group is distinguished by a combative image of boy-girl relationships. They show signs of insecurity that are no longer so common in late adolescence, and they do not have the developed emotional interaction with boys that still older girls have.

Their defensiveness is most clearly visible in their approach to the question about a girl's fiance asking her to change. In this group we find the highest proportion of girls who say that the girl should not change, who think that such a criticism is a legitimate basis for breaking an engagement, and who interpret it as a sign that the boy does not love the girl. More often than either younger or older girls, the 14- to 16-year-olds treat the criticism as a threat to the integrity of the girl's self, and react aggressively.

Their anxiety and vulnerability vis-à-vis boys appear in a somewhat different form in response to the question about the boy who starts paying attention to his date's girl friend. First, they are more likely than either of the other two age groups to say that the girl should do nothing, act as though she does not notice, not let the boy know she is jealous. Girls at this age, as we have already noted, are busy building a dating personality—and they base this construction or fiction on a large measure of denial of feeling. They are somewhat less likely than older girls to deal directly with the boy in an effort to solve the problem (for example, by trying to see his side, by talking it over with him, or even by breaking up with him). When they do try to solve it they turn more often to the girl friend, and try to settle the issue with her. The essential feature of this approach is to manipulate the boy in collaboration with the girl friend. Along with their stress on social skill as a basis for successful relationships with boys, this finding supports the view that early dating is a manipulative game rather than a real relationship based on mutuality and emotional interaction. It is consistent with many other findings in the area of friendship, and tends to support the observation that in the first stages of dating, girls turn very heavily toward dependence on loyal girl friends. We have noted the importance they attach to loyalty in defining the meaning of friendship.

We can summarize the attitudes of girls in early adolescence in this way. They are pleased and excited about their new experiences in dating, but they are somewhat anxious about their success, and react to boys as though they were slightly dangerous, to be handled with skill in order to be subdued and won. In their anxiety about boys, they concentrate on building a defensive dating facade, and their real friendships continue to be with girls.

By late adolescence (seventeen and eighteen) much of the danger and defensiveness has faded from girls' relationships with boys. By this time most girls have found a place in the dating scheme, and many of them have already formed genuine, trustful, love relationships with boys. The greater maturity and emotional depth of their friendships with boys are manifest in almost all of our questions. They enjoy dating, and almost all of them do date. Their conditions for dating and for steady dating concern the relationship between the boy and girl (they should respect each other, plan to marry, really like and enjoy each other). When they disapprove of steady dating, it is again on a relational basis, or on the basis of individual preference for variety and activity (you miss too much fun, do not get to know other boys). They tend to disapprove of going steady more than younger girls do, although a much larger proportion of them actually have steady boy friends (31%, compared to 13% at fourteen to sixteen and 2% earlier than fourteen). Their opinions toward dating and steady dating are more articulate and definitive than those of younger girls.

Two findings bear particularly on older girls' more interactive relationships with boys. In evaluating popularity with boys, they give more weight to a girl's sensitivity and understanding than younger girls do. That is, they more often think a girl will be popular with boys if she tries to have relationships based on emotional sensitivity and mutuality. She should be friendly, loyal, and sensitive to his needs, and not too aggressive (41% of this group give such answers, compared to 33% of the early adolescents and 28% of the preadolescents). When they think of a boy friend paying attention to someone else, they are more likely than younger girls to try to maintain the relationship with the boy and to see his point of view.

One finding from our analysis of girls' attitudes toward dating points to an interesting aspect of the dating arrangement and adolescent heterosexual relationships. In general, girls stress mutuality and stability much less in their concepts of dating than they do in their discussion of like-sexed friendship. Dating is a formal relationship which makes little demand on intimate emotional characteristics. In girls' attitudes toward dating, the primary emphasis is reserved for their own emotional needs rather than for interaction with the boy or for his needs. The dating relationship, unlike the like-sexed friendship, does not contain a heavy identification element or emphasis on the relationship itself.

Dating as an Index of General Social Development

For both boys and girls we find a general relationship between dating and other areas of social activity. Those who date are more often members of organized groups, more frequently hold jobs, and have a greater number of leisure activities. The relationships in all cases are positive but of low order. Among older girls we also find consistent relationships between dating behavior and other areas of social development, particularly development in conceptions of friendship and the handling of interpersonal conflict.

The most interesting findings in this area came from an analysis of off-phase dating patterns, an analysis prompted by certain of Helene Deutsch's observations and speculations about the importance of time-phasing in adolescent development. She suggests that any really anachronistic elements in adolescence are dangerous: that the presence or absence of particular themes is not in itself crucial, but that presence or absence at a particular point in the sequence is critical. So, for example, she suggests that homoerotic friendship between preadolescent girls should cause less anxiety than too great a heterosexual involvement, because intense like-sexed friendships are appropriate to this developmental phase. The younger girl is both physically and psychologically immature for serious heterosexual interaction on the other hand, and may suffer serious permanent damage from a premature experience.

We have no direct information about the sexual experience of our subjects. But we felt that anachronistic behavior in the dating realm would have serious consequences of its own on a social level, and that an extreme dating pattern would reveal something about the child's sexual development as well. For these reasons we conducted an analysis of dating patterns in relation to age.

The beginning of dating brings with it certain changes in all areas of the child's social life, in like-sexed relationships as well as heterosexual ones. Once a girl begins to date, her interests change and she finds little to share with girl friends who have not yet entered the dating phase. Even when girls are developing apace, dating may inject certain disturbing elements into their established friendships. The girl may find that now her girl friend is not only a loyal and supportive helper, but also a competitor, temptress, or measuring rod. She may begin to feel ambivalent about the intimate sharing that has until now been the key element in the friendship. She now wants to move toward certain experiences alone; at the same time, she fears desertion by her old friend.

When a friendship circle moves into these problems together, each girl can gain some support from observing that her friends are all having the same new experiences and problems. But the girl who is out of phase will probably suffer special anxieties and a sense of isolation.

The very young girl who commits herself precociously to heterosexual friendships creates for herself special problems of impulse management, and also probably loses the benefit of some crucial experiences that accrue from a more extended period of relationships with other girls. If Helene Deutsch is correct in her assessment of the importance of the like-sexed intimate friendship in the girl's emotional development, then the omission of this experience should bring about an impoverishment in her emotional life. If a young girl expresses her emotional needs only in relation to a boy friend, she is also foregoing valuable training in the skills of relating to other girls. She is losing the one chance for intimate contact with other females that normally intervenes between a girl's tie to her mother and her adult love relationship with her own daughters. This seems a particularly regrettable loss when we look more closely at the function of these normal transitional ties to other girls. One of the key functions they perform is to neutralize the ambivalence that marks the adolescent girl's relationship to her mother.

If the girl for some reason misses her chance for working through her negative feelings toward her mother, she will come to her own daughters with only a competitive model of feminine relationships, a model inappropriately burdened with undiminished infantile hostility.

Premature commitment to heterosexual relationships may also stem from a splitting of Oedipal ambivalence toward the mother. While the average girl has some negative feeling toward her competitor-mother, she also feels strong counterbalancing love for her. If, however, the relationship with the mother is dominated by hostility, then we might expect the girl to have difficulty with any female who is potentially a rival, and to avoid friendships with girls. One path that would permit this and yet provide an outlet for emotional sharing is an early engagement in intense heterosexual friendship.

We thought that going steady very early might also serve as an escape from the insecurity of the competitive dating situation—a flight from the danger of not being chosen in the popularity contest—and that it would result in some deprivation in social learning about casual dating relationships with boys as well as more intimate friendships with girls.

The other deviant pattern, the girl who has reached late adolescence and does not yet date, offers less interesting possibilities for dynamic interpretation. Here we also anticipate a fault in social development, but one of more general proportions. The very late dater, whether she falls in this category because of initial psychological problems, severe unattractiveness, a restrictive family, or a generally limited environment, is missing one of the critical experiences of adolescence. She is not learning the varied lessons for which the dating institution is designed, and she will also very likely be excluded from many experiences in friendships with other girls of her age as well. As her friends begin to date, the girl who does not date will have more and more difficulty finding friendships that satisfy her particular needs. She may well find herself isolated from girls her own age and unable or unwilling to move into established groups of younger girls. Her difference from her age-mates in this important area may affect the late dater's membership in formal organizations and participation in group activities. We suspect that she will have little social life and will be retarded in broad areas of social development. We expect, further, that girls in this group will be more dependent on their families than the average late adolescent—their dependency may be an underlying cause of their inability to keep pace with their peers in social development, or, at least, their social isolation will throw them back on to the resources of the family for their social interaction.

To test some of these ideas about anachronism in heterosexual development, we formed groups on the basis of girls' ages and dating patterns. With our three broad age categories, and three categories with respect to dating behavior (that is, nondaters, daters, and steady daters), we had nine possible analysis groups. Of these, we were interested in preadolescents who go steady and in late adolescents who do not date. We wanted, in each case, to compare girls who are out of phase with other girls of the same age. The 14- to 16-year-old group was not useful in this particular analysis, since all three dating patterns are common enough in this period to disallow any definition of one or another pattern as anachronistic. We found, however, that the 14-year-old group was similar to girls 11 through 13 in the proportion of steady daters, and that no dating was as uncommon at 16 as it was at 17 or 18. Therefore, to increase the number of cases in our deviant categories, we dropped 15-year-olds and regrouped age categories for this analysis. Early steady daters include all girls 11 through 14 years of age who report this pattern, and late nondaters are girls 16 or older who have not started to date.

Our analysis groups for the age-dating relationships are small, but the data give some clues about the meaning of anachronistic patterns. On the issue of dating itself, we find, as might be expected, that the late adolescent who does not date has relatively superficial and immature attitudes compared to other girls her own age. She fixes much more than her peers on age criteria for dating, and puts the appropriate age for beginning dating much later than other girls do, as though rationalizing her own deviant position. She has little to say about the dating relationship, and only superficial notions of what makes a girl attractive to boys. On all of the questions that pose problems in boy-girl relationships, this group is distinguished from other late adolescents by a lack of awareness of the relationship itself. They are not very aware of the boy's needs, apparently have no conception of a stable and trusting friendship between a boy and a girl, do not try to solve problems by looking to resources of the relationship itself. A trusting and mutual friendship with a boy, the normal conception for girls this age, is not within the ken of this group. Their answers in the area of dating and heterosexual friendship look like the answers of much younger girls.

In general, the late adolescent who has not yet begun to date presents a picture of pervasive psychological problems. She is not only retarded in social development vis-à-vis her peers, but shows signs of poor development in all areas of social interaction. Here we find a girl who is overtly dependent on the family, who is insecure and self-absorbed, who knows clearly that she is out of phase with her age group and is worried about her deviance.

Their conceptions of like-sexed friendship are equally immature, and they are peculiar in certain respects. In defining friendship, the late nondating girls give fewer and less sophisticated answers than others in their age group. They refer to emotional interaction and mutuality less often than other late adolescents (50%, compared to 70% of their age-mates), and they rarely refer to a friend's emotional sensitivity. The one criterion they mention more frequently than other girls do is what we have called moral courage. This means specifically that they think a friend should be ready to defend a person when he is attacked by peers (42% of late daters, and 12% of other late adolescents give this answer). The crucial quality of the response, we suspect, is the anticipation of attack by peers. We shall see in other findings that the girls are aware of their own deviance, and we suspect that their sensitivity to the notion of peer attack is closely tied to this sense of deviance.

They think of popularity, both with girls and with boys, in superficial terms. They do not look to sensitivity and response-to-the-other as sources of popularity; nor do they show the typical late adolescent concern with gossip, morality, and the ethics of dating. They more often think of popularity flowing from physical attractiveness (good looks) and from specific social skills like conversational facility. A peculiar finding in answers to the question about popularity with boys is that the girls who are not popular say more often than other girls that boys like girls who are not too sexual. Probably they have been taught that the way to success is proper behavior, but we also wonder if this answer might reflect a sense of guilt attached to sexual fantasies. We find other indications that these girls have rather intense conflict about sexual matters, and apparently some guilt.

In the question of avoiding friendship with some girls, the nondaters more often say that they would not go around with girls who are too boy-oriented or too sexy, or have bad reputations (24% of the late non-daters, compared to 11% of other late adolescents). When asked what girls worry about, the girls in this group do not report common adolescent concerns about popularity, school work, and the like as often as their age-mates do (43% of this group compared to 80% of the other late adolescents), and much more often focus on physical charac-teristics (72% compared to 51%). Only in this group do we find refer-ences to sexual matters; a few of these deviant girls (5%) say explicitly that they worry about sex, menstruation, or sexual development.

Girls in this group have little active social life. They do not date, but more than this, they rarely belong to organized social groups, and they report few leisure engagements. Social isolation in their case seems to reflect general immaturity. The girls are generally self-conscious, self-absorbed, and insecure. Interviewers rate them low, as a group, on self-confidence (37% of this group are rated below average, compared to 16% of other late adolescents), on humor (37% compared to 14% of other girls this age), and on the degree of organization they manifest in the interview (43% are rated "disorganized," compared to 18% of their age-mates who date). Their low self-esteem is apparent in answers to the question, "What things that you do make you feel important and useful"? One in six of the girls says that nothing gives her this feeling —compared to one in twenty-five of other late adolescents. When girls in this group give sources of self-esteem, they more often allude to recognition by adults (14% of the nondaters, none of the girls who date), and less frequently mention being part of a group or being ac-cepted by peers (24% compared to 35%).

The girls in this group are generally dependent on adults, particu-larly on their parents. They are rated high on authority reliance, and in answering the series of questions about rules, they show a heavy de-pendence on parental authority. They do not think a friend can be as close as a family member, and they spend most of their leisure time with their families.

The late adolescent nondaters have a lower average score than others in this age group on our index of femininity. They show less interest in feminine themes in their daydreams, the qualities they admire in adult ideals, and in their reasons for choosing jobs. On the other hand, they are not characterized by strong masculine strivings—they do not reject the idea of marriage, and they do not have masculine job aspirations. What apparently substitutes for feminine goals in their dreams of the future is a very literal escape theme. They choose particular job aspirations because they involve travel, and girls in this group daydream of travel more often than other girls of this age (22% compared to 7%).

While they are not oriented toward feminine goals, they have a strong narcissistic orientation. We have seen that they worry about their own looks, and they are generally oriented to physical appearance in their judgments of adult models, the popular girl, and friends.

We wondered, of course, whether these girls were objectively less attractive than average, but interviewer ratings do not indicate any gross unattractiveness in the group as a whole. They are not often thought to be outstandingly beautiful, but neither are they very often judged unattractive.

Because of their general immaturity it seemed possible that they might be less developed or late developing in biological sexual features. In the one index we have—the age at which they first menstruated—this group does not, however, differ from other girls.

In analyzing background characteristics, we found an association between this pattern and a farm background, but the relationship is not large. Among girls from cities and towns, we found no significant relationship between this pattern and any particular social status. The combination of social deprivation and psychological immaturity that we have noted among the girls suggests an impoverished lower-class or rural background. But apparently the pattern is extreme enough that other forces (for example, a pathological family interaction or personal history) must accompany cultural deprivation to produce it.

Many of the more interesting findings from this analysis concern the preadolescent girls who go steady. The girls are enthusiastic about dating and steady dating, but they too have immature attitudes and conceptions about the actual relationship between boy and girl. Compared even to other preadolescent girls, they have superficial and undifferentiated ideas about the characteristics that lead to popularity with boys, and about problems that arise in heterosexual relationships. Even their age-mates who have not begun to date show more awareness of the nature of boy-girl relationships, and think more of the boy as a person with needs and sensitivities than do the girls who are in a sense so precocious in their heterosexual development. We must note at this point, then, a peculiar paradox. The very young girl who acts overtly like older girls (that is, she already has formed a stable and exclusive tie with one boy) is relatively immature in her understanding of heterosexual relationships. In older girls, more permanent relationships seem to bring greater understanding and awareness of the boy, his needs, and the relational process. In its anachronistic form, steady dating does not lead to enrichment of the girl's understanding of the relationship —in fact, it is more often associated with superficial and undeveloped attitudes toward heterosexual friendship and love.

The preadolescent steady dater shows a lack of social development that extends beyond the boy-girl relationship. She has fewer clear ideas about the nature of friendship and popularity with girls, what ideas she has are more often superficial than are those of other girls her age; she does not stress the qualities of trust, confidence, sharing, and mutuality in friendship as much as the average preadolescent. Again in like-sexed friendship, she seems to have less understanding of the interactive aspect of the relationship than do girls her age who are not so precocious in dating behavior.

Still, we must view their immature ideas about boy-girl relationships as a peculiar and provocative finding. We can easily see that a very young girl who isolates herself from other girls her age by an exclusive tie to a boy would miss a great many experiences in like-sexed friendship, and therefore she might have naive and poorly articulated ideas about such friendship. But we would not necessarily expect this to generalize and affect her conceptions of boy-girl friendship. She has more experience in this regard than other girls her age, yet her greater experience does not lead to greater sophistication, as it does in older girls. If a girl has not developed sufficiently in her conceptions of interpersonal relationships, increased overt experience does not apparently add anything to her development.

Here is one final set of findings about the social development of these girls who enter steady dating so early: they are less socially active as well as less sophisticated about social relationships. They belong to fewer formal groups and organizations than do other preadolescent girls. Their leisure activities tend to be nonsocial. They are active, energetic girls—they have a high overall activity index—but when we look at the kind of leisure engagements they report, we find that early steady daters have fewer activities that require the existence of a group (for example, team sports, parties, and hayrides) and more activities that are essentially individual in nature (for example, sewing and reading).

General psychological characteristics that distinguish the early steady daters from their age-mates can be summarized in this way: they are active girls, apparently well organized and integrated. They are strongly oriented toward adult feminine goals, and not very interested in personal or individual achievement. They are apparently not very closely tied to their parents, yet they seem somewhat dependent on other adult authorities. We have seen that they are not well developed in social relationships, and we find that they also tend to be nonintraceptive and to have peculiarly sterile fantasy lives.

Now we come to the evidence on each of these points. Compared to their age-mates, the girls who begin steady dating at fourteen or earlier have a high average activity index. The index includes dating as a component and we suspected that this might account for their high scores. But we find, analyzing activity items separately, that the girls report a higher incidence of working than other preadolescents, and that they engage in an equal number of leisure activities. We have indicated earlier that these activities are usually not ones that imply social interaction, but they are more often solitary activities or ones appropriate for two individuals. In line with this, the only component of the activity index that distinctly favors girls who do not go steady is membership in formal organizations. Forty-two per cent of the steady dating preadolescents have no memberships, compared to 26 per cent of other girls this age.

The early steady daters rate high on interviewer judgments of organization of thought, a measure we have reason to interpret as reflecting poise in relating to adults. They are reasonably self-confident. Although they are not judged above average any more than their age-mates, girls who go steady are significantly less likely than other girls of this age group to be rated low in self confidence. They have at least average verbal ability, again they are significantly under-represented in the "below average" category. The precociously heterosexual group, then, shows no sign of problems severe enough to disturb their poise and general social demeanor. Rather, they are somewhat above average for their age group on available measures of personal presence.

The feature most clearly and consistently distinguishing this group from other young girls is a conscious preoccupation with adult feminine goals. Whatever else their early commitment to heterosexual relationships means, we can be quite certain on the basis of our data that girls who go steady this early are girls who actively and eagerly picture themselves in the adult roles of wife and mother, and who enjoy activities associated with these roles. When they think of decisions they will make in the next few years, they more often think of decisions about boys and dates than other preadolescents do (23% compared to 5% of other girls), and they are the only group at this age in which we find an emphasis on marriage decisions. On the question of how they picture their future lives, differences are sharper, and in the same direction. While 55 per cent of the steady dating group explicitly talk of marriage in their plans, only 23 per cent of other young girls do so.

We designed a composite measure of conscious feminine orientation for purposes described in Chapter 7. This measure is made up of questions about what the girl's future goals are and also what she enjoys currently. The score on this measure is a simple addition of the number of items (out of six possibilities) on which she gives answers specifically related to a traditional conception of femininity. We find that the little girls who go steady have a significantly higher femininity index than their age-mates who date a number of different boys or have not yet started dating. One of the items of the index, the job choices girls make, illustrates the difference quite dramatically. The girls who go steady choose almost exclusively occupations which are defined as women's fields—nursing, secretarial work, and teaching. They rarely choose the traditional masculine fields, and they choose all high achievement fields less often than other preadolescent girls. They do not choose medicine and law, but they do not even choose teaching and social work as often as their age-mates. Their choices cluster in the secondary professional and clerical categories. The reasons they give for choosing particular jobs yield similar findings—the steady dating girl gives particularly feminine kinds of job attractions, and seems oblivious to personal success and individual achievement. She likes the occupation because she likes to help others and to be of service to others, and because she likes working with children. She is not as interested as other youngsters at this age in status or success rewards. Girls in this group fairly often (10%) explicitly say that they have chosen a particular job because it is work that a woman can combine with homemaking and child raising.

Other indications that the girls are not strongly oriented toward individual achievement come from their fantasies. They do not daydream of individual success as often as their age-mates, and they less often allude to achievement goals when they talk of the most wonderful thing that could happen to them or things they worry about. The early steady daters have relatively unpretentious educational plans. They do not plan to go to college as often as other little girls. This is not simply a reflection of their lower occupational goals, for, as noted in Chapter 2, many girls who have modest job aspirations want to go to college.

One finding does not fit the nonachievement theme; in fact, it tends to contradict it. When we ask which of two jobs they would prefer—a steady and secure one or one in which they had little security but an opportunity to be very successful, the steady daters choose success more often than other preadolescent girls do (67% of steady daters group and 40% of other girls choose the "success" alternative). In light of our other findings, particularly the lack of achievement content in their actual job aspirations, we think that the choice of open opportunity in this case does not mean that the girls in this group strive for individual excellence and achievement. Rather, we think it indicates an acceptance of risk-taking and a degree of self-confidence or ego-strength. We have seen earlier that the girls are relatively self-confident, and it seems more consistent to conclude that their readiness to risk stems from a confidence in their own resources rather than from a strong desire for outstanding personal performance.

Another area in which the early steady daters consistently differ from their age-mates is the realm of fantasy and general intraceptiveness. They have apparently less contact with the internal world of feeling and dream than does the average preadolescent. This emerges in answers to the question about daydreams—the young girls who go steady say more often than others that they do not daydream (42% of this group; 18% of other preadolescent girls); and when they do daydream, their dreams are very close to reality, only rarely do they report dreams which are true fantasies or have any quality of wonder (no steady daters tell fantastic dreams, compared to 18% of other girls in this age group). Similar results come from the question, "What is the most wonderful thing that could happen to you?" The girls who are precocious in their dating behavior more often say they do not know or cannot think of anything in particular.

Their internal worlds seem sparsely furnished. Painful internal experiences as well as pleasant ones are less familiar to them. They have apparently fewer worries than their age-mates; and they are less self-critical, less often stating ways in which they would like to change. We noted earlier that they take a more superficial view of relationships, both in like-sexed friendships and heterosexual ones. In questions that pose interpersonal problems (for example, a girl hears that a close friend has gossiped about her; a girl's fiancé criticizes her) the early steady daters tend to give abrupt and rather simple solutions, less often delaying overt action or searching for compromise. They tend to discharge problems with direct action, which means that they absorb less conflict internally than do girls who delay action or look at various alternative solutions before acting. We infer that they have less complex and differentiated internal responses, both from their immediate tendency to act and from the fact that they prefer definitive solutions to delaying actions or compromises.

The combination of strong conscious orientation toward feminine goals and lack of fantasy and general intraceptiveness that we find in this group of girls is highly provocative, and provides an important clue to the meaning of early steady dating. The combination is striking, first, because it runs counter to our understanding of femininity and to most of our findings in this area. Usually, as we shall indicate more fully in Chapter 7, the girl who shows a strong feminine bent in conscious anticipation of adult roles is also highly intraceptive and plays actively with fantasy. This association between femininity and the easy access to the internal world is much more in keeping with what we know of feminine psychology—certainly closer to what we would predict from psychoanalytic theory of feminine personality development.

What do we make of the peculiar combination found in the preadolescent steady dater? We suggest the following interpretation based in part on Deutsch's conception of the preadolescent developmental phase. Both in behavior and in conscious goals, the girl who goes steady in preadolescence is making an early and strong commitment to adult feminine identity; indeed, we suggest a commitment which is premature in light of her age and general maturation. Barely emerging from latency, with its absorbing concern for real skills and the physical world, she turns precipitously to a single, exclusive relationship with a boy. She has neither skill nor experience in mature object relations. Her only relationships to this point have been either the original family ties of childhood, heavy with dependency and shaded by infantile emotionality, or the fairly superficial friendships normal in latency. As she enters adolescence, the normal and appropriate training period for skill in object ties, she avoids the essential lessons of the period and insulates herself from her peers by establishing an early and singular relationship with a boy. She is an isolate among her peers and fails to use this normal channel for gradual acquisition of understanding and skill in relationships. She might nevertheless develop apace if she used her tie to the boy friend as an experimental ground for testing the nature and limits of friendship. But we have seen that her early boy-girl relationship is not an adequate substitute for the like-sexed friendship. The reason for this, or at least one crucial reason, is that the boy-girl friendship cannot offer equal opportunity for identification, the means by which the girl normally enriches both her understanding of friendship and her own embryonic self-concept. This acceleration in heterosexual development (or, more accurately, in the behavioral forms of heterosexuality) means that the girl is involved in boy-girl relationships before she has developed a full capacity for object relations. We expect, then, that her relationship to her boyfriend will be relatively superficial, or based on a family model. We suspect, as well, that this early tie to one boy friend stifles development of her capacity for object relations.

The preadolescent girl who forms a relationship with one boy has also, we noted, a clear concept of herself as an adult woman. She has chosen goals that are strongly and traditionally feminine at an age when most girls still have relatively fantastic and contradictory ideas about their adult lives. She is down to earth about the realities of traditional sex role definitions. Paradoxically, this same clear-headed conception of adult reality may bar her from realizing her own aims. Mature femininity (for example, as it looks in the older age groups) implies sensitivity to others, strong introspective and intraceptive themes, a development of the internal world of feeling and fantasy. The normal preadolescent plays with images of adulthood, testing and trying a variety of possible future identities, while the girls who go steady seem already to have settled the issue of their future identity, and to have settled for an image very close to their current life and activity at least in external forms. The crucial point is this—play is appropriate in preadolescence, while serious and realistic narrowing of identity to conform with the facts of adult sex roles and limitations is not appropriate. The younger girls who range in fantasy, who think that they will be doctors or lawyers or merchants or chiefs, will not necessarily become these things in adulthood. Most of them will probably become wives and mothers, and they will, very likely, hold jobs that our society defines as appropriate for women. They will settle for the narrower range having toyed with a broader one, and the play will have added, meanwhile, to their inner resources. Fantasy and introspection are important components in the mature feminine personality.

Both the intimate like-sexed friendship and the open exploration of identity images help to enlarge the young girl's ego and to build her own self-concept. The intimate friendship serves as an important medium for the playful testing of future identities. In her friendships with other girls she tries out various social selves, and together young girls plan and speculate about alternative future roles. When the young girl by-passes this whole area of social learning to push on to an adult-like stable tie to one man-boy, she misses an opportunity for real intimacy, and she inhibits her own capacity for object relations and for the inner enrichment this opportunity offers. Untrained in object ties, her attachment to her steady boy friend, so precocious in form, can at best be a hollow imitation of the real article.

We wonder why young girls should choose such a fast-paced move toward adult reality. We suggested a few possible causes and we can now assess their relevance. A general insecurity and specific fear of standing the test of competitive dating might lead a girl to commit herself to one boy. Having found a haven in this permanent relationship, she might define her goals for the future as a simple continuance of this security. We do not, however, find evidence to support this hypothesis. Our measures of insecurity are inadequate, but we must at least conclude that no generalized insecurity dominates these girls.

Another interpretation we suggested relies on the notion of Oedipal conflict. The girl who has too intense and untempered hostility toward the mother cannot, we suggested, face either the closeness or the potential rivalry that ordinarily characterize adolescent girls' like-sexed friendship. In this interpretation, the girl's choice of a stable heterosexual tie is seen primarily as an avoidance of homoerotic friendship with other girls, although it might also be a re-enactment of the strong feeling for the father implied in an early splitting of Oedipal ambivalence.

Our data are not adequate to test this notion in any definitive sense. We do not know enough about girl's feelings toward their mothers, and what we do know is not at a psychic depth relevant to the psychoanalytic formulation. The few findings we have are understandable within this framework—they are consistent with it although clearly inconclusive. The steady daters among our youngest subjects do not have very close family relationships, and they do not choose the mother as an adult ideal as frequently as other girls of this age do. Their family relationships are also marked by greater open conflict than those of their age-mates. All of these findings, however, might stem simply from the fact that the girls do go steady: that is, they may argue with their parents about this, and turn away from the family because of the conflict. The fact that the little girls who go steady do not show a particularly mature or deep understanding of heterosexual relationships may lend some support to the idea that they seek rather to avoid the intimacy of the homoerotic friendship than to share intimacy with a boy. The girls who choose the steady relationship with a boy clearly do not express as great a need for intimacy as other girls. Whether they are actively avoiding it or simply have less need for intimacy is not an issue we can settle.

One other less likely possibility is that precocious steady daters are girls whose general sexual development is moving at an accelerated pace. This alternative did not seem very reasonable from what we know about their attitudes toward sex and sexual morality. They seem, in fact, a little prudish. For example, they think a girl will be popular with boys if she is a nice girl, not aggressive or overtly sexual; and they quite frequently (more so than their age-mates) say they would avoid a girl who was too fast or sexy, or had a bad reputation. They do not seem particularly concerned with sex and sexual morality as personal issues, as we might expect from girls who are sexually precocious. One projective question tells of a girl who "feels terrible about something she did" and asks the subject to guess what it might be. The steady-dating preadolescents do not think of sexual misdemeanors more often than do other girls of their age. Beyond these psychological indications that they are not particularly precocious in sexual development, we know from our data on the menarche that the girls who go steady show no such early development.

We conclude that the very early formation of a stable and exclusive relationship with a boy reflects some general problem in object ties, that it does not indicate global pathology but a rather specific problem in social relationships, particularly in forming intimate personal relationships; and that it does not stem from precocious sexual development or imply particularly intense sexual experience.

SEVEN

Feminine Development

T*hroughout this book* and in all of our work with adolescents, we have made one key theoretical commitment. We have assumed that adolescent adaptation directly depends on the ability to integrate the future to their present life and current self-concept. We recognize that our goal-oriented society demands a lively sense of the future in every phase of life, and that adolescent adjustment has specifications other than the ability to cope with the future. Nevertheless, we feel that this particular adaptive quality is most important during the transitional era of adolescence and that it is the single best measure of overall integration in adolescent subjects.

For adolescence is a period of transition with little independent reality. It draws its meaning from the past and from its relationship to some future adulthood toward which it aims and unfolds. This indefinite quality, this tentaive aspect remains despite the enormous effort of the advertising world to create a "teen-age culture." The image they have managed to create bears eloquent testimony to the fact that adolescence has little meaning detached from its adult goal. This "teen-age culture," constructed of myth and fancy, is an aimless, incoherent mass of contradictory consumption trends. Separate the present of adolescence from its future in adulthood, and a hollow and superficial picture is about all one can hope to reveal. Adolescence in all cultures, especially in our own, is bound inextricably to adult reality.

We have seen in an earlier chapter how the adolescent boy expresses his concern with a future identity in occupational terms. Boys as young as fourteen reveal an absorbing preoccupation with the world of work, and a marked interest in some of the skills represented in the occupational spectrum. We are struck by the high degree of reality probing apparent in their discussion of potential jobs and of their own talents and interests in relation to these jobs. We noted the value of a boy's occupational plans for predicting his current adolescent adjustment to peers and parents and to his own growing self. We have seen that the boy with a clearly developed view of his future role, who sees channels from his present status to some future work goal, also shows a high degree of ego development and ego integration in his current attitudes and activities.

This is not true of the adolescent girl. The world of work does not apparently claim for her the same central place as a mechanism for integrating her current and future worlds. It is not a major device for expressing her commitment to a future self concept. We have seen signs of ambiguity and paradox in girls' posture toward work, and have concluded that the occupational area is often used by girls as an acceptable, nonthreatening sphere in which to express predominantly feminine goals. The confusion and incoherence in girls' talk of future work derives, we think, from the fact that it serves two functions. For some girls it is a real focus of interest and investment; for others it is a means for indirect expression of needs outside the occupational sphere. Serving two distinct functions and various mixtures of them, girls' work goals cannot bear direct and simple relationships to measures of current activity and interest. A girl may have well-developed occupational plans without having an integrated self-concept. She may, on the other hand, have poorly articulated work plans and be highly active and self-confident in her adolescent environment.

Perhaps, then, the girl uses some other image of the future to orient her fantasy and her developing self-concept. Perhaps an image of her future roles as wife and mother serve to balance and measure the present against the future, to form a bridge between the girl's adolescent identity and her future adult self. We were not certain how the feminine image would serve a girl, but we thought it would hold a position roughly comparable to that which the occupational identity holds in the boy's self concept. We found in fact that it operates differently, but is of an importance comparable to the occupational image of the boy. The girl's ability to integrate a concept of the adult feminine role is central to her adaptability and success as an adolescent. It is this relationship and its complexities that we shall describe in the present chapter.

First, however, let us consider briefly the concept of adult femininity currently dominant in American culture. What is the common image of adult womanhood in our society? What do young girls anticipate when they think ahead and picture themselves as wives and mothers? What kind of life and what kind of person do they see represented in their imaginings?

The most common picture of adult femininity—portrayed in popular media and lived out in actuality by large numbers of young and middle-aged women throughout the country—is of an attractive, youthful, and energetic woman who combines the sophistication and competence of a career woman with the gentleness and warmth, the loving protectiveness of a Victorian lady. She lives her life with the spirit and ease of an agile athlete. Her family, to which she brings devotion and executive ability, is a team cooperating in a spirit of "togetherness," to borrow the advertising term. She and her husband are partners in building a particular life style and in a search for family success. She takes a keen and active interest in her husband's work life; he, in turn, participates in the family venture, at least as a companion in family play. This idealized wife and mother is intelligent and interested in the world around her. While she focuses most of her effort and interest in the family circle, this focus does not narrow her view or her field of operation (as in the case of the Victorian wife and mother who maintained an infantile quality and charm in part because of her intense and exclusive identification with her children). The modern wife and mother centers her attention on the family, but at the same time she uses the family as a source of contact with the larger world. Through the family she brings closer those elements of the outside world which spark and feed her own interests. Her husband's work gives her access to certain social circles; when she has children she joins a nursery school study group and later a parents' organization at the local school. These broader community ties grow out of her love and interest for her children, but come to serve tastes and interests of her own, independent of the family. She achieves stimulation and breadth from the act of focusing on the family circle.

The youthful attractiveness of American women, the characteristic most often striking to people from other cultures, is something we take for granted. It is insured and fortified by our ideology about marital love. Love in the American myth is a romantic concept dominated by unconscious, uncontrollable, mystic forces; but it is this, after all, in most Western cultures. The distinctly American contribution to the myth is the competitive and conditional quality of love. Marriage is based on choice, and the choice is supposed to rest on romantic attraction. This attraction, presumably, is deep but undependable, for romantic love can shift objects rapidly. Unfortified by religious or traditional sanctions, romance provides a highly unstable foundation for monogamous marriage.[1]

Modern divorce laws have been accommodating to unstable love. Love may be given freely and marriages formed freely; but love can also change objects, can be withdrawn, and marriages can be freely dissolved.

The context of romantic love and relatively easy divorce creates a cultural atmosphere and attitude that values personal attractiveness above many human qualities. When a woman has only her wit and beauty to count on, when religion or social pressure or tradition or lack of alternatives do not support and bulwark marriages, then she must concentrate a great deal of energy on maintaining and enhancing her personal gifts. Hence we have the American stress on youth and beauty, and a vigorous cosmetic industry. Beauty, apart from rare perfection of feature, is conceived as an achievable characteristic in our society rather than a gift given or withheld by nature. Regarding even her own body, the American woman must assume a stance of competitive achievement. Even here she will be gauged by her effort and energy.

Now we return to the young girl's concept of womanhood. She looks forward to being an attractive, active woman in the family setting we have described. She will be married to a man of her choosing with whom she shares a romantic and permanent love. In order to insure this future, she will turn some of her energy and executive talent to the task of becoming and remaining physically attractive. And her success as a woman will be measured in part by this achievement, along with the various other achievements implied in the phrase "the well-rounded woman."

Our evidence indicates that young girls do actually conceive their future womanhood along dimensions suggested by the popular image.

---

[1] The universal symbol of romantic love, Romeo, is also the perfect representation of unstable cathexis. We find Romeo intensely moving and convincing in his commitment to Juliet. We agree with his arguments against Friar Lawrence's conservative suggestion that the couple separate for a year until the fury of family antagonism has spent itself. We are committed to Romeo's idea of life and the exclusive quality of love, we are captured by his view of reality, and we agree that separation is tantamount to death of the soul. Only as we get older does the sense of Friar Lawrence's suggestion begin to probe through this captivating view. We then notice what may have slipped our attention before: that a few days before this fateful and symbolic argument, Romeo was equally convinced that he would shortly die of love for Rosamond. Romantic attraction is indeed fleeting in its attachments, for all its depth and gentle oppressiveness.

Further, although the image itself is distinctly middle class our data indicate that acceptance of the image is not closely tied to social status. Regardless of the status of her parents, the young girl in our culture looks to this middle-class image of womanhood for her guides to the ideal way of life.

We know, first, that most girls do expect to combine a life of work skill and a life of feminine fulfillment. Most of them plan to continue training beyond high school, and to hold regular jobs at least during some period of their lives. Yet we have seen that their plans for education and work are not dominated by a long-range or binding commitment to a special skill or talent. The adolescent girl does not look at the occupational sphere as a source of a life meaning or life work. Her life plan is contained in her feminine goals of marriage and motherhood, and her education and work are conceived as providing access to these goals or making her more competent and well-rounded in the roles of wife and mother. She will work for a while and then marry. She will help out with family finances, particularly in the early years of marriage before she has children. And her education and work experience before marriage will increase her efficiency in meeting the complex demands of an active family life.

Most girls expect their life pattern to follow one of two paths: education and work followed by marriage and work until they have children; or education and work followed by marriage and immediate child bearing. We find variation in the amount of educational preparation they expect to get, but not much in the degree of commitment to the jobs they choose. They all plan to give up their work, whatever it is, in favor of marriage and family life.

The common adolescent fantasy of marriage and family life follows closely the lines of the popular image. We asked two questions about girls' pictures of marriage: What kind of young man they expect to marry, and what kind of work they would like their husbands to do. We asked the second of these questions specifically to check the class aspirations of our subjects—to see what social status surrounds their picture of married life.

The large majority of girls who think about the status characteristics of their later lives hope for a middle-class pattern. They choose this pattern irrespective of present social class position—that is, whether or not they have experienced it at first hand in their parents' home. This universality of the middle-class choice leads us to conclude that girls' ideas about their future lives are strongly influenced by the popular image, more strongly even than by their experiences at home.

Status symbols are common in girls' descriptions of their future mates. When the American girl dreams of her future husband she apparently has a clearer picture of the kind of clothing he will wear (a white collar and decorous suit) than of his handsome face. Only the little girls are romantic enough or old fashioned enough, or, perhaps, uninhibited enough to care about the young man's looks. The majority of girls equip their dream men with the personal characteristics and roles of the middle class. They want young men who have skills and education, and who have the ego qualities to insure achievement in middle-class jobs—independence, attractive personalities, high standards, and competence.

Beyond the class theme which so strongly emerges in girls' discussion of their future husbands, we also learn from their answers quite a lot about how they visualize the marriage relationship. Here again we are struck by the degree to which their ideas adhere to the popular image. Over half of the total sample of girls refer specifically to the kind of marriage relationship they want in describing the kind of men they hope to marry, and this stress on the marriage interaction increases with age (44% of the under 14 group, 54% of girls 14 to 16, and 70% of those over 16).

The kind of relationship girls want is based on mutual love, respect, consideration, and shared interests, in which the husband cooperates in the home. Success and proven competence, the image of the established and fatherly man, do not play an important part in girls' fantasies. Rather they seek a partnership of peers—a cooperative and congenial marriage based on equality. A fifth of the sample refers explicitly to the family attitudes of the husband as important—he should like children and be a companion to them, or help in rearing them.

In speaking of the husband's work role, a minority of girls bring up their desire for a highly interactive marriage in the modern style of togetherness. About one girl in ten hopes that her husband will have a job that is not too demanding, so that he will have plenty of free time to spend with the family. This is a long way from the traditional conception of the husband as the provider and worldly representative for the family. The crucial thing in the old concept is how well the man acts as a representative and protector of the family vis-à-vis the broader world. When the girl defines the husband's work by saying that it should not interfere with family interaction, she has reduced work and providing to a secondary role. The man is no longer, in this scheme, primarily defined by his work. His work is defined by the demands of his family roles.

A striking bit of evidence about the authority of the "togetherness" image of family life—the extent to which it has affected girls' ideas of adult femininity—appears in the results of a small exploratory study conducted among sophomore students in one of our leading women's colleges. Here the girls were asked to write a short essay describing the way they expected to be living in ten years. The similarity of goals revealed in these essays is impressive testimony to the weight and uniformity of the popular image. Between forty-six and forty-eight of the total group of fifty girls included each of the following elements in their picture of future life:

1. Marriage to a successful professional man or junior executive.
2. Three or more children.
3. A home in the suburbs.
4. Daily activities including chauffeuring, shopping, and food preparation.
5. Family income of $20,000 a year or more.
6. A station wagon.
7. Membership in community organizations.

When subjects in this study confronted the outcome of their collective efforts, their first reaction was a mixed surprise and dismay. Each of them felt somehow that the other girls had copied or poached on her own dream. Two girls reacted differently when they found themselves sharing a common fantasy. The two disclaimed the goal, saying that the life described was not really what they wanted, but the only one they knew and so it was all they could realistically look forward to.[2]

We may question this study as a basis for drawing conclusions about popular images. After all, the sample is extremely class-biased; the girls who attend Eastern women's colleges are a homogeneous group. Although this is true, we would nonetheless argue that the findings bear on the image. The group of upper-middle-class talented girls in this study have much greater access to alternative patterns of feminine adjustment than any other group in our culture. They have talent and training which open professional possibilities to them; many of them are daughters of women who took an active interest in increasing women's rights; they certainly have greater opportunity than most girls for choosing life goals that are glamorous or in the grand manner of deviant ladies in earlier historical periods. But even they have been swept by the force of the popular image into strongly conventional

[2] This study was reported to the authors in a personal communication from Susan M. Ervin.

choices. The good life, liberated from any compulsion to realize a consuming talent or interest, free to try a little of everything and be well rounded—this is the compelling dream of young women in our society today. The dream is an attractive one, no doubt, and we are not objecting to it. But we would hold that the young girl today is more concerned with living a series of roles, by the idea of adapting gracefully to a life pattern, than by becoming herself or acting and choosing out of an awareness of her unique qualities and desires.

Data from the Vassar studies support this view. In their studies of alumnae, Sanford and his co-workers (1956) were able to establish fairly clear alternative patterns of adjustment to college and later life. The high achiever, overachiever, the social girls and the deviant or neurotic—these types were distinguishable in late adolescence and maintained themselves as the women grew older, contributing a coherence and continuity to each woman's life pattern. When the same set of types was applied to a current population of undergraduates, lines of distinction blurred markedly. The young woman in the class of 1957 or 1958 does not fit any single pattern neatly. She more often combines features from a number of types; she is, in short, more well rounded than her opposite number in the class of 1937 or 1938.

The pattern today, then, seems to be one of greater diversity and variety within each individual's development, and greater uniformity among individuals in their choice of the diversified pattern. The commonness of the pattern, we suspect, is in part a function of the development of mass media and the broad distribution of an image of the desirable style of life. When there was no means for distributing a common image, young women concerned themselves with working out life goals more directly from the one or two talents or interests or tastes which were most highly developed in themselves. When goals follow a common image, they are likely to deal with aspects of form and style more than with individualized content, and to stress only that content which holds for all women rather than that which distinguishes among them. Feminine goals centered in family life are a more reasonable focus for a popular image than are any of the unique and individual talents that may mark a particular girl with a particular developmental history.

How do feminine goals enter into adolescent development? We expected that just as the boy gains psychological coherence from attaching his hopes and goals to an image of an adult job, the girl might gain coherence and richness in adolescence by focusing on her future functions of wife and mother. Or to look at the process from its other side, the girl who does not have such a picture of future roles may be postponing the step ahead, defending against adulthood because she is unable or unwilling to cope psychologically with the complexity and responsibility which adulthood implies. For the girl, adult identity implies a special problem since it is so clearly tied to sexuality. The girl who postpones consideration of adulthood even as she approaches it may well be having difficulty adapting to her own sexual and impulsive self. We suspect that such a girl would be relatively immature and psychologically undeveloped, whether because she is simply growing at a slower pace or because of pathological features in her development.

In a first approach to the analysis of feminine identification, we constructed a simple index of traditional feminine interests, based on the number of times a girl indicated feminine goals and interests in response to seven questions. The measure consisted of two kinds of items: those that revealed an interest in current activities that reproduced aspects of the adult feminine role, and those that indicated a conscious consideration of feminine goals in the girl's plans and expectations for the future. An example of the first was a question asking girls to suggest activities for a girls' club, to think of the things they like to do best. If the girl suggested any homemaking activity like cooking, sewing, or gardening, she was given one point on the femininity index. An example of the second kind of response that contributed to the index was the choice of a traditional feminine occupation like nursing.[3]

We segregated high and low femininity groups with this measure and compared them on various responses and indices in areas theoretically relevant to feminine identification. The results of the analysis were interesting and useful. They indicated that girls scoring high and low on the femininity index differed in intraceptiveness, receptivity, and other factors which psychoanalytic theory ties to feminine development, and also in areas suggested by our view that a forming concept of future femininity is the anchor for a girl's adolescent integration. The highly feminine girls scored hgher on measures of adolescent ego functioning like time perspective, activity level, poise, and sense of self. The differences, which we shall summarize shortly, are stable when we factor out social class and verbal ability. We seemed, at least, to have gained some purchase on the issue of feminine development.

But the analysis also left a great many questions unanswered, and provoked still other questions that we had not thought of at the outset.

[3] The series of questions and scoring categories on which the index is based appear in Appendix C, page 459. The measure was formed by adding the number of points a girl got on the seven items. All girls who failed to respond to more than one of the critical questions were dropped from the analysis. Scores on the index ran from 0 to 7, with a modal score of 3 for the total sample.

In particular we found ourselves asking questions about the meaning of a low score on the index, about the possible alternative choices a low score might imply. So we proceeded in our next analysis to use an additional set of criteria to isolate more refined patterns of feminine development. The specific items used were these:

1. Choice of a traditional masculine occupation.
2. An active desire to be a boy.
3. Belief that a boy's life is more desirable than a girl's.
4. Rejection of marriage.

Two of the questions from which this information came were included in the original index, but for that purpose the opposite response was crucial. For the nonfeminine girl, then, we were asking the question "What specific form does this girl's nonfeminine adaptation take?" For the highly feminine, we also gained some refinement, since it was possible for a girl to score high on the original index and at the same time give one or two of the crucial nonfeminine responses. Only a few of the possible combinations ever occurred. No girl high in femininity ever rejected the idea of marriage. On the other hand, some highly feminine girls did choose masculine job aspirations, and some, despite their pleasure in looking forward to adult feminine roles, think they would like to be boys.

We did an extensive analysis of the patterns produced by this refinement, and gained some clearer understanding of the meaning of high and low femininity. Before we present the pattern analysis, however, we shall review briefly the results of the basic femininity analysis.

The results of this original analysis fall roughly into three areas: those findings that tend to substantiate the index as a measure of forming femininity; those which show connections between the explicit integration of a feminine image and more subtle and implicit dimensions of feminine character; and, finally those that bear on the relationship between feminine integration and aspects of current adolescent adjustment.

Our data are rich with evidence that the index is, in fact, measuring an explicit preoccupation with femininity and future feminine goals. In general we find positive relationships between scores on the index and other signs of conscious commitment to feminine goals, and the relationships are substantial.[4]

Girls who score high on femininity are more explicitly interested in

---

[4] In the interest of clarity, we shall present data for extreme groups. The reader may assume, however, unless specifically warned, that the relationship holds across the range of scores. That is, the higher a girl scores on the index, the higher (or

boys and in popularity with boys than other girls are. They are more clearly preoccupied with thoughts of marriage and family life, and their ideas about marriage (the kind of man they hope to marry, the kind of family life they expect to have) are both more detailed and more sophisticated than those of other girls.

The femininity index shows interesting and somewhat complex relationships to other aspects of feminine development. Whether we think of these other elements of femininity stressing psychoanalytic concepts like passivity, masochism, narcissism, or emphasizing the perspectives of ego psychology (intraceptiveness, the nature and quality of object relations, clarity of self-concept), we find that the girls who are integrating femininity into their personal identities differ from those who are not, in all aspects of underlying feminine development. The differences are not, however, always as simple as orthodox theory might suggest. The highly feminine girl does have a strong narcissistic component in her make-up, and seems to seek and hold in consciousness certain kinds of painful experiences.[5] She is not, on the other hand, selfless or passive in any ordinary sense. She has a rather highly devel-

lower) she is in the other characteristic described for extremes. Extreme groups, for which percentages are presented, were defined as follows: High: those who score 5, 6, or 7 on the index ($N = 164$). Low: those who scored 0 or 1 ($N = 349$).

[5] Feminine girls list physical appearance as a source of worry more than other girls do, and they more frequently wish for changes in their physical appearance, although interviewers rate them higher on physical attractiveness than nonfeminine girls. We measure narcissistic orientation by an additive index—in this case the girl was scored each time that she alluded to physical appearance in describing another person (for example, a girl who is popular, the adult ideal, adult club leaders, girls who are popular with boys, the kind of man she would like to marry). Feminine girls score much higher on this index than do those who are not consciously concerned with feminine goals.

Our evidence regarding masochism is less compelling than the findings on narcissism, but supports the psychoanalytic notion that feminine women tend to accept and tolerate, even take pleasure in, a measure of pain. We find that feminine girls are more intrapunitive, more selfblaming than nonfeminine girls. In the series of questions about interpersonal problems (for example, a boy criticizes his fiancee, a girlfriend gossips, a girl's boyfriend seems interested in her best friend) the feminine girls less often externalize aggression, they show greater self-analysis and self-blame, and they exert greater effort to maintain the relationship despite conflict. These answers, however, all indicate general intraceptiveness and ego control as well as intrapunitiveness. Feminine girls worry more than other girls, and name more disappointments they have suffered. According to their reports, the feminine girls have more often experienced a major tragedy: illness, death, or divorce in the family. We know from other information that femininity groups do not differ in incidence of parental death or divorce. It seems that they hold on to the experience longer and more consciously than other girls do. We also find a consistent relationship between femininity and reported discomfort during menstruation.

oped sense of self, and her adolescent adjustment (which we shall discuss in more detail) is an active and energetic one. She is passive, if at all, only in interpersonal situations, and here the passivity holds only at the level of overt activity. While she is less given to active disruptive gestures and to aggressive assertion of individuality in relationships, she is very active on a psychological level in trying to maintain existing relationships by handling problems and conflicts that arise, by absorbing some of the burden of these conflicts rather than expulsively shunting her own hostility or anxiety into the relationships.

Our findings in the area of interpersonal skills fit the modern conception of feminine integration, and are supported by other data from the study. The measure of an effective and feminine woman in our culture is skill and grace in relating to other people, in forming and maintaining satisfactory relationships. In all of our data about friendship, we find that feminine girls, those who are actively building a feminine identity, place great value on interpersonal relationships and have highly developed attitudes about personal ties. They are, we have noted, more sophisticated and subtle than nonfeminine girls in handling conflicts that arise in personal relationships. They bring highly differentiated thought and skills to bear on solving such conflicts, and they show how strongly they value existing relationships in the fact that they choose to resolve problems within the relationship rather than withdrawing or breaking out of its nexus. By this choice they also reveal a deeper and more complex conception of friendship—for them such a tie holds the potential for resolving conflicts; it is not simply a tenuous alliance that exists only so long as no problems and no tensions arise.

We find that feminine girls also reveal a greater maturity in their ideas about what friendship is. When we ask what a friend should be or be like, they stress the friend's capacity for a mutual, interactive relationship (High femininity group 31%; Low femininity group 10%), and they less often want a friend who is solely an amiable parallel actor (High femininity group 20%; Low femininity group 56%). Their view of friendship more often requires sharing of confidence and mutual support; they have, in short, a fuller and richer conception of friendship than do nonfeminine girls.

The girl who is consciously integrating feminine goals is also generally more intraceptive than other girls, and has a richer, more articulated fantasy system. In response to interpersonal problems the feminine girls bear more conflict internally, and in their search for compromise solutions reveal a more differentiated psychological system. They tend to be more aware of internal stimuli and more tolerant of their own feelings, wishes, anxieties, and fantasies. In two questions, about worries and disappointments, we find the nonfeminine girls more often saying they have not had any disappointments and that girls do not worry. Even when they recognize worries and disappointments, the nonfeminine girls name fewer, on the average, than do the feminine girls.

A distinguishing feature of feminine girls is their acceptance of internal conflict. The most striking single example of this comes from the third scene of our picture-story measure—the picture in which the conflict is clearly posed between parental demands and the desire to go along with peers. The feminine and nonfeminine groups do not differ significantly in the absolute proportion of girls who adhere to the parents' stricture and go home—but they differ markedly on explicit recognition of the conflict involved in their choice. Thirty-four per cent of the high feminine group, compared to 8 per cent of the nonfeminine, say the girl would go home but would feel bad, or sad, or reluctant, about having to give up the fun. These references to internal conflict are spontaneous, and so yield a measure of salience. The internal environment is clearly a salient force in the feminine girl's life, more so than for the nonfeminine girl.

Fantasy is similarly more acceptable to the feminine girl, and more highly developed. She can tell us what she would like to change about herself, she can suspend existing reality in this way, while the nonfeminine girl very often cannot. She is more likely to say that she has wished at times to be a boy. Feminine girls more often give some response, and in many cases more than a single answer, to each of the following questions:

What is the most wonderful thing that could happen to you?
Do you ever daydream? Could you describe a daydream for me?
What kind of person would you like to marry? [6]
What kind of thing gives you a feeling of wonder?

The dimension these questions share is the admission of fantasy, the ability to suspend for the moment the grasp on reality as it exists, and as one knows it. In each case, the feminine girl shows a keener ability to play with reality and a greater acceptance of fantasy. The inner

[6] We excluded girls who do not want to marry from the nonfeminine group before analyzing this question.

world of dream and feeling has for her a livelier reality than it has for the nonfeminine girl.

The last area in our analysis of femininity is girls' current social adaptation. In this sphere we come to the question posed at the outset of this chapter. Does an integrated concept of her adult feminine role serve the same anchoring function for the girl in transition that the occupational role provides for the boy? Does the capacity to achieve such feminine integration act as both a symptom and a mechanism of adolescent adjustment? From our data on the social adjustment of feminine and nonfeminine girls, we conclude that the answer to both questions is yes.

Feminine girls, compared to those scoring low on the index of femininity, reveal a high level of ego-integration on practically all of our measures. Specifically they are distinguished by the following characteristics:

1. A high level of social activity: the feminine girls have tried a greater number of leisure pursuits, and they belong to more clubs and other voluntary organizations.

2. An extended time perspective: in answer to open questions about future plans and decisions, the feminine girls look farther into the future than do the nonfeminine.

3. Poise and social skill: interviewers rate the feminine girls higher on self-confidence and organization of thought in the interview.

4. Self-esteem: the feminine girls name more sources of self-esteem than do nonfeminine girls, and less often say that nothing they do makes them feel "important and useful."

5. An integrated ego-ideal: the feminine girl can name some adult or group of adults she would like to emulate, while the nonfeminine more often reject all adults as models.

It seems that the feminine concept does function for girls in much the same way that the occupational concept serves boys—in freeing attention and energy for current activities, and as a symptom of a highly developed ego.

We find specific contrasts between boys and girls in only two areas, contrasts that reflect different identity problems in the two sexes. While in boys we found that a well-integrated concept of occupational goals was associated with a precocious thrust for autonomy and a well-developed internal control system, the feminine identity shows no comparable associations in girls' development. The girl who is clearly oriented toward feminine goals is no more concerned with independence than the girl who has little explicit interest in adult femininity; nor is she functioning any more autonomously. Extreme groups on the measure of femininity do not differ either in the degree to which they are consciously concerned with personal controls or in their actual integration of personal standards.

Many of the connections and relationships we have reported are linked to social class; many of the characteristics that distinguish the feminine girls are more common in the middle class, and the index is class linked. We might suspect that the relationships are spurious, arranged for us by the underlying class factor. To check this possibility, we ran the femininity analysis separately for each of the two major social classes, and concluded that the femininity factor has a force of its own, apart from its association with middle-class status. Our control for class position did not destroy the relationships we have noted. In all cases the direction of relationship is unchanged, and in most cases the size of differences is about the same.

Verbal ability, another possible culprit variable, is not strongly related to scores on the index. However, we ran the analysis separately for girls rated high and low in verbal ability, and again the relationships between femininity and ego variables hold true within each of the groups.

Patterns of Femininity

The patterns we isolated with the index of femininity and the non-feminine critical responses listed on page 238 are as follows:

1. Unambivalent, feminine girls—those who score high on femininity and give none of the critical masculine or antifeminine answers.

2. Ambivalent or omnipotent feminine girls—those who score high on femininity and also wish to be boys, or envy boys, or choose traditional masculine jobs, or give any combination of these nonfeminine responses.

3. Neutral girls—girls who stress neither feminine nor masculine goals and interests.

4. Boyish girls—those who are low on femininity, and would like to be boys.

5. Achievement-oriented girls—those who do not focus on future femininity, but rather on masculine occupational goals.

6. Antifeminine girls—all girls who do not want to marry.

Since not all the groups are equally interesting in each area of analysis, our most efficient presentation is a series of descriptive profiles of the types, emphasizing the ways in which each is unique or significantly different from some other patterns. We shall compare the ambivalent and unambivalent feminine groups, for here we have two patterns that share feminine goals. The remaining groups, all of which indicate little active interest in feminine roles, will form a second cluster for descriptive-comparative purposes.

Unambivalent Feminine Girls

The two groups of feminine girls are similar in a numbers of ways. Both groups show highly social, well-integrated adolescent adjustments. They share the feminine qualities of narcissisim, intraception, and a complex internal environment. Maturity in interpersonal development marks both patterns.

But the unambivalent feminine integration is unique in certain respects. The girl with this adaptation is most thoroughly focused on the social and personal aspects of reality. Compared even to other feminine girls, she is consistently outstanding in this respect. She gains self-esteem from helping others and playing a succorant role; she typically chooses an adult ideal on the basis of interpersonal warmth and sensitivity. She shows little motivation for personal achievement. She prefers security to success, she does not daydream about achievement, but rather exclusively about popularity, dating, marriage, and family goals. Her educational goals are lower than those of the ambivalent feminine girl. When she does choose higher education as a goal, it is with sights fixed on a vocational purpose, for example, her desire to go to college is likely to be expressed as a wish to go to teachers' college. Her vocational orientation is highly feminine—toward teaching or nursing. Of all our groups, the unambivalent feminine girls are most eager to have children and to care for children.

The second area in which this group reveals exceptional attitudes and behavior, clearly different from other feminine girls, is family relationships. We noted that femininity in itself has no particular implications in the area of autonomy and developing independence from the family. When, however, we refine our patterns of feminine integration, quite striking relationships emerge within the high feminine group. The unambivalent feminine girls are clearly identified with their mothers, and apparently have close and amiable relationships with strong traditional parents. Of all groups in this analysis, the unambivalent feminine girls most often choose their own mothers (50% compared to an average of 32% for all other groups) or some other feminine relative (22% compared to 14% of all other girls) as an adult ideal. They report fewer disagreements with their parents than do other girls, and they more often spend some part of their leisure time within the family circle. Helping at home constitutes one of their major sources of self-esteem.

The girls are distinguished by a compliant, dependent relationship to their parents (for example, they also gain self-esteem from being praised by adults more often than do ambivalent feminine girls), they observe parental regulation with caution and in a spirit of identification with the parents' point of view. Apparently compliance is also an important part of the parents' expectations—this group reports, more often than any other, that their parents expect them to be obedient and "respect authority." Their parents, at least as the girls portray them, do not stress independence or resourcefulness as qualities important for their daughters to develop. They expect, rather, a combination of respect for authority, skill and popularity with the peer group, and social grace ("manners," "that I'll act like a lady"). Girls in this group are not typically given a part in making rules at home—again, indicating that their parents do not strongly encourage autonomy. On the other hand, their parents are not harsh. The unambivalent girls report psychological punishment more than any other group, and rarely say they are punished physically. Their parents, according to the picture we get, are strong and clear in stating requirements. Since the girls apparently comply with their demands, little occasion for conflict or harshness occurs.

As far as background factors are concerned, we again find that the two highly feminine groups are similar in some respects, and different in others. We were not able to predict some of the differences; in fact, we had predicted opposite findings in some cases. The major difference in background, and the one we expected least, concerned social status. We rather expected the unambivalent feminine pattern to be primarily a lower-middle-class pattern. The measure of femininity rests heavily on a traditional conception of sex roles, and this conception is ordinarily associated with the lower-middle class. The unambivalent choice of feminine goals would, we thought, not only indicate certain harmonious psychological features (for example, a good relationship with the mother), but also a relatively limited environment (that is, the girl chooses one sex role unambivalently because no other pattern occurs to her or is offered by her surroundings). The more encompassing pattern that combines a desire for feminine goals with a wish for the freedom and range of the traditional male role might well indicate internal conflict, but we expected that it might also grow out of a more indulgent and open environment which offered the girl at least the hope of having both sets of advantages. We expected to find this pattern primarily in the upper-middle class, among the more privileged daughters of professional and managerial families.

However, we find the opposite to be true in our data. The unambivalent feminine girls are more often from stable upper-middle-class families, while the ambivalent feminine pattern occurs more often in the lower-middle class. Whether we use the father's education or occupation to measure social status, we find that the higher-status girl is more often settling on a feminine identity that excludes conflicting goals, that is more clearly integrated around homemaking and personal relationships and does not pretend to an integration of feminine goals with the strongly individual themes of achievement, freedom, or self-realization. Lower-middle-class girls, on the other hand, more often aspire to the more complex integration.

We can suggest several explanations for this unexpected finding. The lower-middle class may define the feminine role in a way that is narrower and more restricted than the upper-middle-class definition. If this is true, then our finding can be explained in this fashion: when the upper-middle-class girl chooses and anticipates adult femininity, she chooses a role broad enough to encompass individual aspirations for challenge, self-development, and freedom. But the highly feminine lower-middle-class girl with equal individual ambition, knowing only a more confining interpretation of femininity, must say in effect "I want the goals of marriage, homemaking, and motherhood; I also want freedom and self-development which I cannot find in the feminine role. Therefore I choose a masculine job or daydream of the boy's freer life, or in one way or another make clear that femininity alone, as I know it, does not encompass all of my hopes." [7] The main difference between the patterns, according to this interpretation, would lie not in what the two groups want, but in what they see available in the feminine role from their day-to-day experience.

Another possible explanation is that all of these girls aspire to an image of femininity that is biased toward upper-middle-class content. The girl who is from a professional or managerial home can expect that simply by choosing feminine goals, she will achieve her dream,

[7] We are indebted to Lois W. Hoffman for her helpful interpretive suggestions in this discussion. Dr. Hoffman has findings which indicate that the narrower the definition of sex roles, the more girls will tend to reject the feminine role.

while the lower-middle-class girl must combine a higher level of personal ambition or greater beauty or some other distinguishing characteristic to reach her goal—that is, to marry a professional man who will provide her the context for the kind of adult feminine role she hopes to assume. Her ambition, expressed often in our interviews as an unusual or ambitious occupational plan, may be mainly a means of moving into the social circles where such young men gather.

Again, it is conceivable that our data reflect an historical change—that in a culture shift from feminism back to a more traditional acceptance of differences in freedom and power for men and women, the upper-middle class has led the return to older values, and that the trend has not yet affected the lower-middle class. Our data permit no critical tests of these interpretations, but we judge that the first and last are somewhat more plausible than the middle view. We find no evidence that the ambivalent feminine girls are more talented or more resourceful than the consistently feminine ones, as we would expect if we assume that the lower-middle-class girl needs more resources than the upper-middle-class girl to attain a common image of adult femininity.

Both groups of highly feminine girls have relatively well-educated mothers, but the mothers of unambivalent feminine girls are usually less well educated than their husbands, while a fairly large group of the ambivalent feminine girls are from families in which the mother is more highly educated than the father. Again it seems that the unambivalent feminine girls are from more established upper-middle-class homes. The question of models cannot be ignored here, however. The ambivalent girls, who are often ambitious to achieve masculine goals, have mothers who are also apparently ambitious, and who may provide a more active model to their daughters. A larger number of the ambivalent feminine girls are daughters of working women.

The groups do not differ in age—in fact, none of the femininity groups vary significantly in this respect. The nonambivalent feminine pattern is more common among Protestant girls, the ambivalent adaptation more frequent among Catholic and Jewish girls. But this difference is very likely an artifact of the status variation already noted. Farm girls in our sample never fit the ambivalent pattern, whereas they take the directly feminine position quite frequently.

Ambivalent Feminine Girls

The ambivalent pattern, we recall, combines an explicit integration of feminine goals with a desire for certain aspects of the role traditionally assigned to men. These are girls who, although strongly feminine, can and do recognize attractions in the masculine role. The term ambivalent feminine may be misleading, for we have no direct evidence that the girls who fall in this group have conflicting feelings about femininity. It is only that feminine goals are apparently not full enough or open enough, in their view, to offer all of the satisfactions they seek.

Our first suggestion about this group was that they would come from an indulgent, nontraditional upper-middle-class background. The picture we developed was of the girl who spends her childhood in an atmosphere of progressive suburban schools, in which each child is taught to think of himself first as an individual with unique talents to develop, and in which, according to some observers, sex-role distinctions have become blurred.[8] We thought that the double aspiration of these girls might be the product of an ideology and of specific training in the growth-dominated value system of modern suburban culture. We have seen, however, that the data do not support this view of the social background of ambivalent feminine girls. They tend to be from lower-middle class homes rather than from the upper-middle class.

The distinguishing features of girls in this group cluster in the areas of achievement and autonomy. While these girls are similar to the unambivalent feminine girls in their concern with marriage and motherhood, in their developed ideas about marriage, and in general social development, they also maintain a lively interest in personal achievement now and in the future, and are focused on individual development. Of all groups in the analysis, the ambivalent feminine girls most often plan to go to college, and most often daydream about future success in school and work. They worry and daydream about boys and dating (What is the most wonderful thing that could happen to you?), but they also give high priority to concerns and fantasies about success. They are not as consistently or totally oriented toward people and the feminine-social area as are girls in the other highly feminine group. They show a greater interest than other feminine girls in jobs and in real skills (as distinguished from social skills). They choose masculine models more than the unambivalent feminine girls do, and the women they choose are more often nonfamily figures who are selected for admirable traits of character, talent, work skills, and personal attractiveness. These girls apparently choose their models on more objective grounds than do the other feminine girls, who choose mainly family figures with whom they have, after all, more emotional ties.

[8] Our own data support the picture of suburbia as a culture that tends to homogenize sex roles, at least as these are expressed in leisure activities. (Compare our discussion of population density in Chapter 9.)

A finding that reveals both their achievement strivings and their autonomy comes from the question in which we ask girls to choose between a job that is secure and one which offers little security, but an opportunity for success. While the nonambivalent feminine girls are characterized by a strong security orientation, the girls in the ambivalent feminine group confirm their interest in masculine success goals by a marked preference for the riskier, more open job. They have, we judge, a greater sense of their own competence, a greater readiness to rely on their own resources than do other feminine girls.

The family milieu in this case is one which emphasizes autonomy. Parents of this group, we find, encourage their daughters toward independence and self-reliance to a greater extent than do parents of the unambivalent feminine girls. They apparently treat their daughters as we would expect traditional families to treat only boy children. According to the girls' reports, their parents typically give them some share in setting rules to govern their own activities (over two-thirds of this group have a hand in rule-making, compared to 50% for the rest of the population). When we ask them to describe "the most important thing your parents expect of you," girls in this group often allude to ego skills and independence. Compared to other groups, they more often say their parents expect them to "stand on their own feet," "have good sense and good judgment," and "stand up for their own opinions." At least as the girls report it, their parents are not so concerned with the idea that their daughters be popular and get along well with their age-mates, nor do they demand respect for age and authority as often as the parents of unambivalent feminine girls.

Both groups of feminine girls are more often from small families than from large ones. Even when we control for social status (that is, when we run the relationship separately within each of the two major social classes) this relationship holds up. Small families, in general, may imply a closer relationship of parents to each child, and greater attention from the parents in matters of goals and modeling.

We now summarize the contrasts between our two feminine types. The ambivalent feminine girl, along with her conscious integration of feminine goals, maintains a strong interest in success and individual achievement. She has a sense of her own competence, and looks forward to exercising talent and skill in search of personal goals. She is more often from a lower-middle-class background than is the girl who concentrates exclusively on feminine goals. Her family background is likely to include an ambitious mother; one who has achieved greater education than her husband, and who works outside the home. While girls in this group do not choose the mother as an ideal as often as girls who have a more exclusive feminine orientation, it seems evident that their active and energetic mothers stimulate them to strive for personal success in school and work. Both groups of feminine girls look forward to sharing in the material rewards and advantages of the middle-class life. The unambivalent feminine girls hope to reach their goal only through the channel of marriage, while the ambivalent feminine group sees at least two available means—individual achievement and an appropriate marriage.

The Nonfeminine Patterns

The one characteristic that all of the nonfeminine patterns share is a problematic social development. In most general terms, all of them show some flaw in this area, although the specific forms of the problem vary widely, from simple immaturity to difficulties of seemingly pathological proportions. The boyish girls and those who have neither strong feminine nor strong masculine goals (that is, our "neutral" category) seem primarily to be slow developers. The achievement-oriented girls have relatively specific adolescent social problems (that is, they are not successful in the competition for popularity and dates) and seem to use the future as an escape from (perhaps a sublimation for) their problems. The antifeminine girls show more general and more serious problems in all areas of social development.

Except for this one area of common difficulty, the patterns vary widely, each having its own distinctive features. Only the antifeminine group, those girls who actively reject the feminine goal of marriage, prove consistently homogeneous. The other patterns, although less clear or homogeneous types, show some interesting variations that lend themselves to consistent and meaningful interpretation.

The Achievement-Oriented Girls

These girls are similar to the ambivalent feminine girls in some respects. They are bright, ambitious girls who show an unusual investment in the occupational sphere and a strong desire for individual achievement. They gain self-esteem from job performance, they hold jobs more often than other girls do, they tend to choose nonfamily women as adult ideals, and to choose these ideals on the basis of work skills and personal attractiveness. A large proportion of this group plan to go to college, and they stress personal achievement in their plans and daydreams of the future.

Girls in this pattern do not reject the idea of marriage, but they do not, on the other hand, make marriage and feminine goals central to their future plans. Their ideas about marriage are less detailed and less mature than those of highly feminine girls. They are in general less socially developed than the feminine girls. They are less mature and articulate in their ideas and attitudes toward friendship; they do not worry or dream about boys and popularity as much as the feminine girls do.

Data on their actual popularity indicate that they are less popular than other bright active girls. They begin dating somewhat late, and they date less often than girls in any but the antifeminine pattern.

Their lack of popularity is not attributable to a lack of personal attractiveness or poise. They are, according to interviewer ratings, reasonably attractive and highly poised and organized. The fact that they impress the adult interviewers favorably, combined with their frequent choice of teachers and club leaders as adult models, suggests that these girls find relationships with adults easier and less problematic than friendships with their own age-mates.

Girls in this group are frequently from lower-middle-class backgrounds, and they reveal a desire for social mobility in their own job aspirations and in describing the jobs they would like their future husbands to hold. Their mobility striving seems to express a positive drive toward a different way of life rather than a rejection of family background, or of a reaction to difficult family relationships. Their relationships with their parents seem placid enough and even pleasant. We find that these girls have no sign of unusual conflict with their mothers or strong identification with their fathers. They do not, apparently, use their mothers as models in thinking of their own future lives, but their mother-daughter interaction seems normal.[9]

We think there may be a crucial connection between the two distinctive characteristics of this group—that is, between their adolescent social problems and their strong mobility desires. But we are not by any means certain of the nature of the relationship. Their lack of popularity may push them into a preoccupation with a fantasy future where life will be much happier, or their concern with the future may block normal involvement in adolescent preoccupations. Perhaps the two

[9] They choose their own mothers as ideals less often than other girls. In addition, their mothers do not look like high achievement types. They infrequently work outside the home.

factors interact in some more complex way. From what we know about adolescent clique structure, we may speculate that these ambitious girls have no access to the peer groups that would satisfy their status desires. They may find boys of their own status, who are most likely to ask them out, unacceptable or uninteresting. To minimize day-to-day frustration, the girls may focus on a future dream in which they have more of the prestige and pleasure they want. This living in the future may in turn decrease their investment in the present and in all kinds of adolescent values and goals. A finding from the question about daydreams adds some support to this view. The girls who have masculine job aspirations are the only nonfeminine group who report daydreams with any frequency. They are much more like the highly feminine girls in this respect than like other nonfeminine groups, although the content of their dreams centers strongly on individual achievement rather than on popularity and dating. They do indeed seem relatively uninvolved in adolescent values, focusing their attention and life instead on an image of the adult future.

The Boyish Girls

This pattern and the achievement orientation we have just discussed share a general attraction to the male role. In the case of the boyish girls, however, the attraction is expressed more naively—the girl says simply that she wishes she were a boy. Our guess was that this simple expression would come from younger girls. It implies no strong commitment to masculine goals. It may simply express the annoyance of a young tomboy that she lacks certain freedoms and bears certain social obligations because she is a girl. As such it would not necessarily imply a permanent nonfeminine stance. The active girl who clings to boyish interests in adolescence can emerge in young adulthood as a warmly feminine type.

We expected this group to be young, boyish, and energetic, and perhaps somewhat resentful of parental regulation. Our data bear out some of these expectations but complicate the picture somewhat, too, as data so often do.

The boyish girls are not significantly younger than any of the other groups, although the trend is in this direction. They do, however, seem psychologically immature; in some respects they seem more like children in latency than like fully developed adolescents. In answer to all of the general questions—about worries, sources of self-esteem, plans, hopes, and daydreams—these girls consistently emphasize current activities and boyish interests. They feel important and useful when playing competitive sports and games, they worry about current adolescent problems like getting parents' permission for activities, they daydream about doing well in school, but also about very concrete and immediate problems like being invited to a particular party or having to choose between two school activities. In discussing plans for the future, they reveal a time perspective more restricted than that of girls in any of the other groups. They are not much concerned with sexual morality, but show a kind of latency concern with other moral values like honesty, loyalty, and courage. One indication that they are late in developing is the fact that they begin menstruating, on the average, somewhat later than other girls do. They reveal consistently boyish interest patterns, preferring team sports and active outdoor entertainments more than other girls, and eschewing more passive or social activities.

Our data are somewhat inconsistent on the question of the boyish girls' family relationships. Their parents do not seem objectively more restrictive or harsh than parents of other girls. But they react to their parents as though they were unusually strict. We know from the questions on punishment techniques, parent expectations, and the girls' role in rule-making, that their parents are not extraordinarily restrictive. If anything, they are more lenient than average. The boyish girls make them out to be unreasonably strict. In the picture-story series, they portray parents as forbidding, and when they think of how a girl might want her parents to be different, they stress the wish for greater leniency, and greater freedom.

This tendency to picture parents as harsh and restrictive, when in fact their own parents seem quite average, fits a general impression we have that the boyish girls are irritable and rebellious. We find (although we had not predicted) that in any parent-child question in the interview, the girls are likely to take a view of the situation that assumes conflict, and to respond with a defiant, rebellious tone. They assume that if a girl wants her parents to be different, she wishes they were less restrictive. When they list the reasons a girl might break a rule, they suggest rebellion as a motive more than other girls do. They less often say they would confide in their parents if they had done something shameful or failed to obey. In general they consider rules as part of the parents' weapons in a struggle for power. And they are peer-oriented in a boyish sense, often regarding the peer group as a cluster of loyal partners pitted against the wit and resource of adults.

The desire to be a boy, then, reflects a collection of boyish interests and attitudes. The girls who express this wish prefer boyish activities, and also tend to look at relationships with parents and peers in a way that is more characteristic of boys than of girls. Although not significantly younger than the total girl sample, this group seems psychologically less mature. We have no clear understanding of the meaning of their immaturity—whether it indicates a retreat from developing sexuality or simply a slower pace of development—but the fact that girls in this group do want to marry some day seems to contraindicate a retreat from femininity.

Neutral Girls

A sizable group of girls who score low on the index of femininity give none of the critical nonfeminine answers. They neither wish to be boys nor aspire to masculine jobs, and they accept the idea of marriage when the interviewer asks them specifically about it. The girls are nonfeminine only in the sense that their future plans and current activities do not focus around marriage or feminine roles.

We explored two possible explanations for this lack of strong sex-linked goals. The first was that these might be girls who are generally immature, who have not yet developed any defined stance toward the future. We thought they might be young girls who are absorbed in adolescent activities and have not yet begun to connect the present and future aspects of adolescent identity.

A second possible hypothesis is that these are nonverbal girls. In an analysis based on the presence or absence of particular interview responses, we always face the possibility that the low end of the scale represents simply a low overall response to the interview. In the present case, this would mean that the neutral pattern is not an indication of lack of sex-role orientation, but simply lack of intelligence or verbal ability.

Our data support the first of these suggestions. The neutral girls are most like the boyish girls in all respects except in their attitude toward authority and in specific activity preferences. We noted that the boyish girls sounded a rebellious note whenever they referred to parents and parental regulation. The neutral girls do not seem nearly as uncomfortable with their parents' authority. In fact, they are rather more compliant and close to their families than the average girl. In activity, they differ from the boyish girls in that they much less commonly take part in active sports and games.

Except for these differences, the neutral girls are similar to the boyish group in their apparent absorption in early-adolescent concerns and their immature conceptions of social relationships. Most of these girls do not yet date, and their social orientation has not undergone the radical revisions and the maturing influences which dating normally brings. They are slightly younger than the sample as a whole, but the difference is not significant. Girls in this pattern, like the boyish girls, begin menstruating somewhat later than other girls.

They clearly are not of low intelligence. They are judged average on intelligence and verbal ability by interviewers, and they give as many answers to questions as the average girl in the sample. As a group they have a lower nonresponse rate than either the boyish girls or the antifeminine girls. This seems, then, to be a slow developing group, but one which shows no particular pathology or fear of growth.

Antifeminine Girls

This group includes all girls in the sample who say they do not want to marry. The American adolescent girl who consciously rejects the feminine goal of marriage is, we think, deviant in a number of senses. First, she takes a position that is statistically very rare. Only 5 per cent of adolescent girls do not want to get married. More important, she is deviant in that she rejects a status prescribed as the single most important goal for women, the only status aside from the religious life which assures a woman acceptance in our society. Realization of her feminine nature in child bearing is legitimately available only to the woman who marries, and a woman's access to conventional social circles depends on being married or having been married. To reject the goal of marriage, then, implies a turning against society and its regulated rewards. We suspected that it might also signal a fairly severe personal pathology, since it means in most cases that the girl is giving up the idea of feminine realization. Unless these are all very young girls, their rejection of marriage would, we thought, indicate a rejection of, an alienation from, the self. We expected this group to show signs of self-rejection, and especially rejection of feminine sexual identity. We did not have any formulated predictions about the background characteristics of this group, but we suspected that their family relationships would be unsatisfactory. A milieu that produces self-rejection and problems in the acceptance of sexuality and sexual identity must have strong pathological features.

The antifeminine girls are distributed through the age range about the same as the total sample. Not wanting to marry may mean different things to girls at the two extremes of our age range, and ideally we would analyze these differences. But the size of the total group did not allow this refinement, and we have had to treat all girls who reject marriage as a group.[10]

Our findings indicate with striking clarity and regularity that the antifeminine girls are psychologically deviant. They are in fact the only group of girls in all the analyses who show signs of severe pathology. They are extremely constricted, but this is not their most critical symptom. Despite their constriction, which, in general, leads to sparse interviews, they give certain responses significantly more often than other girls, and these responses are uniformly bad signs, symptomatic of poor adjustment and self-rejection. If sparseness alone characterized the interviews, we might argue that the antifeminine girls were simply low in intelligence.[11] But in combination with symptomatic responses, the sparseness takes on the aspect of pathology, and we conclude that these girls are seriously troubled. Their pathology apparently interferes with all levels of ego functioning, including the way they react to the interview.

Impoverishment marks their answers to all questions that deal with the future or call for fantasy and introspection. They apparently hold little commerce with the internal environment of wish, hope, and dream. So, for example, a third of this group say that they never daydream (compared to 15% of the total population), and only one in twenty of them reports a daydream which has the slightest fantasy quality. Over a quarter of the antifeminine girls cannot think of anything when asked to tell the most wonderful thing that could happen to them. An even larger proportion have no picture or plan of what their future will be like. Even on such relatively specific questions as

[10] One other problem caused us concern in this analysis. Most of the girls in this group are choosing the ambiguous and unsatisfactory position of the single woman, but a few are giving up marriage for the more established station of the religious. In the latter case, the girl responds to a calling, makes a positive choice for a way of life, and does not necessarily choose against marriage. Ideally we would separate these groups in analysis; but here again we had to lose a distinction if we were to realize any analysis at all.

[11] Girls in this group are also probably relatively low in verbal intelligence, although our data are not consistent on this point. Interviewers rate them low on organization of thought, but average on verbal ability. Coders, on the other hand, rate them low on verbal ability, and the coders judged each girl against a broader group of interviews. This peculiar contradiction in the data may reflect impairment in intellectual functioning rather than lack of intelligence. The relationship between IQ and personality is complex, and we are not convinced that IQ alone can explain the peculiar personal and interpersonal features of the antifeminine girls, although it undoubtedly contributes its share to their problematic adjustment.

their adult ideal, decisions they will need to make in the near future, and sources of self-esteem, a surprisingly large proportion (between 15% and 20%) of this group either say that they do not know or give no answer. They have trouble projecting themselves into imaginary situations more often than other girls—this difference appears consistently on all of the problem situation questions and in the picture-story series.[12] They have extremely limited ability in situations demanding empathy or imagination. We have the impression that these girls for some reason have constructed a dense defensive wall against the internal world. Theory would suggest that heightened adolescent impulsivity has forced a defense crisis in them. Youngsters sometimes use global repression and detailed attention to external reality as a defense against the intense impulses of this era. The reality they fix is a drab one because it has been purged of emotional color. Anna Freud and Helene Deutsch both describe this defense system. Deutsch views it with special concern in the girl since the free flow of intuition and introspection sacrificed in the process is so critical to feminine integration. She suggests that girls who have no adequate means of parrying and gradually accommodating the rush of adolescent sexual impulses use this self-denying system as the only alternative to being overwhelmed. It is a primitive defense system, and the fact that it comes into play at all indicates a severe lack of resources or considerable pathology or both.

A clue to some of the psychological difficulties of antifeminine girls can be found in their family relationships. They are, we find, from large families and are often first children. Their parents tend to be traditional and restrictive toward their daughters, and are considerably more punitive than the parents of any other group in this analysis. Over a third of this group report that they are physically punished when they do something wrong, compared to 13 per cent of the total sample. The antifeminine girls portray parents as suspicious (for example, on the picture-story series, only girls from this group think the parents would be suspicious of the girl's statement that she is going to join her friends), and express an almost unanimous wish for less restriction when asked how a girl might want her parents to be different.

Their parents apparently discourage autonomy. Girls in this group least often say they take part in rule-making at home. In answering the question about what their parents expect of them, they emphasize obe-

---

[12] See Questionnaire, Appendix A, for a list of the problem situation questions.

dience and respect for authority. They rarely mention independence and autonomy. Coders rated their parents highly traditional more often than the parents of any other group.

Their home life is characterized not only by strictness, but also by conflict. In the series of questions about parents' rules, we find evidence that the antifeminine girls resent their parents' regulation and that they both rebel against and rely on this external control. They indicate a conflict-laden family atmosphere when asked if they ever disagree with their parents and whether they have conflict with their brothers and sisters. In particular they seem to have strong conflict with their mothers.

One further outstanding feature of their family relationships is the very heavy burden of responsibility the antifeminine girls have in the home. A large proportion of the group (31%) have major responsibility for maintaining the household. In general, the antifeminine girls carry more home duties than other girls do.

Girls in this group almost all wish they were boys. The reasons they give refer either to the greater freedom they would have, or to some distaste for femininity (for example, if they were boys, they would not have to worry about clothes or grooming). A few antifeminine girls would be boys to escape basic feminine functions—menstruation and childbirth. They are the only girls in the sample who express this open rejection of biological femininity. A large proportion of this group started menstruating later than average, but they do not report unusual difficulties during their menstrual periods.

Antifeminine girls are unlike boyish girls in most respects. They are not like the boyish girls, so involved in current activities that they cannot yet concentrate on the adult future. Their rejection of femininity, or the underlying conflict which it symbolizes, affects their current activities adversely too. They have either little opportunity or little energy for adolescent activity. They have the lowest average activity index of any of the groups. They do not date, they are less likely than other girls to hold paying jobs, and they have very few leisure interests. While these findings may all be attributed to harsh environmental circumstances, psychological problems are probably at the root of their awkward performance in the interview. Interviewers rate them low in self-confidence, organization of thought, and personal attractiveness.

In discussing jobs and future occupational plans the antifeminine girls stand out from other groups by virtue of an overriding concern with security. They strongly prefer a secure job to a risky but more promising one, they choose stability over other job characteristics (high pay, travel, and interesting work) more than any other group, and a few girls from this group spontaneously give as a reason for choosing a particular job the fact that "there are lots of jobs in that field" or "it's easy to get that kind of work." A striking insecurity about one's own resources must, we think, underlie such an unimposing basis for choosing a job. It is as though they feel fortunate to find any work, and are too intimidated and unsure to make demands for anything more from the environment.

They apparently also have problems in the area of friendship and peer relations. They are relatively undeveloped in concepts of friendship—as are all of the less feminine girls. But they also have idiosyncratic ideas about friendship that reflect again the nature of their psychological adjustment.

The same lack of self-esteem, the same insecurity they express in their future plans appears in the area of friendship. In answer to the question "Are there any girls you would not be friends with?" the antifeminine group least often would exclude anyone. Security is their dominant concern in friendship. They most often think a friend should be loyal, and should have the moral courage to defend a friend when someone else attacks her. They feel themselves, accurately, to be outside the solid peer culture, and so in need of friendly defenders and loyal companions.

We have suggested that these girls are self-rejecting, and particularly that they do not accept their own sexual development. They tend to deny sexuality in their discussion of interpersonal relations and friendship. When they suggest reasons why a girl might be unpopular with her peers, or popular with boys, when they discuss reasons for their own exclusion of some girls from friendship, and in answering the projective question about what a girl might have done to cause a sense of shame—they consistently refer to sexual issues less than other girls do. At any point in the interview where sexual references are conceivable, this group is distinguished by the fact that they make such allusions less often than other groups in the femininity analysis.

The picture emerging from these data, then, looks something like this. The oldest girl in a large and economically deprived family [13] lives a confined and difficult life. She shares the sense of deprivation with brothers and sisters, but has an additional burden by virtue of her sex and ordinal position. Inevitably she is given heavy responsibility in

[13] We found, although we did not predict, that girls in this group were predominantly from lower class families.

the family—helping with housework and with the younger children; she becomes a kind of assistant mother. The first child in a large family, if he is a boy, may be pushed rapidly toward independence and self-support. And younger children in a large brood have the advantage of being nurtured by a mother who already has assistants. But the oldest daughter is very likely to be rushed into responsibility without any of the advantages of independence and choice. If, in addition, a girl is unlucky enough to have parents who are both traditional and punitive, her problems are compounded. She is introduced too early to the hardest and most burdensome aspects of a traditional version of adult femininity. It is not surprising that girls who grow up under these conditions are not as eager to marry and have children. They have already been surrogate mothers prematurely, and have known too much of the disadvantages of the role without any of its gratifications. They are aware of the fact that their brothers receive more desirable treatment, and this almost certainly adds another basis for their rejection of the feminine sex role.

We may conclude our discussion of femininity with a summary of our findings. There is, we find, an image of adult femininity broadly held among adolescent girls. This image draws its features from the picture presented in the mass media—a picture of an active, attractive woman who plays a number of roles (wife, mother, companion, and citizen) effectively in the setting and style of upper-middle-class suburban culture. The formal qualities of life are more crucial to this concept of adult femininity than is any specific content. The girl's image of adulthood contrasts with boy's in which we find a greater stress on specific work content and individual taste and skill.

This difference, we should emphasize, reflects the essential difference between the identity tasks confronting the boy and girl and is appropriate to the different identity resolutions they must make. The boy designs his own identity in answer to the questions "What will I do?" "What will my work be?" For the girl this identity question must also be answered, but the answer is very general (I will be a wife and mother). The content of being a lawyer is fairly specified; much of the content of being a wife and mother will depend on whom one marries and so must wait to be filled in at some later date. The formal features of the image, those which deal with life style, lend themselves more easily for concretizing an image of the future.

The integration of a concept of adult femininity—a clear orientation toward feminine goals—plays an important anchoring function in the girl's adolescent adaptation. This function is roughly equivalent to that served by the boy's occupational aspiration. We have seen that girls who look to future femininity with pleasure and anticipate some of the aspects of the feminine role in current activities show strong feminine features in other areas of thought and behavior and active, effective ego development.

Our pattern analysis yielded a refinement in our understanding of adolescent feminine development, particularly of girls who do not have a strong feminine orientation. Clearly the lack of explicit feminine goals can mean three quite different things in adolescence. It may mean simply that the girl is psychologically immature and not yet ready to concern herself with any adult role. It may reflect a somewhat masculine concentration on individual achievement and occupational plans —which, however, may still serve basically feminine needs in girls who cannot express these needs openly. Finally, the lack of conscious feminine goals may represent a rejection of femininity and a serious problem in the girl's self-concept and self-esteem. The last of these meanings implies a serious degree of pathology, and it is the only nonfeminine pattern which seems to be more than a minor variation in form or pace of normal feminine development.

EIGHT

Family Structure

In the two chapters that follow, we alter somewhat the analytic perspective we have used up to this point. Our emphasis has been largely "psychological"—that is, we have stressed developmental, intrapsychic, and interpersonal frames of reference. In these chapters "objective" variables are highlighted. Although our dependent variables remain, on the whole, psychological, we look at the influence of situation on motive, attitude, and experience. This chapter examines the effects of variations in the composition of the family. What is the influence of a broken home—broken by divorce or by the father's death? What differences, if any, are produced by family size? What are the effects of birth order? And finally, what does it mean in the adolescent experience if the mother works? These are the simple questions this chapter will pose; the answers are, for the most part, anything but simple.

The Broken Home

We begin with those instances in which there is a traumatic variation in family structure—families disrupted by death or divorce. It is patent that these are potentially pathogenic events; yet it is our impression that the quality and the extent of disturbance arising from broken homes remain uncertain, anecdotal matters. Much of what we know comes from observations of families so disturbed by these events that they receive professional attention. Our study, sampling the total population, allows us to explore families and children not so acutely damaged by these situations.

262

We cannot claim too much for our findings: the interview may capture some but surely not all of the effects of the broken home on the adolescent. A further limitation is that all instances in each group, divorce and parental death, are treated together; that is, we do not distinguish, in either case, between recent and long-standing events. Nevertheless, the results are, we feel, suggestive. Finally, we included in the following analyses only those subjects who are living with the mother. There were very few instances where the father had custody of the children of divorce, and few where the mother had died and the children were living with the father.

Children of Divorce—the Sons

These boys present a rather sharp distinctive picture. Let us begin by summing it up—they are overconfident, defiant, overassertive —somehow we can almost see them swaggering about, as some adolescent boys do, in what is nearly a parody of masculinity. They seem to have problems in several areas—in the internalization of standards, in coming to terms with authority, and (perhaps) in self-control. Here are some of the findings which make us think so.

When we compare them with boys who come from intact families they more often tell us the following things: that they cannot think of a rule they would never break; that parents make rules for their own benefit, rather than the child's; that a boy might break a rule for impulsive or rebellious reasons. Coder judgments rate them high on reliance on adult authority, generally a sign of the authoritarian syndrome, and on rebelliousness. On the projective pictures they say more often than other boys do that the hero would go home out of fear, and they do not as frequently allude to ideas of trust and responsibility.

We have seen failures in internalization in other groups of boys, particularly the downward-mobile, but we have never seen so consistently rebellious a picture as these boys show. One telling example is in their rather exaggerated response to the question "Have you ever broken a rule?" Most boys answer with a matter of fact "yes." These boys emphasize the point, by saying "Of course" or by referring to the frequency of their misdeeds. Another instance comes in response to the question about when a boy might break a rule. More than most boys, even more than most who are poorly internalized, they give answers denoting impulsive and rebellious motives. This assertive mood comes together with other ego qualities that we shall discuss shortly.

Why are these youngsters bristling so? They seem to feel that they are being treated harshly, and very likely they are right. In the projective pictures they portray the parents as "very strict" more often than other boys do. They are more likely to disagree with the mother and they more frequently report physical punishment. It is not hard to imagine what may be going on in these homes. The mother, alone and uncertain, afraid of what may happen to a boy in the absence of paternal authority, bears down too hard. Her discipline is too heavy and too externalized. The son reacts with hostility, perhaps also sensing the uncertainty in his mother. He may then tend to rebel against her authority, which in turn reinforces her uncertainty, to initiate another phase of the cycle.

Very likely this is not all there is to it. If it were, we might expect to find similar dynamics in the case of homes broken by the father's death, and as we shall see, we find a very different pattern there. What must be lost for the boy in a divorced family is not only the sheer presence of the father but also the father's presence as an ideal of masculinity, the father as a certain type of "good object." Much of the time, we suspect, the mother will have devalued the boy's father, whether consciously or not, to subvert any tendency the boy might have to identify with a man toward whom she harbors bitter feelings.

We have one finding that bears on this question. We learn that these boys do not choose their fathers as ideals as often as other boys do. By itself this is probably not too significant, since many of them may know their fathers only dimly. What is significant, we feel, is that these boys tend to reject any adult ideal. More than other boys they are likely to say that there is no adult they want to be like. We may argue that this points to a general difficulty in finding and using masculine models. Without a viable model the boy may retreat to grandiose imaginings of manhood; a defensive, excessive, pseudomasculinity may result. (Add to this the likelihood that in some cases the mother might covertly encourage this, by investing in her son the wish for a forceful and manly protector.) Let us look at some of the evidence which supports this line of conjecture.

Boys from divorced families are more likely to be lone wolves. They do not very often belong to clubs or organized groups, and they claim to have "one or two very close friends" less often than boys from intact families. Although they have as many leisure activities as others, they choose isolated individual activities more than social ones, and they do not share activities with their families very often. What is probably more important than any one of these items is the fact that they tend to protest too much about their independence. When asked whether they would seek advice from their parents or their friends on a series of problems, these boys more often reject advice from either quarter. A similar independence of spirit appears in their attitudes toward work. They are more likely to prefer a risky job with great opportunities than a safe and secure one. In other contexts we interpreted this choice to indicate that self-assurance born out of a knowledge of one's talents. But here one generally found other evidences of ego strength. In these boys we fail to find this sort of supporting evidence. Their energy level is not unusually high; they are not well-internalized, nor do they seem to have established a genuine autonomy. They do not appear to be as poised to the interviewers, or as organized, or as interesting as adolescents in general. We argue then that the bold self-assurance we see in them stems not from a sense of their capacity but reflects instead a denial of weakness, an exaggerated masculinity.

Some other findings lend support to this view. They are more likely to say that given the chance they would not want to change anything about themselves. Although they read a good deal they are more likely to choose comic books and adventure stories, and less likely to read literature, poetry, or intellectually demanding material. On the draft their attitudes are strong and stereotyped. They feel they ought to go into the army for patriotic reasons and to defend their country. The one social activity in which they rank high is dating—they begin dating earlier than other boys do and date more actively.

When taken separately none of these items is decisive; taken together they confirm our earlier picture of stereotyped and driven masculinity. We can only speculate as to why things turn out this way. We do know that the mother is more likely to be authoritarian; and we imagine that she may, on the one hand, idealize certain male qualities and, on the other hand, devalue the masculine image. Another possibility is that the son may feel himself forced to be "the man of the family" and thus driven to assume the shell of masculinity. However it transpires, the result for the boy's development is fairly clear. Behind the mask of masculine assertiveness there are problems in the development of ideals, autonomy, and social life; authority relations, the internalization of values, and behavior controls are retarded and problematic.

Children of Divorce—the Daughters

We have seen that divorced mothers treat their sons strictly. It is immediately evident in the data on girls that the same climate of authority is reported by the daughters from divorced homes. Parental strictness emerges in the same items as in the study of boys. For the girls study we had additional measures available—and on all of these the daughters from divorced families more often give answers reflecting strict parental control. They do not as often have a part in making rules at home as do girls from intact families. When asked what their parents expect of them, the girls more often mentioned obedience and respect for authority. In answer to an indirect question about a girl's dissatisfaction with her parents they more often cite her unhappiness about parental restriction and harshness, and less often mention a desire for a closer relationship to the parents. We have noted that sons react to this heavy-handedness of control by impulsivity and defiance, by problems in internalization, in the relation to authority, and in self-control. We sense that the boy, attempting to salvage his independence, overasserts that rebelliousness not uncommon in adolescent boys. But girls react differently; on the surface, at least, they acquiesce to the mother's authority. They do not differ from other girls in their responses to questions about rules, promises to parents, or reactions to adult authority—those questions to which boys from divorced families gave defiant and externalized answers. The girls, again on the surface, are no more annoyed or disgruntled with their mothers' rules than other girls are. They tell us just as frequently that they feel their mothers' rules to be right.

Yet this is the surface, and just below it is some chafing, some alienation. We have seen that they fix on the issue of harsh restriction when they think about what would make a girl wish her parents were more like the parents of friends. Even more important, we feel, is the evidence which indicates that although they comply with the mother's authority, they do not as frequently identify with it. The reader may recall that in response to the projective pictures, a sizable group of girls have the heroine reassure the parents who have imposed a restriction—saying that "Of course she will behave like a lady." A smaller group have the girl shocked that the parents think it necessary to remind her how to behave. We took both of these answers as signs of sensitivity to and identification with the parents' point of view. We find that girls from divorced families do not give either answer as often as other girls do. Another datum in the same direction is that when asked why parents make rules, they less frequently give answers which indicate an identification with the parents; they do not as often think parents make rules to help children mature, or to protect them, or to let children know what is expected of them. And they do not as often justify the parents' position in answer to the question about our projective "Jane," who wishes the parents were more like the parents of other girls.

We have argued earlier that an increasing degree of identification with the parents' viewpoint characterizes feminine character development during adolescence. Girls seem to move from a simple and direct acceptance of external rules, to a more complex and self-aware compliance, in which they accept regulations they consider appropriate and in keeping with their own desires. Younger girls obey their parents because they should and because the parents are right; older girls because they learn to agree with the parents about how children ought to behave. In this respect girls from divorced families do not keep pace with other girls. Nevertheless this relative absence of identification, if that is what it is, does not seem to reflect severe problems in the areas of authority and control. The girls do not show flaws in their internalization of values and controls; they differ only in the style of compliance.

What seems to happen is that girls in this group handle their troubles with their mothers not so much by ambivalence as by withdrawing from them psychologically. We recall that the boys from divorced homes did seem to be ambivalent. They saw mother as punitive, and responded by defiance; yet they were apt to feel that a friend cannot be as close as a family member. Daughters from divorced homes, on the other hand, are more likely than those from intact ones to opt for the friend as against the family. This is one of a number of signs of psychological distance from the mother. The girls are also less likely to name their own mothers as adult models. In response to the question about the girl with a good job away from home who is asked by mother to return home, they reject the mother's plea out of hand more frequently than other girls do. When suggesting confidantes for the girl who has "done something she thought she would never do," they tend to think either of a close friend or some adult woman outside the family; they do not as often think the girl would confide her troubles to her mother.

Fortunately, this apparent coolness toward the mother does not seem to generalize to others. Instead, the girl seeks other adult models, and cultivates peer friendships. When we take these one at a time: girls from divorced backgrounds do not, as equivalent boys tend to do, reject adult models in general; instead they relocate the model function, picking women teachers and other women outside the family. They do not more often say that there is no adult that they want to be like.

Girls from divorced homes also rely on and are mature in the ways of friendship. We have already seen that these girls more often believe that they can be closer to a friend than a family member; and that a girl would confide a secret to her best friend. In other respects as well these girls are mature in their understanding of like-sexed friendship. Their conceptions of friendship involve ideas of trust, mutual support, and sympathetic understanding. More than other girls they see a friend as someone with whom to share feelings and confidences. They believe that popularity is gained through a sensitivity to the needs of others, and they value loyalty to a girl friend above occasional dating opportunities, more often than other girls. We have already indicated —although the data are suggestive rather than definitive—that boys from divorced homes may have problems in relations both to peers and to adult males. This is not so with the girls. They seem to develop intimate friendships and demonstrate, as far as we can tell, a sense of affiliation and identity with adult women.

Aside from the coolness they seem to feel toward their mothers the girls show problematic signs in only one area—general social participation. Their dating patterns are similar to those we find in other girls. But neither do they belong to clubs and formal organizations as often, nor hold part-time jobs as frequently, nor have as many leisure activities. There is reason to believe that this reflects situational rather than intrapsychic difficulties. The girls report heavier home responsibilities than other girls do, not only in homes where the divorced mother works, but also when she does not. In either case the daughter's help is needed to maintain the home when the father is absent. These responsibilities no doubt diminish the girl's social life by absorbing a major portion of her time. Certainly the girls from divorced families do not show those signs of impoverishment we would find if their inactivity were largely a reflection of psychological factors. Nor do they give signs of personal demoralization, for they are thought by the interviewers to be as poised, self-confident, and personally attractive as other girls.

One important question remains. Do the seemingly strained relations between mother and daughter—the coolness, the tenuousness of identification—lead to problems in achieving a feminine identity? As far as our measures can tell us, they do not. On the index of traditional femininity the girls obtain an average score slightly, although not significantly higher than girls from intact families. They daydream about marrying and having children more frequently than other girls do, and less often about achievement, jobs, and future plans in general. In our measures of antifeminine attitudes we find that the girls stand out in two respects—they see advantages in being a boy more often than other girls do (although they express less frequently the wish to be boys), and they choose masculine jobs less frequently. Our evidence, then, does not suggest marked problems in feminine identification.

In summary, our data suggests that boys suffer more visibly than girls do as a result of a divorce in the family. The boys in this group seem to be affected in a great many areas of their lives—in their use of adult models, in their stance toward achievement and independence, in their relation to authority, in the development of standards and controls, and in some phases of interpersonal experience. The girls seem to survive the family breakup rather less disturbed—a strained relationship with the mother, compensated in other ways, is the most apparent negative outcome. We also find a reduced level of social activity but, as we have said, this may be due to reality pressures. Without the opportunity for a close clinical appraisal, we can only guess at what makes the difference; but we would guess that it is the loss and devaluation of the like-sexed model that troubles the boys' adolescent development.

The Death of the Father

Those subjects whose fathers have died provide a control for those whose families have been broken by a divorce. We can ask whether it is the brute fact of the father's loss, or the context of that loss, which is responsible for the apparent difficulties suffered by the sons (and less so, the daughters) from divorced homes. This section will show that the effects of paternal death are of an entirely different order from the effects of divorce.

For both sexes the results of the father's death seem to be largely situational. Financial pressures are intense and visible, and they produce a diminution of leisure, of frivolity, and—relative to other adolescents—a premature seriousness. Yet in other respects the youngsters seem to be emotionally intact.

The families live in straitened circumstances; and the children bear more than the usual burden of domestic and financial responsibility. Both boys and girls are more likely to work at part-time jobs than other children; and they work longer hours and in more adult-like jobs. The girls report heavier home responsibilities, more often sharing with their mothers the major tasks of homemaking. The boys more often contribute to family support, or maintain themselves with their earnings.

There is, as we would expect, an ever-present sense of financial exigency. When asked what boys worry about, the youngsters more often allude to financial problems; when they think about college they are likely to allude to potential economic obstacles. When the girls are asked how a girl might like her parents to be different, they more often think of changes in living standards. When asked how they would change their lives if they could, both sexes are more likely to mention easier life conditions.

It is also not surprising to find that these children have less opportunity for leisure than other youngsters. They report fewer recreational activities and fewer group memberships. Yet it is most interesting to note that they are not as low in group membership as are children from divorce-broken homes. The youngsters more often belong to a single club or social group, while children of divorced parents (especially the boys) are more likely to be completely without formal group affiliation. If we look at overall activity level, the children whose fathers have died are not strikingly different from others, since they more often work, and date about as frequently as other children do.

The gravity which marks the children can be discerned in several areas. When the boys talk about work they are more than ordinarily concerned about security, more frequently naming it an important criterion in choosing a job; and when offered a choice between a secure job and one that is riskier but offers more possibilities for success, they are likely to prefer the steady one. When they discuss their own vocational aspirations they mention concrete considerations. They think a job in the field of their choice will be easy to get, or always available and secure, or that the pay will be good. We see a similar seriousness in their reading habits. This is one leisure activity they list more often than do youngsters from intact families, and they are attracted to newspaper and magazine reading, and to more serious nonfiction books. They do not as often read comic books, travel or adventure stories, or books about sports and hobbies. These differences are especially strong for the boys, but they hold to some extent for the girls as well.

The girls whose fathers have died show their seriousness in the realm of fantasy. Their daydreams differ from those of other girls in two respects: they are less narcissistic and romantic, and they focus more often on unsolved personal problems. It is not simply that they allude more to the father's death or to family finances, although they do, but even in realms removed from these topics they seem more serious in their daydreams. They mention realistic and emotional problems more often than other girls do. For example, they may say they are not as happy as they would like to be, or they may refer to some unresolved misunderstanding with a friend. We see here a heightened introspectiveness and self-criticism which is by no means modal for adolescent girls.

The important thing to note is that in most other respects these boys and girls seem very similar to those from intact families. They do not differ on measures of time perspective, self-confidence, poise, or personal attractiveness. They are similar in moral development and in the growth of autonomy. Their mothers have expectations and methods of discipline similar to those of parents in intact families, and they are considered by their children to be reasonable in their application of authority. This group does not differ at all on questions and indices dealing with authority relations and parental control. They are not distinguished in the way they relate to adults or in their choice and use of adult models. They choose adult ideals from within and beyond the family circle in proportions similar to those children from normal families, although the girls more often choose the mother as an ideal, and less often choose other female relatives. Boys and girls whose fathers are dead almost never say they have no adult ideal.

In regard to friendship the youngsters are in general very much like others, although we find an interesting variation. On the whole, their understanding of friendship develops along a path and at a pace similar to those of children from unbroken homes. We find for girls a normal growth of sensitivity and understanding, and the boys report having close friends as frequently as others do. They are more likely to feel that a friend can be just as close as a member of their family; in this respect they are somewhat more advanced. They also spend more leisure time with friends than do children from normal families. Yet at the same time, they seem to reserve a greater degree of authority to the family in the case of problems. The boys more often would seek family advice on decisions; and in talking about a serious misdeed, the girls more often suggest the mother as a confidante. When asked the "lonely mother" question, girls whose fathers have died more often suggest that the mother come to live with her daughter and less often reject the mother's request out of hand. What we seem to find, then, is a strong sense of family loyalty, on the one hand, and yet a high degree of reliance on friends and friendship on the other.

The strong family cohesion suggested here probably grows out of the tragic event the family has endured, and the continued need for mutual support under adverse economic circumstances. At the same time the families have probably had more than ordinary experience with the function and value of friendship; friends will have played a major and a supporting role during and following the crisis of the father's death. Also the mothers probably have too little time for play and companionship with the children, and not enough money for certain forms of leisure. We suspect that in many instances the mother must rely on friendly families to offer her children the recreation and "good times" she cannot provide. The very conditions, then, that cause strong family loyalty may lead to a strengthening of friendship ties.

Family Size

Do adolescents raised in large and small families differ from each other, and if so how and why? The question is more difficult to answer than we might at first imagine. To begin with, size of family is related to both social class and religious affiliation; Catholics and fundamentalist Protestants have larger families than those in the major Protestant sects, and working class families are larger than middle class. Any analysis of the effects of family size must therefore control for class and religion, and in doing so, we reduce sample size and thus the precision of the analysis.

Even more vexing is the problem of finding an interpretive approach. Since our data are limited to the reports of the children, our grasp of family dynamics, here as elsewhere, will be largely inferential. When we speculate on family dynamics we discover that it is fairly easy to argue both sides of the question. Suppose we assume that the style of family discipline differs in large and small families—it is possible to reason, on the one hand, that the parents of large families will be more lenient, if only because their disciplinary energies must be dissipated over a larger number of children; or on the other hand, that given a large brood to control, parents will be forced to use sterner methods of authority. Or the question of affect: we might say that having a great many children produces an inevitable attenuation of affective resources; or we might conjecture that parents who choose to have many children do so because they deem children to be very important, more important than either success or pleasure. In addition there is the problem of determining whether the differences we may find between large and small families are situational or predispositional in origin; that is, is it family structure that makes the difference, or is the fact that different sorts of people, with different values and attitudes, have large and small families?

These uncertainties made us wary of proposing an elaborate hypothetical schema and keep us hesitant about claiming too much for our findings. Nevertheless, a persuasive and plausible picture of differences between children from large and small families does emerge. Perhaps the most striking finding is that children from small families, boys as well as girls, are consistently higher on measures of ego skill and development than those from larger families. The relationships are generally straight-line. As family size increases, we find a decrease in the trait or behavior being measured. The largest differences occur in those cases between the family with three children and the family with more than three children, although there are also large differences between one- and two-child families.

Children from small families have a higher activity level and seem to be more poised, and self-confident with adults. They date earlier, and report a larger number of leisure activities and memberships in organized social groups. As a group, these children show most of the qualities we have seen earlier in our studies of the upward-aspiring. They show a longer time perspective; they are more preoccupied with educational plans; they refer to personal achievement more frequently in daydreams and in thinking about the most wonderful thing that could happen to them. They are more often upwardly mobile, and the boys, at least, use achievement criteria in judging future jobs more often than do boys from large families. Fundamentally, children from small families tend to be active, energetic, and future-oriented.

These differences do not hinge on social class, although class and family size operate in the same direction. Within each of the two major social strata, family size maintains its effect on activity and other ego variables. Although we could not control for class and religious affiliation simultaneously and retain adequate sample size, we feel fairly certain that the reported findings are not merely an artifact of religion. Controlling for class imposes a rough control on religious affiliation, since the majority of Catholic and Fundamentalist families fall in the lower stratum. For Catholics we did run an analysis which controlled both class and religion and here family size seems to operate in much the same way as in the total sample.

We also find clear differences in the family atmosphere reported by (or inferred from) adolescents from large and small families. The children of small families seem to be close to their parents and in some respects more closely identified with them. They more frequently share leisure time with their parents, tend to rely on parental advice, and use parents and other adults as confidantes more commonly. They are more likely to have absorbed the parental viewpoint, although as we shall see later, this does not mean that they have failed to develop an autonomous value system. Boys and girls from small families, in this case families with one or two children, are more likely to say, in response to one of the projective pictures, that the adolescent would adhere to a promise to his parents because of a sense of trust or obligation he feels toward them. The girls in this group more often have the projective heroine reassuring her parents about her behavior, a response which we have taken to suggest a high degree of identification with the parental point of view. When they are asked why parents make rules, children from small families again show an identification with parental authority by stressing the parental wish "to protect children, to give them standards to live by, to help them mature."

In contrast, youngsters from large families are more likely to state or imply a sharp separation between parental interests and their own. They are much more likely to say that parents make rules to protect their own welfare and prerogatives, an answer uncommonly given in the samples as a whole. They are also more oriented toward peer values. On the picture-story questions they more frequently have the hero or heroine responding to peer pressure and breaking the promise to parents. When asked when an adolescent might break a rule they mention peer pressure more frequently. On issues of personal taste and behavior they more often tell us they would seek the advice of friends rather than parents, and are more likely to think of a peer in the role of confidante. Even in the choice of models, when we ask specifically about adults, children from large families name a larger proportion of models in the young adult category, older siblings, and other young acquaintances.

From what we have reported so far, we might come to the conclusion that adolescents from small families, so closely tied to the parental point of view, are less independent than those from large families, who are more invested in the world of peers. Yet this would be rather too simple-minded a formulation. The youngster from a large family tends to be less independent than ambivalent in regard to his parents and adult authority, and as we have seen again and again throughout this study, the ambivalence is essentially a mixture of dependency and resentment. Youngsters from small families, one or two children, have absorbed the parental perspective; but this does not mean that they have submitted to it unthinkingly. We find, in fact, that they are more likely to give evidence of well-developed and autonomous internal controls, more so than those from large families. These findings, we should say, are not artifacts of the social class difference between the two types of family; the relationships hold within each of the two major social strata.

Let us look at some of the findings here more closely; they are more impressive for boys than for girls, which is generally the case when we treat questions of authority and internalization. When we compare the groups, boys from small families score higher on the index of internalization; they less frequently yield to peer pressure in the projective situation, and they less commonly show an externalized view of parental authority. Boys from large families rely more heavily on adult authority, and conceive of it in more external terms (for example, Why do parents make rules? When might a boy break a rule? What rule would you never break?). And although they are more dependent on adult control they show signs of rebellious resistance to it.

The findings for girls are less clear but generally move in the same direction. We have already seen that girls from smaller families tend to adopt the parental perspective. They see the parents as protective, they have the girl in the picture-story reassure her parents, they cite the sense of trust and obligation to the parents. Girls from larger families rely more on authority and yet give some signs of an underlying resistance against that authority. When asked how a girl might wish her parents to be different, they more often mention a relaxation of parental strictness; and in discussing when a girl might break a rule, they are more likely to describe the strategy a girl might use in order to break a rule and get away with it. We have interpreted this last response as a decorously feminine form of rebellion.

From our earlier analyses of family dynamics we might expect these differences to be related to the style of family power and authority. This is indeed the case. The parents of large families, to judge from their children's responses, are more traditional, strict, and punitive in their exercise of authority. Their youngsters are less likely to have a say in setting the rule at home; they expect obedience and respect for authority more frequently; their children on the projective pictures more often portray parents as strict, and when asked directly are more likely to characterize their parents' rules as hard. Finally the parents punish their children physically more often than do the parents with fewer children.

The distinction between small and large families is nearly equivalent to what we have already seen between lenient and strict families. We find what appears to be a strikingly similar arrangement of findings, and we are led to propose a similar interpretive framework. As we mentioned at the beginning of this discussion, we cannot determine whether the parents of many children are drawn to authoritarian methods of control because of the peculiar structure of the large family, or whether more fundamental differences between these types of parents, in values or personality qualities, are responsible for the differences in family style and ultimately in their children. Our own disposition, is to emphasize a difference in values. We would guess that the parents of small families more commonly share a complex of values characterized by a stress on personal responsibility and individual achievement. In raising their children they would stress early independence and the internalized sense of morality which supports that independence. Very likely they believe that the parents help to develop the child and devote themselves conscientiously to the child's training. They emphasize achievement, success, and the kind of "full life" that is to be found through vocational and social mobility. We would guess that they have, consciously or not, determined to commit their resources, both emotional and financial, to maximizing the child's educational and social opportunities.

It is extremely important to keep in mind that our adolescent subjects were conceived and born, for the most part, at the end of the depression and before our country's entrance into the second World War. Their parents are of a generation in which a large family did not have quite the cachet it enjoys today and when it was more commonly a part of middle-class practice and ideology to limit families in order to provide "opportunities" for one's children. It may well be that the differences between large and small families are diluted in the present generation of adolescents—those born in the period of postwar affluence. Or it may be that the differences we have described maintain themselves, but that the cutting point has changed, that, for example, differences now are to be found between families with up to four children and those with more than four children. It is also possible that the postwar era has seen general changes in values, particularly in the meaning of work and achievement, that erode the relationships we have cited. Some social commentators have argued that a general attenuation of the achievement ethic has taken place, that a family-centered, leisure-centered ethos is replacing it. We are ourselves frankly skeptical that anything of this sort is in fact occurring, but if it is, it would act to change the meaning of the child, the significance of family size, and the pattern of findings our study has disclosed.

Ordinal Position

Ordinal position has proved to be a perplexing psychological variable. As our knowledge of it has increased, our understanding of its influence has become, on the whole, less certain, more ambiguous and qualified. Most developmental psychologists have long since given up the hope that ordinal position, taken alone, will add much to our knowledge of intrafamily dynamics. We are by now fully aware that the influence of ordinal position is modified by such factors as family size, and (perhaps most important of all) the sex of other siblings. Nevertheless, certain recognitions, some of great interest, are beginning to emerge. For example, it now appears fairly certain that the first-born are more often achievement-oriented, conscience-ridden, and identified with the parents. Our own findings on this topic are presented modestly; they are not particularly strong, but they do confirm some previous findings, and in some areas may suggest new paths of study.

The First-Born

Anecdotal accounts, clinical observations, and empirical studies concur: the first child is likely to be the recipient of pressures, hopes, and anxieties that later children are more apt to escape. His parents will generally be overattentive and overambitious, excessively eager that the child validate their worth as parents, excessively fretful that he may depart from some ideal standard, overstern and yet overindulgent. This close absorption of the parents in the child leads, on the whole, to the "first-child" pattern we alluded to earlier. First-borns are far more likely to achieve eminence, and, in fact are more likely to receive higher education; superego internalization, sometimes of an inhibiting sort, is a conspicuous feature of character; they are more often sensitive, withdrawn, "nervous," and less often gregarious and popular with peers.

Our findings confirm many of these expectations. Although differences between first-born and others are relatively small, this is in large part due to restricted sample size after simultaneous controls on social class and family size.

First-born children, both boys and girls, are more often achievement-oriented. They are more frequently upward-aspiring and have more ambitious educational goals. They give achievement-related answers to a number of questions: in their spontaneous reasons for choosing a job, in selecting among criteria for jobs, and in their discussions both of current concerns and future decisions. First-born girls more often daydream about career goals and personal achievement. All in all, these data support previous findings on the drive and ambition of the first-born.

A high degree of identification with parental values is also evident, as well as a tendency to assimilate themselves toward the adult world. First children are more likely to take the parental attitude in regard to rules. They state that parents make rules to help and guide their children, and that children would be confused and lost without rules. In response to the picture-story item, they have the child reassure the parents. They tell us they would never break a rule that would cause pain to the parents, and first-born girls stress their positive feelings about parental rules. For the first-born, sources of self-esteem cluster in two categories—taking adult-like roles, and receiving praise and recognition from adults.

The first-born show an atypical pattern in one other area—social skills. Interviewers rate them high on poise, self-confidence, and attractiveness (which may reflect their ease with adults). They date early, and report a greater number than most of group memberships. These findings in some sense contradict the picture of the first-born child as withdrawn, not too popular, and not too gregarious; but then our findings, on dating and group membership, may reflect this group's drive and eagerness to succeed. Here, as elsewhere, we must be cautious about apparent contradictions of other findings, because of differences in measures, sample, and so on. In general, our findings clearly lend support to the fairly well established picture of the first-born child, as responsible, "adult," and oriented toward success.

The Middle Child

The literature on middle children is less consistent and coherent than what we find on first children, not surprisingly, since the middle child position is intrinsically more variable than that of the first, more subject to influence by sex of older and younger siblings, spacing between siblings, and so on. Our general assumption, however, was that middle children would show some signs of demoralization, having suffered from competition with older children, and having experienced displacement by the younger. We guessed that these children might well demonstrate some difficulties of adjustment during adolescence, although our expectations were, it should be said, rather unspecific.

The analysis of the data produced some interesting findings that lend partial, but only partial, support to this view. Middle children are distinctive in two areas—mobility aspiration and the development of internal controls. Middle children are significantly over-represented in our group of boys whose vocational goals are downward mobile. Among girls, middle children are less likely than either first-born or youngest to aspire to upward social movement.[1] Downward-mobility aspiration is one of the most important signs of demoralization we discovered in the entire analysis of interviews with boys, and the fact that middle children fall in the group more than others has, we think, a good deal of importance.

Since downward aspiration is generally associated with faulty development in processes of internalization and behavior controls, it is not surprising that the middle-child group shows signs of this developmental failure. In boys the findings are both striking and consistent. Boys who are middle children rate low on the index of internalization, and give a higher proportion of noninternalized responses to almost all of the individual questions about rules, values, and personal controls. They think a boy would break a rule when he could get away with it or when he was pressed by his peers to do so, and they do not think that the boy in the picture-story test could withstand peer pressure to break his promise to his parents. They rarely think that children could manage without parent regulation, and often say that if parents were to stop making rules, dire consequences, crime and delinquency, would increase. In all of these respects, they show less internal control and less certainty about their own controls than do either oldest or youngest children. They also—more often than children in other ordinal positions—say there is no rule that is absolutely unbreakable in their view.

Among girls we have less consistent findings, but again the general trend is for middle children to show less well-developed internal controls when any differences appear. The middle-born girl scores lower than other girls on the internalization index, and is more likely to give noninternalized answers to two questions aside from the index—the question about consequences that would follow if parents did not make rules, and the question that asks girls to think of an unbreakable rule.

[1] There were virtually no cases of downward-mobility aspiration among girls.

The middle-born girls do not show as strong an identification with the parents' viewpoint as the girls who are the oldest or the youngest in their families. This comes out most clearly when we ask why a girl might want her parents to be different. Girls in the other two groups say fairly frequently that the girl is probably just exaggerating normal dissatisfactions or chasing a shadow, but the middle-born girls almost never assume this parent-oriented pose.

In these two areas, mobility-achievement and internalization, the middle-born children seem to have more than normal problems. On the other hand, analyses of general social development, attitudes toward friendship, independence from the family, and the integration of feminity in girls did not reveal any significant differences that would indicate greater problems among the children in the middle position. We can only conclude that our evidence fails to support most of our original expectations, and suggest that our inconclusive findings may be a function of lack of refinement in our analysis. Perhaps an analysis that took account of the sex of siblings as well as the child's birth order might uncover more meaningful differences.

The Youngest Child

A consistent pattern of findings about the youngest child emerged from our data—in this case, a pattern we neither predicted nor suspected in advance. The youngest child seems to have more strongly developed friendship ties than his older siblings, and seems to rely on the family less for his social interaction. Boys and girls who have only older siblings share their leisure more often with friends and less often with family members, compared to first- or middle-born children. They have highly developed and mutual concepts of friendship and more often think that a friend can be just as close as a member of their own family. In the girls sample, youngest children reveal a strong sense of loyalty to their friends (that is, they would not forsake a friend for a blind date, and they are more reluctant than other girls to inform a teacher that a classmate has cheated), and they have a greater commitment to work out problems within a friendship rather than withdrawing from a relationship when problems arise (that is, they give more relationship-maintaining solutions for the problems). Among boys we find the youngest-child group more compelled by peer pressure than boys in earlier birth positions. They think a boy would break a rule under the influence of his gang more than other boys do, and in answering the picture-story questions they more commonly say that the boy would stay with his friends when they press him to break his promise to be home. Youngest boys also say they would seek their friends' advice in issues of taste—more so than either first- or middle-born boys. Youngest children in both samples share one other common response that we think reflects a strong social orientation. More than either of the other birth-order groups, our youngest children refer to being part of a social group and being accepted by peers as sources of self-esteem.

We cannot make a strong case for these findings. They did not follow from any idea we had previously held about development in the youngest child, but emerged fortuitously from an analysis designed for other purposes entirely. Nonetheless, we can suggest a conception that accounts for them, and hope that in some future research this conception may be tested systematically.

The findings for the youngest children are consistent with one of our original suggestions about the difference between first children and those who follow. The first child, according to this conception, will absorb a disproportionate share of the parents' emotional needs, while younger children will be freer to develop in various directions. We have noted a dependent quality in the first-born group, a tendency to orient toward parents and other adults in their social relations. This contrasts quite sharply with the peer orientation (perhaps even domination) that characterizes adolescents who are the youngest in their families. The last-born children generally are less adult-oriented than other youngsters and they invest peer relationships with greater significance and greater emotional energy. Their tendency to center personal relationships in the peer group may be a product of several related features of the family situation. Their parents may have less need to bind later children to themselves, and so permit the child a greater range to develop critical relationships outside the family. Parents may also be unable to give the same companionship and emotional intensity to later children that they have offered the first-born. In some cases, at least, the youngest child will have been born when the parents are approaching middle age with its special demands and problems. In addition to simple physiological changes which the parents have undergone, other life problems may now demand a greater portion of their time and energy.

By their late thirties and early forties, men who have strong career investments are faced with the immediate demand to make their final maximum effort to establish a level of success. Other fathers who have no great professional aspirations may be pressed at this point by the financial problem of providing for their children's educations and for their own security in later life. Mothers who have several children and are beginning to orient toward the larger community through school contacts and demands, have less time to devote to the late-born child than they offered to the first. The last-born of a large family may have to supply fewer parental demands for emotional supplies, but he is also very likely to be offered less intense and abundant emotional gifts from his parents. He is in this event not only free to develop critical relationships outside the family, but encouraged to do so. His experience in the family gives him a background of skills and models for peer relations which may serve to channel his critical social needs in this direction rather than toward relationships with adults. Often the last-born child in the large family will have had his most formative relationships with older siblings rather than directly with the parents. And this special feature of his background seems bound to affect his later social development both by giving him special skills in peer relations and also by establishing certain patterns for realizing critical social and emotional needs.[2] Any or all of these conditions—more likely to mark the development of youngest children than of children born earlier, might contribute to the peer ties which our findings indicate are highly developed in this group of adolescents.

Sex and Ordinal Position: An Example

We shall conclude our consideration of ordinal position with a close analysis of a single problem—the effect of position on girls in two-child families. Our choice of this problem is essentially fortuitous. This was the only case where, after appropriate controls for family size and the like were made, a sufficient sample was available to examine the various patterns of sex and position. Even so, as we shall see, the findings are frail, apparently because of insufficient cases. Nevertheless, the data are of some interest, if only to suggest the potentialities of ordinal position as an independent variable.

Because of unique features of the first-child position, because parents are likely to invest their first-born with the large measure of their own needs and aspirations, including their unrealized personal ambitions, it seemed to us that a first-born girl might be at some disadvantage in the integration of an appropriate and satisfying feminine identity. An in-

[2] The extreme example of children who formed their central emotional ties to peers rather than adults is represented by the refugee children studied by Freud and Burlingham (1943).

tense interest in individual achievement, the distinguishing characteristic of first children, is a trait highly valued in our culture in the male child, but disapproved and discouraged in the female. If we can assume that parents will tend to press the first child more than later ones into precocious achievement and instrumental use of competitive skills irrespective of the child's sex, then we should be able to predict that first-born girls will be both somewhat less feminine than other girls and also somewhat less adapted to the culture's expectations of girls. This latter expectation might lead us to predict that girls in the first-born position would show more problems of personal adjustment than other girls.

When we look more closely at the implications of birth order for the girl child, however, we find both positive and negative features of the first-child position. Our culture, for all of its changes in values regarding women, remains highly traditional about the desirability of male and female progeny. Most couples hope their first child will be a boy. This does not mean that parents feel intensely disappointed with a first-born girl, but it does hold implications for the parents' treatment of the first-born girl and for her relationship to later children. As to the former, we have indicated that we expect parents to encourage a first girl toward competitive achievement and that they will be less likely to do so with girls born later.

As to the child's relations to siblings, the first-born probably has unique difficulties in yielding and sharing with later children, since this birth position is the only one which includes the experiences of the only child. In families where a first-born girl has to yield to a baby brother, we might expect her to have pronounced hostile-competitive reactions, particularly if the parents reveal strong traditional feelings of pleasure at the birth of a son. Dominance and competition, the adaptive responses to displacement, are again characteristics suited to masculine development but not to the culture's concept of attractive and acceptable femininity.

The girl who is born second, who learns early that she cannot succeed in competition with a sibling both bigger and more experienced, learns to forsake the privileges of power or to use techniques other than direct dominance to gain advantage. In either event she learns things which are functional to the feminine role as our culture defines it. She learns to yield to someone stronger or to win favor by being little, appealing, beseeching, and by using techniques of the less powerful.

There is one reservation to this view of the first-born position as the one which is the most likely to create problems in feminine adjustment. The older sister may, if her identification with the mother is particularly strong and effective, gain unique experiences in mothering. She may act as an assistant mother in relation to younger siblings, and in this way find a feminine way by which to convert her position and activity into an adaptive resource. Even in this case, we would expect her pattern of integration to be somewhat more active than the traditionally conceived feminine one, although her adjustment might be excellent.

As we said earlier, there was one case, two-child families containing daughters, where we could describe all the patterns of sex and position with four categories. Here we hypothesized that the girl who comes second after a brother will develop the clearest feminine identification. The older sister with a younger brother, we thought, might have the greatest difficulty in this respect. She would presumably experience envy toward the brother who displaced her, feel disadvantaged by him, and at the same time have certain competitive advantages over him by virtue of her superior knowledge and skill. As a first child, she will be the focus and dramatic embodiment of many of her parents' ambitions.

For all of our speculation and fond expectations, the analysis of birth order yielded modest results. This seems to us in part a function of lack of information. Some of our findings hint that there are important relationships here, but that they demand a study designed to probe certain relevant areas more thoroughly than we were able to do. So, for example, in the analysis of two-child families, we find that girls who are first children with younger brothers do have certain problems in feminine development and are clearly different in this area from girls who have older brothers. Yet the two groups are also alike in some ways, in contrast to girls who have no brothers at all. For example, girls who have a brother are more narcissistic than those who have only a sister, and they say that their parents expect them to be ladylike and mannerly more often than do girls who have only sisters. We suspect that the presence of both a boy and girl child in a family leads to sharper distinctions in certain areas of parental behavior and more direct and simple expressions of sex-linked expectations. The girl who has a brother may learn early that she must distinguish her behavior from her brother's, and that she has unique areas or techniques she can and must prefer in her appeal for parental affection. She must be ladylike while her brother can be rough; on the other hand, she can devote care and attention to her own physical attractiveness and her brother will be discouraged from showing too lively an interest in such matters. The day-by-day experience of contrast may lead to more sharply defined sex roles in these families than in families where both children are girls. We can only speculate about this, for we have no clear picture of the sex-role expectations parents hold for their daughters or the way in which they structure comparisons and contrasts between children. The few suggestive findings indicate that there are areas of family interaction and of a girl's development which are strongly affected by the sex of her sibling. But we have no information or too little information in the appropriate areas.

The other factor which we see behind our relatively disappointing findings is the problem of sample size and control requirements in this kind of analysis. We have, again, a number of provocative findings which must be set aside because they could so easily be a function of some variable like age or social class which cannot be controlled without reducing analysis groups to a hazardous point. Girls who are younger sisters (of either an older brother or sister) are physically punished more often than older sisters, and they tend to see parents as strict and restrictive. We cannot, however, make use of these findings until age has been factored out, and this reduces the critical categories to such small numbers that the findings are no longer reliable. Even with a large initial sample we meet the problem of diminishing cells in analysis of family composition. The solution for this problem lies in purposive sampling for narrowly defined analysis, and this, of course, is not a technique practical for our main purposes.

After this apologia, the reader may be surprised at the richness of our findings rather than their sparseness. We have, if you will recall, two major hypotheses: first, that the girl who is first-born will have greater difficulty with feminine integration than those born in later positions; and second, that where we can look at more specific patterns of family composition (that is, in two-child families) we shall find that the first-born girl displaced by a younger brother will have the greatest disadvantages in feminine development, and the girl born second after an older brother, the greatest advantages.

There is little question that the first-born girl develops an integration that is distinctive in certain respects, and this is true whether she is first of two children or from a larger family. First-borns are, as we have already indicated, adult-oriented and interested in personal achievement, more so than girls in other birth positions in families of the same size. Girls who are only children stand out in these respects even more than other first-born girls. On the specific issue of feminine identification and feminine development, however, our data are less consistent. We note a split in our findings concerning femininity. First-born girls in large families show greater ambivalence about femininity and less adequate feminine identification than do girls born in later positions in equal-sized families. But the relationship does not hold in two-child families, where we find no consistent differences between first and second-born girls in the various areas of feminine development. There is an inescapable class element in this break—two-child families are much more commonly middle class while large families are characteristically of lower social status. But when we control for the class factor, essentially the same pattern emerges in each class, although actual rejection of femininity appears most commonly among first daughters of large lower- and lower-middle-class families.

In three-child families and those that have four or more children, first girls score lower on the index of femininity than do girls later in birth order. This difference is sizable (63% of first-born girls score two points or fewer, compared to 40% of other girls in large families; the proportions scoring five or more points are 4% for the first-borns and 17% for others), and it holds in each of the major social classes. Girls who are first in large families are less narcissistic than their younger sisters, and they give fewer responses indicating a feminine orientation on a number of individual questions. They daydream less than their younger sisters, and indicate less active play with the internal world of feelings when asked how they would like to be different and what would be the most wonderful thing that could happen to them. They choose their own mothers as ideals less often than girls in later birth positions do, and they choose their models more often for skill and abilities or because they have traditional character traits. Although they do not apparently model themselves to their mothers' image, the oldest-girl group shows a traditional conception of family relationships more often than other girls from large families. They less often say that a friend can be as close as a family member, and they feel more often that a girl should yield self-interest in favor of her obligation to her lonely mother. This group seems somewhat less advanced in the development of friendship than do girls in later birth positions. They do not stress concepts of mutuality and intimacy in their ideas about friendship, and their solutions to problems in friendship reveal a more limited appreciation of the strength and durability of the relationship.

The last important group of findings concerning the oldest girls in large families comes from our pattern analysis of nonfeminine integrations, and here we find an important class difference that intersects birth order differences. In the two social classes we distinguish in this analysis,[3] we find some clear differences in nonfeminine and antifeminine patterns. First-born girls in each class are low on the index of femininity, but the alternative integrations they choose differ depending on class level. Middle-class girls who are first born fall into two femininity patterns more often that their younger sisters—the masculine-achievement pattern and the boyish pattern. First-born girls in large working-class families are different from their later-order sisters, and outstanding in masculine achievement and antifeminine patterns. The two groups of first-born girls, from the middle class and the lower class, hold masculine job aspirations in common, although the middle-class first girl chooses this alternative path even more than her lower-class counterpart. The critical difference between the classes lies in the choice of other nonfeminine goals. The middle-class choice is an open and naive fantasy wish to be boys, which, you will recall, is an immature choice apparently based on slow psychosocial development. The working-class first girl is much more likely to reject the central feminine goal of marriage. In fact, this group of girls accounts for 80 per cent of the cases in the entire sample in which girls say they do not want to marry.

From the point of view of our initial hypothesis, the findings for first-position girls in large (three or more children) families are consistent and supportive. But in light of the fact that the relationship between femininity and birth position does not hold up for girls in two-child families, we will need to reformulate our ideas to include family size as a factor in the relationship. Before we do this, a brief review of the findings for two-child families is in order.

The fact that a girl is the first or the second of two children will not predict her score on the index of traditional femininity. The two groups are indistinguishable in this respect as they are on most other measures of femininity, for example, they do not differ on the measure of narcissism, in the qualities of fantasy or intraceptiveness, or in friendship development. First-born daughters in these small families, like their counterparts in large families, are more active, more adult-oriented, and more interested in personal achievement than are girls who have an older sibling. And the single large difference we find between the two groups in feminine development reflects these differences in ego integration, particularly the first-born's high energy and interest in achievement. With respect to femininity patterns, the first-

[3] There were too few upper-middle-class families with four or more children to allow separate analysis for this group. Upper- and lower-middle-class families were therefore combined.

born girls cluster in the ambivalent feminine pattern, and less often (compared to the second-born group) in the nonambivalent feminine category. When we control social status, the same differences hold in the two social classes, although they are more striking for the middle-class group. Except for these two differences, the groups are essentially the same in their feminine adaptations. Girls who are only children follow the pattern of the first-born girl in two-child families. They are the most outstanding of any group in the frequency with which they appear in the ambivalent-feminine category.

This dual finding from the analysis of small families adds to the picture of large families, and, we feel, clarifies the difference in the first-born girl's position in the two settings. The girl who is first in a small family does develop certain attitudes and goals traditionally considered masculine, but she does so without apparent cost to her feminine integration. In the large family, internalization of masculine patterns does apparently inhibit development of explicit feminine goals. To some extent this difference may be a product of the heavier pressure which besets parents of large families and the traditionalism we have noted among these parents. The kind of complex integration that characterizes first-born daughters in small families, the successful blending of active, individual striving and feminine goals, probably requires a good deal of active involvement and concern from parents.

The first-born girl falls heir, we think, to a legacy of parental ambitions which orients her early growth toward a somewhat masculine-competitive pattern. Displacement by a younger sibling exacerbates the tendency to seek gratification and recognition by means of dominance and competitive skill. In order for the girl to yield this advantageous but somewhat nonfeminine path, or to learn to integrate socially prescribed, feminine-passive forms of gratification within it, probably requires active and conscious efforts by the parents to encourage and reward the specifically feminine patterns of giving and yielding. To take pleasure in more subtle, less active appeals for love and gain, the girl must be encouraged to use indirect paths when she has already learned more direct and active ones. This encouragement and teaching must come from the parents, and it probably requires, for its effective outcome, both devotion and a clear sex-role conception on the parents' part. We are suggesting that in large families no one of the children gets quite so much of the parents' attention as this outcome requires. If the first child in a large family, a girl, has learned in her early years to bid for recognition and reward by active and assertive means—she will in all likelihood not learn to convert to less direct and active forms.

Her parents will have too great a stake in her achieving autonomy and too many pressures from subsequent children to worry about the rather special problem of her feminine identification.

In addition to this, the first daughter in a large lower-class family apparently meets other pressures which turn her actively against a feminine integration. We have suggested (in Chapter 7) what we think these additional factors are—the premature and excessive responsibilities of surrogate motherhood which the first girl in a large family is likely to be asked to assume, particularly where the family has no financial resources for outside help. The girl who experiences the responsibility of motherhood under such pressing circumstances—where she must yield the ease and freedom of childhood for the hard work of adulthood, without at the same time realizing any of the advantages of adult status—may feel that the traditional feminine role has little to offer in the way of gratification. Other factors, the mother's inability to serve as an effective identification model, severe Oedipal conflicts continuously rearoused by the arrival of new siblings, the intensification of hostility toward the mother, and the need to repress competitive urges—these too may contribute to the peculiar stress of the first-daughter role in large, lower-status families. But they are forces we cannot assess directly with our data. In any event, reality pressures must be critical in determining the antifeminine attitude, since birth order alone will not predict it. Only where first order of birth and low status are combined do we find this particular development.

The analysis of two-child families, our special effort to investigate the interaction of birth order and sex of sibling, produced some interesting findings, but no consistent support for our speculations.

The first part of our speculation—that being the second of two children with an older brother would provide the greatest stimulation for feminine development—realized quite a lot of support. Of the four possible family situations represented in the analysis, these girls score highest on narcissism and on the index of traditional femininity. They begin dating earlier than girls in any of the other patterns, and they very rarely fall into any of the nonfeminine or antifeminine categories in the analysis of integration patterns. They are the least likely of any of the groups to wish they were boys, and no girl in this group said she did not want to marry.

Our thoughts about the family constellation least likely to provide an easy feminine development, the family in which a first-born girl is displaced by a brother, proved much less satisfactory. The girl with a younger brother is more likely than those in any of the other three family patterns to say she does not want to marry, and to wish that she were a boy. These are the only two measures on which this group shows signs of sex-role conflict. We have indicated already that they are high in narcissism—apparently the fact of having a brother at all urges this orientation—and girls in this group seem to have particularly strong and rewarding relationships with their own mothers. They choose the mother as ideal figure and confidante more commonly than girls from other two-child families.

In some ways the girl who is born second in a family of two girls seems to have greater problems with feminine integration than her first-born sister does. She is almost as likely as the first-born girl with a younger brother to wish she were a boy and to reject the idea of marriage. In addition, girls in this situation are low on the index of traditional femininity and the narcissism index, they are more likely than other girls in two-child families to choose masculine models. They choose their own mothers as ideals and confidantes less often than other girls from small families. Apparently the second girl in families which are limited to two children feels the weight of whatever traditional feelings and disappointed hopes the parents may have had about a son. The first daughter does not seem to feel this pressure as strongly, and realistically she has less reason to. The first girl disappoints the parents only in the minor issue of preferred order, if at all. But the second girl represents a threat to the parents' hopes for a boy-child, especially in cases where they plan in advance to limit their families to two children.

Apparently when a girl is the less powerful and skilled of two girls, she gains little of the advantage for femininity which we thought would result from learning to yield in competition and to use more subtle and passive techniques in appealing for parental affection. Yielding to an older and more sophisticated female may not provide a basis for feminine development, or the possibility of taking an assertive-competitive path may simply be greater where her competitor is another girl. We noted in our data some hints that the presence of a brother tends to sharpen parents' sex-role expectations for their daughters, and it may be that in a two-girl family, the younger daughter is not discouraged from assertive competition as strongly as the girl who follows an older brother. The parents may also, in their disappointment at not having a son, subtly encourage their second daughter to gratify some of their wishes by adopting a more masculine-aggressive pattern. This path may be even more appealing to the child because she cannot adopt the more feminine surrogate-mother role her older sister has assumed. She may, out of a simple need to distinguish herself from her advantaged competitor, hit on a more aggressive-assertive boyish adjustment.

We now see another reason for the breakdown in the relationship between birth order and feminine development when we move from large families to small. In the small family where the parameters of interaction are so narrow, we cannot consider birth order as a separate factor from the issue of sex. The fact that a child is first or second has little independent significance. At least in the matter of a girl's integration of a satisfactory feminine identity, it seems to be more advantageous to be first-born in a family of two girls, but second-born in a family consisting of a boy and a girl.

The whole analysis of birth order might assume other interesting dimensions if we were able to control for sex of siblings in large families as well as small. A breakdown as detailed as this, however, requires a study designed specifically for the purpose and one with a larger sample than we had. At this stage we can only assess the results of our own investigations as useful but by no means definitive. We have found interesting relationships, some of which correspond to prior expectations. But we have uncovered many more paradoxes and questions than we have been able to answer.

Mothers' Employment

Here again we deal with a variable that has a long history in sociology and child development. Beginning with the social movement that urged the desirability of woman's maintaining a double role—as individual worker as well as homemaker-mother, there has been a continuing and growing interest in the effects of maternal employment on children's growth and integration. Welfare bureaus have devoted considerable thought and money to the problem. The questions asked in these investigations are often highly practical. Does the mother's absence from the home encourage delinquency in the children? Does it affect the health and welfare of the family? How do women manage the practical problems of child care while they are working? Do family concerns contribute to absenteeism on the job (a wartime concern)? Finally, can a mother-substitute, either an individual or agency, adequately perform the essential functions of the mother's role? Can there, in fact, ever be a substitute for the full-time mother?

Research on the problem of maternal employment is not nearly as simple as it may first appear. There are many important distinctions to be made about the nature and extent of the work the mother does, the age of the child, and the kinds of arrangements which are made for child care during the mother's working hours. A good bit of the practically oriented research has ignored such refined specifications, and has suffered in consequence. Recent and more sophisticated studies have begun to distinguish among various types and conditions of maternal employment (Nye and Hoffman, 1963).

Our data on this issue have one important limitation—we cannot tell from them how long the mothers of our subjects have been employed or unemployed, since we asked only whether they work now. We cannot distinguish between children whose mothers have always worked and those cases in which mothers have returned to the labor force after raising their children to school age or later. This obviously is a crucial problem, and bars us from any definitive test of many aspects of the theory of maternal employment. Nonetheless, we can report some interesting findings about the relationship between the mother's employment and adolescent development. We can suggest a theoretical scheme to account for the findings, one which knits them into a coherent pattern.

Two things are clear from our findings. First, that the mother's employment has much more significant implications for the life of an adolescent girl than for the boy; and, second, that full-time and part-time work imply different motivations and meanings for the woman herself and for her adolescent children.

The analysis we have done is limited to youngsters from intact families in which the father is employed. Two preliminary findings about the distribution of women who work in major population groups should be stated at the outset since they are crucial to the validity of all of our interpretations. We do not, to begin with, find any consistent or striking relationship between the social class position of the family (gauged by father's occupation) and the likelihood that the mother works outside the home. Except in farm families, where only about 15 per cent of the mothers work, the proportion ranges between 32 and 45 per cent for all status groups in both of our samples.[4]

[4] In the girls sample, the range is 33 to 41 per cent, and the direction of difference is not the same as we move down the ladder of skills represented by the father's occupation. So the figure is 33 per cent for the wives of professional men and business executives, 41 per cent among wives of white-collar, sales, and clerical workers, 38 per cent for the skilled and semiskilled blue-collar class, and 41 per cent in the families whose heads are unskilled workers. In the boys study, we found the

The second finding concerns the relationship between mother's employment and the age of the child, and it also is a negative finding—that is, there is no relationship between the age of the child and the likelihood that his mother works outside the home. We know that there is a significant association in studies of younger children, but apparently within the adolescent range this breaks down.[5]

Most women probably make the commitment to return to work when the child enters school. By the time the child is eleven the mother is no longer delaying her return to work because of the child's age. A woman may delay the decision beyond this point for other reasons, including the fact that she has other younger children, but these delays will not bear any significant relationship to the age of our subjects.

These two findings reduce the need to exercise special controls in the analysis of the mother's employment. Yet we were interested in making separate analyses for the two major social classes on the grounds that the meaning of maternal employment must be quite different when the general economic position of the family is good or poor. We shall discuss the results of this controlled analysis after a description of our basic findings. We shall describe the results from the study of girls first, since girls seem most crucially affected by the mother's employment.

Adolescent Activities and Employment

On the basis of previous research and our own analysis of adolescent activity patterns, we developed certain conceptions about the meaning

highest proportion of working mothers in families of the professional class (45%), and the lowest proportion outside the farm group, in the skilled and semiskilled blue-collar group (32%). All other status groups are practically identical in the proportions of working and nonworking mothers (38% of wives of business executives, 40% in the white-collar group, and 38% in the unskilled blue-collar group). The largest difference in the analysis, between the professional and skilled worker groups in the boys' sample, is the opposite from any expectation we would have on the basis of economic necessity.

[5] Since the entry of mothers into the labor market has been shown to have multiple sources—economic necessity and the woman's desire to absorb increasing leisure are among the more critical factors that urge mothers to work—we might expect the child's age to have a greater effect in higher social classes where, presumably, the mother has a choice of working or not working, where simple economic pressure is not so decisive a force. When we analyze maternal employment in relation to the child's age in the higher social strata, however, we again find no relationship.

of full-time and part-time maternal employment—its impact on family life, the motivational factors that underlie the mother's work, and the significance of these factors for performance of the maternal role, particularly in relation to adolescent children. We looked at data on adolescent development and family life for tests of some of these derivations.

The analysis of adolescent activities that led to our formulations about full-time and part-time maternal employment can be summarized briefly. Both groups of working-mother daughters are active in some sense (daughters of nonworking mothers are never the most active on any index in our study), but the spheres of their activity are quite different. The single area they share, and in which they contrast with girls whose mothers do not work, is household responsibility. The proportion of girls who carry major responsibilities at home is larger where the mother works either full-time (22%) or part-time (17%) than in homes where the mother is not employed (5%). Girls whose mothers do not work most often report that they do token jobs or none at all (59%, compared to 43% of girls whose mothers work part-time and 42% of girls whose mothers work full-time).

Daughters of women who are employed full-time work hard at home, carry some kind of paying job, and date actively; in particular, they go steady more often than other girls at each age level. On the other hand, they report very few of the kinds of engagements we conventionally think of as "healthful leisure activities." They do not as commonly belong to clubs or other organized social groups, nor do they have as many group attachments as girls whose mothers work part-time or not at all. They have tried significantly fewer of the leisure activities suggested in a fixed list (compared to girls in the other two groups), and they have less interest in trying new sports, games, or hobbies. Fewer of these girls report any leisure reading. We gain the impression that the daughters of women who hold full-time jobs are active girls, but that their activity has a serious character. They work hard and their social life consists primarily of dating. They begin dating earlier than girls whose mothers are at home part- or full-time, and they go steady earlier and more commonly than other girls. Even in leisure they seem bent on early assumption of adult-like patterns.

Daughters of women who work part-time are outstandingly active girls, no matter what measures we employ. They are almost as responsible for home tasks as the girls whose mothers work full-time, and they often have jobs outside the home—not, again, as frequently as the full-time group, but more than girls whose mothers do not work. Practically all girls in this group have some formal group affiliation, and they belong to a larger number of clubs and organizations than girls in the other two categories. They date early and actively; they date as much as girls whose mothers work full-time, but they do not as often go steady. At each age level girls in the part-time group are less likely to go steady than are girls in the full-time category. Only after sixteen do they approach the full-time group in this regard.

The part-time group also has the largest number of specific leisure activities. They are enthusiastic about sports, games, and hobbies already experienced (compared to girls in either of the other categories), and they suggest a greater number of other activities they would like to try. In short, the daughters of women who work part-time are active in every sphere. They are different from the girls whose mothers work full-time in that they have a broader range of social and leisure activities.

Another difference among our groups in the area of leisure commitment is that the girls whose mothers work full-time spend relatively little leisure time with the family. They, more often than other girls, spend time "alone," and they share leisure activities with a friend more often than with family members. Girls from families in which the mother works part-time most often report that they spend their leisure with their families—more, even, than do the girls whose mothers do not work. Girls in the nonworking-mother group fall between the other two groups in the distribution of time spent with family and with friends.

From their daughters' activities, we can infer something about the mothers who work full-time. They do not apparently spend much time with their daughters or take a highly active role in promoting and supervising a varied program of leisure activities for their children. The out-of-school activities which their girls most often report, part-time jobs and dating, do not make as many demands on parents as some other activities. They require no special parent involvement, as a child's group memberships often do, and they require no special facilities or equipment as many leisure sports and hobbies do. Both part-time working and dating can be carried on outside the parents' sphere. We may have in the daughters of full-time working women a precocious separation of the child from the family. Their early and frequent steady dating and the fact that they spend little time with the family suggest that they have shifted some major portion of their emotional involvement away from the home. We might suggest further that they form these extrafamily involvements in order to supply emotional needs which have not been met at home, perhaps because their mothers are overextended in their own commitments outside the home. In short, we thought that a pattern of neglect might mark the families of women who carry full-time jobs.

Part-Time Group

The activities of girls whose mothers work part-time suggest quite a different family pattern. Specifically we get the impression of active parents who participate energetically in the child's life. They spend a good deal of time with their children, according to girls' reports, and their children's pattern of leisure engagement is one which implies parent involvement.

The fact that a mother works part-time in itself implies certain things about her psychological make-up—more, it seems, than can be inferred from a full-time job commitment. Economic factors do not, we suspect, contribute as simply or forcefully to the decision to work in the case of part-time work. Very likely all women who look for employment are motivated by economic desires of some order—either they must supplement the husband's income to make ends meet at all, or they choose to work in order to increase the family's level of living and enlarge the number of luxuries the family can enjoy. We suspect that women who work part-time are less often directed by economic interests of a bare subsistence kind. Since full-time jobs are generally easier to find than part-time jobs, we assign relatively greater weight to personal motivation as a determinant of this choice, and assume that the women themselves limit their work commitment. We suggest that these are women who, while they want to contribute to the family's economic well-being, are at the same time bound by a sense of responsibility to reserve their major emotional investment for direct care of the family.

This group may also include a relatively large proportion of women who seek in work some measure of personal fulfillment. Again, assuming that they are less economically pressed, and considering that it takes a degree of initiative to find part-time jobs, we might expect these women to be active and energetic, the kind of women who need some individual fulfillment beyond that provided in the roles of wife-homemaker and mother.

If these speculations are correct—and the high energy level of mothers in this group gains some support from the data on girls' activities—we might expect the part-time working mother to feel split loyalties and to have a rather complex personal integration based on a high level of energy and on a personal goal system in which one seeks challenges in the environment and takes pleasure in mastering them.

Women of this type would be similar to the "guilt-motivated" working mothers that Lois Hoffman has described in her study of younger children (Nye and Hoffman, 1963). These are women who enjoy their outside jobs and feel some measure of guilt because they choose to spend part of their time away from the family in a personally gratifying activity. To reduce the guilt over what they conceive to be a self-indulgence, women of this type show a pattern of overprotective concern for their children, tend to demand less from them, and to provide few opportunities for the child to learn through doing or meeting challenges unaided. They tend, in other words, to supply the child's needs too readily and completely through their own activity. Their children show the effects of maternal overprotection in dependency and an impaired capacity for individual problem-solving.

Our adolescent girls whose mothers work part-time do not seem overprotected. They are highly active youngsters. Their activities are too many and too varied to permit any conclusion except that they have a great deal of initiative and responsibility. Yet for several reasons we cling to the view that the part-time working mother is like Hoffman's guilt-motivated mother at least in her high activity level, her strong sense of responsibility, and in the fact that she works primarily because she wants to work and enjoys the work role. We could explain the difference in effects on the child, between our subjects and Hoffman's, largely on the basis of the age difference in the two groups. Many of our working mothers may have returned to work only when their children approached adolescence. Even women who work while their children are young may feel less guilt as the children gain maturity and self-sufficiency, so that by the time their children reach adolescence, most working mothers may be more realistic and less selfless in their expectations vis-à-vis the child. The active woman who overprotects a younger child may become a model of activity for the older one.

The girls in our sample whose mothers work part-time certainly seem to be using some high energy model. From the fact that they spend a good deal of time with their families, and from the parent-involving activities they engage in, we ventured the not very radical speculation that the mother is the model they use. If this is the case, and if modeling is the process involved, we would expect these girls to be independent and responsible as well as energetic.

Our data generally support these speculations about the girls whose mothers work part-time. They are unusually developed in the area of autonomy. They show an independence of thought and values generally rare among girls, and their autonomy is apparently permitted and encouraged by the parents. Altogether this group can be said to show a pattern of development more common to boys than to girls in our culture.

Their independence shows itself in many forms. For one, they have more open disagreements with their parents than girls in either of the other groups. They name more disagreements in answer to the general question, and in each of the specific areas probed—clothes, dating, hours, driving, friends, and ideas—this group is consistently lowest in the proportion who say that a particular issue is not a source of disagreement between them and their parents. They are particularly likely, compared to the girls whose mothers work full-time or not at all, to say they disagree with their parents about ideas. In a series of picture-story questions, girls in this group think the heroine would question a parental restriction more than other girls do. Thus, we get a picture of considerable verbal discussion and argument in the home. This pattern is apparently accepted and stimulated by the parents. According to girls' reports, parents of this group frequently expect their daughters to be self-reliant and independent; yet, at the same time they stress good manners and ladylike deportment. They allow their daughters a share in rule-making more often than other parents, at the same time that they maintain a clear and strong personal authority. The girls in this group picture parents as "strict and reasonable" in their exercise of authority more than girls in the other groups. They less often see their parents as lenient.

Another fact also leads to the conclusion that their self-assertion is encouraged. Although these girls argue and assert themselves with the parents, they apparently have close and happy relationships with them. They spend a good deal of time with their families and they show both love and respect for their parents. Girls in this group very often choose their own mothers as an adult ideal. Both groups of girls who have working mothers choose the mother more often than do daughters of nonworking women, but in the part-time group this looks less like a dependency sign than in the full-time group. These girls do not choose other relatives very often—their choices are not narrowly restricted to the family group. They show other signs of independence from the family—they think a friend can be as close as a relative more than girls in either of the other groups, and they are least likely of any group to say (in response to a projective question) that a girl should leave a good job to return home to her lonely mother. They try most often to work out some alternative solution to this problem. In light of their general autonomy—in these instances and in the apparent ease with which they disagree with their parents—we take the choice of the mother as a model to indicate uncomplicated respect and affection.

Two other series of findings fill out our picture of girls with part-time working mothers. They are, in the first place, highly developed and mature in their ideas about friendship. For all their warm and apparently satisfying relationships within the family, they are not retarded in friendship development.

The other set of findings relates to something we mentioned earlier —that the girls in the part-time working mother group may be developing an integration which does not adhere closely to traditional concepts of femininity. They score relatively low on an Index of Traditional Femininity—as do all of the girls whose mothers work. But this group shows certain other signs of a nonfeminine orientation—they choose traditionally masculine occupational goals more than other girls do. In line with this last finding—although not the same finding, since it is based on the jobs they want their future husbands to hold—girls in this group aspire to upward social mobility more often than other girls. They choose their fathers as adult models somewhat more often (although still infrequently), and they show some signs of moral development that are more characteristic of our boy sample than of the general population of girls.

They are slightly higher on an index of internalization, and markedly different on responses to two individual questions in the index. The daughters of part-time working women more often say that the girl in the projective picture-stories would obey her parents because she had promised, because of a sense of trust, and they are much more likely than other girls to feel that if the girl did break her promise to her parents, she would tell them of her misdeed later. They show, in our view, a sense of commitment to the promise they have made— more than do the girls in other categories.

These findings can be interpreted in light of our earlier speculations about the part-time working mother and her relationship to her adolescent children. We suggested on the basis of the adolescents' activity patterns that family relationships in these cases were strong and actively cultivated by energetic mothers. We find the daughters of these woman to be, on one hand, warmly related to their families and apparently strongly identified with active mother-models. On the other hand, they show a degree of autonomy in relation to the family which is rare indeed among girls in our sample. The modeling concept forms the theoretical bridge between these two findings:—the girls have warm and close ties to families which provide them a feminine model of unusual energy, independence, and responsibility. In modeling themselves after their mothers, they develop an autonomy which seems at first to contradict their close family ties. But this autonomy grows out of an identification with an independent mother and is encouraged by the parents. It implies not a rejection of the parents, but rather an internalization of their values.

The part-time working mothers apparently offer a model of integration that is not primarily based on traditional concepts of femininity and the feminine role. Daughters of women in this group express somewhat masculine predispositions in their occupational aspirations, their independence, and their desire for social mobility. Girls in this group not only aspire to social mobility more than other girls, but also they more often fit the pattern we designate as a masculine mobility model. That is, they expect to acquire high status at least in part through their own efforts to achieve high prestige positions. They apparently conceive future achievement as a family enterprise which they will share with ambitious husbands.[6]

Full-Time Group

We can turn at this point to the other working mother group—that is, to those girls whose mothers hold full-time jobs outside the home. We speculated on the basis of the activity pattern that characterizes this group, that the girls whose mothers work full-time receive somewhat inadequate attention and companionship from their families and that they turn to friends and boyfriends for the warmth and closeness they fail to find at home. Our findings in this case are not, however, consistent or strongly supportive of the initial hypotheses. We find no indication that parents in the full-time working mother group neglect their children or deny them emotional support. We have suggested that they do not enter very actively into their children's leisure lives, but,

[6] Another finding fits this general interpretation. When asked what kind of man they hope to marry, girls in the group whose mothers work part-time tend to stress ego skills and family values. They would like the men they marry to have talent and drive and also strong family values—to like children, enjoy family life, and spend time with the family.

apart from this, they apparently fulfill their obligations very much as other parents do.

We expected, for example, that signs of parental neglect might show up on measures of discipline and strictness, or in the attitudes adolescents express toward their parents. But we find no evidence of peculiar harshness or of rejection, or any signs of excessive family conflict among girls whose mothers work full-time. In fact, they tend to disagree with their parents somewhat less than other girls do. They show no special resentment toward their parents, nor do they express an unusually strong desire for a closer relationship with their parents (on a projective question about a girl who would like her parents to be different). Girls in this group admire and respect their mothers more than the daughters of nonworking women. They choose their mothers as models more frequently than do the girls whose mothers are not employed and about as often as girls in the part-time group. They think of their mothers in the role of confidante more than other girls do, and they are more tied to the mother emotionally if we can judge from their answers to the situation in which a girl is asked by her lonely mother to return home. They more often say the girl should go home than do girls in either of the other patterns.

The daughters of full-time working women show a mixed pattern of developed autonomy and unresolved dependency. The only interpretation which seems to lend any coherence to the findings is this—these girls are developed in ego skills which equip them for managing practical aspects of reality well and with ease, but emotionally their major commitment is still to the family. In this latter regard (that is, emotional dependency) they appear to be less autonomous than other girls in this age group.

We have seen evidence of their autonomy in practical affairs in the unusual work load they manage. They share in rule-making at home more than girls whose mothers do not work, and about as often as those whose mothers work part-time. Their parents expect them to be independent and self-reliant, and they are least likely of all three groups to rely heavily on adult authority.

With respect to emotional dependence on the family, girls in the full-time working mother group distinguish themselves on a number of items. In addition to their responses to the question about the lonely mother who asks her daughter to return home, daughters of full-time working women choose their adult models exclusively from within the family more than girls in either of the other groups. They have fewer conflicts with their parents than the part-time group, and are similar in this regard to the nonworking group. They also are less likely than the daughters of part-time working women to think that friendship can be as close as a family relationship. When we ask them to think of the person to whom a girl might confide a misdeed, these girls most often think of the mother.

Impact of Employment by Social Class

This peculiar combination of ego autonomy and affective dependence—and it is peculiar in that ordinarily we find adolescents moving toward independence at about the same pace in the two areas —leads into our second analysis of the differential impact of maternal employment in the two major social classes. It seemed highly probable to us that the meaning of maternal employment would be different in the two classes, and, in the case of the full-time working mother, this is borne out in the analysis. A part-time work commitment has a relatively stable meaning and implication in both the middle and working classes, but full-time maternal employment apparently depends upon different motivational sources in the two groups, and has distinct meanings for family interaction. The findings we have reported for this group represent a combination of two quite different patterns.

Middle Class

In the middle class the girls of full-time working women seem more like those whose mothers work part-time: they are relatively active, autonomous girls who admire their mothers but are not unusually closely tied to the family. They have a high rate of participation in leisure activities and in organized groups—higher than either working-class girls whose mothers work full-time or middle-class girls whose mothers do not work. They do not have as active leisure lives as girls in the middle-class part-time group, but the differences between the two patterns are not large on our measures of leisure activity.

The serious and adult-like activities decrease in this group when we factor out class. Middle-class girls in the full-time pattern do not have as much responsibility at home, and they do not hold part-time jobs as often as girls in the working class whose mothers work full-time. They date just as actively, but again look more like other girls of their class level whose mothers work part-time. They do not go steady as often as their counterparts in the working class. They spend more time with their families than the daughters of full-time working women in the lower class, and their relationships within the family seem like those we have described for the part-time working mother pattern. Their parents expect them to be self-reliant, give them a share in rule-making, and apparently permit discussion and open disagreement. In all these respects, girls in the middle-class full-time group are more like those in the part-time patterns and different from girls in the working class whose mothers work full-time. They choose their mothers as ideals more than daughters of non-working women—this holds for all the working mother groups at both class levels—but they do not choose in-family models as exclusively as do their working-class counterparts. They think of the mother as confidante, but they also think that a friend can be as close to them as a family member. They do not characteristically think that a girl should yield personal work interests to return home to a lonely mother.

Working Class

The dependency which distinguished the total group of girls whose mothers hold full-time jobs is primarily a feature of working-class girls in the pattern. Here we find both a strong positive affection for the mother and a strong dependency component. The working-class girls in families where the mother works full-time show the primary characteristics of premature seriousness, deprivation in social and leisure activities, and emotional dependency. Compared to other working-class girls or to middle-class daughters of full-time working women, they have fewer group memberships and leisure activities, and they are more often responsible for major housekeeping tasks and part-time jobs. They are not striving toward emotional independence, nor are they encouraged by their parents to be self-reliant. In this regard they look most like girls whose mothers do not work and differ from all of the other working mother groups.

Compared to any other group in this analysis, the working-class girls whose mothers work full-time have strong emotional ties to the family. They admire and feel close to their mothers, and seem psychologically highly dependent on the family. In choosing an adult ideal, girls in this group name their mothers as often as girls in other working mother categories, and when we consider all in-family choices, they are by far the group most family-oriented (76% of this group name an ideal from the family group, compared to 60% of the working-class nonworking mother group, the second highest of all categories in this respect).

They have fewer disagreements with their parents than any other group of girls, and they more often reject the notion that friendship can be as close as kinship. When answering the question about the lonely mother who wants her daughter to come to live with her, girls in this group give the traditional response of loyalty to the mother more than girls from any other constellation. The contrast is again a striking one—56 per cent of this group think the girl should return, compared to 42 per cent of the next highest group.

On the other hand, these girls do not spend a great deal of time with their families. They are more likely than other girls to say they spend most of their free time alone or with a friend. In many cases, this friend may be a steady boyfriend since a large proportion of these girls go steady. If we take steady dating to indicate a transfer of emotionality from the family, then we are faced with the paradoxical fact that girls in this pattern are both very tied to their families and at the same time more likely to have shifted the focus of their emotional lives. Another indication that at least in some spheres they do not in fact rely on their mothers as much as we might think from their attitudes toward family relationships is that they do not think of the mother as a confidante as often as girls in the other working mother groups.

Patterns of Effects

The analysis of maternal employment within social classes has distinguished two patterns of effects that may accompany a mother's full-time work commitment. The patterns break on class lines in the following manner—in the middle class the effect of the mother's working full-time appears to be similar to the effects of a partial work commitment in either class group—family interaction is high and is geared to training children toward autonomy and self-reliance. Girls in such families are active in both organized and nonorganized leisure activity, spend a good deal of time with their families, and are relatively autonomous in issues of judgment and authority. They admire their mothers but do not seem particularly dependent on them.

The lower-class girl whose mother works full-time is not like other daughters of working women. The girls in this pattern come closest to our original conception of the girl who is neglected and suffers a serious loss in family life because her mother is overextended in her commitments, harassed, and perhaps resentful. Here we find girls who carry very heavy responsibilities, lack normal leisure commitments, and apparently find in extrafamily relationships (that is, the steady dating relationship) the secure and stable companionship which they do not find at home. Although in fact they share very little time with their families, the girls in this group have a strong and sentimental conception of the importance of family ties, continue to be emotionally dependent on the family at an age when other girls have begun to break their ties of dependency. This last set of findings does not, we think, contradict our original notion that full-time maternal employment might imply neglect. One reason girls from such families might be sentimental about the family and more dependent on it is that their needs for family-based security have never been adequately met. At the same time that girls with such backgrounds take unusual responsibility for daily realities, they may continue to yearn for the closeness and security of more normal family interaction.

Explanation

Why should full-time maternal employment have such different effects in the two status groups? The simplest hypothesis relies on economic factors. The middle-class mother who works either part-time or full-time very likely has some degree of choice in the matter. In the working class the two commitments may reflect quite different degrees of personal choice and financial press—the lower-class woman who works full-time may be responding to a much simpler and more imposing condition of economic need. Two minor findings from our study support this suggestion. When we asked girls to think of ways in which a girl might like her parents to be different, the girls in our working-class full-time group differed clearly from the other three working mother groups in one respect. While the other three groups all stand out for their reference to the parents' life style ("she'd like them to have a nicer home, go out, entertain more"), the working-class full-time group rarely gives such answers. On the other hand, the working-class full-time group gives economic problems as a source of worry for girls much more than any of the other working mother groups.

If in fact this is the case—that the working-class full-time pattern is the only one of our four working mother groups that represents serious economic deprivation—then we can make some ordered interpretations of our findings. The mother who works because of serious economic need is not necessarily one whose psychological make-up prepares her for the dual roles of homemaker and worker. She may feel herself taxed by the demands of a life complication which she did not choose and does not feel up to. Sheer economic deprivation adds a further burden of concern, and in many cases we might expect to find such women both harried and resentful or passively resigned to an unsatisfying and burdensome life situation. The pattern is similar to the one Lois Hoffman has characterized as guilt-free (Nye and Hoffman, 1963). Such women feel no special obligation to their families because they are pressed themselves. They expect to get their children to take a good deal of responsibility at home; they spend very little time and energy in managing or sharing their children's leisure affairs; and they engender in their children a strong sympathy and sentimental loyalty.

We are reminded of the mothers who so regularly appear in the short stories of Frank O'Connor and other Irish authors—the strong and stable support in a family whose father deals primarily in alcoholic charm and irresponsibility. The key for such a woman is to convert the children to her side as emotional suppliers and supporters in the real problems of life. She inspires her children with both the strength to cope with reality and also the dependency that assures her some emotional gratification in an otherwise bleak life. To be sure this fictional Irish mother is an exaggerated form, but we suspect that some such pattern is the paradigm for understanding the emotional nexus that dominates many lower-status families in which the mother's employment is a condition for family survival.

We have already described the motivational pattern that we think underpins part-time maternal employment. The distinctive features here are that the woman herself chooses to work and that she maintains a vivid sense of obligation and responsibility toward her family. She chooses a complex rather than a simple life pattern, but the conditions of the pattern are set by her primary commitment to her family role. We see this as a pattern requiring unusual energy and one which results in a high degree of family interaction. Derivative effects of the pattern we note in the degree of parent participation in the leisure lives of their adolescent children and in the energy, autonomy, and responsibility that characterize girls from this family setting. These psychological features of the girls develop, we suggest, from a modeling process in which the girls identify with and draw their ideals from their own active and autonomous mothers.

The only pattern remaining to be accounted for is the middle-class mother who works full-time. We found this group of girls to be indistinguishable in most critical respects from the daughters of women who work part-time. We must now ask how a full-time work commitment might for a middle-class woman be the same, have the same meaning, as part-time employment. We suspect that economic need alone does not distinguish the two kinds of employment for middle-class women, and the woman of higher social status who works full-time does so, at least in part, because of personal choice.

Maternal Employment and Adolescent Boys

We would expect, from the findings in the girls' study, that maternal employment might be a less important factor in the life of the adolescent boy. If we are right in our view that much of the influence of maternal employment comes about through a modeling process in which the girl fashions her ego-ideals and activities in keeping with the pattern set by her mother, then we can expect that this pattern will be less effective in predicting the boy's developing integration. For the boy, the model provided by his father will be the key to ego development, and the mother's activity or employment should be a comparatively minor factor.

Our interpretations of the meaning of work to mothers in the part-time and full-time patterns gain some general support from our data on boys. Here again we find that the lower-class family in which the mother works full-time has more pressing financial troubles—or, at least, that financial problems come through to the children more clearly. Boys in this group think of financial problems as a source of worry and also as something they would like to change about their own lives more often than do boys in any of the other working mother patterns, and more often than those whose mothers do not work at all. The other three types of working mother (that is, higher-status women who work full-time and women of either high or low status who hold part-time jobs) again seem to be women who are unusually conscientious, active mothers. Their sons, like their daughters, report sharing leisure activities with their parents more than other boys do, and they have a larger number of leisure activities of the kind that imply parental involvement (that is, membership in organized groups and active sports and hobbies).

Beyond these few findings, the working mother variable shows relatively little power to predict the boy's activities and psychological characteristics. When the mother's work stems from personal choice —or so we infer, at least—the boy has a relatively high leisure activity index, but he differs in no other area from boys whose mothers do not work. He is not less likely to work or date; he shows no signs of unusual achievement striving,[7] of special forms of ego development, or of precocious loosening of dependency ties.

The boys from families in which the mother's work is the product of economic necessity, that is, lower-status women who work full-time, do differ from other boys in some respects, and this seems to us interesting in light of the fact that this is the one case in which maternal employment implies something about the father as a model. The fact that a mother "must" work, irrespective of her personal wishes, does not speak well for the father's capacity as a provider. When we consider the importance of economic prowess in the American definition and evaluation of the male, a father who cannot or does not support his family adequately can hardly serve as an effective ideal for his son. It is in the area of modeling that the boys differ most clearly from their age-mates. They choose their own fathers significantly less often than other boys do, and they more frequently say that they have no adult ideals. Beyond this we find that boys in this group are somewhat rebellious in response to adult authority, and that they show signs of poor ego-integration. They have a relatively short time perspective and a low level of general activity. Only in dating are they especially active. They do not have part-time jobs as often as other boys; they have very few organizational ties and active leisure engagements. Our information on their family attitudes is limited. We did not ask boys as many questions in this area as we did girls. But boys in the lower-class full-time group do not seem to be emotionally dependent on the family in any way that compares with our findings for girls from similar family backgrounds. They do not think that family ties are always closer than friendships, and they do not rely heavily on parental advice or on in-family models more than other boys do. We would like to have information on the boy's relationship to his mother distinguished from his attitude toward his father, but in this our data on boys are specifically lacking.

We can say, by way of a general conclusion, that the effect of maternal employment on the boy's development is significant only when

[7] When we consider only urban boys from lower-middle and upper-middle working-class homes, we do find a relationship between the boy's mobility aspirations and maternal employment. Boys who aspire to upward-mobility more often report that their mothers work part-time than boys do whose orientation is nonmobile or downward-mobile. While maternal employment is generally a less imposing force in the life of the boy, this finding suggests that in certain cultural settings, the fact that a boy has an ambitious mother may crucially affect the direction of his development. Kahl's work (1953) supports this suggestion.

it serves to inform us about general features of family integration and, specifically, about the relationship between the boy and his father. When the mother's work rests to any significant degree on factors of personal choice—when, that is, it reflects qualities and motives of the mother but does not yield specific information about the father—it fails to predict a unique pattern of adjustment in the boy, although it appears to be an important force in the girl's integration. This difference in the findings for boys and girls supports our earlier view that the kind of woman who assumes an occupational role through a desire for some self-realization exerts an influence on her daughter's development through a modeling process in which the girl identifies with and incorporates in herself many of her mother's ego characteristics.

NINE

Subcultures

In this chapter we shall look closely at the demographic side of our findings. Throughout this account we have remarked on demographic factors in their relation to other variables: sometimes offhandedly, as in reporting that a certain relationship holds up when, say, social class is controlled; sometimes systematically, when we have explored the interaction between a demographic factor and other variables. We have just seen, as an example, that the meaning of full-time maternal employment differs for middle- and lower-class girls; we also saw that ordinal position, size of family, and social class, when taken together, can illuminate the psychological meaning of demographic "position." Thus, the first-born girl in a large and low-status family tends to be antifeminine and gives signs of emotional disturbance; the first-born girl from a large but high-status family shows no signs of personal difficulties, and a different posture toward femininity.

In some instances we have noted that demographic factors seem to enlarge or diminish relationships. For example, low-status girls who have some share in making rules at home are more independent than low-status girls who do not; yet they are less so than middle-class girls who report having their say about rules. Similarly, middle-class boys who are physically punished have a lower energy-level than others of equal social status, yet are more active than lower-class boys who are so disciplined. In these cases, the family's specific practices are apparently supported by other elements in the class culture. When the family deviates from class norms the effect on adolescent development is not as striking as in those cases where the family's ways are in tune with the norms.

Before we get to the substance of this chapter, we would like to say a few words on the strategy which will guide our report on demographic variables. We are wary of the misplaced encyclopedism which can tempt the investigator, particularly now that computer resources are so readily available. Demographic analyses in a study such as ours—with a large sample and a great number of variables—can yield literally tens of thousands of "findings." If sanity is to be preserved, some principle of selection is essential. We shall report relationships when we believe they add to our understanding of the ways in which demographic characteristics are translated into the adolescent's experience. In some cases we are led by—or, as it may turn out, misled by—established findings and theory on the connections between social structure and experience; in other cases, we follow, informally, our sense of relevance.

Urbanization

Two geographic variables were analyzed in relation to specific features of adolescent activities, interests and development. One of these, geographic region, proved disappointing. As far as we can determine, clear regional differences exist only in highly specific activities which depend on climate or special geographic features. Adolescents in the South do not know winter sports; those in the urbanized East report active leisure centered on camping or field interests less often than do children in the West. We found other more interesting differences (for example, in some areas of family interaction and independence training) between adolescents in the North and the South, but almost all of these differences fade when social class or urbanization is controlled. Traditional concepts of child raising are not significantly more common in the South, nor are Southern girls oriented toward a traditionally conceived adult feminine role. These and other stereotyped notions of a more stable and tradition-tied Southern culture may have some validity for a very small upper-class segment of the South, but no general validity can be claimed for them. At least in areas covered by our studies, the unique Southern culture, if it exists, does not have a visible effect on adolescent development.

The second geographic variable, urbanization, gives more interesting findings. Here too we find obvious differences in activities—city youngsters do not camp, and those from farms have less access to organized social activities and the arts—but we find other differences too. Two groups stand out in this analysis—adolescents from suburban communities in the major metropolitan areas and youngsters from truly rural areas. These two environments have an impact on adolescent development more comprehensive than any simple density factor can explain. They seem to represent rather separate and coherent cultures with distinctive styles of family life and child raising; other points on the urbanization scale look more like variations on (certain definable and) relatively narrow themes.

Perhaps this is a clue to the most efficient presentation in this section. We shall first consider findings that most clearly tie to the density variable, those that change directly with community size; we shall then describe the special characteristics of suburban and farm children.

Generally, adolescents from smaller communities have more active, diversified, and organized leisure lives. Adolescents in large cities spend less time with their parents and report somewhat less congenial family relationships. They are more often either rebellious or overdependent on adult authority. And they show an eagerness for adult status in several ways. When asked what age group they would choose as companions in a club, big city youngsters are much more likely than those from smaller communities to want to be youngest in a group of older children. When they suggest activities for a club, they give a much narrower range of activities and concentrate specifically on social activities—parties and dances. They rarely suggest outdoor programs, which is to be expected, but neither do they mention any of the arts and crafts, hobbies, or individual sports as often as adolescents from small communities. City youngsters do not hold jobs as often as do boys and girls from smaller cities and towns, but when they do, they work longer hours and in more adult-like positions. City girls have heavier home duties than girls in small communities, and they begin steady dating at an earlier age; although dating in general is more common and begins earlier in the smaller towns. City girls more often do not date at all or date only one boy.

The complexity of life in a major city imposes certain pressures on the family and on parent-child relationships. Parents do not have the closer control of adolescent activity that comes with the parent-involving organized leisure and joint family activities that are common in smaller communities. The city child spends more of his free time beyond the range of control of parents and parent surrogates. The less active, less organized leisure of city children seems to reflect the fact that cities are not designed for children. Perhaps this is why city children seem so eager to arrive at adulthood. The city offers most of its advantage to adults.

Suburbs

In this respect—in the degree of orientation to child-rearing—the suburbs are polar to the central city. The environment not only relieves the child of having to adapt to a complex adult life pattern, but in fact seems consciously designed for children. Suburban children differ from those who live in urban centers in all the areas we have described above as distinguishing between city children and those from smaller communities. The large cities, smaller cities (50,000 to 300,000), and towns (10,000 to 50,000) consistently arrange themselves in order of size, with leisure activity increasing as community size decreases. The suburbs are out of order in the sense that they are like the small cities, only more so. It is the suburban adolescents who exemplify what is often taken to be the American pattern of active organized leisure. They stand out in the range and diversity of leisure, in dating, group membership, and joint family activity.

Two features of the pattern are noteworthy. One is that, although suburban children are unusually advantaged in their present lives, they also show the heightened interest in adult status we noted among city children. They are precocious in social development, dating earlier and more frequently than the youngsters in any of the other categories (although they do not go steady as often as city children); they mention social activities first in suggesting programs for a club, although they also suggest other kinds of activities; they clearly prefer coed to like-sexed groups, and they show the same preference that city children do for companions older than themselves. Certain other findings, to be presented shortly, lead us to conclude that in suburban children this eagerness for adult activity is part of a general drive toward maturity rather than a desire to be done with the disadvantages of childhood.

A second feature about the activity preferences of suburban children is that when we look at responses to the questions, "What kind of activities do you think a club like this should have?" "What do you think boys (girls) your age like to do best?" we find that suburban children suggest a profile of activities that is not distinguished for the two sexes; in all other urbanization categories activity profiles do differ sharply for boys and girls. The leisure activities suburban boys and girls actually engage in are also more alike than is true in any of the other urbanization categories. Girls in the suburbs play games and sports more than do city girls or those from smaller communities, and they do not show the marked preference for traditional feminine activities that we find in girls from smaller towns and cities. Boys in the suburbs both know and suggest hobbies and creative activities more than do boys in any other community setting.

Our interest in this group of findings centers on the lack of sex-specific activity prescriptions. Many observers have suggested that American society is diluting the meaning of the sex roles, and that in part this dilution is produced by a socialization system which does not distinguish between activities appropriate for boys and girls. Our data support this contention to a limited extent, as far as it applies to the suburban milieu. The fact that suburban children are those with whom most social critics live and have contact should caution those who generalize easily about American adolescents as a whole.

Beyond the area of leisure activities, suburban adolescents look different from the general population in several aspects of ego development, and in certain phases of family relations. They stand out, as we hinted earlier, in their orientation toward the future and adulthood. When we ask what they do that makes them feel important and useful, suburban boys and girls more often allude to taking adult responsibilities. They tend to have a more extended time perspective than other adolescents, and to have plans for the future which are both well-formulated and strong in achievement themes. They more often plan to go to college and to enter the professions.

Relationships in suburban families show the influence of liberal modern child-raising ideology. We find here both high parent involvement in the child's life and activities and an apparent encouragement of the child's developing autonomy. Adolescents in this setting are generally less authority-reliant than their age-mates from other kinds of communities, and they more commonly disagree with their parents (particularly about ideas). Suburban boys depend less on parental opinion in deciding issues of personal taste; girls more often have a part in making rules at home. In these respects suburban youngsters seem to have achieved greater autonomy and to have done so with their parents' encouragement. A further sign of a distinctive suburban family culture emerges in the area of discipline. Suburban parents use psychological punishment more and physical punishment less than do parents in large cities or smaller communities.

We wonder, of course, whether these findings may be the result of status or education differences, since the suburbs are in all likelihood heavily advantaged in both regards. We do note a dilution of certain of the relationships when we control father's occupation or education.[1] In the activity areas, suburban youngsters at every status level stand out in contrast to those from other kinds of communities, and the difference is especially large in the lower-class levels. In other areas of ego development and in family relationships, some of the variation we have noted is indeed attributable to status. Although differences do not disappear, they are reduced when status is held constant. Our interpretation of these findings follows: the suburban community is dominated by highly educated adults whose conceptions of family relations and of child raising are infused with values on activity, autonomy, and achievement. These families set the atmosphere in the community, encourage community facilities for young people, and press for certain practices and policies in the educational system. The advantages they seek and develop for their own children (for example, advantages in leisure facilities) become advantages for all the children of the community. Activity differences between suburban children and those from other community settings do not disappear when class is controlled, and, as we have said, differences are generally larger in the lower class.

When we look at other areas of ego functioning, we are considering aspects of development less effectively touched by the community. To some extent community leaders affect the orientation and philosophy of the schools, and this in turn may have an impact on the development of all children in the community. This may account for the greater autonomy of suburban children vis-à-vis adult authority. Irrespective of social status, the suburban children tend to be more independent in their stance toward unrelated adults. The areas in which suburb-nonsuburb differences depend largely on status differences all involve close family interaction, specific behaviors or patterns of behavior which would presumably be less open to the effects of the educational system or other community agencies.

Farm

By and large we find, as we have reported, that the smaller the community in which an adolescent lives, the greater his advantages in leisure activities, opportunities for independence, and other areas of personal and social development. At the lower end of community size, however, this trend reverses itself; youngsters from rural areas are as

[1] The relationship between suburban residence and status is not as striking as we might expect.

deprived as those from the meanest urban environment. They have fewer opportunities in all areas of life—in leisure activities, organizational membership, part-time employment, and friendly interaction with unrelated adults. And they show a pattern of unique characteristics that goes well beyond community factors, a pattern that indicates a distinctive subculture with a family style and ideology of its own. The only group in our studies which shares even part of the pattern is the extreme lower-class urban group, those children who represent unskilled working-class families.

Farm children seem to be less at ease socially than city children. They are less poised in the interview, less confident, and less organized. They embarrass more easily than other adolescents, and they are rated lower in verbal ability both by interviewers and by coders who read their transcribed responses.

In the crucial adolescent areas—autonomy, internalization, and attachment to peers—they also look less advanced than their urban peers. We find among farm families a strong and traditional parental control, slow to give privilege or loosen reins, often enforced by physical punishment (although, peculiarly, farm children often report psychological punishment too). Farm children rely heavily on adult authority and generally on external controls. They are usually dependent on the family—they choose their models within the family; they have few disagreements with their parents. Farm boys look to their parents for advice on issues of taste; farm girls spend their leisure time within the family more commonly than do other girls. On most of the items used to measure independence from the family or internalization, farm boys and girls are significantly less developed than city children. And their parents do not apparently encourage autonomy. Farm girls infrequently have a part in making rules at home, and they do not think of self-reliance or independence as the thing their parents want or expect of them as often as other girls do. Farm children, both boys and girls, are disciplined with physical punishment more commonly than adolescents from any other community background.

Thus, the rural group seems the most distinctive of our geographic categories. Adolescents in this setting present a remarkably uniform picture of traditional conceptions of family life and of their limited effects on adolescent development. The most conspicuous effect of the farm environment and culture seems to be a severe limitation on the adolescent's social growth. Beyond this we find a marked inhibition of fantasy. Farm children, as we have said, have a more difficult time in the interview, and are less verbal than city youngsters. These differences, in combination with their less highly developed fantasy life, might lead us to conclude that American farm families are a low IQ group.[2] Although this may be the case, we doubt it. For one thing we do not find gross differences in educational achievement between farm and nonfarm parents. If we exclude from urban families the professional group of highly educated parents, the distributions of fathers' education for urban and rural samples are indistinguishable. We believe that farm youngsters are less developed both socially and internally because their environment either fails to stimulate (in the case of fantasy) or actively inhibits (in autonomy and internalization) this development.

Social Class

Social status is surely the most thoroughly explored variable in all of the social sciences. Even if we limit ourselves to studies conducted on adolescent samples, the number of references which report class differences is nearly overwhelming. Among the more important reports and analyses are those of Hollingshead (1949), Himmelweit (1955), Centers (1949), Lipset and Bendix (1960), Coleman (1961), to mention but a few.

What can we expect to find? Obviously, the mere fact of privilege, and its effects, should make its way into the findings. Higher-status children will have had greater opportunities for leisure and in groups devoted to it, and this should have some influence on their social relationships both with peers and adults. Socialized to middle-class standards, at home in a world of middle-class premises, we expect them to show greater poise in an interview with an adult middle-class interviewer. Their sense of the future, their sense of themselves in the future, should be firmer, and more articulated. The middle-class is future-oriented, and in any case they can count on parental support to ease and guide their way in the future. The values of achievement and self-determination, although generally felt in American society, are more forcefully implanted in the middle-class family and milieu, and in addition are buttressed by a more favorable material climate, by the fact that opportunities to achieve and to determine one's fate are more likely to be present. Another source of differences between the classes will be found in the ideology and practice of child-rearing. Our find-

[2] Compare this to Terman's norms, which do indicate a relatively lower intelligence among rural populations.

ings have led us to expect an authoritarian parental climate in the working class, and an easier (although internally perhaps more rigorous) one in the middle class. This difference may well influence the child's sense of his freedom, the way he views authority, and ultimately the moral style he composes.

On the other hand, we did not expect class differences to be quite as sharp as much of the literature has seemed to suggest. Both life styles and ideological modes overlap strata, and there is, we felt, an American consensus which in many areas overrides the marginal differences associated with social status. There is, of course, a world of difference between a physician's son and an unskilled laborer's son; but perhaps there is not so much difference, if any at all, between the bank teller's boy and the electrician's boy. Furthermore, class differences, we thought, might be stronger when tested in adults than in adolescents. We were impressed by the extremely strong effects associated with mobility aspirations. Many of those in the working class are aimed upward, and have absorbed the attitudes and viewpoints of the middle class; and some middle-class youngsters seem to be drifting downward. The fluidity of status among adolescents, the contamination of position by aspiration would, we suspect, act to weaken class effects in our sample.

These, then, were the expectations with which we initiated the social class analysis. We shall look at the results of the analysis shortly, after one additional comment, about measurement and the relative effectiveness of various class indices.

In our studies we had three potential measures of social class— father's occupation, father's education, and a crude economic index based on the family's possession of certain consumer goods. We did not have information about family income since we found in pretests that adolescents rarely have such information. Of the three available measures, father's occupation is by far the most useful and yields the most significant findings. We cannot place farm families in a social class category on the basis of occupation, but these are virtually the only cases lost. Almost all children know what work their fathers do, while a large (13%) proportion do not know the father's educational background. Even when the adolescent claims to know, we find many cases in which the information he gives seems factually unreliable.

The economic index we used distinguishes very poor families from others, but is not effective in differentiating middle-class families from the large body of blue-collar working-class families. Owning a home, having a telephone, and owning a car are so common in our society that they no longer provide a meaningful measure of status. We did find the economic index useful in assigning farm families to two rough status categories, and we used it for this purpose.

The class findings that follow all refer to the occupational analysis unless otherwise noted. At the end of the section, we shall present a few interesting results of a special set of runs in which the relative education of the father and mother is taken as an independent variable, an indication of status pressures in the family.

Activities

Status is related in a clear and simple way to activities and interests. Girls and boys from upper-middle-class homes report more leisure engagements than do youngsters of lower-middle-class background; these in turn have more activities than the children of blue-collar manual workers. For boys the same relationship holds for specific activity categories—higher-status boys more often report any particular leisure activity. Among the girls, however, we find that certain activities are more characteristic of lower-class girls. They more often engage in organized team sports. Passive leisure engagements, watching television and going to movies, are common in both groups. Middle-class girls more often take part in individual sports, hobbies, and arts and crafts.

Both boys and girls from high-status backgrounds show that precocious social development which is so prominently encouraged in the popular child-raising literature and depends so strongly on active parent guidance and cultivation. Middle-class boys and girls date earlier than lower-class children; they belong to more organized groups, and they have greater experience in organized social activities like dancing.

Presentation of the Self

The relative social poise of middle-class adolescents is strikingly apparent in their approach to the interview situation. When face to face with a strange adult, the high-status youngster is much more at ease than the lower-class child. In fact, the largest differences in the entire class analysis emerge on some of the interviewer ratings of confidence during the interview. Middle-class subjects are rated much higher on self-confidence and on the clarity and organization of their ideas. The latter finding is particularly interesting when taken together with ratings of verbal ability. Both interviewers and coders rated subjects for verbal power and both ratings show some relationship to social status.

But these relationships are significantly lower than those between social class and the youngster's rated capacity to organize and present his ideas clearly to the interviewer. We suspect that the critical component in this capacity is poise and the ability to interact confidently with a strange adult. The relationship may also depend on the perceived status of the adult, but we have other indications that lower-class youngsters are in general less socially skilled and less at ease with adults outside the family, irrespective of the adults' status characteristics. Middle-class subjects are, according to interviewer ratings, more at ease by the following criteria—they more often look directly at the interviewer and show some humor. Embarrassment and blushing show no association with status.

Friendship

We had not expected friendship development to be strongly class linked, except in certain formal respects tied to the child's experience in organized groups. Conceptions of friendship, attitudes toward the intimacy of friendship, conceptions of the ethics of friendship, and ideas about the resolution of conflict within peer relations—all these are relatively free of social class influence. Boys in different status groups do not differ in the fact of having one or two best friends, and girls in all status groups show the same primary allegiance toward like-sexed as against opposite-sex friendships. Development in the conception and significance of friendship follows the same pattern in the two major social class groups—from a parallel, activity-centered relationship in early adolescence to a more mutual, interpersonal, and interaction-centered relationship in late adolescence. Girls in both strata have more mature conceptions of friendship than boys.

In girls we found only two clear class differences in the area of peer relations. The first is that middle-class girls more often spend their spare time with friends rather than with the family, while the reverse is true for lower-status girls. No doubt this is partly due to the fact that middle-class children spend a larger portion of their leisure in organized groups of teenagers. Furthermore, middle-class parents probably encourage the child to form strong peer ties as part of a general belief in early training in social skills.

This in turn bears on the second striking status difference in girls—that those of middle-class background show a persistent preoccupation with popularity and social success. These girls, and especially those of upper-middle-class origin (professional and business managerial), daydream of popularity more often. They more often cite popularity as a cause of worry; they would like, if they were to change themselves, to have greater social skill and be more popular; and they more often list peer acceptance—the ability to get along with other youngsters and to be liked—among the things their parents expect of them. This obsession with popularity, which has frequently been noted by observers of American middle-class norms, is in all likelihood prompted by parental pressure; in any case, the middle-class girls are quite different in this respect from lower-class girls and also quite different from boys, regardless of background. Nevertheless, in the conception of friendship —which, to the girl, is likely to mean an intimate relationship between two girls, and is likely to be more important than the peer group as a whole—high-status girls show no distinctive ideas or attitudes. It is almost as though the two areas—the popularity contest in the society of peers, and the more mutual and intimate interaction between friends— were rather separate areas of social reality.

Achievement and the Future

The second area in which we predicted specific class effects embraced the child's conception of future time and his orientation toward personal achievement. We expected middle-class children to show a stronger investment in the value of individual achievement and to organize their time in terms appropriate to this value.

Our data yield class differences in these dimensions, but somewhat to our surprise, the differences are uniformly small. They contrast strikingly with the differences that emerge in the other major status analysis we ran, that based on the adolescent's own orientation toward status, his mobility aspirations. The most substantial class differences in adolescents' orientation toward the future occur in those aspects of planning clearly linked to real opportunity. Middle-class boys and girls expect to go to college and to train for professional jobs much more often than do children from lower-class homes. Also they feel more confident that they will achieve their educational and occupational goals.

But where measures depend less on specific opportunity, class differences, although stable, are much less impressive. Middle-class boys have a more extended time perspective than lower-class boys—they tend to encompass a longer time period in their planning and decision making. The difference is not a marked one, however, and, in girls, it is not even reliable. High-status boys, compared to boys of lower status, have a more detailed concept of the steps required to reach their job goals, but this is largely a reflection of the fact that their goals imply more preparation—generally the completion of some form of higher education. Their conception of the training they need is no clearer than lower-class youngsters' ideas; nor are their educational plans more appropriate to their job goals. It is simply that the jobs they aspire to fill demand greater training, and they know what that training is.

The desire for personal achievement plays a more important role in the hopes and plans of middle-class boys. They think of achievement more often than lower-class boys do when they are asked to tell what things worry boys, what is "the most wonderful thing" that could happen to them, what qualities they admire in their adult models, what gives them a feeling that they are "important and useful," and what things they would change about themselves if they had a chance. In none of these cases are differences large, however, and in none do we find achievement as salient a concern for the middle-class as we had expected. Only a small minority refer to achievement values or concerns in answering any of these questions.

Middle-class boys see their future jobs as sources both of intrinsic satisfaction and of achievement opportunities. They are more likely to aspire to a job for its intrinsic interest; lower-class boys more often adduce security as attracting them to the jobs they choose. Middle-class boys state the interest of the work and the rewards of leadership and recognition to be central criteria for choosing jobs; lower-status boys more often emphasize high pay and security. Similar class differences appear in answer to the forced-choice question asking boys whether they would prefer a secure job or one with little security but an open opportunity for great personal success. This finding may also be taken to indicate the boy's sense of effectiveness—middle-class boys may be willing to accept a greater risk as a price for greater opportunity because they have more confidence in their own power to affect the future.

Yet in all of these items on jobs and achievement, class differences among boys, although consistent, are smaller than comparable differences previously reported for adult populations, and much smaller than those we have found within social classes when mobility aspiration is used as the analytic variable.

For girls we find few consistent class differences in achievement. Middle-class girls are more likely than those of low status to mention achievement as a source of worry, but they most often mention school grades in this connection (and this contrasts with boys' achievement concerns which center on both school and job). Aside from this response, middle-class girls do not distinguish themselves by a preoccupation with individual achievement. They plan to attend college and prepare for professional jobs somewhat more than low-status girls do, but the lower-class girls show much the same thrust toward mobility —they choose semiprofessional and white-collar jobs, and hope either to go to college or to continue their training in secretarial school. Girls from neither social class aspire to jobs primarily for their achievement opportunities. They want "interesting" jobs, but they mean that they hope to have nice coworkers and to be able to work with people or help others. Fame, leadership, high pay, and status are among the characteristics they consider least important in choosing a job. On the forced-choice question, middle-class girls are in fact somewhat less likely than lower-class girls to choose the risky job that offers a chance for a major personal success, preferring instead a job they can be sure of.

The last aspect of achievement motivation we considered, postponement of gratification, was only slightly touched in our studies, but the single bit of evidence we have is consistent with findings already presented. Middle-class boys more often save some of their own money than do boys of lower status. In girls we find no comparable difference; and for the boys the difference is more remarkable for its modest size than for its occurrence.

Family Style and Personal Development

We turn now to the last area, or combination of areas, in which we specified class predictions—family relationships, the development of autonomy, and the internalization of standards and controls. We expected middle-class parents—the primary target and market for the child-raising literature—to be distinguished by a strong commitment to the virtue of autonomy, to encourage the child toward early independence in making decisions and governing his day-to-day activities. We thought these parents would exercise a relatively moderate and rational authority over their children, an authority characterized by Cousins (1960) as denying the parent status its nonrational powers of achieving socialization goals. We expected them to enforce their control by deprivation and guilt-inducing verbal punishments rather than by physical punishment.

Children from middle-class homes would, we thought, be different from those of lower-class background in ways which follow from and parallel these differences in family interaction. We expected to find in middle-class youngsters a precocious loosening of family ties, an early move toward autonomous social functioning and toward location of significant emotional relationships outside the family.

We thought that internalization processes might show some class variation because of different family authority patterns in the two-class groups. To the extent that an authoritarian pattern, reflected in the use of physical punishment, is class related, we could expect a class difference in the pace of internalization. Aside from this relatively extreme pattern, we did not expect the class variable to produce many differences in this area of adolescent development. If, as we hoped, our measures were relatively free of the bias that may occur because of class differences in verbal skills, we expected to find the consolidation of personal, internal standards and controls proceeding in much the same way in both social classes.

Our findings show that middle-class parents most consistently differ from lower-class parents in their encouragement of autonomy in their male children. Their sons stand out in self-reliance and in emotional independence from the family. Parallel differences in our data on girls are less consistent. In the areas of family authority and the adolescent's internalization of controls, we find only the single difference that lower-class families continue to use physical punishment when middle-class families have abandoned it. Otherwise, only a few differences appear in the style of family authority and in the child's reactions to authority.

Middle-class boys report more disagreements with their parents than do lower-class boys. Also they less often rely heavily on their parents' advice on issues of taste and judgment. The interesting difference here is not that middle-class boys substitute friends' advice for parents', but that they more often say they would rely on their own judgment in such questions. This difference recurs on each of the six individual issues discussed.

Boys from upper-status homes choose their own fathers as models more often than do lower-class boys, but they give a larger proportion of nonfamily models as well. The lower-class boy is more likely to choose some family member aside from the father, or to choose no adult ideal at all. Middle-class boys less often rely heavily on nonfamily adult authority.

Middle-class parents do not differ from those of the lower class in what they expect in their daughters' behavior, but they do permit them a larger voice in rule-making. And middle-class girls seem more autonomous both in their willingness to disagree with their parents and in their allocation of time. They more often spend most of their leisure with a friend or friends, less often with the family. They do not differ from lower-class girls in the choice of adult models. Neither the choice of the mother nor the choice of models within or outside the family differentiates the two class groups. Judgments of girls' authority reliance—based on their discussion of adult club leaders—indicate that middle-class girls are more likely to rely heavily on adults than are lower-status girls.

The pattern of family discipline differs for the two classes, and this difference applies to both sexes. Verbal punishment is less common in the lower than in the middle class; physical punishment is more common in the lower class. The groups do not differ in the child's perception of parental strictness, and among girls we have two pieces of evidence to corroborate the impression that parental authority is not strongly linked to social status. In the question on parent expectations, the class groups mention respect for authority equally often, and they are indistinguishable on a modernism-traditionalism dimension on which parent expectations were judged. Girls from both classes generally approve of their parents' rules; we find no status difference here.

Our internalization measures—the index as well as single items other than those included in the index—yield no class differences for either boys or girls. The one interesting difference that appears concerns peer relations. Both boys and girls from middle-class homes more often mention peer influence, the pressure of the gang, as a reason why a boy or girl might break a rule.

Two general observations emerge from this analysis—social class, defined either by father's occupation or education, has less influence on adolescent behavior and family patterns related to adolescent behavior than a great deal of previous research might lead us to expect. We do find class differences which are consistent with the expectations that previous research and theory stimulate. But they are small differences for the most part; substantial differences appear only for specific social activities and skills, where the variables in question are tied specifically to opportunity and the family's economic resources. The status variable per se contrasts quite sharply with the mobility variable in its predictive power. When we take the adolescent's motivational stance toward status (rather than his actual status derived from the family) as an analytic base, we find large, consistent, and psychologically significant differences in most areas of boys' adolescent development. Mobility differences for girls, although less impressive, are nonetheless larger than straight class differences, and they form a pattern which is meaningful and understandable when we use a more complex model of the meaning of mobility for girls.

The second general point about the class analysis is that among adolescents, social class seems to be a more important force in the boy's life than it is for girls. Both sexes are affected by status in the opportunity for certain social experiences. But boys feel the impact of the class culture more directly than girls do in areas involving parent attitudes and ideology—achievement, autonomy, and methods of discipline. Middle-class families stress achievement and encourage autonomy in their sons more consistently than they do for their daughters. The boys from upper-status homes differ from lower-class youths in both of these respects, while differences for girls are not only smaller in size but, more important, lack the coherence and consistency we note in the data on boys. The class subculture has apparently less influence on the disciplining of girls than for boys. Here our data suggest that the lower-class parent distinguishes punishment for the two sexes more sharply than middle-class parents do; that they abandon the use of physical punishment for their daughters even when they continue to discipline their sons in this way. In part this may result from girls' generally more compliant relationship to adults, but it may also reflect the parents' response to girls' developing sexuality. For the father, the girl's heightened sexual-symbolic value may act as a bar to any physical contact.

The analysis of status based on father's education produced a pattern of findings generally similar to the analysis based on occupation. In most cases, however, differences were smaller than comparable differences from the occupation analysis.

Educational Discrepancies Within the Family

One interesting set of findings related to status stems from an analysis of girls' interviews based on the relative education of the two parents. We were prompted to look at this variable by earlier work and discussion (compare, particularly, Allison Davis, 1957) suggesting that behind every mobile child there is a mother whose status aspirations have been thwarted by her marriage. Our own mobility analysis gave hints of the same kind of relationship. For example, the mothers of those in our upward-aspiring groups more often hold part-time jobs, compared to those whose children are not oriented toward upward mobility. In the study of adolescent girls, we obtained data on the educational background of both parents—as we did not, unfortunately, for boys—and so were able to test some of the effects of educational discrepancies between parents.

The analysis and the pattern of findings are complex, in part because it is an analysis of girls' aspirations. We noted earlier that the expression and meaning of status and mobility aspirations are more complicated and subtle in girls than in boys; it also seems likely that the status-oriented, ambitious mother would express her hopes more directly and simply in her training of a son than a daughter. Raising a daughter to realize mobility drives is complicated—we must implant the wish for mobility without endangering that feminine desirability which ultimately is her best resource in the status game. We must give her autonomy and ambition, but protect and control her at the same time.

Our results can be grouped meaningfully into two clusters—those that relate specifically to the issue of social mobility and those that imply something about the larger question of the role of the educated woman (or the woman educated more highly than her husband). One group of differences holds for all educational levels; the other findings —those which go most directly to the issue of mobility striving—hold only at those levels where mobility aspirations are meaningful and prevalent, where the father has a grade school or high school education.

In all families where the mother is more highly educated than the father, we detect a stress on child autonomy. Girls from these families report that their parents expect them to be independent and self-reliant more than other girls' do; and they are less likely to say that their parents want them to be obedient and to respect authority. In that latter category, we find a disproportionate number of girls whose fathers are clearly superior to their wives in educational background. Girls in the "educated mother" group are less reliant on adult authorities generally, and they seem to be less tied to the family emotionally than other girls. They more often think a friend can be just as close as a family member; and they more often say that the girl in the projective situation would not give up her job to return home to her lonely mother. They are active children—they more often belong to clubs and organizations and have more leisure activities than other girls. And their mothers apparently release them from other responsibilities in order to encourage these social and leisure activities. They have heavy home responsibilities much less often than girls from families where the parents have equal educational backgrounds or where the father's education is superior.

The one respect in which these girls appear less independent than others is that they have fewer disagreements with their parents. On each of the disagreement items, including the open question, girls from father-dominant families more often report conflict, those from mother-dominant homes least often say they disagree with their parents. The largest differences occur, both on the open question and among the specific items, around differences in ideas. There are two possible explanations of this finding which contrasts with other more general indications that girls whose mothers are educationally dominant have greater emotional autonomy than those whose families fit other educational patterns. First, there is the possibility that the mother-daughter relationship is unusually close in these families and that open disagreement (unlike the prospective future disagreement hypothesized in the "lonely mother" question) is too threatening to be acknowledged. The other possibility is that the mother who is educationally advanced plays a more central role in the training of her children—deciding how they will be treated, what they will be allowed to do, and so forth—and that this produces a "softer" child training regime which, in fact, creates fewer disagreements. In most families the mother will yield more privileges to children and will allow them more rein than the father will. This, and the close mother-daughter tie may very well combine to produce the peculiar finding we have described.

Beyond these differences among the various family education patterns that hold across status levels, other differences occur on lower-status levels which, we think, reflect special mobility pressures. Girls whose fathers have grade school education and whose mothers have gone to or completed high school, and those whose fathers have been to or completed high school and whose mothers have more than a high school education (that is, either technical training or college) seem most likely to be the ones in which an educational discrepancy will reflect pressures toward upward social aspiration. Both of these groups differ from others of equivalent status (determined in this case by the father's education) in the following ways—they are higher in all areas of activity except home responsibility. They have more leisure activities and belong to more clubs, but also more often hold part-time jobs. In addition to the signs of autonomy we noted (at all status levels) among girls whose mothers are more highly educated, these groups also have a larger voice in setting rules at home; in this respect they are like the daughters of college-educated parents. (Once we get to the college level, the fact that the mother has had more schooling than the father no longer seems important.)

In several specific responses the lower-status groups with educated mothers express the special mobility pressures they feel. In answer to the question about how a girl might want her parents to be different, "more like the parents of her friends," they mention the family style or standard of living more frequently than do other girls of the same status. In describing their daydreams, these two groups of girls more often refer to themes of personal achievement, less often to marriage and children. These girls tend to choose job aspirations which are high in status and education, and are usually considered masculine fields. They more often choose the traditional professions (for example, medicine, law, and architecture).

A number of questions in the area of internalization indicate a somewhat masculine integration. The girls with more educated mothers have more highly internalized standards than other girls from lower-middle and lower-class backgrounds. They score higher on the index of internalization, and give a higher proportion of "internal" responses on each of the items included in the index. They also reveal a close identification with parental rules in their picture-story responses and in answer to the question, "What would happen if parents didn't make rules"?

One finding seems to corroborate our earlier impression of a close mother-daughter tie in cases where the mother is relatively highly educated. The girls in each of the two groups under analysis choose their own mothers as an ideal adult more often than do other girls at comparable status levels.

Our impressions from this analysis correspond to Davis's conception of the meaning of this kind of educational discrepancy in lower-middle and lower-class families. The mother who values education (and, we assume, the status rewards of education) but fails to realize her status quest in marriage does apparently build strong status desires in her daughters, along with the middle-class attitudes and values which will be instrumental for achieving them. They do so, we gather, by stressing status gain through personal achievement rather than through marriage. (Perhaps they themselves regret giving up a career in favor of marriage.) At any rate, their daughters have absorbed, more than girls of comparable class level, the values of achievement. They have professional aspirations, they wish for personal achievement, and they daydream about individual success. They less often daydream about marriage and family life.

We conjectured that these might be the girls who make up the individually oriented mobile group discussed in Chapter 3. Although we had not thought of the educational discrepancy variable as a key background factor when doing the mobility analysis, we found it to be extremely important. Of the individually oriented mobile group, no fewer than 75 per cent come from homes in which such a discrepancy exists, while the figure for the total sample is only 32 per cent. The education of the mother, in relation to that of the father, is significant in determining both the degree and style of the girl's mobility orientation.

Religion

We focused our analysis of religious differences on the areas of autonomy, achievement, internalization, and response to authority. All of these topics, central to individual development during the adolescent period, have been linked in theory to religion—particularly to the Protestant ethic. Orthodox Protestant concepts of a direct individual contact with God, the primacy of the individual conscience, personal responsibility and guilt, contrast with the emphasis the Catholic church places on the role of the church as an intermediary between man and his Creator; an intermediary which offers relief and absolution of guilt in exchange for acceptance of its authority and infallibility in all matters of religion, ethics, and conscience.

The two major religious groups form subcultures within American society, but the society as a whole—its institutions and traditions—is dominated by the Protestant ethic. Many observers—including official representatives of the Catholic Church—note what they consider a secularization of life among American middle-class Catholics, a tendency to adopt the values and attitudes of American core culture at the expense of close adherence to their faith and religious practices.

In general, then, two separate hypotheses are suggested by previous research and observations about religious cultures in American society. On the one hand, that social and psychological differences will exist between the two groups in those areas in which socialization follows the direction of values and ethical concepts in which the two religious doctrines differ; and, on the other hand, that differences between the religious subcultures will be less striking in the middle class than at lower-status levels. Both suggestions offer testable, specific hypotheses about behaviors and attitudes falling within the scope of our studies. Any analysis of religion in American society must control social status because of the concentration of Catholics in later immigrant groups and thus in the lower classes. Since all of the religious analyses are run separately for the two major social classes, we are able to note differences in the meaning of religion at different status levels.

An additional refinement seems appropriate in analyzing religious differences in our culture. This involves segregating orthodox Protestant sects from the neo-Fundamentalist groups which deviate sharply from the central body of Protestantism in theological interpretation and doctrines governing individual behavior. The significant differences for our purpose lie in the fundamentalist tendency to control the individual by stimulating fear of a harsh and retributive God. Rejecting the orthodox emphasis on the personal, internal authority guiding each man's daily activities, Fundamentalism replaces this authority with a vengeful God who will mete out severe punishment (as well as public scorn) to those who sin against Him. Because the two systems differ in the crucial area of authority, we held them separate in our analyses. Again, class controls must be imposed because of the concentration of neo-Fundamentalist sects in the South and among the economically deprived. We shall summarize findings for the Fundamentalists briefly, but will be concerned primarily with differences between Catholic and orthodox Protestant cultures. When we refer to Protestant characteristics, we mean characteristics of children from orthodox-Protestant backgrounds.

Protestant youngsters, by and large, show greater independence from the family, and a more developed internal authority system than do adolescents from Catholic homes. Protestant parents apparently stress independence training more than Catholic parents do; they are less traditional and authoritative in their relationship to their children; they rely more heavily on the child's internal resources and less on external rewards and punishments as the means for controlling child behavior.

Catholic boys and girls have fewer disagreements with their parents than do Protestant youngsters. Catholic girls more often spend their leisure time with their families and less often with friends, and they are more likely to say that a girl should give up a good job and return home to her lonely mother. Among boys, we find Catholics more often turning to parents for advice on issues of taste and judgment, while Protestant boys more often turn to friends or rely on their own judgment. The latter difference is particularly striking. Catholic boys and girls choose the like-sexed parent as an ideal more than Protestant youngsters do, and they less frequently choose an ideal outside the family circle.

Measures of internalization, when they yield differences, also favor the Protestant subjects. They think of emergencies as the cause of rule-breaking more often than Catholic children do; and they are less likely to think that a boy or girl would break a rule for the sake of rebellion when there was little chance of being found out. On the picture-story series, Protestant youngsters refer to a sense of trust and a feeling of responsibility for their promise when they say that the hero or heroine would not yield to peer pressure. Catholic boys and girls more often say that the hero would not tell his parents about his misdeed if he did disobey, and they are rated more authority-reliant in their discussions of the role of adult leaders.

Parents of the two major religious groups are pictured differently by their children. Protestant girls report that their parents expect them to be independent and self-reliant more frequently than Catholic girls do, and they much more often say that they have some part in making rules at home.

Protestant boys and girls report that their parents punish them with verbal and psychological techniques more often than Catholic youngsters do. They are slightly (although not significantly) less often disciplined physically, and their parents use deprivation techniques less than Catholic parents do.

We also found certain interaction effects between religion and social status. These findings cluster in the areas of authority reliance and family authority patterns. In contrast to our original expectation that in the middle class, religion would have little effect on family relations and child development, the two variables interact in a way that seems to indicate that increased status has very different consequences in the two religious groups. The pattern generally is one in which upper-status Protestant youngsters are more autonomous and internalized than Protestant children of lower status, and their parents stress independence training and lenient discipline more than do Protestant lower-class parents.

In the Catholic group, the effect of increased status is just the opposite. Middle-class parents are stricter and more traditional than lower-class Catholic parents. Their children are more closely tied to the family and more dependent on external controls than are lower-class Catholic youngsters. So, for example, on ratings of authority reliance, middle-class status in the Protestant group is associated with less reliance on adult authority, while among Catholic youngsters, those from middle-class homes rely more heavily on adult authority than do those from lower-class backgrounds.

Protestant boys in the middle class rely on their parents' advice less often than those from lower-status homes, but higher status in the Catholic group brings greater reliance on parents. The same kind of relationship occurs for the girls in the area of leisure time ("Do you spend most of your free time with your family, with a friend, or by yourself?" and for both boys and girls on questions about disagreements with parents.

In the area of internalization, we find signs of a similar reversal. On the Index of Internalization and on each of the individual items, high status is associated with greater internal development in the Protestant group; low status is associated with internalization in the Catholic group.

Protestant high-status parents expect independence and self-reliance from their daughters more commonly than Protestant low-status parents; and they more commonly allow their daughters a share in rule making. These relationships are reversed for the Catholic group—low-status parents more often give and expect greater independence than parents of the middle class. Techniques of discipline do not show an actual reversal, but increased status does not have the same effect in the Catholic culture that it has for Protestant families. The use of physical discipline diminishes with increased status in the Protestant group, but stays at exactly the same, relatively high, level across classes for the Catholic group.

Two other clusters of findings outside the autonomy-authority area follow the same pattern. In the area of peer relations, we find that higher-status Protestant youth are less likely than those of lower status to compromise a commitment to their parents because of peer pressure, and they less frequently think of peer pressure as the reason a boy or girl might break a rule. The reverse is true in the Catholic group—higher status is associated with greater sensitivity to peer pressure. And among girls we find a similiar result on the question about parental expectations. Protestant middle-class girls do not list popularity with their age-mates as one of the most important things their parents expect as often as lower-class Protestant girls do. But middle-class Catholic girls mention it more often than do Catholic girls from lower-class homes.

A few questions focusing on achievement motivation produce similar differences. Among middle-class Protestant boys, high status is associated with a preference for a job offering risk and opportunity rather than security. This alternative is chosen more often by low-status

Catholic boys. In both the boy's and the girls' samples, worry about achievement is positively related to status among Protestants and negatively related to status for Catholics.[3]

The only area in which we find middle-class Catholic youngsters behaving more like middle-class Protestant children than do the lower-status Catholic youth—and even here the evidence is by no means unequivocal—is in specific areas of leisure activity. High-status Catholic adolescents read more, date more, and belong to more organized groups than do Catholic children of lower status. But status and religion operate in the same direction in these instances, and Catholic middle-class youngsters are no more "like" Protestant adolescents of equal status than are Catholic youngsters in the lower class. We find, then, little support in our analysis for the view that the Catholic middle-class family is being secularized or being absorbed into American middle-class core culture. In the areas most crucial for our analysis (and for the large body of social theory on religious differences) the higher-status Catholic families seem to deviate markedly from the values of the core culture, and seem to stress traditionalism in authority and in parent-child relations generally. They are, as far as we can tell from our analysis, the strong adherents and bearers of more orthodox and traditional Catholic concepts of authority and the individual.

It appears, then, that increased status—and the increased opportunity for education and individual development available to higher-status groups—functions primarily as a catalyst to religious commitment, as a reinforcement of the individual's investment in the essential and distinctive qualities of his religious faith, whatever that faith may be. Protestants in higher-status groups emphasize and value the essential Protestant beliefs in individual conscience and authority, in independence and responsibility, more than do lower-status Protestants. On the other hand, high-status Catholic families, compared to those of lower status, are characterized by adherence to the central themes of Catholic doctrine—submission to an authority external and superior to the individual conscience; and the maintenance of a strong, traditional family structure.

Our analysis of the neo-Fundamentalist sects provides some inde-

[3] Veroff, Feld, and Gurin (1962) report a similar finding for Catholics in their national study of adults. They predicted a positive relationship between income level and the strength of achievement motives, and found a small positive relationship among Protestants. In the Catholic group, however, they found a clear reversal of the expected difference, with low income respondents having stronger achievement motives than those with higher incomes.

pendent support for this interpretation. These groups, which rest so much of their case for belief on an image of a punitive deity, are nonetheless variants of the Protestant system and hold the essential notions of direct communication between man and his God, and an unrelieved and irreversible individual responsibility.

The adolescents from neo-Fundamentalist backgrounds as a group look in most cases more like the Catholic boys and girls than like other Protestant youngsters—in their relatively heavy dependence on the family circle and the parents, in their tendency to respond to external authority rather than an internal system of values and controls, and in the nature of their interaction with their parents. In a few cases (for example, the parents' use of physical punishment and their demands for obedience) the neo-Fundamentalist group shows greater traditionalism than Catholic families do.

Only when we look at the interaction between religion and status, and in this case status was defined by the father's education,[4] do we find a basic similarity between the two Protestant groups. Unlike the Catholic group whom they resemble so closely, the neoFundamentalists change with increased education in the same direction as the orthodox Protestant group does. The family values in the more educated Fundamentalist homes focus more clearly on individualism and on rational authority; children from the educated Fundamentalist families show greater autonomy and more internalized value systems, compared to those of the Fundamentalist low-education group. In this religious culture, physical punishment decreases as education increases; verbal disagreement between parent and child increases, as do most signs of adolescent autonomy and internalization. Despite the differences between the Fundamentalist sects and more orthodox Protestant groups at a descriptive level, increased education appears in both groups to intensify commitment to essential Protestant interpretations of man and of man's relation to authority. This apparent similarity in the use and meaning of education and privilege in the two groups may be the result of some extraneous factor—for example, the more highly educated Fundamentalists may be only nominal members of their churches and be less subject to Fundamentalist doctrines than less educated and (perhaps) more devout believers. Or it may reflect a basic similarity in the two major Protestant systems which increased sophistication clarifies. The finding, in any case, seems to us an intriguing one, and one that merits further exploration.

[4] Education was used as the measure of status because the neo-Fundamentalist group includes a large proportion of farmers.

The Family in the Community

We had two items of information on the family's community ties: whether the family has been geographically mobile or has lived in one community for ten years, and whether the parents belong to any organizations in the community. Each of these measures proved to be an effective predictor of certain facets of adolescent behavior. Although geographic mobility is not closely tied to social class, we suspected that its meaning would vary sharply for the two major classes. Organizational membership of parents, like that of the children, is strongly class-linked and requires class control. Both of the analyses in this section, then, were conducted separately for the middle and lower-class subjects.

Geographic Mobility

Irrespective of social status, geographic mobility has important consequences for the child's social development. In both social classes, the geographically stable children are more integrated socially than those who have moved at least once during that period. They belong to more clubs and organizations (the parents do too) and have experienced a larger number of leisure activities, particularly those activities which require the participation of others. Boys from more stable families are more likely to have "one or two close friends—boys (they) spend most of (their) time with," and among girls the geographically stable more often spend most of their leisure time with friends, less often spend time alone (compared to girls who have moved one or more times in ten years). In general, the adolescents who have moved about seem less developed in the forming of peer ties. Their ideas and attitudes about friendship are less complex and less differentiated than those of the adolescents who have lived in one place, and they are somewhat less subject to peer pressure. Despite this, they are, as a group, no more or less close to their families than other adolescents.

When we split the geographically mobile into class groups, we begin to get a more differentiated picture of the meaning of geographic movement to the child. Mobile middle-class children are relatively solitary, intellectual, and close to their families. They are not tied to the peer group either through close friendship or through organizational membership. They spend more time alone, and they are readers. The boys in this group particularly distinguish themselves from others of equal status in the amount and level of reading: they read more novels, history, poetry, and fewer comic books, animal stories, travel and adventure.

The mobile adolescents seem socially poised and mature. Interviewers rate them high in poise, organization and self-confidence. They are relatively autonomous according to most of our indices. The girls in this group have a part in making rules at home and say that their parents expect them to be independent and self-reliant more than other middle-class girls do. Mobile middle-class boys, compared to those from stable families, more often assert that they would rely on their own judgment in making decisions. These youngsters appear to be what we have called "adult-oriented" adolescents. They are close to their own parents—sharing leisure with the family, choosing their own parents as models, thinking of their parents as confidantes—but do not seem unusually dependent on them. They are loosening their emotional ties to the family, but apparently are not using the peer group as the medium of transition from dependency to autonomy. They seem, rather, to be moving directly toward an independence and individuality which they are taught and encouraged toward by the parents.

Lower-class adolescents who have moved show quite a different pattern from the mobile middle-class youngsters. While they are socially less developed than lower-class adolescents from stable families, and more solitary, they are neither close to their own families nor autonomous. They are socially awkward with the interviewers, and they are rated lower than other low-status adolescents in self-confidence and verbal ability. They are somewhat rebellious toward authority, and tend to reject the idea of an adult model. Were we to assume that geographic mobility was causal, we would have to conclude that for lower-class youngsters, movement exaggerates all of the disadvantages of low status and all of the negative developmental features more common among lower-class youth. We do not, of course, draw this conclusion; rather, we see geographic mobility and the developmental features as joint products of some other characteristic of these families. In the lower class, it is probably the most disadvantaged and the least integrated, who move. This makes good sense—the less effective and less integrated workers, those least capable of holding a steady job, are also least likely to provide the kind of family life that encourages easy and positive adolescent growth.

The upper-middle-class families who move obviously do so for very different reasons. Movement itself does not in this case imply negative background features. Movement brings a certain dislocation in the child's social development, particularly in regard to close, stable peer attachments. But the family provides a substitute for these attachments and encourages the child in his movement through the adolescent transition. A stable family life and a strong independence training are the resources offered to the child as substitutes for lasting community ties.

Organizational Membership

Parental commitment to the community, in the form of organizational membership, has a relatively uniform meaning across class lines. The class differences we find in this case are differences of degree rather than in the direction or nature of relationships. The central difference is that parents' organizational membership makes a greater difference in the lower class than in the middle class. In those areas where it has implications for adolescent development, this measure of 'the parents' community ties is a relatively powerful variable, and is particularly powerful for the low-status group. It seems to signify that the parents have adopted and identified with the middle-class values. This, in turn, has a potent effect on family relationship and adolescent development.

Parent membership is strongly related to adolescent membership and to all forms of social activity. Adolescents whose parents belong to organizations have more leisure activities, date more, and more commonly have part-time jobs. They share leisure activities with their parents more often than other adolescents do, and seem generally to have congenial family relationships.

When we look beyond the area of social activity and the development of specific social skills, the impact of the parents' organizational ties concentrates primarily in the lower class where, as we have said, it seems to imply an identification with middle-class values. We find, for example, that these adolescents have more ambitious educational and vocational goals than youngsters of equal status, and that they express a greater concern with personal achievement and achievement of adult status. They have a more extended time perspective, and are generally more interested in, and preoccupied with, the adult future. They are more autonomous than other lower-class youngsters and their parents seem to encourage their independence. In all of these ways, we should say, these youngsters are very different from the lower-status group as a whole, and very much like middle-class adolescents. In the middle class, on the other hand, the fact that parents do or do not belong to organizations makes relatively little difference in the adolescents' future orientation or concern with achievement. Only slight differences occur, and although generally in the same direction as lower-class differences, these are too small to be of significance.

In the double area of internalization and response to authority we found interesting but inconsistent differences for the lower-class group. Lower-class parents who belong to organizations have adopted some middle-class patterns—they very infrequently prefer physical punishment and they tend to allow children a greater measure of self-regulation—compared to unaffiliated lower-class parents. But the effect of this family style is not so clear in their children's concepts of authority or developing internal controls. On one item in the internalization index, the youngsters in this group stand out—they think a boy or girl who had disobeyed his parents would in all likelihood confess his misdeed later. And they are somewhat less likely than other lower-class youths to conceive parental authority either as excessively harsh or as a means of maintaining parents' rights in a system structured as a struggle between opposing parent-child interests. In other items centered around authority and internal control, we find no differences between the two groups (those whose parents are affiliated and those whose parents are not) of lower-class adolescents.

On the question of authority reliance, the group from more integrated families are significantly more dependent on adult direction than are other lower-class youth. This is partly because the group from affiliated families are less rebellious (according to coder ratings of subjects' conception of the role of an adult leader of a youth group, and also in their answers to questions about rules). But the lower incidence of rebellion does not completely explain the difference. This group seems, in fact, to be quite dependent on unrelated adults. They want an adult leader to be directive; they gain self-esteem from the fact that teachers praise them or ask them to fill some special role. And, in line with this pattern, they tend to choose models outside the family— teachers or other adults whom they have known in leadership roles. The children in this group, whose parents seem to identify with middle-class values in so many ways, are in much the same situation as our upward-mobile subjects (and, indeed, many of them are aspiring to upward mobility). Encouraged by their parents to seek a way of life which the parents themselves have not attained, they are almost forced to reject as models the parents who have encouraged their ambitions. The dependency which they show in relation to adult leaders and teachers is also understandable. These adults, usually from the middle class, represent all that the adolescent has been taught to want and work toward. It is not surprising that he should try to ingratiate himself, to win favor with such adults, even if the effort involves some dependency and obsequiousness. These, after all, are the adults who can show him how to become the kind of adult both he and his parents want him to be.

TEN

Integrating Themes

There remain only the tasks of summarizing major conclusions and findings and of tying together the main threads that run through our observations of American adolescents. Most of what we have to say in this final chapter has been stated somewhere earlier in the book, or is at least implicit in the book's structure and organization. At this point we hope to draw the various themes together, to clarify and interpret some of the major findings.

The adolescent in our view is both pushed and pulled toward the future. The psychic conflicts of the period, with their regressive dangers, assemble the power of the past to urge the child to leave family and childhood. The prospect of independence and adulthood urges him to become his own man. He will move on the strength of this attraction, but if it should fail, he still has behind him the tail wind of all the childhood dangers to be escaped. We suggested at the beginning of our studies that this thrust to the future is crucial to the adolescent experience, that without some such tie to adulthood, the adolescent experience has no substance, and that the child's ability to integrate a concept of his adult future would be a key solution on which a great part of his adolescent adaptation would depend.

Our studies have confirmed and strengthened this general conception. The future is by no means a remote or irrelevant prospect to American adolescents. It is crucial as it is absorbed, integrated, and expressed in current activities and attitudes. In one form or another, the future orientation appears again and again as a distinguishing feature of youngsters who are making adequate adolescent adaptations. A faulty time perspective consistently marks the groups in our studies who were isolated analytically by other measures of ego weakness or lack of personal integration.

The style and focus of future orientation differs sharply for boys and girls. The two groups focus their interest on different aspects of future identity, and they differ also in the style of expression. Boys tend to concentrate on the vocational future and their style is all business—concrete, crystallized, tied to reality, if not always realistic. They think of job preparation and channels, and of their own capabilities and tastes for particular work roles. They think of the future in an instrumental way—"This is what I think my future will be because this is what I think I am and what the job world looks like to me." It is not surprising to find that boys' vocational goals are not much colored by dreams of glory. For the most part the jobs boys choose represent modest advances over their fathers' positions, and they are jobs with which the boys have had some personal contact. Boys who have no clear vocational plans or whose job goals are deviant in some way (for example, downward-mobile or glamour-based) have less instrumental and realistic notions of steps toward their goals, and are likely to show a pattern of personal maladjustment in their current lives.

Girls focus on the interpersonal aspects of future life—on marriage and the roles of wife and mother. They are not without notions about channels and instrumental acts appropriate to their goals, but the ideas they have are less concrete than boys'. They are less concerned with real skills than boys are, and more concerned with social and interpersonal reality, as we would expect from the nature of their goals. Their reasons for choosing particular jobs reveal that girls want jobs that express feminine interests and provide a social setting for meeting prospective husbands.

Beyond this interpersonal emphasis, girls seem to bridge the present and future much more with fantasy than with reality-tied or concrete plans. The girl is less likely to say of the future, "This is what I think I will be," than she is to say, "I hope my life will be like this." The boy checks and conditions his goals by the step-by-step instrumental procedures they imply; the girl leaps more directly in fantasy to the goal. And this makes good sense—for her the procedures are equally ambiguous, whether the goal is simple or grand. What she will become does not depend in any direct or simple way on her own instrumental acts, it depends rather on the man she marries.

A clear concept of her adult femininity, of feminine goals and interpersonal skills, functions for the girl like the vocational concept for the boy. It bridges the worlds of adolescence and adulthood, brings the future concretely into current life, and allows the future to contribute meaning and organization to adolescent activities and interests. Girls who have relatively clear notions about and goals in adult femininity show a high degree of personal integration. Those girls who specifically reject a feminine future are troubled adolescents.

The different stances boys and girls assume toward the future is expressed most simply and directly in our analysis of mobility aspirations. Mobility aspiration for the boy is no idle dream, it is rather the concrete expression of a boy's faith in himself. The goal he chooses is realistic in light of his talent and opportunities, but is not overblown. And it is cast in the phrasing of reality—What is the job like? What activities and demands does it encompass, what training does it require? What are my abilities and opportunities, do they provide me access to the field?

The girl's mobility aspirations are less formed and less fettered by reality. She need not test her desire against her own talent and skill, since these will not be crucial determinants of her future status. Her access to higher status will come through marriage. For most of these girls (except those few older girls who have already experienced a lasting, meaningful relationship with a boy) marriage itself has so little reality that the difference between a "good" or socially advancing marriage and any marriage at all is not significant. Since it is all a dream, in any case, one may as well dream big. Girls' mobility plans are less careful than boys', less cautioned by an assessment of opportunity. They are more simply dreams.

The imminence of adulthood, the imposing need to master and incorporate some elements of adult identity into current life (at least in fantasy), means that the child must alter his relationship to his family in some important ways. He must begin to detach himself from the family and develop some measure of independence in behavior, emotions, values, and beliefs. The process of detachment has traditionally been described as high drama—the rebellious adolescent pressing for enlarged independence and continually confronting conservative, dynastic parental control. We shall have more to say later about the detachment as it seems to develop in American adolescents, and about the appropriateness of this traditional model to the reality of American family life. At this point it is enough to say that the process as we observe it seems less dramatic and full of conflict than tradition and theory hold, and to point out again a significant difference between boys and girls.

Our findings regarding the issue of independence indicate that the urge to be free, to be one's own master, is almost exclusively a masculine stirring. Up to the age of eighteen girls show no great press for independence, certainly no need to confront authority or insist on the right to develop and distinguish independent beliefs or controls. The difference appears in our descriptive findings about adolescents' attitudes toward themselves and their family relationships. It also emerges analytically when we look at the relationship of developing independence to other areas of personal growth. In boys, the measure of independent functioning achieved relates clearly to other areas of development—to the integration of a future concept, to upward-mobility aspirations and general achievement strivings, to current adolescent adjustment. These relationships do not hold for the girls. Feminine integration does not demand a strong bid for independence during the adolescent period. Indeed we find that girls' attitudes toward parental control do not even relate very strongly to the nature or style of that control.

Close to the issue of detachment, and theoretically the central mechanism for realizing separation, is the issue of adolescent peer group ties. Here again we have the impression that the importance of the peer group has been exaggerated in theory and in much of popular complaint about adolescents. Our data again indicate that boys and girls differ both in the extent of their allegiance to the peer group and in the particular uses they make of peer ties. Boys more often hold allegiance to the group as such, conceive the group as a coherent and loyal band offering support to members and having an authority of its own. Boys recognize "the gang" as a force that could lead a boy to break rules; they think of getting into a "bad gang" as a danger to be avoided.

Girls use peer relationships differently. They are not as tied to a group as such, nor are they as sensitized to the pressure of "the gang" (except possibly in issues of taste). In general girls are more attracted to close two-person friendships. The loyalty of the best friend is the loyalty the girl depends on, needs, and seeks. In belonging to groups, the girl does not seek a band to support her as she makes a play for freedom—rather, she uses the group as a resource for finding close individual friendships. She is always on the lookout for prospective best friends. The individual friendship transcends the group (although it may exist in a group setting), and becomes the center of mutual self-exploration through shared intimacy. In their concepts about friendship and in the intimacy of their friendships, girls are more highly developed than boys. In fact, the interpersonal seems to be the central area of growth for girls during adolescence. Our evidence indicates that the girl's development in the interpersonal sphere is the pivotal feature around which her adolescent adjustment focuses. A measure of interpersonal development was our best predictor of ego integration in girls.

We have stressed the importance of the future in adolescent adjustment, but we do not mean to underestimate the impact of the child's past on his resolution of adolescent tasks. His particular past in a particular family with its own style of interaction enters and critically affects the youngster's encounter with all of the adolescent problems. Two clear family patterns appear in our studies—the democratic family style and an autocratic or authoritarian style. In the democratic family, parents allow the adolescent a fair degree of autonomy, include the child in important decisions affecting his own behavior, and tend to use psychological and verbal discipline. Authoritarian parents set rules without consulting the children, allow little autonomy, and tend to use physical techniques for enforcing discipline. The effects of the family pattern on the adolescents are apparent, strong, and consistent. The democratic families produce adolescents who are unusually self-reliant, poised, and effective. They are free to criticize and disagree with parents, but have generally warm companionship with them. In the authoritarian families the adolescents are on the surface compliant; beneath the surface (in responses to projective measures) they are rebellious and impulsive. They tend to have an externalized morality, to define morals as what one can get away with. They are less effective and less poised in their general bearing.

The findings from our studies point to the homogenization of American adolescence across regional boundaries and, by and large, across social class lines as well. We were struck by the lack of impressive differences among these population groups. It seems that the peculiar conflicts of the age itself and the force of modern mass communications have combined to cast a universal form for the adolescent experience—a form heavily invested with middle-class values. Adolescent interests and activities, family patterns and moves toward independence, are much the same in all regions, in all social classes. Among standard background variables, only religion yielded differences that are large, consistent, and consistently interesting.

These, briefly, are the substantive findings from our studies. Beyond these conclusions supported directly by data, what can we say we have learned from the studies? We like to think that years invested bear a yield in wisdom and insight that extend beyond the relatively narrow range of empirical findings. Some broader conclusion and speculation should be part of the reward for so much demanding attention to detail.

We have two such broad comments to make, both representing insights we gained from the research, both having to do with the aptness of standard theoretical formulations of the adolescent experience. The two areas that focus these comments are first, the importance of sex differences in adolescence; and, second, the nature of the adolescent experience as it occurs in the middle range of American children.

Our initial approach to the study of adolescence, while tied theoretically to psychoanalysis, rested also on developmental descriptive notions that have dominated child psychology and particularly the study of adolescence. We hoped to go beyond the mere description of change, and to use theory to clarify sources of variation in the form and pace of adolescent change. Nonetheless, we conceived these changes, however they might vary, as organized around certain developmental tasks posed for all children in our culture somewhere near the close of childhood. The tasks we noted were the ones we have described in earlier chapters—regulating instincts; dissolving infantile dependencies and integrating new areas of autonomy; developing stable object ties, particularly heterosexual ties; coming to terms with the superego; and exploring identity possibilities.

This conception of adolescent challenges established the outlines of our investigation, and we had at the outset some notions about the factors, including sex, that would determine different forms of the developmental crisis and its outcome. We were quite sure that achievement and occupational choice would be more crucial to the boy, that social and interpersonal issues would play a larger role in girls' preoccupations and would more surely gauge the girl's personal integration at adolescence.

What we did not anticipate was the force of the sex variable, the extent to which it defines and shades all aspects of the developmental crisis. Since all children undergo radical biological changes at puberty, and presumably also derivative instinctual changes, we assumed that the new task of regulating these instincts would also be met by all children. This would require some reworking of internal controls, some changes in self-regulation. The nature of the solutions might vary, but they would all be responses to a unifying problem and would share at least the rough outline and structure that this problem establishes.

In fact we find that the adolescent crisis for boys and girls differs in almost every regard—in the statement of developmental tasks, not just how they are phrased, but whether they arise during the era at all; in the general direction of solution alternatives available to the child, and in the individual solution expressions achieved by youngsters in our society.

One may see commonalities, of course. But our studies suggest that the observation of similarity in this case requires such a high level of abstraction, and such a cost to the richness of one's description and understanding of adolescent reality, that the transaction loses its relevance and value. So, for example, we know that puberty brings basic biological changes to girls as well as boys. Mead (1955) has even pointed to the more decisive nature of feminine puberty changes. Yet to conclude from this that boys and girls face similar problems psychologically in the regulation of instinctual energy seems to strain too much reality from the situation. At some level the drives increase and must be managed in both sexes, but our findings point to the conclusion that the drive is so successfully excluded from consciousness by the large majority of girls that they do not in any relevant psychological sense confront an impulse problem comparable to boys' during the adolescent years. This difference, in turn, influences the reworking of controls, the development of autonomy, and the resolution of dependencies—producing sex-determined differences in both pace and process.

The key terms in adolescent development for the boy in our culture are the erotic, autonomy (assertiveness, independence, achievement), and identity. For the girl the comparable terms are the erotic, the interpersonal, and identity. Differences between the two sets of problems are larger and more complex than a single discrepancy implies; for this discrepancy is so central that it reverberates through the entire complex. For the girl the development of interpersonal ties—the sensitivities, skills, ethics, and values of object ties—forms the core of identity, and it gives expression to much of developing feminine eroticism. Feminine sexuality, consciously inhibited from active and direct expression, seeks more subtle, limited, and covert expression. The search for popularity, the effort to charm, all of the many and varied interpersonal ties which serve as setting for the girl's practice in winning and maintaining love—these engagements filter and express a good deal of the girl's erotic need. We have noted the greater intensity and importance of girls' like-sexed friendships when compared to their friendships with boys or to boys' like-sexed friendships. And we have held that the intimate friendship between girls serves a number of functions, all tied to the girl's need to explore and understand her sexual nature as well as her individuality. It is primarily through these serial, episodic, intimate two-somes that the girl comes to terms with her sexual nature and gradually sorts elements of identification from aspects of individuality to form an identity. The tie to objects is both the key to her erotic realization and also the mechanism through which she arrives at an individuated personal identity.

For the boy, on the other hand, the integrated capacity for erotic ties and the solution of the identity challenge demand separation and autonomy. What the girl achieves through intimate connection with others, the boy must manage by disconnecting, by separating himself and asserting his right to be distinct. His biological sexual nature is more explicitly and individually stated than the girl's. It has less compelling interpersonal features, depends less on the existence of a fully developed object relation and it insists on the resolution of certain authority problems in order to gain expression. The boy can know sexual gratification outside a full or fully developed love relationship, but his sexual realization depends on severing infantile ties and asserting his independence of them. Without autonomy, the boy's sexual realization suffers the constant hazard of crippling castration fears. To achieve full status as a sexual adult, the boy must clarify the difference between himself and his father and assume the status of the father's independent peer. The girl's adult sexuality, on the other hand, depends on an intricate and little understood process of consolidating a satisfactory identification with her own mother.

The identity problem is also phrased differently for boys and girls in our culture, and the distinction again revolves around their different requirements for object love and for autonomy. We have noted that feminine identity forms more closely about capacity and practice in the personal arts, and we have seen in our findings evidence that the girl's ego integration co-varies with her interpersonal development. Masculine identity, in contrast, focuses about the capacity to handle and master nonsocial reality, to design and win for oneself an independent area of work which fits one's individual talents and taste and permits achievement of at least some central personal goals. The boy's ego development at adolescence already bears the mark of this formulation and reflects his progress in mastering it. Identity is for the boy a matter of individuating internal bases for action and defending these against domination by others. For the girl it is a process of finding and defining the internal and individual through attachments to others.

The normative descriptive approach to adolescent psychology is not the only one in which sex variation has been overlooked. When we look at the developing literature on identity and the self-concept, we note again the predominance of a masculine formulation. The most advanced psychoanalytic theorists often fail to note what seems to be an imposing distinction, at least to judge from the results of our studies and other recent research.

In Erikson's statement of the developmental tasks of adolescence and early adulthood, the problem of individual identity is put before that of intimacy—and there is a compelling logic to this order. For how, one asks, can the individual form a genuine tie to another, a contact of depth and intimacy, unless the outlines of his individual being have been established and fortified; how can we speak of two individuals merging in intimacy unless we start with two individuals?

Yet psychic phenomena do not always follow logic in so orderly a manner. We know that in many people, the working through of identity issues continues well beyond the early adult years and that in some cases, at least, intimacy has been achieved in some degree before the individual has developed the kind of continuity and integrity of self which an identity resolution implies.

This, we would argue, is much more commonly the tone of feminine identity formation. The girl is more likely to gain a developed identity in consequence of intimacy rather than as a precursor of it. Out of her intimate connections to others, through processes of identification and projection, the woman comes to know her own individuality and to solve the question of who she is. The reasons for this arrangement lie both in the nature of feminine psychic development and in the much simpler and more obvious realm of social reality. For the fact is that in our culture at least the need to marry and find acceptance and love exert such pressure on the young girl that we can hardly imagine her having the time and energy to invest in identity-resolution until she has gained some measure of security in a stable love relationship. To do so may even involve hazards to her marriage eligibility. Too sharp a self-definition and too full an investment in a unique personal integration are not considered highly feminine; they are often thought to be unattractive in a young woman.[1]

The girl, then, is likely to arrive at an identity resolution through the interpersonal, and, then, only after she has reached some relatively satisfactory integration of intimacy and the erotic. The boy's tasks are ordered differently—his identity depends on his achieving autonomy —an acceptable integration of assertiveness and self-direction. His

[1] Mirra Komarovsky (1946) has reported interviews with college women in which the girls themselves reveal that they are consciously avoiding too clear and invested self-definitions because of the fear of becoming ineligible for marriage.

identity demands and forms around these qualities; beyond this, no erotic resolution except denial is available to him until he has established a degree of freedom from external control.

We have perhaps overstated the difference between boys and girls. The girl has experienced some degree of separation before she enters the intimate friendships of adolescence—after all, all social development consists of rhythmic and complementary processes of differentiation and integration, of separating from and connecting with objects. The boy, on the other hand, has been tied in more or less intimate (although immature) relationships with others up to the adolescent strike for autonomy. But the tone and order of development that begins in adolescence and concludes in maturity—these, we contend, differ sharply for the two sexes. We have seen the derivative effects of the difference in our studies—the areas of achievement, autonomy, authority and control focus and express boys' major concerns and psychological growth; the object relations—friendship, dating, popularity and the understanding and management of interpersonal crisis—hold the key to adolescent growth and integration for the girl. The internalization of feminine goals also has important implications for the girl's development. Here too the goal is to form a lasting tie to another, and is not an individual achievement in the sense that the boy's vocational goal is.

We conclude, then, that there is not one adolescent crisis, but two major and clearly distinctive ones—the masculine and the feminine. If we are to think of adolescence as a relatively delimited period, we must conclude that some of the traditionally conceived problems of the period (for example, detachment from external authority, the resolution of primitive object ties) are not a part of the feminine phrasing of adolescence. If we conceive impulses to be drives that have some reasonably direct impact on conscious thought and behavior, we may even question the traditional concept of adolescence as a time of turbulent instinctual struggle as far as the girl is concerned. While we cling to the notion that somewhere beneath compliance and repression there lies a heart of fire, our impression from the study of girls is that for them adolescence is less infused with impulse and more focused on form than any traditional conception of the era could have led us to expect.

If sex differences led us to reconsider traditional conceptions of adolescence, the normative findings from our studies also made us think twice about the received version of the period. Most contemporary comment on adolescence focuses on two conspicuous but atypical enclaves of adolescents, drawn from extreme and opposing ends of the social class continuum, and representing exceptional solutions to the adolescent crisis. These are, on the one hand, the delinquent, and on the other, the sensitive, articulate, middle-class adolescent on whom the psychoanalytic view is almost exclusively based.

Now in most ways these types could not be more dissimilar. The estranged lower-class youngster relies largely on alloplastic solutions to the adolescent crisis, living out mutely, in urgent yet aimless acts of violence or bravado, a sullen resentment against the middle-class world and its values. The estranged upper-middle-class youngster is largely autoplastic in response; subject to acute intrapsychic upheavals which are expressed in neurotic symptoms, affect storms, character eccentricities, and a general value ferment. Paradoxically, these two extremes are alike, and their likeness is in being different from the normative adolescent—the adolescent of the core culture. The extremes are alike in showing an unusual degree of independence from the family; they are alike in disaffection, in acting out or thinking out a discontent with the social order; they are alike, above all, in that they adopt radical solutions to the adolescent task of ego-synthesis.

We want to suggest that one cannot generalize these processes to the adolescent population at large. The adolescent at the extremes responds to the instinctual and psychosocial upheaval of puberty by disorder, by failures of ego-synthesis, and by a tendency to abandon earlier values and object attachments. In the normative response to adolescence, however, we more commonly find an avoidance of inner and outer conflict, premature identity consolidation, ego and ideological constriction, and a general unwillingness to take psychic risks. The great advantage of the survey technique is that it allows us to study these adolescents who make up the middle majority, who evoke neither grief nor wonder, and who all too often escape our notice.

Let us begin with the question of autonomy and conflict. In the traditional view, the child at puberty is under great pressure to detach himself from the family emotionally, to find a pattern of disengagement. The instinctual revival brings with it a return of Oedipal dangers and temptations. The home is a "hothouse" and the boy at least must discover a way out, a means of escaping his dependent status in the family, and even more urgently, the dimly recognized drives and feelings toward his parents. This is the psychosexual irritation which pushes the child from home, leading him to negotiate or battle with the parents for greater freedom. The conflict of generations is joined. We add to this a psychosocial pull—the child's need to forge an individual identity—those needs which draw the child toward the future. These forces give the peer group at adolescence its critical importance. Peer group and culture supplant the family as the locus of authority and the giver of norms. Through his immersion in the peer group, through the incorporation of peer ideals and values, the youngster gains the support he needs to win autonomy from the family. And the peer group provides a haven in which the delicate task of self-exploration and self-definition can be accomplished.

This view of adolescence has a good deal to recommend it, but our reading of the interviews suggests that it needs revision in some important particulars if we are to apply it to the middle majority. This view exaggerates the degree of conflict between parent and child; it wrongly estimates the autonomy issue; and it misinterprets the role of the peer group. The normative adolescent tends to avoid overt conflict with his family. Now this is not to say that conflict is not present; but it is largely unconscious conflict, those under-surface resentments which do not necessarily liberate or enlarge the personality, but which, paradoxically, increase the child's docility toward his parents. Even when we do find overt conflict one senses that it has an "as if" quality to it, that it is a kind of war game, with all the sights and sounds of battle but without any blood being shed. More often than not the conflicts will center on trivia, on issues of taste—clothing, grooming, and the like. One can argue that these issues are trivial only to the adult, that they are, however, of great symbolic importance in the adolescent's quest for autonomy. True; but one can reply that parent and child play out an empty ritual of disaffection, that they agree to disagree only on token issues, on teen issues, and in doing so are able to sidestep any genuine encounter of differences.

Much the same is true of autonomy. There are autonomies and autonomies. The American adolescent asks for and is freely given an unusual degree of behavioral freedom—the right to come and go, to share in setting rules, and so on. But it is far more problematic whether he asks for or achieves a high degree of emotional autonomy, and it is even more doubtful that he manages much in the way of value autonomy. Indeed, the ease with which the adolescent acquires behavioral freedom may tend to interfere with the achievement of emotional and ideological freedom, for reasons we shall turn to in a moment. As to the peer group, its supposed functions—as an arena for the confrontation of the self, for the testing and trying out of identities—are present for many adolescents, but for many more the peer group is used for the learning and display of sociability and social skills. The peer culture is all too often a kind of playpen, designed to keep the children out of harm's way and out of the parents' hair. It may not work out this way; the children may begin throwing toys at each other, or, what is worse, may begin throwing them at the grownups in the living room. But generally it does work out just this way. The peer group, with its artificial amusements and excitements, more often acts to hinder differentiation and growth.

This is especially evident in the area of values and ideology. The traditional idea of the adolescent experience has it that the youngster becomes involved in an intense concern with ethics, political ideology, religious belief, and so on. The moral parochialism of early childhood was thought to be smashed by the moral fervor and incipient cosmopolitanism of adolescence. The youngster's need to detach himself from the family and its view of the moral and social order, his need to redo the ego-superego constellation, his need to find new and more appropriate ego ideals, his need to use ideology as a solution for instinctual problems—all these needs came together, so it was thought, to produce a value crisis somewhere in the course of the adolescent career. This pattern can be found in adolescence, but it is found in a bold, sometimes stubborn, often unhappy minority. Our interviews confirm a mounting impression from other studies, that American adolescents are on the whole not deeply involved in ideology, nor are they prepared to do much individual thinking on value issues of any generality. Why is this so? We would guess this is true because to think anew and differently endangers the adolescent's connection to the community, his object attachments, and complicates the task of ego synthesis.

We can sum up in the language of personality theory. The inherent tensions of adolescence are displaced to and discharged within the matrix of peer group sociability. Intrapsychically the defenses and character positions adopted are those which curtail experience and limit the growth and differentiation of the self—repression, reaction-formation, and certain forms of ego restriction. These two modes of dealing with inner and outer experience join to produce a pseudoadaptive solution of the adolescent crisis, marked by cognitive stereotypy, value stasis, and interpersonal conformity. It is a solution which is accomplished by resisting conflict, resisting change, resisting the transformation of the self. It settles for a modest resynthesis of the ego—closely along the lines of the older organization of drives, defenses, values, and object attachments. It is characterized by an avoidance of identity-diffusion through identity-coarctation.

These rather dismal conclusions on the contemporary adolescent character are akin to those stated by Edgar Friedenberg in his brilliant book, *The Vanishing Adolescent*. Adolescence, he says, is disappearing as the period in which the individual can achieve a decisive articulation of the self. Nowadays the youngster, in his words, "merely undergoes puberty and simulates maturity." If this amiable but colorless form of adolescence is indeed a new thing in our country, then we would have to single out as one important reason the extraordinary attenuation of today's adolescence. Given the long preparation required for advanced technical training, given the uselessness of the adolescent in the labor market—parent and child settle down for a long, long period of time during which the child will, in one way or another, remain a dependent being.

Traditionally, adolescence has been the age in which the child readied himself to leave home; and when we read accounts of adolescence in the earlier part of this century we very often note between father and son a decisive encounter, a decisive testing of wills, in which the son makes a determined bid for autonomy, either by leaving home, or threatening to do so, and meaning it. The adolescent then had little of the freedom he has today; he was kept under the parental thumb, but he used his captivity well, to strengthen himself for a real departure and a real autonomy. Nowadays the adolescent and his parents are both made captive by their mutual knowledge of the adolescent's dependency. They are locked in a room with no exit, and they make the best of it by an unconscious *quid pro quo*, in which the adolescent forfeits his adolescence, and instead becomes a teenager. He keeps the peace by muting his natural rebelliousness through transforming it into structured and defined techniques for getting on people's nerves. The passions, the restlessness, the vivacity of adolescence are partly strangled, and partly drained off in the mixed childishness and false adulthood of the adolescent teen culture.

References

Ackerman, N. W., and Jahoda, Marie. *Anti-semitism and emotional disorder*. New York: Harper, 1950.

Adelson, J. Psychology and the humanities: a discussion. Presented at the Seventeenth International Congress of Psychology, Washington, D. C., August 1963.

Adorno, T. W., et al. *The authoritarian personality*. New York: Harper, 1950.

Agee, J. *Agee on film*. New York: McDowell, Obolensky, 1958, p. 168.

Axelrod, M. Urban structure and social participation. *Amer. Sociol. Rev.*, 1956, **21**, 13–18.

Beardslee, D., and O'Dowd, D. Students and the occupational world. In N. Sanford (Ed.), *The American college*. New York: Wiley, 1962.

Blos, P. Preoedipal factors in the etiology of female delinquency. In *The psychoanalytic study of the child*, Vol. 12, 229–249. New York: International Universities Press, 1957.

Blos, P. *On adolescence: a psychoanalytic interpretation*. New York: Free Press of Glencoe, 1962.

Centers, R. *The psychology of social classes: a study of class consciousness*. Princeton: Princeton Univer. Press, 1949.

Coleman, J. *The adolescent society*. New York: Free Press of Glencoe, 1961.

Couch, A., and Keniston, K. Yeasayers and naysayers: agreeing response set as a personality variable. *J. Abnor. soc. Psychol.*, 1960, **60**, 151–174.

Cousins, A. N. The failure of solidarity. In N. W. Bell and E. F. Vogel (Eds.), *A modern introduction to the family*. Glencoe: The Free Press, 1960, pp. 403–416.

Davis, A. Personality and social mobility. *Sch. Rev.*, 1957, **65**, 134–143.

Deutsch, Helene. *The psychology of women*, 2 Vols. New York: Grune and Stratton, 1944, 1945.

Erikson, E. *Childhood and society*. New York: Norton, 1950.

Erikson, E. The problem of ego identity. *J. Amer. Psychoanal. Ass.*, 1956, **4**, 56–121.

Freud, Anna. (1936) *The ego and the mechanisms of defense*. New York: International Universities Press, 1946.

Freud, Anna. Adolescence. In *The psychoanalytic study of the child*, Vol. 13, 255–278. New York: International Universities Press, 1958.

Freud, Anna, and Burlingham, Dorothy. *War and children*. New York: International Universities Press, 1943.

Freud, S. Doestoevsky and parricide. (1928) *Collected papers,* Vol. V. London: Hogarth Press, 1950.

Friedenberg, E. *The vanishing adolescent.* Boston: Beacon Press, 1959.

Goffman, E. *The presentation of self in everyday life.* Garden City: Doubleday Anchor, 1959.

Goodman, P. *Growing up absurd.* New York: Random House, 1960.

Gurin, G., Veroff, J., and Feld, Sheila. *Americans view their mental health.* New York: Basic Books, 1960.

Hartmann, H. On rational and irrational action. In *Psychoanalysis and the social sciences,* Vol. I. New York: International Universities Press, 1947.

Havighurst, R., and Taba, Hilda. *Adolescent character and personality.* New York: Wiley, 1949.

Himmelweit, Hilde. Socioeconomic background and personality. *Int. soc. Sci. Bull.,* 1955, **7**, 29–34.

Hollingshead, A. B. *Elmtown's youth.* New York: Wiley, 1949.

Johnson, Adelaide M., and Szurek, S. A. The genesis of antisocial acting out in children and adults. *Psychoanal. quart.,* 1952, **21**, 323–343.

Kahl, J. A. Educational and occupational aspirations of 'common man' boys. *Harvard Educ. Rev.,* 1953, **23**, 186–203.

Komarovsky, Mirra. Cultural contradictions and sex roles. *Amer. J. Sociol.,* 1946, **52**, 184–189.

Lewin, K. *Resolving social conflict.* New York: Harper, 1948, pp. 3–33.

Lipset, S. M., and Bendix, R. *Social mobility in industrial society.* Berkeley and Los Angeles: Univer. of California Press, 1960.

Lipset, S. M., and Rogoff, Natalie. Class opportunity in Europe and the U. S.: some myths and what the statistics show. *Commentary,* 1954, **18**, 562–568.

Lynn, K. S. *The dream of success.* Boston: Little, Brown, 1955.

McClelland, D. C., Atkinson, J. W., Clark, R. A., and Lowell, E. L. *The achievement motive.* New York: Appleton-Century-Crofts, 1953.

Mead, Margaret. *Male and female.* New York: Mentor, 1955.

Nye, I., and Lois W. Hoffman (Eds.). *The employed mother in America.* Chicago: Rand McNally, 1963.

Parsons, T., and Bales, R. F. *Family, socialization and interaction process.* Glencoe: The Free Press, 1955.

Pearson, G. *Adolescence and the conflict of generations.* New York: Norton, 1958.

Sanford, N. (Ed.). *Personality development during the college years, J. soc. Issues,* 1956, **12**, No. 4.

Schachtel, E. *Metamorphosis.* New York: Basic Books, 1959.

Shapiro, R. L. Adolescence and the psychology of the ego. *Psychiatry,* 1963, **26**, 77–87.

Spiegel, L. A review of contributions to a psychoanalytic theory of adolescence. In *The psychoanalytic study of the child,* Vol. 6, 375–393. New York: International Universities Press, 1951.

Stone, L. J., and Church, J. *Childhood and adolescence.* New York: Random House, 1957.

Strodtbeck, F. L. Family interaction, values, and achievement. In M. Sklare (Ed.), *The Jews: social patterns of an American group.* Glencoe: The Free Press, 1948, pp. 147–165.

Tocqueville, A. de. *Democracy in America.* New York: Knopf, 1948.

Trilling, L. The last lover. *Encounter*, 1958, **11**, 9–19.

Veroff, J., Feld, Sheila, and Gurin, G. Achievement motivation and religious background. *Amer. Sociol. Rev.*, 1962, **27**, 205–217.

Waller, W. The rating and dating complex. *Amer. Sociol. Rev.*, 1937, 727–737.

Whyte, W. H., Jr. *The organization man.* New York: Simon and Schuster, 1956, pp. 350–365.

Winch, R. *Mate-selection: a study of complementary needs.* New York: Harper, 1958.

Wolfenstein, Martha, and Leites, N. *Movies: a psychological study.* Glencoe: The Free Press, 1950.

Wyatt, F., and Hoffman, Lois W. Social change and motivations for having larger families: some theoretical considerations. *Merrill-Palmer Quarterly of Behavior and Development*, 1960, **6**, 235–244.

Explanatory Notes

Numbering of Tables

Each table bears a two-digit number. The first digit refers to the chapter to which the table corresponds, the second digit to the table's position in the sequence of tables connected with that chapter. Consequently, Table 6.1 is the first table for Chapter 6. As a rule the first table for each chapter presents the most general and complete summary of findings for the chapter on either developmental data or differences between boys and girls on all of the relevant questions or indices our studies include. Later tables in the sequence for a chapter present findings from special analyses within the area of concern of the chapter. These special analyses vary from chapter to chapter, and we can give no general rule about the meaning of the fourth table in each sequence. We have ordered these later tables to correspond to the analysis presentations in the text of the chapters.

Tables for Chapters 8 and 9

Because of their prohibitive number and size, we have not included the tables for the family structure and demographic analyses in the book. They are available in mimeograph form from the authors on request.

Response Categories

The total number of response categories for open questions may be very large. In summarizing the data for the tables, we have presented only those response categories relevant to the analysis being considered; for example, respondents answer the question about their future decisions in many different ways. However, in one analysis (e.g., of mobility aspirations) we may be interested only in responses having to do with personal achievement; in another (e.g., patterns of femininity) we may be interested only in answers about marriage. In each table, then, we present only relevant categories. The full set of categories for any question will usually be found in the first table in a sequence.

Responses to open questions often total more than one hundred per cent because boys and girls gave more than one answer.

Italicized categories and figures indicate a summary statement for a broad class of responses. These categories are often immediately followed by a more refined break down of the responses included and the appropriate percentages. In Table 2.1, Item 3, we present both the total of all vocational aspirations classed as "professional" and individual listings for specific professional jobs (e.g., lawyer, doctor). The sum of all individual listings should equal the total for the class.

Questionnaire Forms

To keep the length of interviews within reasonable limits, we used a system of deletions. Three forms of the questionnaire were used, and certain questions were omitted from one or another of the forms. Since the use of the forms was varied systematically, and our samples were large, data for the two-thirds sample still give reliable estimates of true figures for the population. A few questions were asked of only one-third of the sample. All form-linked deletions are noted in the tables.

Notes and Symbols in the Tables

Note, Symbol	Meaning
(*B*14; *G*14) after item heading	Source of data: in the example the data derived from responses to question 14 on the boys' interview schedule and question 14 in the girls'.
(*IR*) after item heading	Data derived from an interviewer rating.
(*CR; B*12, 12*a*, 12*b*)	Data derived from a coder rating based on boys' answers to questions 12, 12*a*, and 12*b* on the boys' schedule
* Asterisk	Less than one half of 1 per cent
Index listings	These refer to measures obtained by combining questions. The development of all such measures is described in Appendix C.

TABLES

Table 2.1. Boys and girls of three age groups compared on questions about future plans and fantasies

Item	Boys, % ($N = 1045$)	Girls, %		
		Under 14 ($N = 844$)	14–16 ($N = 822$)	17–18 ($N = 259$)
1. Decisions in the next few years (B10; G10)				
a. Vocational: choice of work	66	52	73	64
b. Service-related: decisions concerning period of service, armed forces	20	—	—	—
c. Educational: whether to go to college, choice of college	76	57	84	66
d. Marital: when to marry, whom to marry	12	23	30	41
e. Other interpersonal	2	15	5	2
f. Other miscellaneous	13	6	11	22
g. Don't know	1	6	2	*
h. Not ascertained	2	1	*	1
2. Picture of future life (G11)				
a. Occupation		36	30	24
b. Education		8	7	7
c. Marriage		4	2	2
d. Occupation and education		20	23	21
e. Occupation and marriage		9	11	16
f. Education and marriage		3	4	4
g. Occupation, education, marriage		8	13	17
h. Other		3	2	2
i. No plans, don't know, not ascertained		9	8	7

	Boys	Girls		
		Under 14	14–16	17–18

3. Vocational choice
   (B14; G14)

	Boys	Under 14	14–16	17–18
Professional	*40*	*30*	*30*	*24*
a. Engineer	16	*	—	—
b. Doctor	4	4	2	*
c. Arts-writer, musician	4	3	5	5
d. Public-salaried teacher, coach	6	21	17	15
e. Lawyer, diplomat	2	1	1	1
f. Architect	2	—	*	—
g. Dentist	2	—	—	—
h. Forester, conservationist	1	—	—	—
i. Social worker	—	—	2	2
j. Other	3	1	3	1
Secondary professional	*14*	27	*25*	*16*
k. Nurse	—	25	21	10
l. Medical technician	2	2	3	4
m. Accountant	1	—	—	—
n. Other	11	—	1	2
Business-owner, manager	*8*	*	*1*	*2*
White collar, sales	*5*	*30*	*40*	*45*
o. Secretary	—	26	34	39
p. Bookkeeper	1	*	3	4
q. Sales	2	4	3	2
r. Other	2	*	—	—
Farmer	*14*	—	—	—
Manual	*29*	*3*	*1*	*5*
s. Craft skill	7	1	1	—
t. Manual, skilled	15	—	*	—
u. Manual, semi- and unskilled	7	2	*	5
Service	*1*	*4*	*5*	*7*
v. Beautician, barber	1	2	4	7
w. Waitress	—	2	1	—
Transitional armed forces	*5*	*2*	*3*	*2*
Religious	*1*	*4*	*2*	*1*
Glamour	*3*	*13*	*10*	*10*
x. Fashion designer	—	3	3	3
y. Model	—	1	1	3

Table 2.1 (*Continued*)

| | Boys | Girls | | |
		Under 14	14–16	17–18
z. Dance band; dancer, singer, actor	1	3	2	2
aa. Pilot	2	—	—	—
bb. Stewardess	—	6	4	2
cc. Housewife	—	5	2	3
dd. Don't know	8	12	7	6
ee. Not ascertained	1	*	1	—
4. Vocational aspirations classed by status (*B*14; *G*14)				
a. Professional	40	30	30	24
b. Secondary professional (e.g., nurse, model, stewardess)	14	40	35	26
c. Business	8	*	1	2
d. White collar, sales	5	30	39	45
e. Farmer	14	—	—	—
f. Personal service	2	4	5	7
g. Manual; skilled	22	1	1	—
h. Manual; semi-skilled and unskilled	7	2	*	5
i. Not ascertained, not classifiable	11	8	4	5
5. Vocational aspirations: clarity of choice (*B*14; *G*15)				
a. Have one job clearly in mind	73	57	66	70
b. Name several jobs as possibilities	18	26	24	21
c. Housewife, no other vocation	—	5	2	3
d. No choice	9	12	8	6
6. Educational plans (*B*13, 13*a*, *b*; *G*12)				
a. Does not plan to finish high school	5	2	2	1
b. Will finish high school, no further plans	25	13	14	22
c. Will finish high school, further				

	Boys	Girls		
		Under 14	14–16	17–18
plans indefinite	19	22	20	16
d. Will go beyond high school: vocational, trade school (Secretarial school)	4	11	21	24
e. Nurse's training	—	14	11	5
College level	*46*	*37*	*34*	*32*
f. College	22	33	31	28
g. Professional school	4	—	*	*
h. Agricultural school	5	—	—	—
i. Engineering school	10	—	*	—
j. Military school	2	—	—	—
k. Theological Seminary	1	—	—	—
l. Other	3	*	—	—
m. Teachers' college	0	4	4	4
7. Congruence: education and occupation plans (*CR: B*13, *B*14; *G*12, *G*14)				
a. Educational plans inappropriately high	7	21	24	28
b. Educational plans inadequate	4	24	19	12
c. Educational plans congruent with occupational goals	69	38	44	47
d. No basis for judgment	20	17	13	13
8. Clarity of *R*'s conception of vocational preparation (*CR: B*20) [a]				
a. Clear and detailed	22			
b. Clear, not detailed	44			
c. Unclear	18			
d. No training required	2			
e. Not ascertained; no job choice	14			
9. Work models (*B*19) [a]				
a. Father	15			
b. Other family member	10			
c. Acquaintance	15			
d. No one *R* knows	24			

Table 2.1 (*Continued*)

	Boys	Girls Under 14	14–16	17–18
e. *R* has a model, not identified	22			
10. Reasons for job choice (*B*17; *G*14*a*) [b]				
a. Interest in work	70	49	59	66
b. High pay, status	18	3	2	3
c. Security	6	8	12	11
d. Outdoor work	10	8	7	1
e. Independence, own boss	7	—	*	*
f. Meet people	6	11	17	21
g. Social service	6	24	23	14
h. Like children	—	15	11	8
i. Appropriate for women	—	1	2	3
j. Travel	—	2	4	8
k. Easy work, easy to get	12	5	9	15
11. Most important job criteria (*B*22, *B*23; *G*15, 15*a*) [a,c]				
a. Steady job	52		48	44
b. Interesting work	49		57	68
c. Nice people to work with	32		53	58
d. Be your own boss	13		3	2
e. Outdoor work	13		1	1
f. Be looked up to by others	5		6	4
g. Be a leader of people	2		1	2
h. Good chance for promotion	14		9	11
i. High pay	14		7	5
j. A job in hometown	6		4	3
k. Not ascertained	*		10	2
12. Two least important job criteria (*B*24; *G*15*b*) [a,c]				
a. Steady job	1		1	3
b. Interesting work	1		1	1
c. Nice people to work with	2		1	1

	Boys	Girls Under 14	14–16	17–18
d. Be your own boss	31		48	48
e. Outdoor work	29		32	48
f. Be looked up to by others	31		28	18
g. Be a leader of other people	36		24	21
h. Good chance for promotion	7		8	6
i. High pay	13		18	13
j. A job in hometown	41		28	34
k. Not ascertained	1		15	7
13. Certainty about job choice (B15)				
a. Very sure	4			
b. Sure, pretty sure	52			
c. Might change plans	17			
d. Very likely to change	12			
e. No job choice	9			
f. Don't know, not ascertained	6			
14. Interest in vocational counseling (B16) [a]				
a. Strong interest	5			
b. Moderate	81			
c. Weak or no interest	12			
d. Not ascertained	1			
15. Desire to marry (G13)				
a. R is married		—	*	2
b. Yes		81	84	87
c. Yes, qualified		7	9	7
d. Maybe, depends		3	3	2
e. No		6	3	2
f. Don't know		3	1	*
g. Not ascertained		*	—	—
16. Occupation for future husband (G13b) Middle-class high-status occupations				
a. Professional, general		2	4	3
b. Doctor		16	11	6
c. Lawyer		4	5	4

Table 2.1 (*Continued*)

	Boys	Girls		
		Under 14	14–16	17–18
d. Engineer		2	5	6
e. Business, general		5	5	2
f. Business owner		4	1	5
g. Other		5	5	7
Middle-class medium-status occupations				
h. White collar, office work		12	10	13
i. School teacher		2	2	2
j. Salesman		3	1	2
k. Bookkeeper		1	1	*
l. Other		1	1	2
Manual occupations				
m. Trade, craft work		5	2	4
n. Factory work, general		7	3	1
o. Farmer		4	5	4
p. *Glamour occupations*		1	1	1
q. *Leaves choice up to husband*		24	27	34
r. *Stresses working conditions* (not too demanding)		8	11	10
s. Don't know		6	6	3
t. Not ascertained		4	4	4
17. Personal characteristics desired in future husband (*G*13*a*)				
Middle-class characteristics				
Reciprocal marriage relationship		44	54	70
a. Considerate		23	29	32
b. Share *S*'s interests		6	9	17
c. Love, respect for *R*		5	5	5
d. Other		10	11	16
Family attitudes		15	14	13
e. Likes, good with children		13	12	12
f. Cooperative, helpful at home		2	2	1
Social skill		11	19	15
Autonomy and resources		25	36	39
g. Responsible		3	7	9

	Boys	Girls		
		Under 14	14–16	17–18
h. Active, ambitious, successful		15	20	18
i. Intelligent, educated		7	9	12
Working-class characteristics				
j. Steady worker, good provider		16	18	20
k. Respect for institutions, marriage and family		4	3	3
l. Control of negative impulses (drinking, swearing)		13	10	6
Other				
m. Physical appearance		37	25	18
n. Religious faith, activities		14	17	17
o. Social status, money		6	4	3
p. Don't know		5	2	1
q. Not ascertained		2	2	1
18. Adult ideal (*B*50; *G*55) [a]				
Parents				
a. Father	25	5	3	3
b. Mother	2	38	32	28
c. Both parents	1	*	*	*
Other family members				
d. Uncle	8	—	—	—
e. Aunt	—	9	4	9
f. Grandfather	1	—	—	—
g. Grandmother	—	2	3	3
h. Sister	—	3	3	2
i. Brother	4	—	—	—
j. Cousin	—	2	3	1
k. Other	4	1	*	*
Nonfamily adults				
l. Teacher	*	9	13	14
m. Club leader	7	2	1	2
n. Older adult acquaintance	6	3	5	3
o. Young adult acquaintance	3	3	3	1
p. A work model	4	1	1	2
q. Other	1	4	6	13
Heroic and ideal figures				
r. The President	2	—	—	—
s. Scientists	1	—	—	—

Table 2.1 (*Continued*)

	Boys	Girls		
		Under 14	14–16	17–18
t. Other	2	*	1	0
u. *Glamour figures*	4	5	6	8
v. *Composite*	12	*	3	2
w. No adult	7	8	6	10
x. Don't know	8	4	4	1
y. Not ascertained	1	2	1	—
19. Qualities admired in adult model (*B51*; *G55a*) [a]				
Personal qualities	34	74	76	74
a. Generous, helpful	8	12	11	10
b. Kind, gentle, nice person	12	32	28	23
c. Understanding	3	7	11	14
d. Other	11	23	26	27
Work skills	40	23	22	24
e. Can do things, good at work	13	8	9	9
f. Successful in work	10	—	—	—
g. Good wife, homemaker	0	6	6	5
h. Works hard	9	2	1	—
i. Other	8	7	6	10
Character traits	28	18	18	23
j. Strong moral character	12	6	5	5
k. Determination, drive	8	4	4	7
l. Sound judgment	4	0	0	0
m. Heroic qualities	2	1	1	4
n. Other	2	7	8	7
Social skills	23	12	19	15
o. Good personality	18	2	4	6
p. Popular	5	8	12	8
q. Other	*	2	3	1
Superficial characteristics	6	24	19	18
r. Good looking	1	10	6	7
s. Dresses well	2	5	4	4
t. Other	3	9	9	7
u. Don't know	1	1	*	—
v. Not ascertained, *R* admires no adult	19	14	12	12
20. Desired self-change (*B54*; *G59*) [a]				
Physical characteristics	27	60	59	58

| | | Girls | | |
	Boys	Under 14	14–16	17–18
Personal controls	28	10	16	14
a. Better control of temper	6	6	10	7
b. Better disposition, nicer to my family	1	2	2	3
c. More independent, responsible	18	1	3	2
d. Other	3	1	1	2
Social skills	21	17	37	45
e. Make friends more easily, be less shy	9	6	17	25
f. Better personality	6	5	7	7
g. Better conversation skills	2	2	4	5
h. Other	4	4	9	8
i. *Abilities*	9	3	3	4
j. *Situational change*	6	10	4	4
k. Nothing	38	3	12	7
l. Don't know	3	3	1	*
m. Not ascertained	*	1	1	*
21. Sources of self-esteem (*B*53; *G*54) [b]				
Being part of, contributing to a work group	49	27	33	26
a. Helping at home	37	21	22	21
b. Being part of a team	6	3	4	3
c. Other	6	3	7	2
Achievement and competition	37	28	25	30
d. Doing well in school	8	8	6	4
e. Competition in sports	11	4	3	1
f. Making, fixing something	7	9	10	15
g. Independence in work	4	1	1	2
h. Other	7	6	5	8
Assuming adult roles	30	31	39	53
i. In a job	14	11	15	18
j. At home	10	11	13	18
k. In school activities	4	6	9	12
l. Other	2	3	2	5
Helping others	19	22	23	26
Acceptance by adults	8	20	17	13
m. Recognition, praise				

Table 2.1 (*Continued*)

	Boys	Girls		
		Under 14	14–16	17–18
from adults	1	4	4	2
n. Being treated like an adult	1	1	2	—
o. Being given special responsibility	4	8	5	5
p. Other	2	7	6	6
Acceptance, popularity with peers	*4*	*2*	*6*	*4*
q. Nothing, never feel important	4	3	4	5
r. Don't know	3	4	2	1
s. Not ascertained	1	1	*	1
22. *Sources of worry* (B55; G60) [a]				
Physical appearance	*	*57*	*62*	*66*
Achievement	*57*	*21*	*17*	*12*
Popularity and acceptance	*29*	*44*	*73*	*73*
a. General	8	11	15	11
b. With opposite sex	21	26	45	51
c. Reputation, gossip	—	1	7	4
d. Other	—	6	6	7
Reality pressures	*29*	*5*	*4*	*6*
e. Other	2	4	3	4
f. Nothing	4	2	*	*
g. Don't know	2	4	1	—
h. Not ascertained	1	3	2	*
23. *Daydreams* (G64) [a]				
Future		*46*	*61*	*72*
a. Marriage, home, family		17	23	35
b. College		1	3	5
c. Career		17	17	12
d. Other, general future		11	18	20
Current		*32*	*55*	*32*
e. Boys, popularity		16	23	21
f. Activities		9	13	3
g. Problems, worries		7	9	8
Money, material concerns		*22*	*20*	*18*
h. R doesn't daydream		18	13	14
i. R daydreams, but cannot describe daydream		5	5	3
j. Not ascertained		1	1	1

Table 2.2 Development in boys' concepts of future work, education

Item	Age, %		
	14 (N = 316)	15 (N = 341)	16 (N = 388)
1. Vocational aspirations (B14)			
a. Glamour occupations	7	4	1
2. Certainty about job choice (B15)			
a. Very sure	7	3	3
b. Sure	41	54	62
c. Might change, likely to change	34	29	25
d. No job choice	12	11	5
e. Don't know, not ascertained	6	6	5
3. Clarity of R's conception of vocational preparation (CR:B20)			
a. Clear and detailed	14	19	32
b. Clear, not detailed	34	44	53
c. Unclear	30	20	6
d. No training required	1	2	2
e. Not ascertained; no job choice	20	14	7
4. Reasons for job choice (B17) [a]			
a. Interest in work	64	69	77
b. Achievement, status, high pay	8	20	26
c. Security	10	3	6
d. Work with people	10	6	2
e. Social service	8	4	6
f. Own boss	8	9	4
g. Easy, easy to get work	11	15	10
h. Outdoor work	19	10	2
5. Most important job criteria (B22, 23) [a]			
a. Steady job	58	54	44
b. Interesting work	38	49	57
c. Nice people to work with	36	30	20
d. Be your own boss	12	11	18
e. Outdoor work	16	12	5
f. Be looked up to by others	2	3	10

Footnotes for Table 2.1

[a] These questions were omitted from one form of the questionnaire. Numbers on which the proportions are based are one-third smaller than those listed in the table heading.

[b] This question was omitted from one form of the girls' questionnaire, but was included on all forms for boys. Only the numbers for girls are reduced by a third.

[c] This question was not asked of girls in the sixth and seventh grades.

Table 2.2　(*Continued*)

	14	15	16
g. Be a leader of people	1	2	2
h. Good chance for promotion	10	10	20
i. High pay	12	12	18
j. A job in hometown	12	6	1
6. Two least important job criteria (*B*24) [a]			
a. Steady job	2	1	—
b. Interesting work	3	1	—
c. Nice people to work with	*	2	4
d. Be your own boss	36	34	16
e. Outdoor work	22	28	42
f. Be looked up to by others	36	30	27
g. Be a leader of people	42	34	32
h. Good chance for promotion	4	9	9
i. High pay	18	10	9
j. A job in hometown	35	39	49

[a] These questions were omitted from one form of the questionnaire. Numbers on which the proportions are based are one-third smaller than those listed in the table heading.

Table 3.1. Relationship between boys' mobility aspirations and selected variables

	Mobility Type, %		
Item	Upward (*N* = 277)	Stable (*N* = 168)	Downward (*N* = 73)
1. Qualities admired in adult ideal (*B*51) [a]			
a. Work skills, achievements	56	30	23
2. Reasons for job choice (*B*17, 18) [a]			
a. Interest in work	70	78	58
b. Status	20	9	3
c. Ease of job or ease of obtaining job	4	12	32
3. Most important job criteria (*B*22, 23) [a]			
a. Interesting work	56	51	33
b. Status achievement	44	28	36
c. Security	50	59	65
4. Educational plans (*B*13, 13*a,b*)			

	Upward	Stable	Downward
	%	%	%
a. Beyond high school	69	42	12
b. Not beyond high school	31	58	88
5. Preference—security or success (B25) [a]			
a. Security	48	65	67
b. Success	52	35	33
6. Changes desired in self (B54) [a]			
a. Self-rejecting, major	4	10	15
b. Changes that are impossible	6	7	23
c. Moderate changes, within boy's own power	37	29	5
d. Increase in work-relevant resources, skills	18	10	2
7. Savings (B31)			
a. Save	30	21	18
b. Do not save	70	79	82
8. Conditions for breaking a rule (B45)			
a. Emergency	18	10	10
b. Boy mature enough	11	7	1
c. Rebellion	10	14	22
d. Impulse	5	11	16
e. Parental authority absent	5	10	27
9. Unbreakable rule (B47)			
a. Rules involving responsibility to others	19	12	7
b. No unbreakable rule	3	17	21
10. Projective story: reaction to conflict between parent, peer pressure (B40, 40a)			
a. Adheres to promise because of sense of trust	37	19	16
b. Adheres to promise because of fear of punishment	4	6	14
11. Projective story: honesty with parents (B40b)			
a. Would tell parents of misdeed	55	42	44
12. Advice on decisions (B49) [a]			

Table 3.1 (*Continued*)

	Upward	Stable	Downward
	%	%	%
a. Interjects own judgment on at least one issue	30	21	3
13. Intimacy of friendship (*B*52)			
a. Can be as close as family relationship	59	54	34
14. Adult ideal (*B*50) [a]			
a. Father	24	36	10
b. Other family member	17	14	45
c. Unrelated adult	31	24	18
d. No adult ideal	1	5	23
15. Number of leisure activities (*B*56)			
a. Fewer than 20	52	65	67
b. Twenty or more	48	35	33
16. Dating (*B*39)			
a. Date	66	59	52
17. Leisure reading (*B*56e)			
a. Do not read	17	27	25
b. Fiction-novels, mysteries	32	23	11
c. Travel and adventure	31	20	18
d. Technical, scientific	9	4	1
e. Sports and hobby books	10	9	4
f. History, biography	8	7	5
g. Animal stories	5	4	5
h. Comics, joke books	21	26	27
i. Newspapers, magazines	19	16	19
18. Group memberships (*B*1)			
a. None	25	33	52
b. One	32	38	22
c. Two	23	20	17
d. Three or more	20	9	9
19. Employment (*B*28)			
a. Work	49	47	51
20. Proportion of activities enjoyed (*B*56a)			
a. Fewer than half	45	41	59
21. Additional activities desired (*B*56d)			
a. Suggest activity	63	31	10

	Upward	Stable	Downward
	%	%	%
22. Activities for a boys' club (*B6*)			
a. Suggest one activity	26	44	53
b. Suggest two activities	43	32	33
c. Suggest three or more	31	24	14
23. Self-confidence (*IR*)			
a. High	30	23	18
b. Average	52	57	57
c. Low	18	20	25
24. Humor (*IR*)			
a. Showed some humor	74	67	58
25. Organization of thought (*IR*)			
a. High	60	53	50
b. Average	22	27	20
c. Low	18	20	30
26. Time perspective on decisions (*CR; B*10)			
a. Extended	53	51	26
b. Restricted	17	18	29
27. Sources of self-esteem (*B53*)			
a. Assuming adult-role	31	23	16
b. Belonging, being part of a group	46	56	32
c. Being accepted by peers	3	7	14
d. Nothing, don't know	4	8	11
28. Disagreements with parents (*B41, 42*) [a]			
a. Never disagree	34	44	51
29. Parents' attitude toward *R*'s spending own money (*B32*)			
a. Moderate disapproval	18	11	3
b. *R* has no independent funds	1	1	19
30. Projective story: portrayal of parents (*B40*)			
a. Harsh	1	3	19
b. Strict, very strict	26	32	29

Table 3.1 (*Continued*)

	Upward	Stable	Downward
	%	%	%
c. Lenient	73	62	36
d. Very lenient	*	3	16
31. Leisure activities with family (*B56c*)			
a. Share many	19	11	9
b. Share some	73	74	68
c. Share none	8	15	23
32. Punishment (*B*48)			
a. Physical	2	8	15
b. Deprivation	66	69	65
c. Psychological	32	23	20
33. Age			
a. Fourteen	33	29	31
b. Fifteen	30	36	33
c. Sixteen	37	35	36
34. Verbal ability (*CR*)			
a. High	25	11	3
b. Average	69	75	74
c. Low	6	14	23

[a] These questions were omitted from one form of the questionnaire. Numbers on which the proportions are based are one-third smaller than those listed in the table heading.

Table 3.2. Three mobility patterns in girls contrasted on selected measures

	Mobility Type, %		
Item	Upward-Personal (*N* = 69)	Upward-Marital (*N* = 288)	Stable (*N* = 185)
1. Leisure activity index (*G65*)			
a. High	48	33	28
b. Low	17	26	30
2. Dating (*G27*)			
a. Do date	63	71	54
b. Do not date	37	29	46
3. Time perspective on decisions (*CR: G*10)			
a. Extended	49	36	32
b. Restricted	11	20	28

	Upward-Personal	Upward-Marital	Stable
4. Sources of self-esteem (G54) [a]			
a. Assuming adult roles	58	33	38
b. Achievement	38	23	24
c. Being accepted by peers	—	9	4
d. Nothing, don't know	—	2	10
e. R gives more than one response	34	29	22
5. Self-confidence (IR)			
a. High	53	42	33
b. Average	39	38	44
c. Low	7	20	23
6. Organization of thought (IR)			
a. High	56	45	41
b. Average	36	32	32
c. Low	8	22	26
7. Desired self-change (CR:G59) [a]			
a. Self rejecting, major	1	10	12
b. Changes within R's power to effect	29	15	14
8. Daydreams (G64) [a]			
a. Future achievement	32	9	15
b. Marriage, family	15	23	17
c. Boys, popularity	12	22	26
d. R doesn't daydream	13	11	19
9. Most wonderful thing (G57) [a]			
a. Achievement	56	32	38
10. Worries (G60) [a]			
a. Achievement	28	12	18
b. Popularity	50	65	56
11. Criteria for jobs (G15) [b]			
a. Status, achievement	34	13	18
b. Security	44	56	53
c. Interesting work	74	53	58
12. Adult ideal (G55) [a]			
a. Mother	42	31	34
b. All in-family models	56	55	63
c. Unrelated adult	34	24	31
d. Composite	4	3	1
e. Glamor figure	—	13	2
f. No adult ideal	3	2	8
13. Index of internalization			
a. High	24	15	9
b. Low	9	25	18
14. Projective: Response to conflict			

Table 3.2 (*Continued*)

	Upward-Personal	Upward-Marital	Stable
between parent, peer pressure (*G*29)			
a. Keep promise to parents, trust	18	13	14
15. Part in rule-making (*G*52*a*)			
a. *R* has some role	50	55	48
16. Disagreements with parents (*G*32) ᵃ			
a. None	28	21	27

ᵃ These questions were omitted from one form of the questionnaire. Numbers on which the proportions are based are one-third smaller than those listed in the table heading.

ᵇ This question was not asked of the girls in the sixth and the seventh grades since pretesting indicated that the question was too difficult for many of the youngest girls. The total sample for this question was reduced to 1306, and numbers in the mobility analysis were in this case as follows: Upward Personal (*N* = 54); Upward Marital (*N* = 209); Stable (*N* = 139).

Table 4.1 Developmental changes in girls' responses to questions about values, standards, and personal controls

	Age, %		
Item	Under 14 (*N* = 844)	14–16 (*N* = 822)	17–18 (*N* = 259)
1. Attitude toward dating (*G*26)			
a. Sexual reference: don't do anything bad	1	1	*
2. Attitude toward steady dating (*G*28)			
a. May get too serious	2	5	4
b. May get too involved sexually	—	1	1
3. Parents' expectations (*G*30)			
a. Act decently with boys	4	6	3
b. Not go with bad kids	2	2	1
c. Obedience, respect for authority	33	27	22
4. Rule *R* would never break (*G*51)			
a. Sexual reference	5	4	3
b. Do anything to hurt, bring grief to parents	2	4	11
c. Disobey parents	14	9	3
5. Consequences if parents didn't make rules (*G*48)			

	Under 14	14–16	17–18
a. Sexual reference	1	*	1
6. Reasons for excluding a girl from friendship (G24) [a]			
a. Sexual reference	3	4	4
b. Bad reputation	15	39	18
c. Too boy crazy	17	11	8
7. Projective question: shameful act (G36) [a]			
a. Sexual reference	12	24	20
b. Aggression: hurting a friend	18	23	31
c. Aggression: hurting parents	22	19	13
8. Disagreements with parents (G32) [a]			
a. Control on movements	34	37	29
b. Dating	9	26	31
c. Clothing, personal habits	28	19	11
d. Working, helping at home	11	6	4
e. Relations with siblings	6	4	5
f. Friends	6	6	4
g. Cars, driving	*	2	7
h. Ideas	—	*	2
i. Money	3	3	2
j. Nothing much, no disagreements	26	23	26
9. Disagreements with siblings (G32a) [a]			
a. Intense	4	6	4
b. Moderate	23	29	31
c. Slight or none	49	38	46
d. Not ascertained; no siblings at home	24	27	19
10. Disagreements with parents: specific issues (G33) [b]			
a. Dating	19	38	25
b. Driving	23	48	34
c. Clothing	62	48	36
d. Friends	37	42	35
e. Lipstick	26	18	5
f. Ideas	18	34	41
g. No disagreement on any of issues	30	26	31
11. Reference to gossip in discussion of friendship (G20, 22, 23, 24) [a]			
a. At least one reference	23	37	30

Table 4.1 (*continued*)

	Under 14	14–16	17–18
12. Worries (*G*60) [a]			
a. Mention problems of self-control, autonomy	*	1	*
13. Changes desired in self (*G*59) [a]			
a. Greater self-control autonomy, responsibility	10	16	14
14. Qualities admired in adult model (*G*55*a*) [a]			
a. Responsibility, autonomy	10	9	12
15. Attitude toward parental rules (*G*52)			
a. Positive: they're right, fair, lenient	47	54	56
b. Neutral: they're all right	25	17	13
c. Usually fair, sometimes unfair	21	17	17
d. Negative: they're hard, very strict	4	7	5
e. *R* says parents make no rules	1	3	5
f. Not ascertained	2	2	4
16. Part in rule-making (*G*52*a*)			
a. *R* has some role	45	58	62
b. *R* has no role	51	37	34
c. Parents make no rules	1	2	3
d. Not ascertained	3	3	1
17. Why parents make rules (*G*47)			
a. Children need rules to keep out of trouble	20	17	14
b. For child's welfare, general	14	22	27
c. To give child standards	14	17	20
d. To help child mature	28	29	31
e. To protect children	7	9	10
f. Parents have more experience	5	6	10
g. Other child benefit	14	12	7
h. For parents' benefit	17	17	14
18. Projective: How a girl might want parents to be different (*G*34) [a]			
a. Less restrictive	79	80	69
b. Closer relationship with girl	17	25	32
c. Different in personality	12	11	14
d. Different living style	13	15	15
e. *R* indicates that the girl's criticism is probably minor, unjustified	6	14	26

Table 4.2 Comparative data for boys and girls (age 14 to 16) on questions about personal values, controls

Item	Boys, % (N = 1045)	Girls, % (N = 822)
1. Worries (B55; G60) [a]		
a. Mention problems of self-control, autonomy	12	1
2. Desired self-change (B54; G59) [a]		
a. Stronger personal controls (autonomy, responsibility)	28	16
3. Why parents make rules (B43; G34)		
a. Children need rules to keep out of trouble	36	17
b. To give children standards, help children mature	27	46
c. To protect children	—	9
d. Parents have more experience	5	6
e. R gives more than one response	29	20
4. What if parents didn't make rules (B44; G48)		
a. Children would run wild	45	36
b. Children would stay out too late	15	7
c. Children would go with wrong crowd	40	8
d. Children wouldn't go to school	33	2
e. Effects on children: their lives would be ruined, they would be spoiled, insecure	18	31
f. R gives more than one response	78	41
5. When a boy (girl) might break a rule (B45; G49)		
a. Under influence of peers	32	20
b. Emergency	16	15
c. Boy (girl) mature enough to judge rule inappropriate	15	10
d. Rebellion, impulse	31	25
e. External authority absent	7	2
f. R gives strategy for rule-breaking	—	25
g. R gives more than one response	22	16
h. Never, can't think of a time	4	7

Footnotes for Table 4.1

[a] These questions were omitted from one form of the questionnaire. Numbers on which the proportions are based are one-third smaller than those listed in the table heading.

[b] This question was asked on only one form of the questionnaire. Numbers in this case are as follows: under fourteen (285); fourteen to sixteen (278); seventeen and eighteen (89).

Table 4.2 (*Continued*)

	Boys, %	Girls, %
6. Ever broken a rule? (*B*46; *G*50)		
a. Yes, certainly	30	8
b. Yes	60	66
c. Maybe, no, don't think so	10	26
7. Rule *R* would never break (*B*47; *G*51)		
a. Rule relating to moral code of society	28	15
b. Specific rule governing normal behavior	16	26
c. *R* can't think of a rule he would never break	15	6
8. Projective: response to parents' restriction (*B*40; *G*29)		
a. Question restriction	25	4
b. Reassure parents	*	34
c. Hurt, shocked at parents' apprehension	—	10
d. Accept limit, no addition	65	36

[a] These questions were omitted from one form of the questionnaires. Numbers on which the proportions are based are one-third smaller than those listed in the table heading.

Table 4.3. Extreme groups on an internalization index compared on measures of other ego variables (Boy sample)

	Internalization, %	
Item	High ($N = 221$)	Low ($N = 142$)
1. Achievement		
a. Prefer success to security (*B*25) [a]	64	47
b. Choose job aspiration on achievement criteria (*B*17, 18) [a]	78	62
c. Choose job aspiration because of ease of acquiring job, minimum demands (*B*17, 18) [a]	1	13
d. Upward-mobile aspirations	70	53
2. Energy level		
a. High on index of leisure engagements (*B*56)	49	40
b. Belong to some organized group (*B*1)	77	65
c. Hold jobs (*B*28)	63	42
d. Date (*B*39)	66	52
3. Autonomy		
a. Rely on own judgment in issues of taste and behavior (*B*49) [a]	40	20

	High	Low
b. Have some disagreements with parents (*B*41) [a]	67	49
c. Choose adult ideal outside family (*B*50) [a]	23	14
d. Have no adult ideal (*B*50) [a]	7	16
e. Authority-reliant in relation to adult leaders (*B*9, 9*a*, 9*c*)	23	54
4. Self-confidence		
a. High on interviewer rating of confidence	43	22
b. Low on interviewer rating of confidence	16	35
c. High on rating for organization of ideas	65	43
d. Low on rating for organization of ideas	8	28
5. Self-criticism (*B*54) [a]		
a. Wish for changes that can be effected by individual effort	36	12
b. Wish for changes that can't be effected by individual effort	14	30
c. No self-change desired	27	42
6. Time perspective (*CR:B*10, 10*a*)		
a. Extended	44	28
b. Restricted	14	33

[a] These questions were omitted from one form of the questionnaire. Numbers on which the proportions are based are one-third smaller than those listed in the table heading.

Table 4.4. Comparison of girls scoring high and low on an index on internalization on other questions about values, morality, and controls

Item	Internalization, %	
	High (*N* = 284)	Low (*N* = 351)
1. Rule *R* would never break (*G*51)		
a. Rule relating to moral code of society	23	11
b. Rule involving responsibility to self or others	33	36
c. Rules that reinforce adult authority	24	9
2. Projective: Response to parents' restriction (*G*29)		
a. Reassure parents	41	24
3. Authority reliance (*CR:G*9, 9*a*) [a]		
a. High	26	38

Table 4.4 (*Continued*)

	High	Low
b. Medium	58	43
c. Low	10	13
4. Adult ideal (*G55*) [a]		
a. Masculine figure	14	0
5. Vocational choice (*G14*)		
a. Traditional profession	25	6
b. Feminine profession	30	43
6. Wish to be a boy (*G42, 42b*) [a]		
a. Wishes, sometimes wishes, to be a boy	42	38
b. Did at one time wish to be a boy	25	18
c. Never wished to be a boy	33	44

[a] These questions were omitted from one form of the questionnaire. Numbers on which the proportions are based are one-third smaller than those listed in the table heading.

Table 5.1. Development in girls' family relationships, autonomy

Item	Age, %		
	Under 14 (*N* = 844)	14–16 (*N* = 822)	17–18 (*N* = 259)
1. Employment (*G18*)			
a. Have jobs	42	56	58
2. Dating (*G27*)			
a. Go steady, engaged	2	13	31
b. Date	17	59	60
c. Don't date	81	28	9
3. Household responsibility (*G31*)			
a. Major	5	13	15
b. Moderate	28	36	38
c. Light or none	61	45	41
d. Not ascertained	6	6	6
4. Intimacy or friendship (*G21*) [a]			
a. Can be as close as family relationship	58	61	68
5. Projective: Response to Lonely Mother (*G39*) [a]			
a. Reject request	11	18	24
b. Comply, go home	61	46	39
c. Conditional compliance	13	20	20
d. Attempt at compromise	37	51	49

	Under 14	14–16	17–18
e. Not ascertained	5	3	5
6. Projective: Shameful act, confidante (*G36a, b*) [a]			
a. Parents	28	14	13
b. Mother	37	31	25
c. Girlfriend	12	26	29
7. Adult ideal (*G55*) [a]			
a. Mother	38	32	28
b. Other women in family	18	18	10
c. Masculine family figures	8	5	8
d. Unrelated adult	22	29	35
e. Glamor figure	5	6	8
f. Composite	*	3	2
g. No specific adult, don't know	12	10	11
h. Not ascertained	2	1	—
8. Projective: Response to parents' restriction (*G29*)			
a. Accept restriction	50	36	37
b. Question restriction	5	4	3
c. Question parents' authority	4	4	4
d. Reassure parents	28	36	37
e. Hurt, surprised at parent apprehension	3	10	8
f. Other	5	7	8
9. Projective: Response to conflict between parent, peer pressure (*G29*)			
a. Need oriented: stay with friends to have fun	11	16	15
b. Group oriented stay to avoid friends' scorn	5	7	7
c. Parent oriented: go home	75	63	61
10. Projective: Honesty with parents (*G29b*)			
a. Would tell parents of misdeed	36	41	49
11. Projective: Portrayal of parents (*G29*)			
a. Strict and restrictive	26	36	32
b. Lenient	57	51	58
c. Very lenient	11	8	6
d. Not ascertained	6	5	4
12. Disagreements with parents: Specific issues (*G33*) [b]			

Table 5.1 (*Continued*)

	Under 14	14–16	17–18
a. Dating	19	38	25
b. Driving	23	48	34
c. Clothing	62	48	36
d. Friends	37	42	35
e. Lipstick	28	18	5
f. Ideas	18	34	41
13. Disagreements with parents: Reference to other party (*G*32) [a]			
a. Mother	28	25	13
b. Parents	31	34	43
c. Father	*	5	16
14. Attitude toward parental rules (*G*52)			
a. Positive: They are right, fair, lenient	47	54	56
b. Neutral and conditional: They're all right, usually fair	46	34	30
c. Negative: They're hard, very strict	4	7	5
d. *R* says parents make no rules	1	3	5
e. Not ascertained	2	2	4
15. Projective: How a girl might want parents to be different (*G*34)			
a. Less restrictive	79	80	69
b. Closer relationship with child	17	25	32
c. Different in personality	12	11	14
d. Different in living style	13	15	15
16. Parents' expectations (*G*30)			
a. Independence, self-direction	8	16	25
b. Interpersonal skill, popularity	35	33	28
c. Manners and forms	50	42	42
d. Respect for authority	33	27	22
e. Morality	22	30	31
f. Relations within family	21	22	23
g. Achievement	4	5	5
h. Not ascertained, don't know	5	3	5
17. Part in rule making (*G*52*a*)			
a. *R* has some role	45	58	62
b. *R* has no role	51	37	34
c. Parents make no rules	1	2	3
d. Not ascertained	3	3	1
18. Punishment (*G*53)			
a. Physical	23	8	2

	Under 14	14–16	17–18
b. Deprivation	92	92	80
c. Psychological	30	31	50
d. Not ascertained	1	*	*

[a] These questions were omitted from one form of the questionnaire. Numbers on which the proportions are based are one-third smaller than those listed in the table heading.

[b] This question was asked on only one form of the questionnaire. Numbers in this case are as follows: Under fourteen (285); fourteen to sixteen (278); seventeen and eighteen (89).

Table 5.2. Comparative data for boys and girls (aged 14 to 16) on questions about family relationships, autonomy

Item	Boys, % (N = 1045)	Girls, % (N = 822)
1. Dating (B39; G27)		
a. Date	59	72
2. Employment (B28; G18)		
a. Have jobs	47	56
3. Leisure with family (B56c; G65c)		
a. Share some activity	78	93
4. Adult ideal (B50; G55) [a]		
a. Like-sexed parent	25	32
b. All in-family models	45	55
5. Projective: Response to parents' restriction (B40; G29)		
a. Accept restriction	65	36
b. Question restriction	25	4
c. Question parents' authority	3	4
d. Reassure parents	—	36
e. Hurt, shocked at parents' apprehension	—	10
f. Other	5	7
6. Projective: Honesty with parents (B40b; G29b)		
a. Would not tell parents of misdeed	43	41
7. Ever broken a rule? (B46; G50)		
a. Yes, definitely	30	8
b. Yes	60	66
c. No, don't think so, can't remember having done so	10	26

[a] This question was omitted from one form of the questionnaires. Numbers on which the proportions are based are one-third smaller than those listed in the table heading.

Table 5.3. Girls who spend leisure primarily with family and those who spend leisure with friends compared on other autonomy questions

	Spend leisure, %	
	Family	Friends
Item	($N = 906$)	($N = 566$)
1. Part in rule-making (*G52a*)		
a. *R* has some role	45	62
2. Authority reliance (*CR:G9, 9a*) ª		
a. Relies heavily on adults	38	21
3. Punishment (*G53*)		
a. Physical	18	6
b. Psychological	39	25
4. Projective: Response to parents' restriction (*G29*)		
a. Accept restriction, no addition	53	31
5. Disagreements with parents (*G32*) ᵇ		
a. None	29	15
6. Intimacy of friendship (*G21*) ª		
a. Can be as close as family relationship	52	75
7. Projective: How a girl might wish her parents were different (*G34*)		
a. Less restrictive	83	61
b. Closer relationship with child	14	33
8. Adult ideal (*G55*) ª		
a. Mother	38	27
9. Household responsibilities (*G31*)		
a. Heavy	15	8
b. Moderate	35	29
c. Light	48	55
10. Parents' expectations (*G30*)		
a. Independence	7	22
b. Interpersonal skill, popularity	42	24

ª These questions were omitted from one form of the questionnaire. Numbers on which the proportions are based are one-third smaller than those listed in the table heading.

ᵇ This question was included in only one form of the questionnaire. Numbers are reduced to one-third of those listed in the table headings.

Table 5.4. Boys' dependence on parent advice related to other items about autonomy, family interaction [a]

Item	Dependence, %	
	High (N = 294)	Low (N = 82)
1. Projective: Response to parents' restriction (B40)		
a. Accept limit, no addition	72	53
b. Question restriction	20	34
2. Projective: Response to conflict between parent, peer demands (B40)		
a. Stay with friends	15	34
3. Projective: Honesty with parents (B40b)		
a. Would tell parents of misdeed	48	29
4. Intimacy of friendship (B52)		
a. Can be as close as family relationship	30	64
5. Adult ideal (B50) [b]		
a. Father	32	16
6. Leisure with parents (B56c)		
a. Share some leisure activities	74	90
7. Authority reliance (CR:B9, 9a,c)		
a. High	50	24
b. Medium	41	59
c. Low	7	16
8. Attitude toward draft (B12)		
a. Positive, would like army	24	14
b. Rather enlist, choose	20	37
9. Punishment (B48)		
a. Physical	15	4
b. Deprivational	68	56
c. Psychological	17	36
10. Dating (B39)		
a. Do date	54	75
11. Job criteria (B22, 23)		
a. Interesting work	42	69
b. Security	56	39
c. Nice people to work with	13	4
12. Time perspective (CR:B10)		
a. Restricted	25	11
13. Self-confidence (IR)		
a. High	19	36
b. Average	56	40
c. Low	25	14

Table 5.4 (*Continued*)

	High	Low
14. Age		
a. Fourteen	34	29
b. Fifteen	33	34
c. Sixteen	33	37
15. Social class		
a. Middle class	33	39
b. Working class	51	47

[a] Numbers are reduced because the question on which this analysis is based was omitted from one form of the questionnaire and because only boys at the extremes of dependency were used for the analysis.

[b] Since the form of the questionnaire from which this question was omitted was the same form that excluded the question on dependency, the numbers in the table heading apply to this item.

Table 5.5. Boys who do and do not yield to peer pressure compared on other questions about family relationships and autonomy

Item	Response to peer pressure, %	
	Yield (N = 204)	Withstand (N = 634)
1. Advice on issues (B49) [a]		
a. Depend heavily on parents (5 or 6 issues)	22	49
b. Accept friends' advice on two or more issues	43	24
2. When boy might break rule (B45)		
a. Emergency	9	18
b. Rebellion	24	12
3. Authority reliance (CR:B9, 9a,c)		
a. High	41	47
b. Medium	43	45
c. Low	16	7
4. Adult ideal (B50) [a]		
a. Father	18	28
b. Within-family choice	33	49
5. Leisure reading		
a. None	27	18
6. Dating (B39)		
a. Do date	65	57
7. Group memberships (B1)		
a. None	39	28

	Yield	Withstand
8. Projective: Response to parents' restriction (*B*40)		
a. Accept limit, no addition	47	71

a This question was omitted from one form of the questionnaire. The numbers on which the proportions are based are one-third smaller than those listed in the table heading.

Table 5.6. Boys who say they have never broken rules compared to those who have broken rules on other questions about family relationships, autonomy

	Ever broken rules, %	
Item	Yes (*N* = 929)	No (*N* = 54)
1. Advice on issues (*B*49) a		
a. Depend heavily on parents (5 or 6 issues)	41	67
b. Accept friends' advice on 2 or more issues	31	7
2. Intimacy of friendship (*B*52)		
a. Can be as close as family relationship	44	20
3. Projective: Response to parents' restriction (*B*40)		
a. Accept limit, no addition	64	78
b. Question restriction	27	4
4. Projective: Response to conflict between parent, peer pressure (*B*40)		
a. Boy goes home	73	92
5. Projective: Honesty with parents (*B*40*b*)		
a. Would tell parents of misdeed	41	69
6. Adult ideal (*B*50) a		
a. Father	24	43
b. Within family choices	43	74
7. Disagreements with parents (*B*41) a		
a. None	41	72
8. Authority reliance (*CR: B*9, 9*a,c*) a		
a. High	43	71
b. Medium	45	27
c. Low	10	—
9. Group membership (*B*1)		
a. None	29	52
b. One	29	35
c. More than one	41	13

Table 5.6 (*Continued*)

	Yes	No
10. Dating (*B*39)		
a. Do date	60	22
11. Leisure reading (*B*56*e*)		
a. None	20	41
12. Desired self change (*B*54)		
a. None	36	89
13. Punishment (*B*48)		
a. Physical	10	29
b. Deprivational	65	32
c. Psychological	25	33

ᵃ This question was omitted from one form of the questionnaire. The numbers on which the proportions are based are one-third smaller than those listed in the table heading.

Table 5.7. Girls who have ideological differences with parents and those who do not compared on other questions about family relationships and autonomy ᵃ

	Ideological differences, %	
Item	Yes (N = 171)	No (N = 425)
1. Part in rule-making (*G*52*a*)		
a. *R* has some role	69	43
2. Projective: Response to lonely mother (*G*39)		
a. Would return home	37	59
3. Authority reliance (*CR: G*9, 9*a*)		
a. High	22	35
b. Medium	58	49
c. Low	14	10
4. Parents' expectations (*G*30)		
a. Respect for authority	18	33
b. Independence	29	8
c. Manners	38	53
5. Household responsibilities (*G*31)		
a. Light	55	48
b. Moderate	32	35
c. Heavy	7	11
6. Projective: Honesty with parents (*G*29*b*)		
a. Would tell parents of		

	Yes	No
misdeed	58	32
7. Punishment (*G*53)		
a. Physical	5	16
b. Psychological	40	23

[a] This analysis is based on a one-third sample. Numbers are the same for all items because all of the items presented were asked of at least that one-third sample.

Table 5.8. Boys who do and do not report disagreements with parents compared on other questions about family relationships and autonomy

	Disagree, %	
Item	Yes (*N* = 481)	No (*N* = 309)
1. Advice on issues (*B*49) [a]		
a. Would accept friends' advice on two or more issues	32	24
2. Projective: Response to parents' restriction (*B*40)		
a. Accept limit, no addition	61	70
b. Question restriction	28	21
3. When boy might break a rule (*B*45)		
a. Rebellion	16	7
4. Desired self change (*B*54) [a]		
a. Greater self-control, independence	11	*
b. Personal characteristics	33	21
5. Worries (*B*55) [a]		
a. Self-control, independence	16	5
6. Mobility aspiration		
a. Upward	60	48
7. Educational goals (*B*13,13*a,b*)		
a. College	50	41
8. Sources of self-esteem (*B*53)		
a. Achievement, independence	44	29
9. Employment (*B*28)		
a. Hold a job	51	42
10. Dating (*B*39)		
a. Do date	64	52

[a] This question was omitted from one form of the questionnaire. The numbers on which the proportions are based are one-third smaller than those listed in the table heading.

Table 5.9. Boys who question parents' restriction (Projective Story Series) compared to those who accept the restriction on other questions about family relationships and autonomy

Item	Response to restriction, %	
	Question ($N = 264$)	Accept ($N = 681$)
1. Reading (*B56e*)		
a. No reading	14	25
2. Group membership (*B1*)		
a. None	22	33
b. One	27	32
c. More than one	51	35
3. Leisure activities (*B56*)		
a. Fewer than 20	68	55
b. Twenty or more	32	45
4. Advice on issues (*B49*) [a]		
a. Depend heavily on parents		
(5 or 6 issues)	24	48
b. Accept friends' advice on		
2 or more issues	41	24
5. Intimacy of friendship (*B52*)		
a. Can be as close as family		
relationship	55	37
6. Authority reliance (*CR: B9, 9a,c*)		
a. High	39	47
b. Medium	45	42
c. Low	15	6
7. When boy might break rule (*B45*)		
a. Emergency	25	12
b. Mature enough to evaluate rule	18	8
c. Rebellion	9	17
d. Impulse	2	15
8. Index of internalization		
a. High	30	20
9. Punishment (*B48*)		
a. Physical	6	12
b. Deprivational	60	68
c. Psychological	31	20
10. Projective: Portrayal of parents (*CR: B40*)		
a. Strict, very strict	29	40
11. Projective: Honesty with parents (*B40b*)		
a. Would tell parents of		
misdeed	56	40

[a] This question was omitted from one form of the questionnaire. The numbers on which the proportions are based are one-third smaller than those listed in the table heading.

Table 5.10. Parent expectations related to other questions about autonomy and family relationships (*Girl sample*)

Item	Parents expect, %	
	Autonomy ($N = 233$)	Other ($N = 1539$)
1. Projective: Portrayal of parents (*CR: G*29)		
a. Strict and restrictive	19	32
b. Lenient	77	53
2. Why parents make rules (*G*47)		
a. To help, protect children	97	71
3. Projective: Confidante in shameful act (*G*36, 36*b,c*) [a]		
a. Parents, mother	71	47
4. Part in rule-making (*G*52*a*)		
a. *R* has some role	74	49
5. Punishment (*G*53)		
a. Physical	4	16
b. Psychological	68	31
6. Projective: Response to parents' restriction		
a. Accept limit, no addition	21	46
b. Reassures parents	46	30
c. Hurt, shocked	18	5
7. Projective: How a girl might wish her parents different (*G*34) [a]		
a. Identifies with parents	37	12
8. When girl might break rule (*G*49)		
a. Emergency	43	9
9. Projective: Honesty with parents (*G*29*b*)		
a. Would tell parents of misdeed	62	38
10. Projective: Response to lonely mother (*G*39) [a]		
a. Return home	38	55
b. Compromise	69	42
c. Reject request	3	16
11. Intimacy of friendship (*G*21) [a]		
a. Can be as close as family relationship	77	59
12. Leisure companions (*G*65*d*)		
a. Friends	43	30

[a] These questions were omitted from one form of the questionnaire. Numbers on which the proportions are based are one-third smaller than those listed in the table heading.

Table 5.11. Relationship between participation in rule-making and other questions about autonomy (Girl sample)

	Part in rule-making, %	
Item	Some ($N = 1016$)	None ($N = 686$)
1. Intimacy of friendship (G21) [a]		
a. Friend can be as close as family	68	50
2. Parents' expectations (G30)		
a. Independence	18	5
3. Authority-reliance (CR: G9, 9a) [a]		
a. High	29	38
b. Medium	49	53
c. Low	16	3
4. Projective: Response to parents' restriction (G29)		
a. Accept restriction, no addition	37	55
5. Projective: Shameful act, confidante (G36b,c) [a]		
a. Parents	56	42
6. Projective: Honesty with parents (G29b)		
a. Would not tell parents of misdeed	35	52
7. When might a girl break a rule (G49)		
a. Emergency	18	5
b. Rebellion	6	22
8. Punishment (G53)		
a. Physical	7	23
9. Disagreements with parents: [b] Specific issues (G33)		
a. Dating	23	40
b. Driving	27	46
c. Ideas	34	18

[a] These questions were omitted from one form of the questionnaire. Numbers on which the proportions are based are one-third smaller than those listed in the table heading.

[b] This question was asked on only one form of the questionnaire. Numbers in this case are as follows: Some part in rule-making ($N = 334$); No part in rule-making ($N = 230$).

Table 5.12. Punishment related to other aspects of family relationships, autonomy (Girl sample) [c]

Item	Punishment, %		
	Physical (N = 261)	Deprivation (N = 1197)	Psychological (N = 318)
1. Authority reliance (*CR: G9, 9a*)			
a. High	50	31	23
b. Medium	37	53	59
c. Low	6	10	13
2. Projective: Response to parents' restriction (*G29*)			
a. Accept, add nothing	58	43	33
3. Adult ideal (*G55*) [a]			
a. Within family model	73	56	42
4. Projective: Lonely mother (*G39*) [a]			
a. Return home	69	51	47
5. Parents' expectations (*G30*)			
a. Independence	5	12	26
6. Part in rule making (*G52a*)			
a. *R* has some role	28	60	65
7. Disagreements with parents: Specific issues (*G33e*) [b]			
a. Ideas	14	29	51
8. Projective: Honesty with parents (*G29b*)			
a. Would not tell parents of misdeed	57	38	30
9. Projective: Portrayal of parents (*CR: G29*)			
a. Strict, very strict	28	32	35
b. Lenient	50	54	58
c. Very lenient	15	9	4

[a] These questions were omitted from one form of the questionnaire. Numbers on which the proportions are based are one-third smaller than those listed in the table heading.

[b] This question was asked on only one form of the questionnaire. Numbers in this case are as follows: Physical ($N = 91$); Deprivational ($N = 360$); Psychological ($N = 104$).

[c] Numbers are reduced because some cases of mixed punishment (e.g., deprivation and psychological) as well as those in which no response was obtained were dropped from the analysis.

Table 5.13. Punishment related to other aspects of family relationships, autonomy (Boy sample) [b]

Item	Punishment, %		
	Physical (N = 79)	Deprivation (N = 420)	Psycho-logical (N = 161)
1. Intimacy of friendship (B52)			
a. Can be as close as family relationship	31	40	54
2. Advice on issues (B49)			
a. Would accept parents' advice on five or six issues	55	47	31
3. Adult ideal (B50) [a]			
a. Within family choice	57	47	34
b. No one, don't know	24	14	1
4. Authority reliance (CR: B9, 9a,9c)			
a. High	65	41	38
b. Medium	28	47	54
c. Low	3	9	8
5. Attitude toward draft (B12)			
a. Positive	53	37	35
b. Negative	11	26	31
6. Rule R would never break (B47)			
a. Rules maintaining adult authority	40	35	28
7. Projective: Portrayal of parents (B40)			
a. Strict, very strict	48	34	27
b. Lenient	44	56	71
8. Projective: Response to conflict between parent, peer pressure (B40)			
a. Stay with peers	30	18	16
9. Projective: Honesty with parents (B40b)			
a. Would not tell parents of misdeed	37	30	24
b. Would not tell unless parents asked	15	7	6
c. Would tell because parents would find out anyway	8	2	2
10. Disagreements with parents (B41) [a]			
a. None	43	47	39
11. Index of internalization			
a. Highly internalized	13	26	33
b. Highly externalized	27	12	8
12. Dating (B39)			
a. Do date	41	63	57
13. Leisure activities (B56)			

	Physical	Deprivation	Psycho-logical
a. Fewer than 20	75	60	58
b. Twenty or more	25	40	42
14. Leisure reading (*B56e*)			
a. Do not read	32	19	15
b. Read comics only	33	14	18
15. Group memberships (*B1*)			
a. None	48	28	28
b. One	25	33	28
c. More than one	27	39	43
16. Self confidence (*IR*)			
a. High	16	24	34
b. Average	56	57	48
c. Low	27	19	18
17. Time perspective (*CR: B*10, 10*a*)			
a. Extended	23	42	56
b. Restricted	31	22	13

[a] This question was omitted from one form of the questionnaire. The numbers on which the proportions are based are one-third smaller than those listed in the table heading.

[b] Numbers are reduced because some cases of mixed punishment (e.g., deprivation and psychological) as well as those in which no response was obtained were dropped from the analysis.

Table 6.1. Development in girls' concepts and attitudes regarding friendship, heterosexual friendship, and dating

	Age, %		
Item	Under 14 (*N* = 844)	14–16 (*N* = 822)	17–18 (*N* = 259)
1. Concept of friendship (*G20*) [a]			
Characteristics of friend			
a. Amiable, nice	32	20	16
b. Cooperative, unselfish	20	9	6
c. Not a gossip	18	22	23
d. Decent, good reputation	3	5	3
e. Moral courage	5	11	16
f. Good manners	4	1	1
g. Social status	6	4	5
h. Equalitarian	4	2	2
i. Talented, interesting	1	1	1

Table 6.1 (*Continued*)

	Under 14	14–16	17–18
j. Good personality, fun	4	6	8
k. Independent, autonomous	2	6	14
What the friend gives			
l. Support in trouble	13	17	17
m. Understanding	10	13	13
n. Does favors for you	10	8	6
Nature of relationship			
o. Mutuality: intimate, confiding	9	18	28
p. Security: friend loyal, trustworthy	31	52	44
q. Shared interests	19	16	22
r. *R* gives more than one response	82	84	93
2. Sources of popularity (*G22*) [a]			
a. Sensitivity, understanding	35	40	45
b. Equalitarian	24	38	38
c. Skills, talents, resources	27	40	45
d. Morality	6	4	7
e. External qualities: status, appearance, manners	27	23	20
f. Agreeable, amiable	38	29	26
g. *R* gives more than one response	81	89	92
3. Sources of unpopularity (*G23*) [a]			
a. Hostility, mean, bad temper	23	18	14
b. Selfish, uncooperative	19	13	15
c. Gossip, break confidence	20	21	26
d. Snobbish	18	31	29
4. Reasons for excluding girls (*G24*) [a]			
a. Too boy crazy	17	11	8
b. Bad reputation	15	39	18
c. Sexual immorality	3	4	4
d. Other immorality	28	29	31
e. No shared interests	3	8	12
f. Lack of social skill	12	9	10
g. Snobbish	5	4	5
h. *R* would reject no one	11	24	9
5. Sources of popularity with boys (*G25*) [a]			
a. Appearance	56	39	38
b. Social skills, good personality	25	47	48
c. Sensitive, understanding, interested in boys	28	33	41
d. Morality	7	9	10

	Under 14	14–16	17–18
e. Other	31	32	31
f. *R* gives more than one response	56	68	70
6. Intimacy of friendship (*G*21) [a]			
a. Can be as close as family relationship	58	61	68
7. Spend leisure (*G*65*c*)			
a. With family	64	56	50
b. With friends	28	32	40
c. Alone	7	10	8
8. Projective: Conflict between a promise to girl friend and a chance for a date (*G*29) [a]			
a. Keep promise	65	59	51
b. Take the date	22	25	28
c. Conflict, depends	4	10	14
9. Activities with boys (*G*63) [a]			
a. Active team sports	50	42	34
b. Individual sports	19	28	30
c. Social activities	21	44	50
d. Children's games	18	9	8
e. *R* doesn't play with boys	14	14	12
f. Not ascertained	4	3	4
10. Activities for like-sexed club (*G*4)			
a. Social activities	56	83	71
b. Sports and games	39	33	32
c. Outdoor activities	27	14	8
d. Hobbies	17	9	11
e. Educational activities	39	26	36
f. Organizational activities	13	14	13
g. Community services	12	19	19
h. *R* gives more than one response, crosses categories	50	51	44
i. *R* suggests exclusively social activities	30	45	47
11. Activities for coed club (*G*7)			
a. Dances	38	58	64
b. Parties	31	36	32
c. Other social activities	12	23	20
d. Sports and games	68	61	58
e. Outdoor activities	26	17	15
f. Hobbies	24	14	19
g. Educational activities	6	7	7
h. Organizational activities	3	5	7

Table 6.1 (*Continued*)

	Under 14	14–16	17–18
i. Community services	4	10	14
j. *R* gives more than one response, crosses categories	58	41	38
k. *R* suggests exclusively social activities	34	73	68
12. Position in age range suggested for a club (*G5*)			
a. Top age	4	7	31
b. Upper half of range	12	15	38
c. Middle	22	22	15
d. Lower half of range	29	31	8
e. Lowest age	30	21	4
f. Not ascertained	3	4	4
13. Preference for club membership (*G6*)			
a. All girls	42	32	32
b. Neutral	13	14	28
c. Boys and girls	42	53	38
d. Not ascertained	3	1	2
14. Dating (*G27*)			
a. Go steady	2	13	31
b. Date	17	59	60
c. Do not date	81	28	9
15. Attitude toward dating (*G26*)			
a. Positive	12	31	42
b. Neutral	20	27	25
c. Negative	1	1	1
d. Conditions: age	45	26	24
e. Conditions: parents, school	14	15	9
f. Conditions: relationship	15	26	27
g. Don't know	12	5	—
16. Attitude toward steady dating (*G28*)			
a. Positive	14	19	23
b. Conditions: age	34	27	17
c. Conditions: relationship	19	28	40
d. Conditions: other	9	10	9
e. Negative: limits fun, experience	11	30	29
f. Negative: too serious, too sexual	2	6	5
g. Negative: other	12	19	32
h. Don't know	11	3	—

	Under 14	14–16	17–18
17. Projective: response to boy friend's attention to another girl (G38) [a]			
a. Talk it over with boy, understand his view	21	30	34
b. Talk to girl friend	11	11	6
c. Try to recapture his interest	8	7	6
d. Don't stand in his way if he really likes other girl	12	22	25
e. Break-up, withdraw from relationship, find another	36	26	22
f. Don't let boy know she's jealous, she cares	6	16	8
g. Don't know	6	2	1
h. Not ascertained	3	1	2
18. Projective: response to boyfriend's criticism (G37) [a]			
a. Change, unconditional	23	12	11
b. Change if love him, if relationship strong	25	25	26
c. Change if nothing big	15	17	21
d. Change if criticism justified, if would improve her	28	42	48
e. Suggest compromise	9	13	17
f. Shouldn't change; break relationship	8	9	8
g. Shouldn't change, other	18	25	22

[a] These questions were omitted from one form of the questionnaire. Numbers on which the proportions are based are one-third smaller than those listed in the table heading.

Table 6.2. *Comparative responses of boys and girls (aged 14 to 16) to questions about friendship and dating*

Item	Boys (N = 1045)	Girls (N = 822)
1. Concept of friendship (B34; G20) [a]		
Nature of relationship		
a. Mutuality: intimate, confiding	2	18
b. Security: loyalty, dependability	41	52
c. Shared interests	29	16

Table 6.2 (*Continued*)

	Boys	Girls
Personal characteristics of friend		
d. Amiable, nice	29	20
e. Cooperative, unselfish	15	9
f. Not a gossip	—	22
g. Not a tattle-tale	8	—
h. Decent, good reputation	—	5
i. Moral courage	1	11
j. Good manners	8	1
k. Social status	—	4
l. Equalitarian	1	2
m. Talented, interesting	1	1
n. Good personality, fun	4	6
o. Independent, autonomous	3	6
What the friend gives		
p. Support in trouble	28	17
q. Understanding	5	13
r. Does favors for you	21	8
s. *R* gives more than one response	70	84
2. Sources of popularity (*B*36;*G*22) [a]		
a. Sensitivity, understanding	22	40
b. Equalitarian	30	38
c. Skills, talents, resources	32	40
d. Morality	11	4
e. External qualities: status, appearance, manners	40	23
f. Agreeable, amiable, controls impulses	72	29
g. *R* gives more than one response	79	84
3. Sources of unpopularity (*B*37; *G*23) [a]		
a. Hostility: bad temper, mean	33	18
b. Selfish, uncooperative	5	13
c. Won't go along with crowd	36	3
d. Gossip, break confidence, disloyal	4	21
e. Snobbish	17	31
f. Domineering, bossy	30	9
4. Intimacy of friendship (*B*52;*G*21) [b]		
a. Can be as close as family	42	61
5. Reasons: no group membership (*B*2;*G*2) [c]		
a. Friends don't belong	6	*
6. Attraction to favorite club (*B*2e;*G*2e) [d]		
a. Friends are members	8	2
7. Reasons: dropped clubs (*B*5b;*G*3a) [e]		

	Boys	Girls
a. Friends quit	7	4
8. Conditions for breaking rule (*B45;G*49)		
a. Influence of peers, gang	32	20
9. Projective: Response to parents' restriction (*B*40;*G*29)		
a. Question restriction	25	4
b. Question restriction on basis of peer example	13	*
10. Consequences if parents didn't make rules (*B*44; *G*48)		
a. Children would get in with wrong crowd	40	8

[a] These questions were omitted from one form of the questionnaires. Numbers on which the proportions are based are one-third smaller than those listed in the table heading.

[b] This question was omitted from one form of the girls' questionnaire only.

[c] Percentage figures here are based only on the numbers of subjects who belong to no groups (332 boys; 146 girls).

[d] Percentage figures here are based only on the numbers of subjects who belong to more than one group (381 boys; 470 girls).

[e] Percentage figures here are based on the numbers of subjects who have dropped out of some group (551 boys; 359 girls).

Table 6.3. Extreme groups on an index of interpersonal development compared on other ego variables (Girl sample)

Selected measures of ego variables	Interpersonal development index, %	
	High ($N = 301$)	Low ($N = 266$)
1. Energy level		
a. High on index of leisure engagements (*G*65)	41	27
b. Belong to some organized group (*G*1)	97	75
c. Hold jobs (*G*18)	60	51
d. Date (*G*27)	81	66
2. Self-confidence		
a. High on interviewer rating of confidence	47	32
b. Low on interviewer rating of confidence	17	30
c. High on interviewer rating for poise	38	14

Table 6.3 (*Continued*)

	High	Low
d. Low on interviewer rating for poise	14	29
3. Time perspective (*CR: G*10)		
a. Extended	50	37
b. Restricted	4	13
4. Organization of ideas		
a. High on interviewer rating	51	34
b. Low on interviewer rating	14	28
5. Feminine identification		
a. High on index of traditional feminine orientation	37	11
b. Choose own mother as an ideal (*G*55)	48	30

Table 6.4. Dating patterns related to measures of social development in girls sixteen and older

	Dating, %		
Item	Do not date (*N* = 76)	Date (*N* = 344)	Go steady (*N* = 139)
1. Attitude toward dating (*G*26)			
a. Positive	33	40	45
b. Conditions: age	28	25	22
c. Conditions: relationship	20	25	33
d. More than one response	26	30	34
2. Attitude toward steady dating (*G*28)			
a. Positive	5	15	46
b. Negative	83	72	28
c. Conditions: age	25	19	13
d. Conditions: not too serious	—	4	8
e. Conditions: if plan to marry	3	8	24
f. More than one response	38	43	54
3. Sources of popularity with boys (*G*25)			
a. Appearance	45	39	34
b. Dating personality, social skills	60	51	44
c. Sensitive, understanding, interested in boys	30	39	48
d. Not too sexual	13	2	2
e. More than one response	69	78	85
4. Projective: Response to boyfriend's criticism (*G*37) [a]			
a. Change, unconditional	16	11	8

	Do not date	Date	Go steady
b. Change, if minor	16	20	24
c. Change, if really love him	24	20	26
d. Change, if criticism justified	32	49	46
e. Compromise	7	15	26
f. Break relationship	26	7	2
5. Projective: Response to boyfriend's attention to another girl (G38) [a]			
a. Talk to boy	18	32	39
b. Talk to girlfriend	16	7	4
c. Don't stand in his way	13	24	28
d. Break with boy	46	23	11
6. Concept of friendship (G20)			
a. Mutuality, intimacy, security	50	71	73
b. Sensitivity, understanding	3	12	19
c. Moral courage of friend	42	12	11
d. Superficial characteristics of friend	74	92	88
e. More than one response	7	3	1
7. Sources of popularity (G22)			
a. External characteristics	35	20	12
b. Social skills	55	42	41
c. Sensitivity, understanding	30	43	48
d. More than one response	80	90	97
8. Reasons for excluding girls (G24)			
a. Too boy crazy	14	9	6
b. Too sexual	—	6	2
c. Bad reputation	24	10	14
9. Worries (G60) [a]			
a. Boys, popularity	43	82	73
b. Achievement	5	18	13
c. Physical characteristics	72	50	54
d. Problems: sex, menstruation	5	—	—
10. Group membership (G1)			
a. Belongs to no groups	33	20	22
11. Leisure activity index			
a. High	33	51	42
b. Medium	36	32	40
c. Low	30	16	18
12. Self-confidence (IR)			
a. High	23	44	38
b. Average	38	41	42
c. Low	37	14	19
13. Humor (IR)			
a. None	37	16	11

Table 6.4 (*Continued*)

	Do not date	Date	Go steady
14. Organization of thought (*IR*)			
a. Well organized	38	51	53
b. Moderately organized	19	29	31
c. Poorly organized	43	20	15
15. Sources of self-esteem (*G*54) [a]			
a. Adult roles	36	47	51
b. Peer acceptance	4	9	2
c. Being part of a group	24	37	33
d. Recognition, praise from adults	14	—	—
e. Nothing	16	5	2
16. Authority reliance (*CR: G*9, 9*a*) [a]			
a. High	27	16	18
b. Medium	63	62	65
c. Low	10	22	17
17. When girl might break a rule (*G*49)			
a. Emergency	4	19	16
b. Girl mature enough	5	13	19
c. Peer pressure	18	24	20
d. External authority absent	4	—	—
18. Rule *R* would never break (*G*51)			
a. Rules that reinforce adult authority	24	16	13
b. None	18	6	2
19. Projective: Response to parents' restriction (*G*29)			
a. Reassures parents	13	30	36
b. Shock, hurt	12	4	3
c. Questions restriction	1	4	10
20. Intimacy of friendship (*G*21) [a]			
a. Can be as close as family relationship	56	68	74
21. Leisure companions (*G*65*d*)			
a. Family	67	50	41
b. Friends	24	36	41
22. Index of femininity			
a. High	18	25	31
b. Low	34	22	20
23. Daydreams (*G*64) [a]			
a. Marriage, home, family	24	32	39
b. Boys, popularity	14	24	26
c. Achievement	14	21	18
d. Problems	11	3	2
e. Travel	22	8	4

	Do not date	Date	Go steady
24. Reasons for job choice (*G*14*a*) [a]			
a. Interest in work	58	68	65
b. Feminine themes: social service, children, women's work	11	27	30
c. Chance to travel	22	4	5
d. Achievement themes	—	6	3
25. Qualities admired in adult ideal (*G*65*a*) [a]			
a. Sensitivity, understanding	20	41	37
b. Character traits	16	26	20
c. Skill, achievement	23	32	29
d. Appearance	26	17	15
26. Marriage intentions (*G*13)			
a. Does not plan to marry, uncertain about marriage	5	6	—
27. Job aspirations (*G*14)			
a. Traditional profession	7	4	1
b. Feminine profession	10	20	31
c. Secondary profession	19	30	28
d. White collar, clerical	59	40	43
e. Blue collar, working class	7	5	—
28. Personal attractiveness (*IR*)			
a. High	32	46	44
b. Average	55	36	34
c. Low	13	18	12
29. Community size			
a. Rural	53	40	45
b. Small, medium, city	24	36	33
c. Suburbs	4	18	15
d. Metropolitan	18	6	7
30. Social status			
a. Upper middle class	16	23	18
b. Lower middle class	23	22	29
c. Working class	46	51	47
d. Farm	11	4	5

[a] These questions were omitted from one form of the questionnaire. Numbers on which the proportions are based are one-third smaller than those listed in the table heading.

Table 6.5. Dating patterns related to measures of development in girls fourteen and younger

Item	Dating, %		
	Do not date (N = 810)	Date (N = 265)	Go steady (N = 45)
1. Sources of popularity with boys (G25) [a]			
a. Appearance	50	45	69
b. Sensitivity, understanding, interest in boys	31	36	18
c. Not too sexual, aggressive	8	6	18
d. More than one response	60	64	51
2. Projective: Response to boyfriend's criticism (G37) [a]			
a. Compromise	10	14	2
b. Change, unconditional	20	7	29
c. Conditional: justified, minor	54	57	46
d. Break relationship	10	2	21
3. Projective: Response to boyfriend's attention to another girl (G38) [a]			
a. Try to maintain relationship	61	69	53
b. Do not try to maintain relationship	54	46	64
4. Projective: Conflict between promise to girlfriend and chance for date (G40) [a]			
a. Keep promise	60	57	44
b. Take the date	12	8	24
c. Try to compromise	18	24	11
5. Attitude toward dating (G26)			
a. Positive	10	24	33
b. Conditional: age	41	39	22
c. Conditional: relationship	18	28	20
d. More than one response	21	39	11
6. Attitude toward steady dating (G28)			
a. Positive	12	16	31
b. Negative	42	30	22
c. Conditions: age	31	36	22
d. Conditions: not too serious	*	7	13
e. Conditions: plan to marry	3	10	22
f. More than one response	36	58	24
7. Concept of friendship (G20) [a]			
a. Mutuality, sharing, intimacy	9	19	1
b. Security	31	43	16

	Do not date	Date	Go steady
c. Sensitivity, understanding	9	18	2
d. Superficial characteristics	9	6	20
e. Amiable, not disruptive	49	46	64
f. More than one response	78	96	69
8. Sources of popularity (G22) [a]			
a. External characteristics	25	20	38
b. Amiability	36	26	56
c. Sensitivity, understanding	34	53	31
d. More than one response	82	89	64
9. Projective: Response to disloyalty in a girlfriend (G35) [a]			
a. Ask friend about charge	37	49	24
b. Check truth of charge	10	14	7
c. Break with friend	6	4	24
d. Retaliate	6	2	16
e. Don't know	1	*	9
10. Reasons for excluding girls (G24) [a]			
a. Too boy crazy	21	12	11
b. Too sexual, bad reputation	16	26	38
11. Intimacy of friendship (G21) [a]			
a. Can be as close as family relationship	55	69	49
12. Leisure companions (G65d)			
a. Family	63	61	42
b. Friends	29	30	38
c. Self alone	6	9	20
13. Group memberships (G1)			
a. None	27	24	42
b. One	35	31	29
c. Two or more	38	45	29
14. Leisure activity index			
a. High	28	37	40
b. Medium	46	48	49
c. Low	26	15	11
15. Dominant leisure activities (CR:G65)			
a. Group activities	62	58	33
b. Two person activities	6	15	25
c. Individual, non-social activities	12	3	23
d. No emphasis	20	24	19
16. Employment (G18)			
a. R works	44	54	58
17. Organization of thought (IR)			
a. Well organized	49	54	58

Table 6.5 (*Continued*)

	Do not date	Date	Go steady
b. Moderately organized	26	25	20
c. Poorly organized	25	24	22
18. Self confidence (*IR*)			
a. High	35	31	32
b. Average	40	46	56
c. Low	25	23	11
19. Verbal facility (*CR*)			
a. High	10	8	16
b. Average	74	76	80
c. Low	16	16	4
20. Future decisions (*G*10)			
a. Boys, dating	5	6	22
b. Marriage	20	28	55
21. Picture of future life (*G*11)			
a. Marriage specified	21	30	55
22. Index of femininity			
a. High	20	27	42
b. Low	28	24	11
23. Job aspirations (*G*14)			
a. Traditional profession	8	10	—
b. Feminine profession	20	26	14
c. Secondary profession			
(e.g., nurse, model, stewardess)	40	36	56
d. White collar, clerical	33	32	42
e. Blue collar, working class	2	1	4
24. Reasons for job choice (*G*14*a*)			
a. Interest in work	52	59	40
b. Help others, service	23	20	42
c. Work with children	12	10	27
d. Appropriate for a woman	—	1	11
e. Individual achievement	2	6	—
25. Daydreams (*G*64) [a]			
a. Marriage, home, family	20	19	33
b. Boys, popularity	16	24	31
c. Achievement	19	27	9
d. True fantasy	17	23	—
e. *R* doesn't daydream, report			
a daydream	17	21	42
26. Most wonderful thing (*G*57) [a]			
a. Marriage, family	11	14	29
b. Popularity with boys	4	12	7
c. Achievement	34	46	20

	Do not date	Date	Go steady
d. Don't know, nothing	6	1	15
27. Educational plans (G12, 12a, b, c)			
a. No definite plans beyond high school	25	19	39
b. Nursing	12	8	24
c. Vocational training	14	11	20
d. College	35	44	16
28. Preference for security or success (G16) [a]			
a. Prefers success	39	44	67
29. Worries (G60) [a]			
a. Boys, popularity	50	65	57
b. Achievement	20	23	5
c. Current activities, problems	3	5	—
d. Nothing, don't know	5	2	24
30. Desired self-change (G59) [a]			
a. None, don't know	7	5	22
31. Projective: Response to lonely mother (G39) [a]			
a. Unconditional compliance	63	50	41
b. Compromise	40	45	21
c. Reject demand	11	14	33
32. Leisure with family (G65c)			
a. Share some activities	95	91	82
33. Adult ideal (G55) [a]			
a. Mother	38	33	20
34. Disagreements with parents (CR:G32) [a]			
a. Intense	*	2	13

[a] These questions were omitted from one form of the questionnaire. Numbers on which the proportions are based are one-third smaller than those listed in the table heading.

Table 7.1. Femininity patterns in relation to selected questions

Item	Femininity,[a] %					
	Fem (N = 113)	Amb (N = 44)	Neu (N = 115)	Boy (N = 112)	Ach (N = 46)	Anti (N = 69)
1. Sources of self-esteem (G54)[b]						
a. Helping others	29	17	21	6	4	3
b. Adult roles	47	59	27	33	44	20
b1. at home	26	18	6	8	4	4
b2. in a job	4	16	19	14	27	10
c. Acceptance by adults	19	5	10	21	16	13
d. Peer acceptance	10	—	2	4	—	7
e. Activity: sports	10	2	8	18	—	7
f. More than one response	32	37	18	21	20	5
g. Nothing, don't know	1	2	18	9	2	19
2. Preference: security or success (G16)[b]						
a. Prefers security	73	50	60	52	44	80
3. Educational plans (G12, 12a, 12b, 12c)						
a. No definite plans beyond high school	18	7	34	40	22	36
b. Will continue, nursing	25	11	10	3	—	13
c. Vocational training	8	5	19	16	12	12
d. College	43	64	21	20	59	28
d1. Teachers college	18	5	1	4	—	1
e. Other	2	3	1	12	7	10
4. Sense of wonder (G56)[b]						
a. More than one response	27	36	2	4	19	—

b. Nothing, don't know	18	9	30	24	28	51
5. Daydreams (G64) b						
a. Marriage, family	32	25	18	16	7	—
b. Future, achievement	23	48	40	32	67	33
c. Achievement, school	4	9	3	16	17	1
d. Boys, popularity	40	20	12	14	13	16
e. Current activities, problems	11	11	24	32	7	13
f. More than one response	67	54	33	27	34	8
g. R doesn't daydream	6	9	18	24	7	33
6. Most wonderful thing (G57) b						
a. Marriage, family	20	14	2	10	2	—
b. Popularity with boys	14	11	1	1	2	—
c. Achievement	14	45	39	30	39	16
d. Nothing, don't know	2	—	10	9	7	26
7. Characteristics of future husband (G13a)						
a. Attitude toward marriage relationship	68	62	48	46	60	
b. Ego resources, autonomy	30	41	17	15	28	
c. Social status	—	2	5	4	13	
d. R gives more than one response	41	52	40	30	48	
e. No response, don't know	—	2	7	15	1	
f. R does not plan to marry. Question not asked						100
8. Picture of future life (G11)						
a. Don't know, no response	—	—	1	—	2	28
9. Worries (G60) b						
a. Physical characteristics	75	51	57	64	39	49

Table 7.1 (*Continued*)

Item	Femininity,[a] %					
	Fem (N = 113)	Amb (N = 44)	Neu (N = 115)	Boy (N = 112)	Ach (N = 46)	Anti (N = 69)
b. Popularity with boys	56	44	29	25	20	19
c. Achievement	6	18	17	12	33	23
d. Current activities, problems	3	—	5	18	2	7
e. Nothing, don't know	2	2	5	6	4	21
10. Disappointments (G58) [b]						
a. Life tragedy	14	20	5	8	9	10
b. R gives more than one response	11	7	—	—	2	—
c. No disappointments	16	7	22	30	24	33
11. Narcissistic Orientation [b]						
a. High	26	20	11	3	9	1
12. Self change (G59) [b]						
a. Physical appearance	70	63	56	50	60	43
13. Reasons for job choice (G14a)						
a. Social service	37	25	16	8	11	20
b. Work with children	27	14	7	8	2	—
c. Work specially suitable for woman	14	—	1	1	—	—
14. Job criteria (G15,15a,b) [b]						
a. Security	59	41	44	40	44	77
15. Adult ideal (G55) [b]						
a. Mother	50	42	31	30	24	26
b. Other female relative	22	11	20	13	7	23
c. Unrelated woman	25	41	22	27	49	20

	1	2	3	4	5	6
d. Male model	—	14	4	13	9	1
e. No one, don't know	1	5	17	16	7	21
16. Disagreement with parents (CR:G 32) [b]						
a. Intense	1	2	—	7	2	15
b. No disagreements	31	16	27	10	15	14
17. Disagreement on issues [e] (G33)						
a. High	11		12	24		35
b. Medium	43		54	45		42
c. Low	46		34	31		23
18. With which parent does disagreement exist (spontaneous refs. G32) [b]						
a. Mother	11	20	23	27	24	41
19. Disagreements with siblings (G32a) [b]						
a. Intense conflict	1	5	1	9	11	22
b. Moderate conflict	24	18	29	42	28	25
c. No conflict, disagreements	49	41	44	23	35	29
20. Traditionalism of parents (CR:G30)						
a. Highly traditional	26	14	16	17	18	35
b. Traditional	70	71	78	70	72	60
c. Less traditional	2	14	4	11	6	1
21. Household responsibilities (G31)						
a. Heavy	17	7	5	3	1	31
b. Moderate	40	37	28	31	33	28

Table 7.1 (*Continued*)

Item	Femininity,[a] %					
	Fem (N = 113)	Amb (N = 44)	Neu (N = 115)	Boy (N = 112)	Ach (N = 46)	Anti (N = 69)
c. Light	38	52	61	54	56	33
d. Not ascertained	5	2	6	12	4	7
22. Qualities admired in ideal (*G55a*) [b]						
a. Understanding, sensitivity	45	33	30	28	20	10
b. Character traits	9	21	8	19	22	13
c. Work skills, achievement	20	22	28	27	39	25
d. Physical beauty, attractiveness	28	21	12	10	28	19
23. Time perspective on decisions (*G10*)						
a. Extended	67	52	16	14	41	15
b. Restricted	15	7	20	28	14	32
c. No decisions	—	2	8	7	—	26
24. Parents' expectations (*G30*)						
a. Independence, autonomy	9	32	14	10	19	2
b. Social skill, popularity	42	20	25	25	28	28
c. Social grace, manners	55	48	37	27	44	39
d. Respect, obedience	54	20	41	23	24	44
e. Adherence to specific behavioral rules	15	12	10	36	7	6

	(1)	(2)	(3)	(4)	(5)	(6)
25. Rule R would never break (G51)						
a. Disobey parents	17	5	10	7	4	7
b. None	*	7	3	15	4	1
26. Part in rule making (G52a)						
a. Yes	51	68	48	54	63	29
27. Parental punishment (G53)						
a. Psychological	40	30	33	27	24	17
b. Physical	13	2	13	11	2	38
28. When girl might break a rule (G49)						
a. Emergency	15	11	18	6	13	9
b. Rule inappropriate	7	11	8	14	15	6
c. Peer pressure	10	16	12	35	20	7
d. Rebellion	11	9	4	31	7	23
29. Leisure with family (G65c)						
a. Share some activities with parents	99	77	89	91	78	74
30. Why parents make rules (G47)						
a. To help children mature	45	18	29	24	20	22
b. To protect children	21	2	4	8	2	9
c. For children's own good	12	32	13	17	22	17
d. For benefit of parents	9	18	12	29	9	12
31. Ever broken rule (G50)						
a. Yes, definitely	4	14	7	20	13	3
b. Yes, conditional, don't think so, no	40	24	24	17	26	43

Table 7.1 (*Continued*)

| | Femininity,[a] % | | | | | |
Item	Fem (N = 113)	Amb (N = 44)	Neu (N = 115)	Boy (N = 112)	Ach (N = 46)	Anti (N = 69)
32. Picture-story: girl's response to conflict between parent, peer pressure demands (G29)						
a. Adheres to promise to parents because of sense of trust	24	14	16	15	20	13
b. R refers to heroine's feeling of conflict	38	28	10	5	13	2
33. Picture-story: portrayal of parents (G29)						
a. Strict and restrictive	36	22	30	31	28	32
b. Suspicious	—	—	—	—	—	23
34. Projective question: ways in which a girl might want her parents to be different (G34)[b]						
a. Less restrictive	62	68	71	83	63	93
b. Don't know, nothing	5	—	1	—	3	9
35. Picture-story: would girl tell parents of disobedience (G29b)						
a. Yes	58	30	40	48	46	39
36. Projective question: a shameful act (G36)[b]						
a. Sexual reference	20	21	14	8	30	3
b. Don't know, no response	6	2	12	7	2	25

422

	64	48	58	38	41	33
37. Projective question: confidante after shameful act (G36b,c) [b]						
a. Parents	64	48	58	38	41	33
38. Projective question: response to lonely mother (G39) [b]						
a. Return home	54	36	55	54	41	67
b. Compromise	59	50	38	39	40	20
c. Reject request	4	8	18	25	15	11
d. Don't know, no response	1	—	2	1	—	12
39. Concept of friendship (G20) [b]						
a. Mutuality, stress on relationship	29	35	18	10	4	3
b. Parallel activity	15	31	51	60	71	50
c. Support in trouble	10	16	13	37	20	18
d. Moral courage	1	9	—	13	15	32
e. Security, loyalty	32	52	33	34	41	57
f. R gives more than one response	92	89	78	78	86	74
40. Reasons for excluding a girl from friendship (G24) [b]						
a. Morality (nonsexual)	22	25	23	38	22	16
b. Bad reputation	31	22	27	29	22	10
c. Too boy crazy	12	18	15	10	22	—
d. R would not exclude anyone	17	9	17	11	13	35
41. Index of interpersonal development						
a. High	34	29	14	12	17	10
b. Low	10	11	18	27	22	41
42. Projective question: response to boyfriend's criticism (G37) [b]						
a. Change if love him	36	46	25	19	27	11

Table 7.1 (*Continued*)

	Femininity,[a] %					
Item	Fem (N = 113)	Amb (N = 44)	Neu (N = 115)	Boy (N = 112)	Ach (N = 46)	Anti (N = 69)
b. Unconditional change	18	11	24	37	31	18
c. Should not change	7	9	24	28	29	39
d. Compromise	21	28	11	6	3	—
e. Don't know, no response	2	5	5	4	4	22
43. Projective question: response to boyfriend's infidelity (G38) [b]						
a. Maintain relationship	90	81	55	60	59	40
b. Do not try to maintain relationship	30	36	54	59	54	68
c. Don't know, no response	2	2	—	3	—	16
44. Projective question: response to disloyalty in a girlfriend (G35) [b]						
a. Ask friend about charge	44	32	36	33	30	24
b. Check truth of charge	20	28	9	14	11	5
c. Break with friend	3	—	21	18	20	24
d. Retaliate	2	8	5	6	10	17
e. Don't know, no response	3	5	4	1	—	19
45. Reasons for wanting, having wanted to be a boy (G42a) [b]						
a. Rejection of femininity; relief from menstruation, childbirth	—	—	—	—	—	17
46. Dating (G27)						
a. Goes steady	18	14	7	10	2	—

47. Group membership (G1)						
a. Belongs to no groups	17	12	34	30	27	45
b. Belongs to more than two groups	32	39	15	18	22	8
48. Leisure activities enjoyed (G65a)						
a. Team sports	48	56	51	83	61	57
49. Leisure activity index						
a. Low	18	23	41	33	36	56
50. Leisure reading (G65e)						
a. None	—	2	24	27	20	37
51. Activity index (leisure, dating, work)						
a. High	46	54	40	40	35	28
b. Low	12	2	21	20	30	46
52. Activities for like-sex club (G4) [a]						
a. Team sports			15	38	11	9
b. Dances, parties			70	42	74	61
53. Activities for coed club (G7)						
a. Team sports	10	17	15	38	11	9
b. Dances	80	74	52	37	50	42
54. Personal attractiveness (IR)						
a. High	46	48	36	40	54	25
b. Average	44	37	50	42	28	52
c. Low	10	14	14	17	17	22
55. Humor (IR)						
a. Yes	84	82	78	83	61	54
56. Self-confidence (IR)						
a. High	44	45	30	31	43	9
b. Average	43	42	39	40	30	45
c. Low	12	11	31	29	26	45

Table 7.1 (*Continued*)

Item	Femininity,[a] %					
	Fem (N = 113)	Amb (N = 44)	Neu (N = 115)	Boy (N = 112)	Ach (N = 46)	Anti (N = 69)
57. Verbal facility (*CR*)						
a. High	9	14	8	6	17	10
b. Average	78	80	81	76	70	73
c. Low	13	5	11	18	13	17
58. Organization of thought (*IR*)						
a. Well-organized	55	64	40	44	52	32
b. Moderately organized	28	20	38	22	24	20
c. Poorly organized	17	16	22	34	24	48
59. Age						
a. Under 14	47	41	43	39	50	49
b. 14 to 16	37	43	45	42	33	33
c. Over 16	16	16	12	19	17	17
60. Age at menarche [e]						
a. Under 12	27	20	23	12	30	23
b. Over 13	8	5	7	18	4	28
61. Menstruation [e]						
a. Normal	43	38	54	51	60	59
b. Physical symptoms	45	51	31	38	29	33
c. Mood disturbances	10	9	10	7	6	4
62. Social status						
a. Upper-middle class	34	20	10	13	22	4

b. Lower-middle class	23	36	22	23	35	19
c. Working class	35	43	56	49	40	67
d. Farm	8	—	11	14	2	9
63. Religion						
a. Protestant	79	50	67	62	52	70
b. Catholic	10	37	25	29	30	26
c. Jewish	—	9	3	1	6	1
d. Other, none	11	4	5	8	12	3
64. Family size						
a. Small (1 or 2 children)	44	43	29	30	30	17
b. Medium (3 children)	20	25	29	20	11	19
c. Large (4 or more)	35	32	41	50	59	64
65. Birth order (for families of 3 or more children) f						
a. Oldest	25	30	24	30	26	54
b. Middle	46	52	46	46	56	32
c. Youngest	28	18	29	24	17	14
66. Mother's employment						
a. Mother works	32	41	48	48	20	44
b. Mother does not work	68	59	51	52	80	55
67. Relative education of parents						
Father had high school education or less	*53*	*61*	*69*	*63*	*67*	*72*
a. Father more education	45	32	57	50	58	56
b. Mother equal or more	8	29	12	13	9	16
Father had some college	*32*	*25*	*14*	*20*	*13*	*10*

Table 7.1 (*Continued*)

	Femininity,[a] %					
Item	Fem (N = 113)	Amb (N = 44)	Neu (N = 115)	Boy (N = 112)	Ach (N = 46)	Anti (N = 69)
a. Father more education	20	11	10	14	11	9
b. Mother equal education	12	14	4	6	3	1
c. Not ascertained	15	14	17	17	20	17

[a] The numbers in this analysis are small and wherever they are reduced because of excluded questions, the figures are unreliable for the three smallest categories.

[b] These questions were omitted from one form of the questionnaire. Numbers on which the proportions are based are one-third smaller than those listed in the table heading.

[c] This question was asked on only one form of the questionnaire. Numbers in this case are reduced by two-thirds. No percentages are presented for the ambivalent feminine group or the achievement oriented girls because the size of groups did not permit analysis.

[d] This analysis is based on one of the questions used in scoring for femininity. Since the feminine response and the responses presented in this analysis are not independent, the analysis was not done for the high feminine groups.

[e] Proportions here are based on the numbers of girls who have begun menstruating.

[f] Proportions here are based on reduced numbers, since the analysis applies only to girls from medium or large families.

APPENDIX A

The Questionnaires

Interviewer's name _____ Interviewer's number _____
Date of interview _____ Time taken for interview _____ min.
State _____ County (or metropolitan area) _____
Town or city (if applicable) _____
Name of school _____

LOCATION OF INTERVIEW

If interview taken (or should have been taken) at school, check ☐
If interview taken (or should have been taken) at home, check ☐

TYPE OF SCHOOL

Rough estimate of number of children in the whole school _____
What grades are included in this school? _____
                              (specify)
Check the appropriate description—
  Public school _____ Boys and girls _____ Whites only _____
  Church school _____ Boys only _____   Negroes only _____
  Private, other _____   Both _____

RESPONDENT'S

Age _____ Grade _____
                           (grade he is now in)

Was the interview conducted with the interviewer and respondent alone or
was someone else present?

Alone _____ Someone else present _____ If so, who? _____
                                                           (mother, teacher)
If interview conducted at home

Call No.	1	2	3	4	More (specify)
Time of Day AM or PM					
Day of Week					
Results					

1. First we're interested in the kinds of clubs and organizations boys belong to. What clubs or groups do you belong to in your neighborhood, at school or church, or other places?

IF R BELONGS TO ONE GROUP, SKIP TO QUESTION 2a	IF R BELONGS TO MORE THAN ONE GROUP, SKIP TO QUESTION 2c

IF RESPONDENT BELONGS TO NO ORGANIZATIONS, ASK

2. Some boys do belong to clubs and others don't. What would you say are the reasons you don't belong to clubs?
3d. If you were thinking of joining some club and you found out they had a uniform for members, would this make any difference to you?
3e. How do you mean?
3f. Would it make you feel any different about joining?

IF RESPONDENT BELONGS TO ONE ORGANIZATION, ASK

2a. What do you like best about the (*organization*)?
2b. Anything else?
3. Does this group have anything special that only members can wear to show they belong to the club?
          (IF YES)   3a. What?

IF NO CLOTHING mentioned	IF CLOTHING mentioned
3d. If you were thinking of joining some club and you found out they had a uniform for members, would this make any difference to you? 3e. How do you mean? 3f. Would it make you feel any different about joining?	3b. Do you like the idea of having these special clothes? 3c. How do you mean?

IF RESPONDENT BELONGS TO MORE THAN ONE ORGANIZATION, ASK

2c. If you found you didn't have enough time and had to drop out of some group, which one would you give up first?

2d. Why would you pick that one?

2e. Which would you give up last?

2f. Why?

(IF BELONGS TO SCOUTS AND HASN'T MENTIONED AS
FIRST OR LAST CHOICE)

2g. If you found that you didn't have time to belong to the Boy Scouts, how would you feel about leaving it?

3. Does this group have anything special that only members can wear to show they belong to the club?

(IF YES) 3a. What?

IF NO CLOTHING mentioned	IF CLOTHING mentioned
3d. If you were thinking of joining some club and you found out they had a uniform for members, would this make any difference to you? 3e. How do you mean? 3f. Would it make you feel any different about joining?	3b. Do you like the idea of having these special clothes? 3c. How do you mean?

IF RESPONDENT DOES NOT BELONG TO SCOUTS, ASK

---

4. (Let's take *one* group you don't belong to—say, the Boy Scouts.) Have you ever heard about the Boy Scout program for older boys, called the Explorers?

IF YES 4a. What have you heard about it?

4b. Would you consider joining an Explorer group?

4c. How do you mean?

EVERYONE

5. Are there any clubs or groups that you have dropped out of since you were 12 years old?

IF YES | 5a. Which ones?
(FOR EACH GROUP DROPPED)
5b. Why did you drop out?

6. If someone wanted to start a new club for boys like you, what things should the club do? What do you think boys like to do best?

(IF NO IDEA, USE CARD 1, AND ASK) 6a. Any of these things?

7. Do you think a club like this should have just boys in it or both boys and girls?
7a. Why?

8. What age group works best together—what should be the youngest and oldest ages of members?
8a. Why would you say so?

9. Do you think that groups or clubs for boys your age should have an adult leader or adviser?

IF YES	IF NO
9a. What should the adult leader do?	9b. Why not?

9c. Think of an adult leader you've liked. What did you like about him?

10. Now, looking ahead a little, what are the things you'll have to decide or make up your mind about in the next few years?
10a. Anything else?

11. What about the army—do you think you'll be drafted?

12. How do you feel about being drafted?

13. Do you think you'll finish high school or not?

IF YES	IF NO
13a. Are you planning to go to school after high school? (IF YES) 13b. What kind of school? (What do you think you'll take up?)	13c. What do you think you'll do?

14. What kind of work would you like to do as an adult?

15. Are you pretty sure about this or do you think you're just as likely to go into something else?

*16. Would you like a chance to learn more about different kinds of jobs, or not?

IF RESPONDENT HASN'T MENTIONED ANY JOB IN 14, 15, OR 16, SKIP TO QUESTION 28.

17. You mentioned (job or profession). Why do you think you might go into _____ (job) _____?

†18. What would you like about being a _____ (job) _____?

†19. Do you know anyone who is a _____ (job) _____?

* Indicates questions deleted from Form B of the Questionnaire.
† Indicates questions deleted from Form A of the Questionnaire.

20. How do you think someone would go about becoming a ___(job)___ ?
What preparation or training would you need?
    20a. Anything else?

†21. What do you think your chances are of getting to be ___(job)___ ?
    21a. How do you mean?

*22. Which of these things about a job would be most important to you?
(Card 2)

*23. Which would be next most important?

*24. Which two wouldn't you care about?

*25. Which would you rather have—a job where you're sure you won't
be laid off or one you can't be so sure of but where you have a chance
to be a big success?
    25a. Why?

*26. If a man's a hard and steady worker, what kinds of things might still
keep him from being a success?

*27. Do you think this happens to many people? (They work hard and
still don't get ahead?)

28. Do you have a job that pays money?

IF YES

> 28a. What do you do?
>
> 28b. About how many hours did you work last week?

29. Do you work in the summers?

30. What (besides work) do you do in the summers?

31. What do you use your *own* money for?

32. What are your parents' ideas about how you spend your money?

‡33. Do you have one or two *very* close friends—boys that you spend
most of your time with?

‡34. What are the most important things a friend should be (or be like)?

‡35. When do your friends get mad (angry) at you?

‡36. Think of a boy that everyone likes. Why do you think they like him?

‡37. What do you think are the reasons that some boys are not liked by
other boys?

38. If you were with a group of boys and all of the others were from
families with a lot of money, how would you feel about it?

39. Do you take girls on dates?

IF YES

> 39a. About how often?

IF NO

> 39b. Do many of your friends date?
>
> 39c. Would you like to date?

* Omitted from Form B.
† Omitted from Form A.
‡ Omitted from Form C.

40. Now I'm going to show you some pictures about a boy, his parents, and his friends. In each picture someone has just said something, and another person's going to answer. What do you think the answer would be?

> PICTURE 1.   What would the *parents* say?
> PICTURE 2.   What would the boy say?
> PICTURE 3.   What would the boy's answer be?

  40a. How would the boy feel? (Refer to picture 3.)
  40b. If the boy decided to stay with his friends awhile, do you think he'd tell his parents about it later?

†41. Would you say your parents have some old-fashioned ideas or ideas you disagree with?

†42. What about?

43. Why do parents make rules?

44. Suppose parents didn't make rules; what do you think would happen?

45. When do you think a boy might break a rule?

46. Have you ever broken a rule?

47. What kind of a rule would you never break?

48. If you do something wrong, how do you get punished?

*49. On each of the following questions, would you take the ideas of people your own age or the ideas of your parents? For instance, on:
  a. How you spend your money (would you take your friends' ideas or your parents'?)
  b. The clubs you join
  c. How to act when out with your gang
  d. Personal grooming (how to comb your hair, how to dress, etc.)
  e. What time to be in at night.

*50. What adult do you admire most—who would you like to be when you grow up?

*51. What do you admire about him?

52. Do you think a person can ever be as close to a friend as he can to his family?

53. What things that you do—at home or in school or with your friends— make you feel important and useful?

†54. What would you like to change about yourself if you could—about your looks or your life or personality?

‡55. What things do boys worry about most?

56. Here is a list of things that people do. I'd like you to check the ones that you have done in the last year or two.

* Omitted from Form B.
† Omitted from Form A.
‡ Omitted from Form C.

	Things done this past year	Things particularly enjoyed
Baseball		
Football		
Basketball		
Tennis		
Ping-Pong		
Golf		
Skiing or ice skating		
Horsback riding		
Pool, billiards, etc.		
Roller skating		
Bowling		
Swimming		
Boating, canoeing, sailing		
Fishing		
Hunting or shooting		
Camping or hiking		
Listening to radio or records		
Watching TV		
Going to movies		
Reading (not school work)		
Dancing		
Parties		
Meeting friends at drugstore, soda shop, etc.		
Playing cards and games		
Playing a musical instrument		
Making things—arts and crafts		
Collecting things—stamps, etc.		
Photography		
Raising animals or pets		
Gardening		
Working on a car, motorcycle, etc.		

56a. Now, of the ones you *have* done, would you check those that you have really enjoyed.

56b. Are there any other things that you enjoy doing in your spare time?

56c. Are there any other things you'd like to do if you had a chance? (IF READS)

56d. What do you read for fun?

---

1. Race: White ☐   Negro ☐   Other _____
2. What kind of work does your father do? Could you describe what he does on the job? _____

---

3. 2a. Does he work for himself or for someone else? _____
    2b. (If out of work) What does he usually do? _____

    2c. Does your mother work?
        ☐ Full-time   ☐ Part-time   ☐ Not at all
3. What kind of work did (or does) your father's father do? _____

                            (describe)
4. What is your family's religion?   ☐ Protestant   ☐ Jewish
                                 ☐ Catholic   __Other
5. Does your family go to church?
    ☐ Regularly   ☐ Often   ☐ Seldom   ☐ Never
    5a. How about you? _____
6. How long have you lived here in (city or town)?

    (IF LESS THAN 5 YEARS)

    6a. About how many times have you moved since you were 10 years old?

---

7. Are your parents divorced or separated?   ☐ Yes   ☐ No
8. Do you live with your mother and father?   ☐ Yes   ☐ No

    (IF NO)

    8a. Who do you live with? _____
9. Do you have any brothers and sisters?   ☐ Yes   ☐ No

    (IF YES)

    9a. How many and about how old are they? _____
    9b. Does anyone else live with your family? Who? _____
10. Are you taking (going to take) a college prep or vocational or business training course in high school? _____

    10a. What subject is easiest for you? _____
    10b. What subject is hardest for you? _____

11. Do your parents belong to any clubs or organizations? _____

11a. Could you give me some examples? _____

12. Were your parents born in this country or in some other country?

Mother _____

Father _____

13. About how far did your father go in school? _____

14. HOUSE AND HOME: Does your family have:

A vacuum cleaner?	☐ Yes	☐ No
An electric or gas refrigerator?	☐ Yes	☐ No
A bathtub or shower?	☐ Yes	☐ No
A telephone?	☐ Yes	☐ No
An automobile?	☐ Yes	☐ No

Have you had paid lessons in dancing, dramatics, speech, art, or music,
etc., outside of school? ☐ Yes ☐ No

Did your father FINISH high school? ☐ Yes ☐ No

Interviewer Check List

1. Did the boy blush or show any signs of embarrassment at any time during the interview?   ☐ Yes   ☐ No
2. Did he laugh or giggle at all?   ☐ Yes   ☐ No
3. Did he show any humor—like joking or smiling?   ☐ Yes   ☐ No
4. Did he look directly at you most of the time or did he look away?

___

(specify)

5. How would you rate his self-confidence?
   ☐ Higher than average   ☐ Average   ☐ Lower than average
6. Were his answers   ☐ clear and concise
                    ☐ clear but rambling
                    ☐ somewhat unorganized
                    ☐ other (specify)

Thumbnail Sketch

Please include comments on any unusual characteristics in physical condition or looks, personal qualities, response to the interview, etc.

FACE SHEET (GIRLS)

Interviewer's name _____ Interviewer's number _____
Date of interview _____ Time taken for interview _____ min.
State _____ County or metropolitan area _____
Town or city (if applicable) _____
Name of school _____

LOCATION OF INTERVIEW

| If interview taken (or should have been taken) at school, check ☐ |
| If interview taken (or should have been taken) at home, check ☐ |

RESPONDENT'S

| Age _____ Grade _____ |
| (grade she is now in) |
| Date of birth _____ |
| day   month   year |

Was the interview conducted with the interviewer and respondent alone or was someone else present?

Alone _____ Someone else present _____ If so, who? _____

(mother, teacher)

If interview conducted at home:

Call No.	1	2	3	4	More (specify)
Time of Day AM or PM					
Day of Week					
Results					

1. First we're interested in the kinds of clubs and organizations girls belong to. What clubs or groups do you belong to in your neighborhood, at school or church, or other places? (PROBE) Do you belong to a sorority?

| IF R BELONGS TO ONE GROUP, SKIP TO QUESTION 2a | IF R BELONGS TO MORE THAN ONE GROUP, SKIP TO QUESTION 2c |

IF R BELONGS TO NO ORGANIZATIONS, ASK

2. Some girls do belong to clubs and others don't. What would you say are the reasons you don't belong to clubs?

IF R BELONGS TO ONE ORGANIZATION, ASK

2a. What do you like best about the (organization)?
2b. Anything else?

IF R BELONGS TO MORE THAN ONE ORGANIZATION, ASK

2c. If you found you didn't have enough time and had to drop out of some group, which one would you give up first?
2d. Why would you pick that one?
2e. Which would you give up last?
2f. Why?

EVERYONE

3. Are there any clubs or groups you've dropped out of since you were 10?

IF DROPPED ANY CLUBS

3a. Why did you drop out?

IF "TIME" THE ONLY RESPONSE

3b. What was it that was taking up your time? What did the club meetings take time away from?

IF NO MENTION OF DROPPING CLUBS WHEN CHANGED SCHOOLS (in 3a)

3c. Did you drop out of any clubs when you moved or changed schools?

4. If someone wanted to start a new club for girls like you, what things should the club do? What do you think girls like to do best?

IF NO IDEA, USE CARD 1, AND ASK

4a. Any of these things?

5. What age group works best together—what should be the youngest and oldest ages of members?

6. Do you think a club like this should have just girls in it or both boys and girls?
6a. Why?

7. If a club had both boys and girls in it, what activities do you think would be best? What do girls and boys like to do in a club together?

a8. Do you think a club for girls should have any special clothes for members to wear?

IF YES

8a. What kind of thing?

IF UNIFORM NOT MENTIONED IN 8a

8b. What about a uniform? Would you like that idea?

a9. If a club like this had an adult leader, what do you think the adult leader should do?

9a. Think of an adult leader you've liked. What did you like about that person?

10. Now, looking ahead a little, what are the things you'll have to decide or make up your mind about in the next few years?

10a. Anything else?

11. We find that some girls have a kind of plan or picture of what they'll do when they get out of school. What ideas do you have about the way you want things to work out for you?

IF EDUCATIONAL PLANS NOT FULLY COVERED IN QUESTIONS 10 AND 11

12. Do you think you'll finish high school or not?

IF YES   IF NO

| 12a. Are you planning to go to school after high school?

 IF YES

 12b. What kind of school? What do you think you'll take up? | 12c. What do you think you'll do? |

IF MARRIAGE MENTIONED IN 10 OR 11, SKIP TO QUESTION 13a.

13. Do you want to get married some day?

IF YES   IF NO

| 13a. Could you tell me a little about the kind of person you'd like to marry?
 13b. What kind of work would you like your husband to do? | 13c. Why not? |

IF JOB CHOICE MENTIONED IN 10 OR 11, SKIP TO QUESTION 14a.

14. What kind of work would you like to do as an adult?

14a. Why do you think you might go into (occupation)? What would you like about being a (occupation)?

DO NOT ASK OF SIXTH AND SEVENTH GRADERS

a15. Which of these things about a job would be most important to you (Card 2)?

15a. Which would be the next most important?

15b. Which two wouldn't you care about?

a16. Which would you rather have—a job where you're sure you won't be laid off or one you can't be so sure of but where you have a chance to be a big success?

17. Do you have an allowance?

IF YES

| 17a. How old were you when you first got an allowance? |
| 17b. How much is your allowance? |

IF NO

| 17c. Did you used to have an allowance? |

18. Do you earn any of your own spending money?

IF YES

| 18a. What do you do? |
| 18b. About how many hours do you work a week? |

IF NO

| 18c. Do you baby sit? |
| 18d. Do you work in the summers? |

19. What do you use your *own* money for?

Now, I'd like to ask you a few questions about friends and friendship.

b20. What are the most important things a friend should be?

b21. Do you think a person can ever be as close to a friend as he can to his own family?

b22. Think of a girl that everyone likes. Why do you think they like her?

b23. What do you think are the reasons that some girls are not liked by other girls?

b24. Are there any girls you wouldn't go around with?
24a. Why?

b25. What do you think makes a girl popular with boys?

26. What do you think about dating?

27. Do you date yet?

IF YES

| 27a. About how often? |
| 27b. Do you ever date in groups? |
| 27c. Do you date different boys or always the same one? |
| IF SAME BOY |
| 27d. Do you go steady? |

IF NO

| 27e. Would you like to date? |
| 27f. Do you ever go out with a group of boys and girls together? |

28. What do you think about the idea of going steady?

29. Now, I'm going to show you some pictures about a girl, her parents, and her friends. In each picture someone has just said something and another person is going to answer. What do you think the answer would be?

PICTURE 1. What would the parents say?

PICTURE 2. What would the girl say?

PICTURE 3. What would the girl say now?

29a. How would the girl feel?

29b. If the girl decided to stay with her friends, do you think she'd tell her parents about it later?

30. Most parents have some ideas about how they want their children to behave. What are the most important things your parents expect of you?

31. Do you have any regular work to do at home? Are there some jobs around the house that are your special responsibility?

a32. Very often girls your age disagree with their parents about something. What disagreements do you have with your parents?

32a. What disagreements do you have with your brothers and sisters?

d33. How about dating? Do you have any disagreements with your parents about when a girl should start dating or how often a girl should go out?

33a. Do you ever disagree about teen-agers driving in cars?

33b. Do you ever disagree about clothes?

33c. Do you ever disagree about what girls to be friends with?

33d. Do you ever disagree with your folks about lipstick?

33e. Do you ever disagree with your parents about ideas in—politics or things like that?

Now, I'm going to ask you about some problems that girls your age sometimes face.

34. Jane sometimes wishes that her parents were different—more like the parents of her friends. What does she have in mind?

b35. A girl is told by someone that a close friend of hers has said unkind things about her. What does she do about it?

b36. Gladys feels terrible because she did something she thought she would never do. What do you think it would be?

36a. What would she do about it?

36b. Would she talk it over with anyone?

IF YES

36c. Who?

b37. A girl is engaged to a boy who wanted her to change certain habits and manners. What does she do?

37a. How does she feel?

a38. A couple has been going together but the girl notices that her boy friend is paying attention to a friend of her own who often double dates with them. What does she do?

38a. How does she feel?

a39. A girl has a very good job away from home. She gets a letter from her mother saying her mother is lonely and asking the girl to move back home. What does she do?

39a. How does she feel?

a40. A girl has promised a friend to help her with some work on a certain evening. She is later asked by another friend to go on a blind date with a boy who is supposed to be very attractive. What does she do?

40a. How does she feel?

b41. While she is giving your class a test, your teacher is called out of the room. She asks you to take over the class and to make sure that nobody cheats. You see a close friend of yours copying from someone else's paper. What would you do?

IF WOULD NOT TELL TEACHER

41a. How about if it was someone you didn't know well?

42. Do you ever wish you were a boy?

IF YES

42a. Why?

IF NO

42b. Did you ever used to want to be a boy?
42c. Why?

e43. If you had a choice, would you rather work for a man or a woman?
43a. Why?

Would you tell me whether or not you agree with the following statements.

e44. The husband ought to have the final say in family matters.

e45. It is only natural and right that men should have more freedom than women.

e46. A man should help his wife with some of the work around the house.

47. Why do parents make rules?

48. Suppose parents didn't make rules; what do you think would happen?

49. When do you think a girl might break a rule?

50. Have you ever broken a rule?

51. What kind of a rule would you never break?

52. How do you feel about the rules your own parents make?
52a. Do you have any part in making the rules at your house?

53. If you do something wrong, how do you get punished?

b54. What things that you do—at home or in school or with your friends—make you feel important and useful?

b55. What adult do you admire most—who would you like to be like when you grow up?
55a. What do you admire about that person?

b56. We get a feeling of wonder when something seems to us inspiring or impressive or really important. What things would give you the greatest feeling like this?

b57. What is the most wonderful thing that could happen to you?

b58. What's the biggest disappointment you've ever had?

b59. What would you like to change about yourself if you could—about your looks or your life or your personality?

b60. What do girls worry about most?

c61. What do you enjoy playing?

IF ANY IMAGINATIVE GAME MENTIONED

61a. Tell me how you play (game)?

c62. Are there things you used to play that you don't play any more?

IF YES

62a. What?

62b. Why did you stop playing them (it)?

c63. What do you play with boys?

c64. Think of a time when you are alone. Some girls like to spend the time daydreaming. Some girls spend it in other ways. Do you ever daydream or pretend?

IF YES   IF NO

| 64a. Would you tell me about a daydream? | 64b. What do you do when you're alone? |

65. Here is a list of things that people do. I'd like you to check the ones that you have done in the last year.

	Things done this past year	*Things particularly enjoyed*
Team sports, i.e., basketball, volleyball		
Tennis		
Ping-Pong		
Skiing or ice skating		
Horseback riding		
Roller skating		
Bowling		
Swimming		
Boating, canoeing, sailing		
Camping or hiking		
Listening to radio or records		
Watching TV		
Going to movies		
Reading (not schoolwork)		*
Dancing		
Parties		
Meeting friends at drugstore, soda shop		
Talking with friends on the telephone		
Playing cards and games		
Playing a musical instrument		
Making things—arts and crafts		
Collecting things, stamps, etc.		
Photography		
Raising animals or pets		

	Things done this past year	Things particularly enjoyed
Gardening		
Cooking		
Sewing		
Writing stories, poems		
Acting, being in plays		

65a. Now, of the ones you *have* done, would you check those that you have really enjoyed?

65b. Are there any other things that you enjoy doing in your spare time?

65c. Do you do any of these things with your parents? Could you give me one or two examples?

65d. Do you spend *most* of your spare time

        a. by yourself,

        b. with a friend,

        c. with your family?

*IF READS

65e. What do you read for fun?

PERSONAL DATA

1. Race: White ☐ Negro ☐ Other _____
2. Do you live with your mother and father? ☐ Yes ☐ No
3. IF NO, are your parents divorced or separated? ☐ Yes ☐ No
4. What kind of work does your father do? Could you describe what he does on the job? _____
    4a. Does he work for himself or for someone else? _____
    4b. (If out of work) what does he usually do? _____
    4c. Does your mother work?
        ☐ Full-time   ☐ Part-time   ☐ Not at all
    4d. What does she do? _____
5. What is your family's religion? ☐ Protestant   ☐ Jewish
                                    ☐ Catholic   _____ Other
    5a. IF PROTESTANT, what is the name of your church? _____
        IF JEWISH, are you orthodox, conservative, or reform? _____
6. How often do your parents go to church?
    ☐ Regularly   ☐ Often   ☐ Seldom   ☐ Never
7. How long have you lived here in (city or town)? _____

IF LESS THAN 5 YEARS

    7a. About how many times have you moved since you were 10 years old? _____
8. Do you have any brothers and sisters? ☐ Yes   ☐ No
    8a. Specify sex and age. _____
9. Do your parents belong to any clubs or organizations? _____
    9a. Could you give me some examples? _____

---

10. HOUSE AND HOME: Does your family have?

Their own house?	☐ Yes	☐ No
A vacuum cleaner?	☐ Yes	☐ No
An electric or gas refrigerator?	☐ Yes	☐ No
A bathtub or shower?	☐ Yes	☐ No
A telephone?	☐ Yes	☐ No
An automobile?	☐ Yes	☐ No

Have you had paid lessons in dancing, dramatics, speech, art, music, etc., outside of school? ☐ Yes   ☐ No

11. About how far did your father go in school? _____
    11a. How much schooling did your mother have? _____

HEALTH INFORMATION

12. Have you ever had a serious illness? _____
13. How tall are you? _____
14. How much do you weigh? _____
15. Have you had your first menstrual period? _____

IF YES

15a. At what age did you first menstruate? _____
15b. How do you feel around the time of your period? _____
_____

INTERVIEWER CHECK LIST

1. Did the girl blush or show any other signs of embarrassment at any time during the interview? □ Yes □ No
2. Did she laugh or giggle at all? □ Yes □ No
3. Did she show any humor—like joking or smiling? □ Yes □ No
4. Did she look directly at you most of the time or did she look away?

_____

(specify)
5. How would you rate her self-confidence?
   □ Higher than average   □ Average   □ Lower than average
6. Were her answers   □ clear and concise
                      □ clear but rambling
                      □ somewhat unorganized
                      □ other (specify) _____

THUMBNAIL SKETCH

Please describe the girl fully, covering the following points in particular: physical maturity; personal beauty, attractiveness, grooming, and neatness; physical handicaps; poise, femininity, or boyishness; use of make-up, style of clothing.

LEGEND

a These questions appear on Forms A and B of the questionnaire.
b These questions appear on Forms B and C of the questionnaire.
c These questions appear on Forms A and C of the questionnaire.
d This question appears on Form A of the questionnaire.
e These questions appear on Form C of the questionnaire.

APPENDIX B

Sampling and Sampling Error

Sampling Procedure

The boys and girls chosen for these studies are representative cross sections of boys and girls in school in the ages and school grades designated. The 1045 boys interviewed represent the approximately 2.5 million American boys 14 to 16 years old in grades 7 through 12. The 1925 girls represent the approximately 7.3 million girls in grades 6 through 12.

In drawing the two samples, essentially the same procedure was followed. It is described here for the study of girls, with differences between the two samples specified at the end of the section.

The sample was selected by multistage probability sampling. The first stage consisted of the Survey Research Center's basic sample of 66 primary sampling units. Each of these primary sampling units consists of a county or group of counties. Within each primary sampling unit a list of all schools in the area was compiled, and from these lists the sample of schools was selected. Within each selected school a list of all classes in grades 6 through 12 was obtained, and from these lists a selection of classes was made. Finally, a list of all girls within each selected class was secured, and from this list, girls were selected for interviewing.

The list of schools within primary sampling units was compiled from three sources. (1) A list of secondary schools was available from the *Directory of Secondary Day Schools, 1951–1952*, published by the U. S. Office of Education. (2) A list of those secondary schools established since the *Directory* was obtained by interviewers from boards of education in all primary sampling units. These lists of new schools were compared with the *Directory*, and duplicate entries were removed. In this way the list of secondary schools was brought up to date. (3) The interviewers also obtained lists of all primary schools in their areas.

The *Directory* provided information on the size of the secondary school, on race in segregated school systems, type of school (e.g., junior or senior high school), public or private classification, and enrollment. The interviewers obtained similar data on primary schools and those secondary schools established since 1950. In primary schools enrollment data were confined to the total number of students in grades 6 and over.

The data on school enrollment were used for stratifying schools into two groups consisting of (1) private and parochial and (2) public schools. Then group (1) was stratified by Roman Catholic and other private and parochial schools. Group (2) was further stratified by race, size of school, and type of school.

On the basis of these groupings, a systematic selection of schools was made. The probability of selection given to each school within the primary sampling unit was proportional to the number of students in the school.

For each school selected into the sample the interviewers obtained

(1) the grades included in the school
(2) a list of all homeroom classes in grades 6 and above giving
    (a) the grade to which each class belonged
    (b) the number of girls in each class or, if that was unavailable, the total number of students in each class.

Homeroom classes were listed so that each girl was uniquely associated with one and only one class. From these homeroom lists classes were selected with probability proportional to the estimated number of girls in each class. The names of all girls in the selected classes were listed on special forms that designated the girls to be interviewed.

The sample was designed to yield an expectation of four girls from each sample class and an expectation of two classes from each sample school. Any inaccuracies in preliminary reports of enrollment were reflected in variations from these expectations in interviews per sample class and classes per sample school.

In a few schools girls were not assigned to homeroom classes. In such situations another list of classrooms with which the girls could be uniquely associated was used.

Also in some primary sampling units the list of elementary schools was not filed with a central source. In all these instances there was available a list of school districts with some estimate of the number of students in each district. A sample of school districts was selected first and then lists of schools were obtained for the selected districts only, from which a sample of schools was selected.

The over-all sampling rate gave each girl in the study's population one chance in 3625 of being selected for interviewing.

Nonresponse

In all, there were 2004 girls selected for the sample. Of these 2004, interviews were obtained from 1925 which gives an over-all response rate of 96%. For the study of boys the comparable rate was 97.2.

Differences between the Sample Designs for the Girl and Boy Studies

The study of boys had the same sample design with the following exceptions:

1. The boy study was limited to the population of boys 14 to 16 years old in grades 7 through 12. The girl sample included girls in school grades 6 through 12 with no age limits.
2. The study of boys had 34 primary sampling units, whereas the girls study had 66.
3. Elementary schools were selected in only 13 primary sampling units for the boys study. In the girls study primary schools were selected in all sample points.
4. The sample of boys did not include boys in schools established since the *Directory of Secondary Day Schools, 1951–1952,* was published. The proportion of the secondary school population attending these schools was estimated to be about 5%, and these students were not represented in the sample of boys.

Sampling Errors

Survey results are subject to two major kinds of error. First, there are inaccuracies that occur in the respondent's answer and in the way they are recorded by the interviewers—so-called reporting errors. In most cases the magnitude of these errors can be surmised only from the quality of the interviewing. A second type of error is called sampling error. It results from the fact that the survey is based on a sample rather than interviews with the entire population. There is always the possibility that by chance the sample will contain too many or too few boys in the 16-year group, too many or too few boys in a particular organization, and so forth.

The extent to which sample findings may overestimate or underestimate the true figures is largely dependent on the number of interviews, but there are other factors involved as well. With a sample of a given size, the smallest sampling error would be achieved if the cases in the sample were widely scattered through the area sampled, with no two interviews taken in the same place. This kind of sample is prohibitive from the standpoint of time and expense, and in practice the interviews are "clustered" within sample points and within schools and classes. Clustering increases sampling error. To some extent, however, reductions in error are achieved through the use of stratification.

The sampling error measures the limits on either side of the obtained figures within which the true population value has a given probability of falling. It is customary to give as "the sampling error" a figure representing two standard errors; this represents the limits within which the true value will lie 95 out of 100 times.

The sampling error varies somewhat for different findings of the survey. Despite these differences, tables representing the approximate magnitudes of the sampling errors of various estimated percentages will give a general picture of the degree of variability that should be attached to the estimates. Tables 1 and 3 represent a generalized compromise result. However, the sampling error for any particular item may in fact be one percentage point lower or higher than that given in the tables.

Tables 1 and 3 may be used to determine the sampling error for the difference of two proportions when comparing two subgroups, both of which are based on all sample points. The n's of the two subgroups and the average size of the two proportions being compared are necessary for entering the table.[1] If, for example, the two groups being compared are based on n's of 200 and 500, respectively, the proper "box" in the table is found in the row marked $n = 200$ and the column marked

---

[1] The average of the two proportions being compared would be obtained by the following formula:

$$\frac{n_1 p_1 + n_2 p_2}{n_1 + n_2} = \text{average proportion},$$

where n_1 and n_2 refer to the sizes of the two groups being compared and p_1 and p_2 refer to the two proportions being compared.

$n = 500$. If the proportions being compared are about 50%, the sampling error is about 10%; if the proportions being compared are about 20%, the sampling error is about 8%; and so forth. Thus the proper "box" is determined by the n's of the two subgroups, and the line within the "box" is determined by the size of the proportions being compared.

Tables 2 and 4 may be used to determine the sampling error for estimated proportions of groups based on all sample points. The size of the group and the size of the proportion being estimated are needed for entering the table. If, for example, the size of the group is 100, the proper "box" is found in the column marked $n = 100$. Proportions around 50% have a sampling error of about 11%; proportions around 20% have a sampling error of about 9%; and so forth. Thus, if a proportion based on an $n = 100$ were estimated to be 45%, the true population value would have 95% probability of falling within the range $45 - 11\%$ and $45 + 11\%$, or between 34% and 56%.

Table B.1. Differences required for statistical significance (probability $= 95\%$) in comparing two subgroups, both of which are based on all sample points (boys)

n \ n	50	100	200	300	500	700	1000	p
50	20	18	16	16	15	15	15	50%
	16	14	13	13	12	12	12	20%
	—	—	—	—	—	—	—	10%
	—	—	—	—	—	—	—	5%
100	18	15	14	13	12	12	12	50%
	14	12	11	10	10	10	9	20%
	—	9	8	8	8	7	7	10%
	—	—	—	—	—	—	—	5%
200	16	14	12	11	10	10	9	50%
	13	11	9	9	8	8	8	20%
	—	8	7	7	6	6	6	10%
	—	—	5	5	5	5	4	5%
300	16	13	11	10	9	9	8	50%
	13	10	9	8	7	7	7	20%
	—	8	7	6	6	5	5	10%
	—	—	5	5	4	4	4	5%

Table B.1 (*Continued*)

n \ n	50	100	200	300	500	700	1000	p
500	15	12	10	9	8	8	7	50%
	12	10	8	7	7	6	6	20%
	—	8	6	6	5	5	5	10%
	—	—	5	4	4	4	3	5%
700	15	12	10	9	8	7	7	50%
	12	10	8	7	6	6	6	20%
	—	7	6	5	5	5	4	10%
	—	—	5	4	4	3	3	5%

Table B.2. Sampling errors (probability = 95%) for estimated proportions for groups based on all sample points (boys)

p \ n	50	100	200	300	500	700	1000	1045
50%	14	11	8	7	6	5	5	5
20%	12	9	7	6	5	4	4	4
10%	—	7	5	5	4	3	3	3
5%	—	—	4	3	3	3	2	2

Table B.3. Differences required for statistical significance (probability = 95%) in comparing two subgroups, both of which are based on all sample points (girls)

n \ n	100	200	300	500	700	1000	1500	p
100	14	13	12	11	11	11	10	50%
	11	10	9	9	9	9	8	20%
	9	8	7	7	7	6	6	10%
200	13	10	9	9	8	8	8	50%
	10	8	8	7	7	6	6	20%
	8	6	6	5	5	5	5	10%
	—	4	4	4	4	4	3	5%
300	12	9	8	8	7	7	7	50%
	9	8	7	6	6	6	5	20%
	7	6	5	5	4	4	4	10%
	—	4	4	3	3	3	3	5%

n \ n	100	200	300	500	700	1000	1500	p
500	11	9	8	7	6	6	5	50%
	9	7	6	5	5	5	4	20%
	7	5	5	4	4	4	3	10%
	—	4	3	3	3	3	2	5%
700	11	8	7	6	6	5	5	50%
	9	7	6	5	5	4	4	20%
	7	5	4	4	3	3	3	10%
	—	4	3	3	3	2	2	5%
1000	11	8	7	6	5	5	5	50%
	9	6	6	5	4	4	4	20%
	6	5	4	4	3	3	3	10%
	—	4	3	3	2	2	2	5%
1500	11	8	7	6	5	5		50%
	8	6	5	4	4	4		20%
	6	5	4	3	3	3		10%
	—	3	3	2	2	2		5%

Table B.4. Sampling errors (probability = 95%) for estimated proportions for groups based on all sample points (girls)

p \ n	100	200	300	400	500	700	1000	1500	2000
50%	10	7	6	5	5	4	4	3	3
30%	9	7	6	5	5	4	3	3	3
20%	8	6	5	4	4	3	3	3	2
10%	6	4	4	3	3	3	2	2	2
5%	—	3	3	2	2	2	2	2	1

APPENDIX C

Measures-Indices

The indices used in this study consisted of unweighted scores obtained by combining responses to a number of questions. The questions and critical responses used for each index are presented here.

Internalization-Externalization

Three questions were used. Responses considered "internal" and "external" are marked I or E. Subjects who gave internal responses to two or three questions were included in the high internalization group; those who gave two or more external responses were grouped in the low internalization category.

1. What would happen if parents did not make rules? (B44; G48)
   (E) Children would run wild, be delinquents
   (E) Children's lives would be ruined
       Children would get in with wrong crowd
       Children would stay out too late, not go to school
       Children would do as they please
       Family life would suffer, parents would worry
   (I) Children would (might) manage, know right from wrong; effects would be minor
2. When might a boy (girl) break a rule? (B45; G49)
   (I) In an emergency
   (I) If rule inappropriate, child mature enough to judge
       Under peer influence
       Forgetfulness
       Rebellion
       Uncontrollable impulse

(E) When external authority absent
3. What does the boy (girl) do (when pressed by friends to ignore a promise to parents)? (B40; G29)
 (I) Adheres to promise, sense of trust
     Goes home, no reason indicated
 (E) Goes home, fear of punishment
     Stays with friends

Interpersonal Development

The score here was derived from responses to three questions. Answers scored are marked with an I. The high category consisted of subjects who gave a critical response to all three questions. The low group includes all who gave no such answer to any of the questions. The analysis was conducted on two-thirds of the total sample.

1. Do you think a person can ever be as close to a friend as he can to his family? (B52; G21)
 (I) Yes
     Maybe, depends
     No
2. What are the most important things a friend should be? (B34; G20)
     Amiable
     Cooperative
     Controlled
     External features
 (I) Talents
 (I) Understanding
     Supports you in trouble
     Does favors
 (I) Mutuality of friendship
     Security of friendship
 (I) Shared interests
3. Think of a boy (girl) that everyone likes. Why do you think they like him (her)? (B36; G22)
 (I) Sensitivity, understanding
     Equalitarian
     Morality
     External characteristics
     Amiability

Femininity

The seven questions and scored responses on which the Femininity Index was based are the following:

1. If someone wanted to start a new club for girls like you, what things should the club do? What do you think girls like to do best? (64)
   Homemaking Activities
   Sewing, knitting, embroidery
   Cooking
   Gardening
   Child care
   General: learning how to keep house, to be a homemaker
2. We find that some girls have a kind of plan or picture of what they will do when they get out of school. What ideas have you about the way you want things to work out for you? (G11)
   Reference to marriage, family future
3. Do you want to get married some day? (G13)
   Yes
4. What kind of work would you like to do as an adult? (G14)
   Nurse
   Social worker
   School teacher
   Secretary
   Housewife
5. Do you ever wish you were a boy? (G42)
   No
   Used to, but no longer do.
6. Here is a list of things that people do. I should like you to check the ones that you have done in the last year. Now, of the ones you *have* done, will you check those that you have really enjoyed? (G65, 65a)
   Gardening ⎫
   Cooking ⎬ have done and enjoyed.
   Sewing   ⎭
7. Are there any other things that you enjoy doing in your spare time? (G65b)
   Knitting, needlework
   Child-care activities
   Other homemaking activities

Narcissism

This index was based on responses to the questions listed. Responses scored for narcissism were those indicating an awareness of and sensitivity to appearance.

1. Think of a girl that everyone likes. Why do you think they like her? (G22)
2. What do you think makes a girl popular with boys? (G25)
3. What do you admire about that person (chosen as adult ideal)? (G55a).
4. What would you like to change about yourself if you could— about your looks or your life or your personality? (G59)
5. What do girls worry about most? (G60)

The narcissism index was obtained only for two-thirds of the total sample.

Leisure Activity

The index here was a simple score of the number of leisure activities the subject reported for the last year. The categories and their scores were as follows:

High   = 20 or more activities
Medium = 10 to 19 activities
Low   = fewer than 10

Activity

In this case we combined the leisure activity information with information about employment and group membership. The high and low categories were defined as follows:

High = 20 or more leisure activities, hold a job, and belong to more than one group.

Low = fewer than 10 leisure activities, do not hold job, belong to no organized groups.

AUTHOR INDEX

SUBJECT INDEX